1842

Gentlemen of the Press

Profiles of American Newspaper Editors
Selections from the Bulletin of the American Society
of Newspaper Editors

Edited by
Loren Ghiglione

The Poynter Institute
For Media Studies

R. J. Berg & Company, Publishers
Indianapolis, Indiana

To Gene Giancarlo

Contents

List of Abbreviations Used in "Profiles"

ASNE	American Society of Newspaper Editors
APME	Associated Press Managing Editors
API	American Press Institute
FoI	Freedom of Information (ASNE Committee)
FIEJ	Federation Internationale des Editores et Journaux
IAPA	Inter American Press Association
IPI	International Press Institute
NCEW	National Conference of Editorial Writers
NCPA	North Carolina Press Association
NEAPNE	New England Associated Press News Executives
NESNE	New England Society of Newspaper Editors
SDX	Sigma Delta Chi
SERS	Southern Education Reporting Service
SHNA	Scripps-Howard Newspaper Alliance

Introduction

As portrayed in this collection of 107 profiles, written for the *Bulletin* of the American Society of Newspaper Editors over the past thirty years, the contemporary editor comes in eight flavors.

The newsroom autocrat—the kind of editor who possesses, in Norman Isaacs's words, "infinite capacity for taking pains and giving them"—is exemplified by Alfred H. Kirchhofer of the *Buffalo Evening News.* Kirchhofer bolted the visitor's chair beside his desk to the newsroom floor so that it could not be inched closer to him. When a reporter, in the process of being berated for an error, dared stammer, "But, Mr. Kirchhofer, I think. . .," Kirchhofer replied, "You're not paid to think!" Such an editor is rarely overburdened by modesty or doubt; as Lester Markel, Sunday editor of the *New York Times* explained, he edits to please himself ("You can't scratch every man where he itches") and lifts his nose to those who disagree with him (". . . The bad [reporters] . . . think I'm a stinker. I'll settle for that").

The second category of editor, the crusader, sometimes comes equipped with a .25 automatic and a .30-.30 Winchester, as did Dan Hicks of the *Monroe County Democrat,* a weekly in Madisonville, Tennessee. In return for his newspaper attacks on the Ku Klux Klan, a drive-in that showed "filthy" movies, the board of mayor and aldermen, a teen nightclub, the town's water department, and dozens of other targets, Hicks was beaten up, shot at, robbed, and threatened repeatedly. When told he was about to be burned out, he slept in his office thirty-one nights in a row. "The night I went home," Hicks said, "was when it burned down."

Bigger papers have had crusaders, too—J. N. Heiskell, whose *Arkansas Gazette* lost $2 million while fighting Gov. Orval Faubus and other flaming segregationists, and the liberal J. W. Gitt, whose *York* (Pennsylvania) *Gazette and Daily* was labeled by some "the *Gazette and Daily Pravda.*" Gitt opposed the earliest United States involvement in Vietnam, the sending of advisers, and every step that followed. His reporters learned from their editors a new approach to the five Ws. "At the *Gazette,* there's just one W, and that's J. W. Don't ever forget it."

A third category of editor, the writer, feels he isn't doing his job unless he also produces a front-page column or three editorials daily.

Charles A. Guy, the editor of the *Lubbock* (Texas) *Avalanche-Journal* ("the only man who could strut sitting down"), wrote a daily column, "The Plainsman," representing personal journalism at its best. Guy labeled Texas Gov. Price Daniel "What Price Daniel" and greeted the new mausoleum of a library at Texas Tech with a no-star rating. "It is crawling with hot and cold running maintenance men and automatic nose blowers. It has all the conveniences of a modern jail."

Some writer-editors, like Wallace Lomoe, executive editor of the *Milwaukee Journal,* dream early of producing the Great American Novel. Others, like J. Russell Wiggins, dream of composing poetry. Wiggins wrote a column for the *St. Paul Pioneer Press* that included "Dry Victory," a poem in response to a headline, "Brewers Can't Meet Beer Demand"; the poem read:

> It took the Drys a hundred years
> Of work, and talk, and thinking,
> But Wets have dried the country up
> In just one day of drinking.

Few writer-editors ever wind up forsaking their daily column for other forms of writing. Novelist Thomas Wolfe had one of his newsroom characters say, "Christ! Maybe some day I'll write a book myself—about all the poor hams I've known in this game who were going to write a book—and never did." But many an editor has contributed mightily to the writing of others.

Brodie Griffith, editor-general manager of the *Charlotte News,* taught W. J. Cash (who wrote his classic *The Mind of the South* while producing editorials for the *News*), Harry Ashmore (*Epitaph For Dixie* and *The Negro and the Schools*), and Charles Kuralt.

C. G. "Pete" Wellington of the *Kansas City Star* taught reporter Ernest Hemingway "simplicity through brevity" and flexible narrative. (Hemingway later wrote of Wellington, "I can never say how grateful I am to have worked under him.")

A fourth kind of editor, the reporter, is epitomized by Gene Patterson of the *St. Petersburg Times* (and, in 1962, of the *Atlanta Constitution*). When 122 Georgians were killed in a June 3, 1962, airplane disaster at Orly Airport near Paris, Patterson flew there the next day. He tramped the runway, asked questions, and wrote a narrative that justified his philosophy, "You've got to go see it, smell it, taste it, and feel it."

A fifth kind of editor, the philosopher, often prods his peers with his vision of better journalism.

Herbert Brucker, editor of the *Hartford Courant,* wrote four books critical of the press. J. Edward Murray, whose hobbies are philosophy and comparative religion, developed a list of criteria for an ethical newspaper. (Once, invited to speak on "The Role of the Press," he raised Phi Beta Kappa eyebrows by expounding on existentialism.)

There are other kinds of editors. The community-builder—Miles Wolff, executive editor of the *Greensboro* (North Carolina) *Daily News,* ran the

United Fund, the Chamber of Commerce, the Symphony Society, even the local Whist Club; the entrepreneurial editor—Josh Horne founded the *Rocky Mount* (North Carolina) *Telegram* and John O. Emmerich started the *McComb* (Mississippi) *Enterprise-Journal*.

The groups spawned a new kind of editor, the manager responsible for dozens of papers. He often works quietly, unobtrusively. John Quinn says, "The better I do my work, the less I get noticed." But the groups' news bosses have an impact. Legend has it, Don Shoemaker wrote, that Knight-Ridder's Lee Hills had people at the *Charlotte Observer* so much on their toes that "the urinals in the gentlemen's walk had to be raised a clear foot."

* * * * * *

What does it take to be a successful editor? The profiles that follow suggest Ten Commandments.

1. Thou Shalt Come From Humble Beginnings. That way you won't be disappointed. To get a nine-dollar-a-week reporting position at the *Texarkana* (Texas) *Gazette*, J. Q. Mahaffey had to work nine months without pay. He had been hired with the admonition: "We don't need you, we don't want you, but when you are worth something we will begin to pay you." George W. Healy, Jr., recalled a line from George E. Allen when asked why so many newspaper people (including himself) came from Mississippi. "It's better than plowing." (When Mark Ethridge quoted the same line in a profile about Turner Catledge, it read, "It's a damned sight easier than plowing." So much for journalistic accuracy.)

2. Thou Shalt Think Twice Before Pursuing A College Degree. Some of America's best editors—John Hughes, J. Russell Wiggins, and Norman Isaacs—went without a degree, thereby saving themselves "from that peculiarly impervious ignorance bred only in universities," wrote James S. Pope of the *Courier-Journal and Louisville Times*. Horace Greeley proclaimed that he would not allow a college graduate in his basement, much less his newsroom; his kind of reporter, no doubt, came equipped with the degree in life of a Wallace Lomoe. Before becoming a reporter (and later executive editor, of the *Milwaukee Journal*), Lomoe had been a sheepherder, gravedigger, harvest hand, railroad gandy dancer, Columbia River teamster, and lumberjack.

3. Thou Shalt Not, If Burdened With The Trappings Of A University Education, Let Others Know Your Misfortune. Bury your Ph.D.s and Phi Beta Kappa keys. If you're like Carl Lindstrom, executive editor of the *Hartford Times,* who played half an hour of Bach fugues on the piano before going to work and wrote one hundred words every night in each of six diaries—in English, Swedish, German, French, Italian, and Spanish—it's better to say you're spending the time playing poker. Heed the lesson of

Jonathan Daniels, editor of the *Raleigh News and Observer* (A.B. and M.A., University of North Carolina, LL.B., Columbia, Guggenheim Fellow, novelist, biographer) who insisted he was just a country editor—"a newspaperman with the galluses showing."

4. Thou Shalt Start Young. Louis B. Seltzer, editor of the *Cleveland Press,* quit school at eleven—his family wasn't exactly rich—and began newspaper work. Robert Carver Notson, executive editor of the *Portland Oregonian,* became editor and publisher of the *Heppner* (Oregon) *Budget,* a ditto newsletter, at twelve. Child labor laws, bah humbug.

5. Thou Shalt Learn To Play Golf. Sociologists will marvel at how many editors not only mention golf as a hobby but admit they are "ardent" practitioners. H. L. Mencken, no doubt, is somersaulting in his grave. The idea of a journalist, Mencken wrote, "with any self-respect playing golf is to me almost inconceivable."

6. Thou Shalt Drink In Moderation (Or Not At All). Some editors have contributed their own chapters to the folklore about the editor as souse. Scott Newhall of the *San Francisco Chronicle,* his wife wrote, "was invited to leave school because his unassigned laboratory project had consisted of distilling grain alcohol from tincture of iodine, and bootlegging the product." But many editors abstain completely. And Dwight Marvin, editor of the *Troy* (New York) *Record,* noted, "I never drink between drinks."

7. Thou Shalt Develop At Least One Hobby That Marks You As Eccentric. If your parents didn't leave you an outrageous name—Colbert Augustus McKnight or Vermont Connecticut Royster—then you need to: collect crickets (J. Curtis Lyons, *Progress Index,* Petersburg, Virginia), write "Cheer Leader" and other juvenile fiction under a pseudonym borrowed from your spouse (Graham M. Dean, *Ashland* (Oregon) *Daily Tidings*), fly airplanes at the age of seventy-nine (Marcellus Murdock, *Wichita Eagle*), operate an experimental station for hybrid vines (Philip M. Wagner, the *Baltimore Sun*), or play a bosomy, frowsy witch for an amateur clown organization (Bill Steven, *Minneapolis Star and Tribune*).

8. Thou Shalt Maintain A Messy Office. At ninety-one, J. N. Heiskell regarded his office, a garbage dump of stacked newspapers, magazines, press releases, and correspondence, as a crowning achievement. His wife complained it was unsanitary. "Of course the place is unhealthy," he responded. "That's why I died so young." The process is as important as the messiness achieved. The method used by Harry F. Byrd, Jr., then editor of the *Winchester* (Virginia) *Evening Star* (and state senator), was described by his wife, Gretchen. "He . . . subscribes to forty-four daily newspapers, some of which he reads standing up, letting them drop through his fingers to the floor as he finishes them."

9. Thou Shalt Marry A Spouse Who Shall Keep The Real World From

Impinging On Whatever It Is That You Do At The Newspaper. George Chaplin, editor in chief of the *Honolulu Advertiser,* was prevented by his wife, Esta, from doing anything around the house after an experience many years ago when, as she later explained, "I asked him to open a can of peanuts and thirty minutes later he was in a hospital emergency room getting five stitches in his finger."

10. Thou Shalt Ignore Any Such List Of Commandments. Totally reject the advice of journalists. For example, Walter Lippmann said, "There is nothing to teach in a school of journalism." And A. J. Liebling wrote that Columbia University's Graduate School of Journalism, regarded as one of the best, possessed "all the intellectual status of a training school for future employees of the A & P." It follows, logically, that journalism school is bound to propel all its graduates to executive editorships at major papers.

*   *   *   *   *   *

The profiles that follow reveal not only the humor of America's editors but also their strengths—incredible energy, decisiveness under deadline pressure, a desire to get the news and print it, straightforwardness, and more than occasionally, a nonconformist's mind. At the same time, the profiles remind us that editors are usually of their era, rarely ahead of it.

Women journalists are, in several profiles from the 1950s and 1960s, referred to as "girl reporters." An Austin editor two decades ago served as a director of the local Headliners Club which allowed women to enter only after lunch; in its Press Box bar, never.

After mentioning sexism, it's worth noting that this collection describes only white male editors. Fortunately, another volume in this series collects profiles of women journalists. But greater recognition in newspaper management of women and minorities is long past due.

Acknowledging such weaknesses of the trade—and of the editors who are a part of it—one feels compelled, nevertheless, to point to one theme that runs throughout the profiles. Editors have a strong sense of mission. They believe their calling, to report the news, is unequaled. When an associate proposed a fancy moniker for the editor of the *Charlotte News*—to imply, as he put it, "somewhat broader responsibilities than just running the newspaper"—John S. Knight barked, "Hell, there is no title higher than editor."

Loren Ghiglione

November 1, 1983
Southbridge, Massachusetts

Milburn P. Akers, Editor
Chicago Sun-Times

By Frederic S. Marquardt

M ilburn P. Akers has the mind of a politician, the heart of a social worker, and the body of a medieval bishop. He is known as Pete because there is no nickname for Milburn, except maybe Milly, and no one would call him anything that dainty.

Pete comes honestly by any church-like attributes, since his father was a Methodist minister. But I suspect that his bishop's girth is due less to heredity than to a carefully nourished love of food and drink. Few people can equal him in doing justice to a twenty-four-ounce steak, a plate of fried potatoes, and a double serving of bread and butter. Unlike most men who prefer not to get on the scales, Pete isn't sensitive about his excessive weight. But he still has a kindly spot in his heart for the British newspaperman who described him as "burly." His American friends are less polite.

I recall once when Pete apparently forgot that he is the executive suite rather than the outdoor type. It was at the American Society of Newspaper Editors (ASNE) convention in San Francisco in 1957. He casually remarked that he was going to take his wife and daughter to the Grand Canyon and then accompany Judy, who was about fourteen years old, down to the bottom of the canyon. That's more miles of nearly straight up-and-down trail than any man of Pete's girth should attempt. Especially under an Arizona sun in midsummer.

"Pete," I said, "there may be a burro strong enough to carry you down to the bottom of the canyon, but I doubt if either you or the burro would get back to the rim." After taking a look at the canyon, he passed up the chance to play a hero to his daughter.

Pete was born in Chicago in 1900. He learned to think like a politician by associating with some of the best in the business. After breaking into the newspaper business as a reporter on the *St. Louis Post-Dispatch,* he moved to Springfield, Illinois, and went to work on the *Illinois State Register.*

Marquardt was editor of the *Phoenix Republic* when this article first appeared, in 1959.

Springfield is deep in the Lincoln country, but Illinois politicians pay more attention to the examples of Mark Hanna and Boss Kelly than to those of Honest Abe. Because of his apprenticeship in political skulduggery, Akers has given the *Sun-Times* a bipartisan, antipolitics slant.

Pete did a hitch with the Associated Press, working both in Chicago and in Springfield. From 1934 to 1937, according to his biography in *Who's Who in America,* he was "Superintendent of Reports for the state of Illinois." The title didn't mean anything. He actually was handling press relations for Gov. Henry Horner. For six months, while Horner lay at death's door, Pete acted as a buffer between the governor and the public. Some unfriendly newspapers referred to him as the "acting governor," which nurtured his political ego and prepared him for an assault on Washington, where he was assistant to the secretary of the interior from 1939 to 1941.

There's an interesting story as to how Pete went to Washington. Harold Ickes was secretary of the interior, and the Old Curmudgeon took offense at something Pete had written. Secretary Ickes relieved his feelings by dictating a snide letter questioning Pete's ancestry, morality, and sanity. Whereupon Akers locked himself up with Bartlett, Webster, and Roget, poured some vitriol into his typewriter, and wrote a reply that made the paper smoke. Terrible Tempered Harold was so pleased at Pete's literary output that he hired him as an assistant.

At least, that's the way the story goes. I don't know whether it's true or not. But I do know that when Pete and I both went to work for the *Chicago Sun* in 1941, I received a letter from a division chief in the department of the interior saying, "I'm sure glad Marshall Field decided to start a newspaper in Chicago. He at least got that guy Akers out of my hair."

Pete has worked on the *Chicago Sun* and its successor, the *Chicago Sun-Times,* ever since. All except for one day in 1943, that is. I was overseas at the time, but the way I got the story was that Pete decided to quit. He wasn't mad at anyone; just figured it was time to move on. The boys in the newsroom thought this would be a good excuse for a whing-ding, so they hired a suite in a Loop hotel and threw Pete a farewell party.

It was a fine party, but apparently the paper showed the effects the next day. Marshall Field, Sr.—father of the present publisher—wanted to know what had happened. Someone had to tell him about the farewell party for Akers.

"I didn't even know he was quitting," said Field. "Hire him back."

So after being unemployed for one day, Pete went back to work. Feeling a little guilty about the party, he decided to play host at a repeat affair. He invited his co-workers to a second party, same hotel, same suite, fresh drinks. Someone started a crap game, or maybe it was poker, and Pete proceeded to win enough to pay the tab.

Actually, Pete has been up and down the ladder twice. At least he's been up twice. He was managing editor in one of those hectic interludes on the *Sun*—between Turner Catledge and E. Z. Dimitman, if I remember correctly—and was then reassigned to political writing. But it was no particular disgrace to be demoted on the *Sun* in those days. If Pete had known what would become of Catledge (managing editor of the *New York Times*) and of Dimitman (assistant to the publisher of the *Philadelphia Inquirer*) he wouldn't have been worried at all at his reduction in rank. After the *Sun* and the *Times* were merged, Akers was given another crack at the top job.

I wasn't kidding when I said Pete had the heart of a social worker. It has given him a lot of pleasure to be able to hire broken-down newspapermen under a "last chance" stipulation. An amazing number of these gestures have paid off.

Akers also has worked at the other end of the age scale in hiring. He has written to deans of journalism schools and asked them to send along their most likely looking candidates for try-outs. The result has been some top-notch young reporters who are on the *Sun-Times* staff instead of in public relations.

Akers is particularly happy when he can add a good investigative reporter to his staff. He likes nothing better than to direct a campaign against a public official who has gotten out of line. While he was executive editor, the *Sun-Times* published documented exposés that:

1. Forced a Democratic candidate for governor to quit the race before the election.
2. Sent a killer-cop to prison for life and removed from office the Democratic district attorney who tried to cover up for him.
3. Showed up a Republican state schools superintendent who had been careless in handling school lunch programs.
4. Led a Republican clerk of probate court to be repudiated by his party because of irregularities and favoritism.

Wilfred Taylor, a roving correspondent for the *Scotsman* of Edinburgh, recently devoted a column to Akers, calling him a "deceptive scholar-editor." Said Taylor, "Even the gun in his top drawer is deceptive. He just happens to be a small-arms enthusiast." Probably the aforementioned political exposés had more to do with the presence of the gun than Taylor suspected.

No description of Pete Akers would be complete without reference to the memos that used to come—and for all I know still do—from his typewriter. Perhaps the most famous of these was addressed to a city editor—who shall be nameless—in the days when Pete was managing editor of the *Chicago Sun*. It directed the city editor to impress on his staff that they weren't working at a country club. The city editor was so teed-off that he put the memo up on the bulletin board. I don't suppose it was there for five minutes before someone grabbed it for his personal file. Whoever has it should offer to sell it back.

Time magazine once described Akers as "brilliant, blustery . . . as famed for his highhandedness in a rage as for his openhandedness with a raise or a bonus." Pete's reaction was to ask staff members for affidavits to the effect that he was a hard man with a dollar—"just in case the boss wants to call me on the carpet for squandering company funds."

Pete's avocation is history. He has an exceptionally good collection of books about Lincoln—going back to his Springfield days—and he knows the historical lore of Illinois as he knows his own newsroom. When Howard Fast wrote *The American,* Pete wrote a review saying that a lot of the book was copied from Harry Barnard's *Eagle Forgotten.* It was, too, and both Fast and his publisher made a voluntary settlement with Barnard.

I would hate to end this piece leaving anyone with the impression that Pete Akers is an egghead. I wasn't there, but one of the steadier drinkers of my acquaintanceship swears that Akers once put in a person-to-person call to a parakeet in Selma, Alabama. It was during an ASNE convention in Washington, and someone said this particular parakeet could talk plainly. Pete said no parakeet could talk worth shucks. To prove his point, he called the proper Selma number and asked for the parakeet. But the bird's owner refused to bring it to the phone. It was three o'clock and parakeets, in Alabama anyway, are supposed to be asleep by that time.

Robert W. Atwood, Editor and Publisher
Anchorage (Alaska) Daily Times

By Francis P. Murphy

O rdinarily, the northernmost member of ASNE is Robert W. Atwood, editor and publisher of the *Anchorage* (Alaska) *Daily Times,* a prospering afternoon daily.

But he can cross you up. In one year he became its southernmost member by visiting the South Pole. The same calendar year he visited the North Pole. He probably knows why he took on both.

And at other times he has cropped into the news (in the *Anchorage Times,* anyhow) as the easternmost and also the westernmost member. He gets around. The Atwood family album opens easily to advance the argument that you are not really a world famous personage unless you have had your hand shaken, in front of a camera, by Bob.

Here he is, for instance, grasping or being grasped by Kwame Nkrumah at Ghana. Here is the family pacing the Taj Mahal pool just before the visit to Nehru. And on that page—we are still leafing through the album—Atwood with Tom Mboya in Kenya. . . being welcomed by Nasser in Egypt, by the Shah of Iran, Haile Selassie, General Abboud in Sudan, King Mohammed V at Rabat; by—these names are difficult to spell and, moreover, let's get Atwood out of all that heat.

Place him in Anchorage. This is Anchorage as described by Larry Feid, a brand new eye on the *Times,* writing to the *Manchester* (New Hampshire) *Union-Leader,* which paper he had just left:

"You can get parted from your money awfully fast here.

"A shoe shine costs 50 cents; a haircut, $2.50; a one-room efficiency apartment $115 a month, and hard to get. . . .

"The leading movie house charges 40 cents for children, 90 cents for

Murphy was managing editor of the *Worcester* (Massachusetts) *Telegram* when this article first appeared, in 1961.

students (high school age), $1.45 for adults—and the feature picture being shown at this theatre on our arrival was one we had already seen in Manchester.

"As for weather, the word for winter is COLD.

"The average mean temperature in Anchorage in January is 11.2 degrees above; in April, 34.9; in July, 57.

"There are summer days here when the temperature goes up to 80; in Fairbanks the mercury has been known to soar to 95, although Fairbanks is north of Anchorage.

"Winter comes early to Alaska, lasts long; meaning summer arrives late and ends early. But winter does end. And spring does come. And summer is a magic of plant life sprouting without letup in the sixteen to twenty hours of sunlight.

"Finding a native Alaskan, other than an Indian or an Eskimo, can be a real project. For example, the staff of the *Daily Times* comes from New Hampshire, New Jersey, Louisiana, Illinois, Oklahoma, Montana, North Dakota, California, Washington, and Germany.

"Here, instead of serenity, there is bounce; here, instead of day-to-day living, there is history in the making; here, there is a vast land to conquer—one-fifth the size of the lower forty-eight states."

Bob was born in Chicago (March 31, 1907) but was actually brought up in Winnetka, Illinois. He went east to go to Clark University in Worcester for prelaw education. He told his family he wanted Clark because an uncle, Dr. Wallace W. Atwood, was president there. The truth of the matter is he went to Clark because it was at the other end of a one-hour, interurban trolley line. The end in which Bob was interested was that at Wellesley College. A Winnetka high school girl had chosen Wellesley.

That trip east gave Bob his first taste of salt water and his first view of mountains. He has never conquered a love for either since. Here the Winnetka girl fades into the background. The prelegal studies fade in the same direction. Geography became a passion.

Atwood tested newspaperwork as campus stringer for the *Worcester Telegram* when he was a sophomore. He became a man of divided loyalties. One half was forever devoted to geography and the warring half to newspapering. To this hour no man knoweth which is his paramount love.

Graduated from Clark he joined the staff of the *Telegram* at eighteen dollars per week. Either he had something or inflation was on its way because after one week he got a two-dollar raise. Hitherto unheard of.

His apprenticeship eventually behind him, Atwood set out to be the best reporter in the nation with the determination to work six months only on any newspaper that would hire him, and then move on. He worked not six months but six years at the *Illinois State Journal*, Springfield, Illinois, where the Depression caught him and where in that six years he caught his bride—or possibly, she him.

The element of chance enters. His bride's parents were in Alaska. He went up there to meet them. Alaska, he found, was loaded with geography and, to complete the other half of his life, bore a newspaper which wasn't doing so well—the *Times*. It had five employees and a circulation of 650 in a town of 2,500.

Atwood, like most newspapermen, had no money. His bride's father was, by the strangest circumstance, a banker. So, Bob found himself with a bride-built line of credit, a lovely debt, and a newspaper to do with as he wished.

This day his *Times* is the largest paper in Alaska. The immediate area has 100,000 souls. People in Anchorage now figure that Bob doesn't borrow money from bankers anymore; he lends it to them.

Somewhere along the line, Bob got Alaska into the Union. There are available, if you turn the spigot, 100,000 words on why this was done. Basically, he got Alaska in because he discovered in his early days there that if a duck broke a leg in Alaskan geography, the Department of the Interior would send in the 101st Airborne to rescue the duck. But if a man broke a leg, he could damned well get himself out. Atwood changed that.

In the way of personal possessions, Bob has a lovely wife who is author of a hardcover, colorful dustcover type of book on Anchorage. It sells around $4.95 or some such. Her name is Evangeline. He also possesses two of the loveliest daughters man ever set an eye on. Each won a picture-in-all-the-papers beauty prize. One was a Cherry Blossom queen. We forget what the other was. One daughter is Marilyn, the other Elaine.

Bob goes in for brown-type suits. Generally he has been likened in appearance to Dick Tracy or to the Old Man of the Mountain. I suggest he'd prefer the latter comparison. That ancient gentleman sits among a terrific mass of geography.

"The first assignment that Francis Murphy gave me, as a raw recruit, was a real stinker," Bob Atwood recalls. "It was to find out when every church in Worcester was going to have a Sunday school picnic, where it would be, and what they were going to do.

"I counted 110 churches within a block of either side of Main Street plus several hundred more throughout the city. For four days I sat in the office telephoning ministers, Sunday school superintendents, committee chairmen, etc. I found churches the most disorganized organizations and masters at giving reporters the run-around when you want to know about a Sunday school picnic.

"At the end of four days Murphy asked me how I was getting along. I gave him a detailed report on the theory that he asked for it and I would bore him to death. He listened carefully while I went over the situation concerning each church. When I finished he took all my notes and threw them away, with the comment, 'Fine, now do this.' Then he gave me a decent assignment.

"I guess that was my initiation. The others on the staff told me that Murphy did it to see how long I would stick before I quit."

William C. Baggs, Editor
The Miami News

By C. Edward Pierce

E ditor William Calhoun Baggs of the *Miami News* never has been horsewhipped, and, while some of his readers undoubtedly have considered the idea, it's unlikely that he ever will be.

The difficulty in coming to grips with Baggs is that no one, after listening to him for a few minutes, can remember exactly what the argument was about.

Baggs in print is one of the most forthright of editors. His associates sometimes express the wish that he would temper his views a little to coincide with those of the community.

That only prompts him to start his daily column with the statement that a lot of people obviously are all wrong.

In conversation, though, Baggs moves like quicksilver. The person who wants to argue about his liberal racial views suddenly finds himself all wrapped up in the sex life of Thomas Jefferson, the inside story of the Cuban missile crisis or the processes by which the Roman Senate permitted itself to be deprived of power.

Baggs has a remarkable memory, and he picks up anecdotes with the loving care of a collector of rare butterflies.

His choice of heroes is revealing. Two who are near the top of his list are former president Harry Truman and the late Adlai Stevenson. Baggs is equally happy in repeating, from his conversations with the two men, the most down-to-earth remarks of Truman and the most philosophical observations of Stevenson.

Baggs is a character of more than the usual number of sides.

He's deeply involved, for instance, in community affairs. Leaders in efforts to maintain racial harmony in Miami say the public never will know how much Baggs has contributed by his behind-the-scenes work.

Pierce was managing editor of the *Miami News* when this article first appeared, in 1966.

On the other hand, politicians who try to make him a power behind the throne by asking him how they should vote are likely to be told:

"Look, you're the fellow who got elected. You do what you think is right. I'll tell you about it in the paper if I think you're wrong."

He writes folksy columns about a talking raccoon and a wild turkey philosophizing in the Everglades—and he writes thoughtful pieces for the *Encyclopaedia Britannica*.

It comes as something of a jolt, even after long association with Baggs, to hear him break off a story about one of his South Dade farmer friends to take a call from another of his friends at the White House or State Department.

He is aggressive in support of his views, but he plays golf—using one adjustable club—without keeping score. If he kept track of his strokes, he says, he might try not to take so many and thus would spoil the fun of just walking around the course.

Baggs and his friend Ralph McGill, publisher of the *Atlanta Constitution*, are two of the South's most persuasive champions of civil rights for Negroes. The fact that Baggs is a native of Atlanta and a member of an old Georgia family infuriates segregationists who start off by denouncing him in the letters-to-the-editor column as a Yankee carpetbagger.

But Baggs's background makes him much more tolerant of his critics than they are of him. Although he doesn't agree with them, he understands how they feel.

His column reflects his essential friendliness. It never is strident or accusatory. Baggs argues vigorously for his pet projects—civil rights, the preservation of natural beauty spots, the liberal viewpoint in politics—without ever slipping over into a personal attack on the persons who take the other side.

Baggs, who started with the *News* as a general assignment reporter in 1946, wrote his daily column for eight years before being named editor in July 1957. Along with the traditional duties of an editor, he's in charge of the news-gathering operation, but he is scrupulous about leaving the second part of the job up to the managing editor.

As an executive, Baggs has absolutely nothing in common with the typical young corporation man.

A few minutes after his promotion, he ran into two reporters who had been with the paper for years.

"Hey," Baggs said, "I just got to be editor, and the first thing I'm going to do is invent the job of reporter first-class. You guys shouldn't have to write all that crap. Let the kids do it."

When *Time* magazine complimented the *News* on its coverage of the Cuban missile buildup—for which it won the Pulitzer Prize—Baggs would have no part of the predictable "I owe it all to the team" quote.

Said he:

"The best ideas that show up in the paper come from guys out in the newsroom. What we don't have is a team. We have a bunch of individuals."

Baggs operates in an office decorated with—among many other things—a battered brass spittoon, a piece of tile picked up when a house of prostitution was razed and a tile from the lobby of the old Miami News Tower.

On the night when the *News* put out its last edition in the tower before moving to a new plant, Baggs had three kegs of beer delivered to the copydesk. Baggs decided he wanted to take something of the old building with him, so he had a copyboy get him a hammer and chisel and knocked the tile out of the floor of the advertising department.

A guard interrupted him and asked by whose authority he was dismantling the building.

"By the authority of the owner of this newspaper, Gov. James M. Cox," Baggs said.

Governor Cox had died a short time before, but Baggs explained later that he was not being flippant.

"If the governor had been alive," he said, "he'd have been down there with me doing the same damned thing."

Baggs came to the *News* after serving in the air force in Europe during what he describes as War Two. He had worked for the *Greensboro* (North Carolina) *Daily News* and the *Star and Herald* in Panama.

After becoming editor, he criticized the Catholic bishop of Puerto Rico for telling his flock how to vote for governor. The bishop and Catholic leaders in Florida spent a week denouncing him.

"When it was all over," he says, "lightning struck my house. I was in bed at the time, and the jolt threw me to the floor.

"I got up, poured myself a stiff brandy and wired the Puerto Rican bishop. 'You win.' "

That's Baggs.

Robert S. Bates, Editor and Co-publisher
Meadville (Pennsylvania) Tribune

By G. A. Harshman

W illiam Allen White is supposed to have remarked that publishing a newspaper, once a glorious adventure, is now merely a good six percent investment.

We know an editor and co-publisher at Meadville, Pennsylvania, (population, 18,972, circulation, 15,167) who tries to make it both. We pretend no knowledge of his balance sheet but can testify as to the first part.

Or perhaps he fits the Henry Watterson formula of the successful editor owning a chunk of the paper. The *Tribune* is a family-owned paper and thus editor Robert S. Bates is given a free hand on the editorial side. His brother, Edward Irving, handles the management, a task in which he has the aid of Bob's counsel.

There are those who argue that the editor should be confined to his intellectual pursuits, unsullied by the materialism of the business office. Yet a point can be made for the contention that knowledge of what makes the business tick makes a better editor and that conversely, the leaven of editorial viewpoint keeps the pursestrings from being drawn chokingly tight. (Bates would never be guilty of writing such a metaphorical mixture.)

Maintaining a drawn curtain between departments can lead to the charge that editorial people sometimes forget that a newspaper has to have advertising if they are to be paid and if it is to remain free, or that publishers on the other hand may regard the editorial department as a necessary evil and forget that is the reason they are in business at all.

The argument becomes academic to small-town executives, forced to double in brass, as Bob Bates would tell you.

Harshman was editor of the *Sharon* (Pennsylvania) *Herald* when this article first appeared, in 1961.

Nor has the question of the editor's participation in civic activities been a problem to this editor who carries his fifty years and grandfather's status with ease as he does thirty years of editorial service and civic and professional activity.

Bob Bates is typical of those fortunate ones who, born to a newspaper, found it truly their calling and expanded upon their heritage.

His adherence to the objectives of the National Conference of Editorial Writers (NCEW) is reflected in the conscience and quality of the editorial page he directs and to which he contributes daily editorials. His selection by his colleagues as president of NCEW is proof of the measure of his quality in a highly qualified group. He is the only editor of a medium-sized paper to serve as president in the conference's fourteen-year history.

What man of such erudition can be found in so many fundraising activities? Perhaps his ability to stimulate his readers' thought processes is effective in persuading contributors to part with their money. Not content to urge others to civic effort and financial support for community causes by means of his eloquent, hard-hitting editorials, he has been chairman of many educational and charitable drives for which the small-town editor is a sitting duck. And if directorship of a bank and telephone company should threaten to cause him to give too much attention to the mundane life of the business world, he can always compensate by attention to his duties as president of the Meadville Library, Art, and Historical Association.

The Bates home, in its beautiful, tree-studded setting just outside of town, is often the scene of employee gatherings and it has furnished hospitality to many a traveling newspaperman. With Peg Bates as its gracious hostess, its Tudor-style living room is frequently the gathering place of members of the college faculty and friends in the community.

Among many honors was that of having been chosen in 1956 by the Jaycees as "boss of the year," an accolade to which his staff members are known to subscribe, only with them it is "for all time."

Henry Belk, Editor
Goldsboro (North Carolina) News-Argus

By Miles H. Wolff

Members of the ASNE who attended the San Francisco convention may have noticed a very tall man, somewhat stooped and almost handsome, who was always accompanied by a small, dark-haired woman.

If they had stopped to talk with him and had taken a sidelong glance at his badge they would have discovered he was Henry Belk of Goldsboro, North Carolina.

From the red dot on his badge they would have learned he was a new member.

Then, if they had inquired from any of the North Carolina members they would have gained further information. The small woman was Mrs. Belk; the reason she always accompanied her husband was that he is blind.

Perhaps it is not entirely accurate to say he is blind. He does get a glimmer of light in one eye and he can tell when Mrs. Belk is wearing a brightly colored dress. But that is all.

"I cannot remember," Henry Belk said on one occasion, "when my eyes were not a source of pain, of trouble, of distress. Yes, and of fear, if you must. I kept placing that fear out of my mind—there was nothing else to do, you know."

He was born with cataracts on his eyes. Surgeons would not operate until he was adult and his cloudy vision was not corrected until his sophomore and junior years in college. This improved the sight in his left eye but the right eye was left in very poor condition.

After graduation from Duke University, he went into college publicity for two years, taught journalism briefly at New Rochelle College in New Rochelle, New York, and took some courses at Columbia University. He then

---

Wolff was executive editor of the *Greensboro* (North Carolina) *Daily News* when this article first appeared, in 1957.

returned to North Carolina where he has remained since.

He was editor of the *Goldsboro News* for three years and then became managing editor of the *News-Argus* when the two newspapers were merged in 1926. He became editor in 1949.

The crushing blow came three years later. There was a feeling of intolerable pressure in the eyes and a frightening protrusion. The diagnosis was detached retina of the left eye—his good one.

Nine operations followed over the next three years at the Duke University Hospital.

After the eighth operation, Henry seemed to have finally won the battle. Then came a heart attack—a thrombosis—that sent him back to the hospital. While recuperating, he had the final detachment of the left retina and the surgeons admitted defeat.

There was still enough sight in the right eye to warrant a trip to New York for a fitting for microscopic glasses. With these glasses, Henry had a walking and even reading vision for a year. Then an eye infection blotted out this sight.

Last year Henry Belk wrote an open letter to Victor Riesel after Riesel had been blinded by acid.

"I don't know you, Victor Riesel of New York City. But in a way I do. In a way you are my soul brother. For once I could see and now I fumble my way."

Several paragraphs further, he said:

"I had nothing of the terror of your experience but for more than three years I fought to retain some sight. The battle apparently would be won and my spirits soared. Then a new complication would come. Now four years and nine operations later, I accept the verdict. Only a miracle will return to me any vision. But deep inside me there is a conviction that that miracle may happen."

Henry Belk's day starts at six-thirty each morning. He has breakfast and then Mrs. Belk reads the morning paper to him. He is at the office by eight. From then until three-thirty or four o'clock he works steadily, taking time off for a brief lunch and a short rest period made necessary because of his thrombosis.

He considers himself fortunate that he always used the touch system in typing and he is able to write editorials for the *News-Argus* and his column for the *Greensboro Daily News* on his office typewriter.

He usually brings his day's work home for Mrs. Belk to read and to correct any typographical errors. There is another period when Mrs. Belk reads to him—other newspapers and, of course, the *News-Argus* and some of the weekly magazines. A high school senior reads to him for an hour three afternoons a week.

In addition to this he gets records from the Library of Congress and listens to the *Reader's Digest* and to biography, history, and philosophy. He does not get fiction.

Readers of this sketch may have been puzzled by the statement that Henry wrote a column for the *Greensboro Daily News*. He does. It came about in this way. For a number of years the *Daily News* has carried a column of comment on North Carolina affairs three or four times a week. In a day of syndicated columns it is an effort to give a North Carolina "flavor" to the editorial page.

For years, the Raleigh correspondent of the *Daily News* wrote the column. After his death, the dean of the School of Journalism at the University of North Carolina wrote it.

Last year, after the dean's death, editors of the *Daily News* looked around for someone to continue the tradition. They settled almost immediately on Henry Belk. They approached Mrs. Belk somewhat timidly. Would Henry like to do the column? She carried the message to him. He accepted with enthusiasm and has been a steady contributor since then.

North Carolina editors have bestowed on Henry almost every honor in their power. He has been president of the Eastern North Carolina Press Association, president of the North Carolina Associated Press News Council, and president of the North Carolina Press Association.

At home he has been made president of the Rotary Club, president of the county Duke alumni association, and currently is serving on the governor's "Citizen's Committee for Better Schools."

Last year the Rotary Club gave him its outstanding citizenship award for "spiritual, cultural, and economic development of his community and state."

One of Henry's proudest accomplishments is the establishment of College Aid, Inc., in 1954. A loan fund has been set up to help boys and girls from Wayne County (Goldsboro) attend college. He is secretary of the organization.

A Negro high school principal in Goldsboro wrote the editor of the *Greensboro Daily News* to congratulate the newspaper on securing Henry as a columnist. "Few men of our times in Goldsboro, quietly and unobtrusively, have exerted greater influence upon an amicable balance in race relations than has Henry Belk."

Creed Black, Publisher
Lexington Herald-Leader

By Eugene Patterson

W hen I told my wife I was going to write a piece about Creed Black for the *Bulletin* she said, "Tell them he's the funniest man alive."

"What's funny about him?" I asked.

"What isn't?" she explained.

There you have, in essence, your 1983–84 president of ASNE.

"That's just wonderful. I'm glad for Creed," said John McMullan, the executive editor of the *Miami Herald* when I told him I was writing this tribute because Creed's presidency impends. "The last time he was in line to be president he got fired."

Creed and I have in fact discussed from time to time, in low voices, the possibility that he has taken more professional bounces on his way to power than any twentieth-century leader save Deng Xiaoping, and that I've been right up there with him.

Deng knew how to hurt a man like Creed, though. He met our delegation of ASNE editors in the Great Hall of the People and granted us a two-hour interview in 1975 before anybody knew for sure that he would wind up running China (after another couple of bounces) following the then-imminent deaths of Mao and Chou. But we figured we had some very hot stuff in our notebooks as we hurried back to our typewriters at the New Peking Hotel.

Creed wrote long and well, and was nice enough to stop by my room and offer to take my copy to the communist telegraph office along with his own since he was going that way. I said thanks so he filed both of our stories.

You can guess what happened: My interview graced page one of the *St. Petersburg Times* next day. Creed's never got to the *Philadelphia Inquirer*. His colleagues had to scramble to mitigate the embarrassment of having their editor totally blanked. So the *Inquirer* printed some of Mike O'Neill's piece via the *New York Daily News*. This did little to salve Creed's hurts. He still

---

Patterson was editor of the *St. Petersburg Times* when this article first appeared, in 1983.

---

wonders aloud what he wrote that so offended Deng's censors. His *Inquirer* colleagues still wonder if Creed really wrote anything at all.

As you can see, Creed Carter Black has traveled some, since that July day in 1925 when he came into the world at Harlan, Kentucky. By age seventeen he was a reporter on the *Paducah Sun-Democrat* and by age nineteen he was an infantryman winning the Bronze Star for heroism with the 100th Division in Germany.

Our decorated veteran then took a political science degree from Northwestern and a master's from the University of Chicago before going to work on the copydesk at the *Chicago Sun-Times* in 1949. He switched to Chicago's late *Herald-American* in 1950, then moved to Nashville that same year to write editorials for the *Tennessean*. After seven years they made him executive editor and two years later, in 1959, Alvah Chapman lured him out of Nashville to be vice-president and executive editor of the *Savannah Morning News and Evening Press*. Chapman was the new president and publisher in Savannah, on his way up to his present job as board chairman of Knight-Ridder.

Chapman says they did "a lot of exciting things" in the year or so they lasted, trying to introduce modern journalism to a town that likes antiques. "With newspapers that had not been much interested in the twentieth century before our arrival, we had a lot of room," Chapman recalls. "Creed brought a lot of energy and inventiveness to that job. He's a strong-willed editor, yet he and I could cooperate. He still kids me about the time his news budget got stuck financing some dove shoots."

Chapman, it seems, felt they needed to make some influential friends in a community where their investigative journalism was giving hotfoots to fat cats. So they agreed to seduce the gentry with invitations to dove shoots. Creed did not expect to find these activities coming out of his news budget, however, and when he complained Chapman was ready for him. "I told him I had approved his hire of Savannah's first outdoor editor ever, and a dove shoot is an outdoor event," Chapman says.

Both left Savannah before the posse got the tar hot enough to make the feathers stick. Creed managed to run the *Wilmington* (Delaware) *News and Journal* from 1960 to 1964 before he thumbtacked his declaration of independence from the DuPonts to the newsroom bulletin board and moved to the late *Chicago Daily News* as managing editor, 1964–68, and executive editor, 1968–69.

After that he served in the Nixon administration as assistant secretary of health, education and welfare for a year before Lee Hills hired him into Philadelphia to help John McMullan wreck the Annenberg legacy at the *Inquirer* and install Knight quality.

Rolfe Neill, now president and publisher of the *Charlotte Observer* and the

Charlotte News, was editor of Knight's *Philadelphia News* at the time Black hit town. He remembers Executive Editor McMullan's equivocal introduction of the new editorial page editor at a welcoming luncheon.

"The *Inquirer* has always needed a creed," McMullan said, "and we certainly don't have enough blacks."

McMullan recalls, "Creed was just what we needed. We were in a common cause together—brothers working in the same crummy vineyard—trying to straighten out the *Inquirer.* He had just the sort of independence and spirit to redirect those editorial pages. He had a great combination of b.s. and finesse."

Neill agrees. "Creed was able to bring strength of viewpoint to the editorial pages while maintaining good relations with civic leaders he was affronting."

But Frank Rizzo was not charmed. "We took him to lunch to try to talk him out of running for mayor," McMullan recalls. "Creed came at him very smoothly, asking, 'Why would you want to run for mayor, when you've already built your reputation as a fine police commissioner?'"

For the first sixty seconds of the tough cop's response, McMullan said he thought maybe they had misgauged the man. "In a very touching way he said how proud he was that his father had been the first Italian sergeant on the force. Now he was the first Italian commissioner. It could only happen in Philadelphia. So he owed the city so much."

Then suddenly, McMullan recalls, Rizzo glowered fiercely, ground his right fist angrily into his left palm, leaned across the table to Creed Black, and gritted, "Besides, I've got a lot of scores to settle!"

Don't be lulled by that tailored, boardroom look Creed's developed over the years as chairman and publisher of the *Lexington Herald-Leader* in the bluegrass of his native Kentucky—a place where, Alvah Chapman says, "He is doing a really good job."

Don't drop your guard just because he well may be the funniest man alive. He's got a little Rizzo in him.

Lafayette R. Blanchard, Editorial Chairman
Gannett Newspapers

By Vincent S. Jones

W hen Lafayette R. (Fay) Blanchard announced that he would retire at the end of 1956 the news was received with a mixture of shock and disbelief.

Along with scores of expressions of regret came a letter of outright disapproval from an old companion-at-arms, Alexander F. (Casey) Jones, hinting that this was a publicity stunt and calling upon Fay to issue a denial of these "press agent stories."

Back in the 1930s when Blanchard was, successively, managing editor of all three of the daily newspapers then operating in Rochester, his Man of Distinction good looks had made him in demand as a Kodak model in a role which brought him the premature nickname of "Gramp." Today, at sixty-seven, the Blanchard facade still flutters feminine hearts. A brand-new photograph, commissioned especially to accompany the retirement story, elicited comments ranging from open-mouthed admiration to mean-spirited questions as to which brand was being endorsed.

Best evidence of the indestructibility of Blanchard's virility and persuasiveness is the editorial page which he has created for the *Rochester Democrat and Chronicle* over the last six years. The ivory tower of this western New York "bible" has achieved a warm blend of good sense and good humor. It is beautifully attuned to a conservative, successful community which likes to take its Republicanism with a grain of salt and to believe that it is both truly liberal and reasonably progressive. Best of all, Blanchard's undoubted gifts as a writer have become known to thousands instead of being beamed exclusively at fellow executives of the Gannett Group.

In his last year on the job, Blanchard has had the additional

---

Jones was executive editor of the Gannett newspapers when this article first appeared, in 1956.

responsibility of being editorial chairman of the Group, heading up a revival movement which has had a magical effect upon editorial pages of other Gannett newspapers. This has been done by direct study and criticism of other pages and through a weekly bulletin, entitled (with tongue in cheek) "The Sanctum."

For many years, as director of the Group's News and Editorial Office, and later general executive editor, Fay Blanchard worked hard and successfully to help the editors of the Group's twenty-three autonomous newspapers. A whole generation of Gannett editors owes much to the inspiration and guidance they received from him in this critical period when the Group was growing into its present form.

The Blanchard methods revolve about subtle applications of the sounder copybook maxims and shrewd use of practical psychology. As a managing editor he pressed relentlessly for better reporting, brighter writing, and attractive display.

On the *Times-Union*, Blanchard practiced what he preached. His pithy bulletin board memos were so readable that later they were collected into a mimeographed booklet under the title, "Staff, Please Note!" This has become a collector's item. When he moved upstairs to the Group's central News and Editorial Office he wrote (1941–50) "The Bulletin," a weekly letter which goes to about one hundred executives of newspapers throughout the organization.

To editorial writing he brought the same tough standards by which he judged the news as a managing editor. "That sounds like an editorial; let's rewrite it," he told his assistants so frequently that they developed a relaxed style in self-defense. As a speaker, Fay could be equally tough. He did not hesitate to upbraid even the DAR for its share in public apathy about government. He chastised doctors and lawyers for their poor public relations, their addiction to "pedantic mumbo-jumbo," and for shielding the malpractitioners in their own ranks.

One Blanchard secret weapon, the therapeutic nap during the duller portions of afternoon convention sessions, had to be scrapped when his talents were put to work full time by the Associated Press Managing Editors (APME). A needling speech by Fay at the Los Angeles meeting in 1946 brought the inevitable reward—chairmanship of a committee to study Associated Press's domestic report. These labors led to chairmanship of the entire APME study and eventually to presidency of the organization. At about the same time he was "discovered" by the ASNE electorate. He served a term on the board and one year as treasurer.

In addition to a flair for tasteful typography and display, Blanchard takes especial delight in a deft headline or an arresting title. Editors asked to speak at annual conferences of the Gannett Group found themselves listed under topics so challenging that they literally had to speak over their heads. The resultant improvement in conference speeches led to another Blanchard project—*Editorially Speaking,* a pamphlet of newspaper shop talk, now in its fourteenth annual edition of some three thousand copies which go to newspapermen and journalism students all over the United States.

Although an appreciative reader and a sympathetic listener, Blanchard doles out compliments with jealous parsimony. There are none for standard deluxe performances ("that's what you're paid to do, and expected to do"). Associates, however, cherish his rare accolades. A man whose piece was described as "shining like a diamond in a coal-bin" will carry this and a handful of other hard-won tributes to the grave.

Blanchard's interests are wide and he keeps adding to them. A baseball fan, fisherman, and a golfer, he developed a taste for travel and wrote lively accounts of several trips to Europe. He fell in love with France and still works determinedly, with books and records, at learning the language. In retirement, Fay and Beula Blanchard will set out on a leisurely auto trip to the West Coast, where they will take their time selecting a new home—probably within visiting range of their only son, Robert, who inherited Fay's writing talent and now is assistant political editor of the *Los Angeles Times.* The trip is timed to escape Rochester at the beginning of its soul-testing winter climate.

Thomas L. Boardman, Editor
The Cleveland Press

By Irving Leibowitz

F ollowing Louis B. Seltzer as editor of the *Cleveland Press* is like singing "Madame Butterfly" for Renata Tebaldi, pinch-hitting for Babe Ruth, replacing Knute Rockne as coach, and exposing your posterior a la Gypsy Rose Lee.

Thomas Leslie Boardman, forty-six, moved in as editor of the *Press* at a time in January when the paper was in a head-on collision with the *Cleveland Plain Dealer* for circulation, prestige, and power. It was at a time when publisher Thomas L. Vail of the revitalized *Plain Dealer* was challenging Louis Seltzer on the banquet circuit, as a civic personality, as a city-builder, as a newspaper-builder, as an empire-builder, as "Mr. Cleveland."

Jack Howard, president of Scripps-Howard, put it this way: "A newspaper is like a book. We've had the glorious Louis Seltzer chapter. And now we have the Tom Boardman chapter. I'm confident it will be equally magnificent."

One phrase probably best describes the tall, lean, prematurely bald Tom: "quiet determination." He has the alert, logical, searching mind of a scholar (he was an alternate Rhodes Scholar) and an infectious personality that makes staffers, friends, and bigshots in the power structure want to turn handsprings for him.

The day Tom moved into the editor's chair at the *Press*, Louis Seltzer said: "I say that Tom is the logical and natural choice to edit this newspaper. His assumption of this great responsibility brings a sense of comfort to me both for the paper, for its staff, and for my home community in the future."

If Tom was awed by the rugged competition of the *Plain Dealer*, he failed to show it with one of his first utterances as editor. "I am a great believer in

---

Leibowitz was editor of the *Lorain* (Ohio) *Journal* when this article first appeared, in 1966.

23

competitive everything and particularly competitive journalism. We intend to compete by putting out a darned good newspaper."

Some are misled by the mild manner of the new *Press* editor, or by his amusing anecdotes at ASNE cocktail parties. Don't be. He's tough. But not cynical. He believes a newspaper can be critical in a constructive way. He shuns the slambang, "everybody resign" kind of destructive journalism.

Without ranting or raving, without excessive memos and office speeches, he has a curious but effective way of communicating the character of the paper to the staffers and through them to the readers. He hints. He suggests. He questions. He has a way of letting everyone in the huge, modern lakefront *Press* building know what's going on.

Will there be changes at the *Press?* Of course. Every editor wants to put his own stamp on his paper.

You can expect the *Press* to stay in character as the conscience of the community and to push for civic improvements for a greater Cleveland.

"The truth is that the growth and development of our municipalities is controlled as much by the alertness of its leadership as it is by the shifting economic patterns," Tom once said. "To believe that change, good or bad, is inevitable, is at best to invite a dreamless sleep, and at worst to die."

Tom has the same philosophy for the paper as he does for Cleveland: "Change, adapt, or die."

It is an educated guess, based partly on leisurely bull sessions with Tom and partly on what he himself has written, that eventually there will be greater emphasis in the *Press* on foreign affairs, social significance, and science. And less on trivia.

In 1962, at the American Press Institute (API) seminar for editors, Tom wrote back what editors think the readers expect of their newspapers.

"Your interest in world affairs is enlarging, but not as rapidly as the times require," he wrote. "Our job is to improve the presentation so that world events become as interesting to you as local events."

Tom's concern with and alertness to social problems found him saying in 1961, before the Watts riots in Los Angeles and the militant Negro revolution in the North. "Big cities must revitalize to survive the next decade. Negroes, the foreign-born, and Southerners want to carry their share of the load. But if they remain undigested masses, with lack of friendly acceptance, they will become economic and social burdens, draining away vast sums of welfare money and creating social problems."

How do you pick the right editor to succeed a Louis Seltzer? Whom can you trust with the family jewels?

Jack Howard took Tom from the affluence of the *Press,* where Tom had been editor of the editorial page, and sent him for training as editor to grinding poverty—where the alert and pugnacious staff of the *Indianapolis*

Times was battling the entrenched morning and afternoon combination of publisher Eugene Pulliam's *Star* and *News.*

It was a great fight, Mom, but we lost. When Scripps-Howard suspended its Indianapolis paper and plucked Tom for the editorship in Cleveland, the *Indianapolis Times* was gaining in circulation and advertising. Unfortunately, the biggest gains were in production costs.

It was priceless training for Tom, where he could test his weapons, his battle strategy, and his men under combat conditions.

There is a theory abroad that what's wrong with newspapers today is that editors don't understand the mechanical side and are completely mystified by computers and other gadgets that save time and money, reduce costs, and allow you to concentrate your money in the productive part of the newspapers—editorial, circulation, and advertising.

This could be Tom's greatest strength. He's a writer's writer, an editor's editor, and a source of inspiration to anyone who comes in contact with him. But unlike most good editors, he does understand the mechanics of the game. He's a brain.

What does he expect of the *Press?*

"First and most important, to report the news," he said. "To serve as a kind of community bulletin board , . . to serve as a forum for discussion of the major issues of the day . . . to express editorial opinions on these issues, forcefully and fearlessly . . . to keep a watchful eye on government, to be the people's eyes and ears."

Boardman went right to the *Press* as a copyboy when he was graduated from nearby Oberlin College. He met his wife, Cynthia, at college but he waited to marry her during the war on a navy ship docked in New York (but that's another hilarious and precious Boardman anecdote, good for another time). They have two children, Thomas, Jr., seventeen, and Caroline, fifteen.

Tom was an authentic warrior during World War II, entering the navy as a yeoman and returning as a lieutenant commander after hazardous duty all over the world heading demolition teams and piloting planes on special missions. When he was commissioned an ensign, Tom was given a watch as the outstanding graduate of eight hundred midshipmen.

His mother was a teacher who raised him and a sister when Tom's father died. I can still remember a story Tom wrote about his mother.

"My mother has been named Mother of the Year for the whole state of Texas, and as big as Texas is, I'm not the least bit surprised."

I have no idea how the *Press* will do in circulation, or advertising, or net revenue under Tom but I suspect it will be good. More important, though, if people want a paper they can trust, one they can respect, one with integrity, I'm convinced they'll get it with Tom Boardman in the editor's chair.

Herbert Brucker, Editor
The Hartford Courant

By Dwight E. Sargent

He has the bearing of a senator, the conscience of a Congregational minister, the literacy of a college president, and the restless mind of a good lawyer. Many careers would have welcomed him. But he believes that when he became a newspaper editor he found the noblest calling of them all.

He answered that call with an affirmation of faith that has left a mark on his profession and moved him inevitably toward national recognition and a position of leadership in the ASNE. He is a man who has long regarded the press as a lengthened arm of government constitutionally commissioned to guard the democratic process.

This "man who" is a teacher, scholar, author, lecturer, philosopher, world traveler (and an Old Frontiersman who would rather ski than walk), all rolled into the editor of the *Hartford Courant*. If this introduction makes Herbert Brucker sound like one of the driving spirits in American journalism, it is because he is.

Herb would resent my calling him an elder statesman. He is neither old enough nor worn enough. "Jet age journalist" would make him cringe, as it should. Actually he is a bit of each. Instinctively he is both traditionalist and modernist, and has devoted much energy looking for ways for the twain to meet and understand each other.

He is a traditionalist in his devotion to the spirit of our fathers who fought the first battles against censorship and suppression and cleared the way for newspapers to develop as instruments of public service. For him the editor's mission as the community's watchman of the night hasn't changed since John Peter Zenger dared criticize Governor Cosby.

The machinery for carrying out that mission needs frequent retooling, however, if old traditions are to serve a changing world. This is what Herb Brucker hasn't let us forget. With the impatience of a perfectionist he keeps

Sargent was editorial page editor of the *New York Herald Tribune* when this article first appeared, in 1963.

reminding us that what may have been desirable in the day of the Model-T must be changed to fit the television age. We never tire of telling ourselves that we have the best newspapers in the world, but this could not be the truth if voices of reality didn't haunt us, as Herb Brucker's has, with another truth, ". . . there is a lot about our trade that is wrong, and nobody knows it better than we."

Herb has for years been embroiled in every important fight for freedom of information, and has started a few of his own. As ASNE's Freedom of Information (FoI) chairman in 1956 he loosed an echoing volley at Foster Dulles for preventing American newsmen from entering Red China. Said Brucker to Dulles, you're "erecting an iron curtain of your own." No news barrier is beyond his range. Editors, he believes, ought to risk jail more often in defiance of judges who try to dam the flow of news.

This is not the profile of a fire-eating crusader. It is just as well, for fire-eaters don't finish first. Herb's crusading has the quality of responsibility, the power of quiet dignity, the persuasiveness of firm conviction. He's an idealist, yes. But an idealist with a head for figures, as they say, or to put it another way, a practical man who isn't ashamed to have ideals. He has little patience with the assumed incompatibility of conscience and counting-house; a good newspaper, he often says, must be fiscally solvent as well as morally solvent.

It all started in Passaic, New Jersey, on October 4, 1898, when Herb was born to a German immigrant father and a New York mother. He was graduated from Williams College in 1921, then went on to the Columbia School of Journalism, where he did well enough to win a highly competitive Pulitzer Traveling Fellowship. The latter gave him a semester at the Sorbonne and a chance to sharpen his nose for news in northern Africa and Central Europe before returning to the wilds of Manhattan.

After two years with the *New York World*, he went to *World's Work* and the *Review of Reviews* before joining the Columbia School of Journalism faculty in 1932 as assistant to Dean Ackerman. He left, as a full professor, for wartime OWI service before becoming associate editor of the *Courant* in 1944, editor three years later.

He lives in the Hartford suburb of Avon, on thirteen acres which, to a New York commuter, is an indecently short eight miles from the office. He and his lovely wife Elizabeth keep the place shoveled out, or mowed, depending on the whim of the New England skies, for his three grown children, two step-children, and their children are scattered about the countryside from Hartford to Seattle.

Tall, tweedy, and good humored, Herb presides over an editorial page of national influence. Many a paper has copied its style, few have achieved its editorial sting. Typical of the *Courant's* record of community leadership was a three-year fight against entrenched two-party resistance to a much-needed manager form of municipal government. The *Courant* won, and so did Hartford, which is one of the many reasons the oldest (founded in 1764) newspaper in the country is known as one of the most vigorous.

Its editor's citations from colleges, colleagues, and professional organizations bear respectful witness to his standing as one of the nation's most honored journalists. He has traveled the lengths of the earth and twice in recent years has served on the faculty of the Salzburg Seminar for American Studies in Austria.

On the lecture circuit Herb is remarkably nonbombastic for a man of many controversies. His formula is that the shortest distance between orator and audience lies in candor, logic, and mutual confidence. Neither as dramatic as Jenkin Lloyd Jones nor as electrifying as Gene Patterson, a Brucker speech is no less memorable. He talks of the heart and soul of a newspaper in tones of intimacy and in a way to brew his own mixture of drama and excitement.

Herb has a little list of myths he is sure won't be missed. One is that journalism schools downgrade liberal arts in favor of technical courses. Once when Walter Lippmann told the National Press Club that "There is nothing to teach in a school of journalism," Brucker charged from his corner with a cutting counterthrust: "It is all but instinctive with newspaper people to believe that there is nothing to teach in a school of journalism. This belief reflects an ignorance so big, strong, beautiful, and shining that it is impossible to dent it." This foe of the foes of journalism schools has just been elected to a second term as president of the American Council on Education for Journalism.

Herb has not always been right. (At the start of the 1948 campaign he wrote that ". . . all signs point to the long overdue return to the Republicans." Which, I suspect, makes him a bedfellow of a goodly number of his ASNE brethren who also thought they could believe what they read in the polls.) But for a quarter century he has pointed with telling accuracy to the rusty places in the American press and the soft spots in our professional ethics. Three books tell much of that story.

His first, *The Changing American Newspaper,* notes how the mission of the newspaper has changed little since the first, *Publick Occurrences,* appeared in 1690 with publisher Benjamin Harrison's prospectus: "It is designed that the countrey shall be furnished once a moneth (or if any Glut of Occurrences happen, oftener) with an account of such considerable things as have arrived our Notice."

The "Glut" happened and will be with us always, but methods of keeping up with it have changed, and will continue to do so as the "moneths" go by. This is what Columbia's Professor Brucker was saying a quarter century ago when the atom bomb and the unearthly goings-on at Cape Canaveral had not been heard of. Although he did not then know the nature of tomorrow's news he urged preparation to handle it more efficiently via expository writing, better pictorial journalism, news summaries, and constant examination of the moods of the reader.

He talked about *interpretation* when to most people it meant *translation.* He tried to keep *opinion* in its place, and out of the wrong places, before the separatist movement became generally understood. He discussed a newspaper's duty to interpret the facts at a time when it was fashionable to say the facts spoke for themselves. That was in 1937.

Freedom of Information, his second book, found the conscience of the author still concerned with the mores of the American newspaper, and still raising embarrassingly pertinent questions. Only this time they related to the nuclear age—how to adjust, how to inform, how to enlighten, how to serve, how to organize and display the news better, how to make what he calls "The Fourth Branch of Government" a truly responsible segment of society and deserving of its freedom.

One of his theses should be nailed to the door of the New Frontier:

> In passing, one may offer a suggestion to those who themselves become the victims of the newspapers' habit of prying. The best defense is to come clean. If somebody wants your picture, let him take it, even though it seems obvious to you that it is none of his damned business. If a reporter asks a question, answer it frankly. With nothing to conceal, few who respond with honesty and fairness rather than with hostility and a desire to tell the press where to get off suffer greatly from its nosiness. It is with shutting the door that trouble begins . . .

Herb would liberate the word *objective* from the sole custody of the newsroom. Objectivity relates to editorials too, he argues properly, provided they are concerned with searching for truth and not appeasing a prejudice. His point is worth repeating:

> There is no need to fear that papers, by making their editorial pages as objective as their news columns, will stultify themselves with an excess of ifs, buts, and on-the-other-hands. Objectivity in opinion is achieved not by emasculating editorials, but by directing every possible ounce of missionary zeal and hellfire to the service of the entire community rather than merely to a part of it. A news story is made objective by reporting both sides of the controversy. An editorial is made objective by weighing both sides of a controversy with a broad perspective and a deep understanding before deciding

which side to fight for. Editorially, a newspaper should be objective only as to purpose. Once it has determined what is right in a given issue, it should pull no punches . . . . We need more, not less, of the thundering Hebrew prophets in our editorial page.

Speaking of prophets, the ninth chapter in this book is entitled "Managed News." It was published eleven years before President Kennedy held his first press conference.

Last year the third Brucker book, *Journalist, Eyewitness to History,* joined Macmillan's Career Book Series. Although essentially a guide for college men and women wondering about journalism as a career, their elders will find it a rewarding dissertation on the joys and frustrations of a life lived to the accompaniment of rolling presses. It makes lively reading for those who would learn of our profession from one who would trade it for no other, but whose accounts are unblemished by sentiment.

In some respects Herb has always been steps ahead of the rest of us. In others, he is as set in his ways as when he pecked out his first piece of copy in the city room of the old *New York World.* One of those green-eyeshade editors discovered to his horror that the new reporter had a skeleton in his closet—*Journalism School.* Herb confessed, whereupon his mentor came through with the expected counsel: "Now listen. The first thing you want to do is forget everything they told you up there." Herb neither listened, nor forgot, as the old editor shuffled off to oblivion and the young cub grew up to be one of journalism's most widely respected practitioners.

This, then, is the world of Herbert Brucker, editor.

It is a world of good works and great satisfactions, of services rendered and wrongs righted. It is also a world of miles to go and missions unfulfilled, for it is bounded on all sides by challenges and opportunities waiting to be explored by the editor with a sense of destiny.

Herb isn't quite as nimble on his skis as he was during his schussing days at Williams, but his sense of professional duty is as sharp as ever, his standards as uncorrupted, his pursuit of quality as relentless. Unchanged after his embattled years in Hartford (like his comfortable New Jersey accent) is his feeling for journalism as "a vibrant thing, a deeply moral calling for all who are associated with it." Of such are the dimensions of his personal and professional commitment to freedom of information.

This would be a good time to ignore everything Herb ever tried to teach us about the necessity for interpretive reporting, for in his case the facts of a truly distinguished career speak eloquently for themselves.

Gentlemen, the editor of the *Hartford Courant.*

Harry F. Byrd, Jr., Editor
Winchester (Virginia) Evening Star

By Gretchen Byrd

F rom his classmates at the University of Virginia I learned that my husband, Harry F. Byrd, Jr., the editor of the *Winchester Evening Star* and the publisher of the *Harrisonburg Daily News-Record,* both in Virginia, was the only member of his class to have the *New York Times* sent to him at school. That in itself may or may not be significant. But to set the record straight it should be mentioned he also had several Virginia newspapers on his subscription list. Seems Harry, from a tender age, just *liked* newspapers.

Naturally, having newspapers around meant that they had to be perused. So at every opportunity Harry would bury his nose in one of them—in class or out. Few educators, I would imagine, appreciate inattentive students. To have one of them sit before you baldly leafing through the local gazette . . . well, it proved to be too much for one professor. Close to the end of the term he advised Harry there was no need to take the final examination as there was scant likelihood he would receive a passing mark.

Harry took up the gauntlet and, temporarily, set aside his newspapers. For three days and three nights he boned up on the subject, took the final exam, and managed to pull out a cool 96.

At first Harry had no intention of entering the newspaper profession, for it was planned that at the conclusion of his college years he would accept a job with a sulphur company. But one day in May 1935—about a month before he was to take that job—Harry wrote his father a twenty-page letter criticizing the *Winchester Star* and recommending ideas for improving it.

His father, who doubled as publisher while serving in the United States Senate, replied with one sentence: "If you know so much about newspapers, why don't you go to work on the *Star* and find out which of your ideas are good and which are bad?"

Thus ended Harry's potential career in the sulphur industry. That was

This article first appeared in 1964.

twenty-eight years ago. I suppose it's superfluous to add that he's even more intensely interested in newspapering today.

Of course, he's had to squeeze in a lot of other non-newspaper activity on the side, owning and operating six hundred acres of apple orchards, and having more than a passing interest in politics. As an orchardist, he spends most of his afternoons walking through the apple trees while many of his friends are on the golf course. He has been tempted, though, to pick up a golf club occasionally, particularly with Paul Miller and Dick Nixon. But I have never cracked the secrecy about his score.

Keenly interested in politics since he was a boy in the Governor's Mansion in Richmond (his father was governor in the twenties), Harry has served in the Virginia Senate since 1948.

But even among politicians and statesmen, his first love—newspapering—prevails. He feels nonmetropolitan newspapers are obligated to put out a well-rounded publication and to that end he goes overseas frequently, talking with international leaders and studying economic and political conditions in the countries visited.

His favorite international personality is Winston Churchill, whom he first met in Richmond before the wartime prime minister had gained lasting fame.

When Harry was last in England, Mr. Churchill gave him—and me—a personally conducted tour through the House of Commons and House of Lords.

Incidentally, Mr. Churchill gave Harry two pieces of advice regarding the construction of a legislative hall. Mr. Churchill was discussing the bombed out House of Commons, which he insisted be restored in its original form. His advice was this: One, have an oblong chamber and put one political party on one side and the other political party on the other side "and make them stay there." (Mr. Churchill did not mention that he had changed political parties several times.)

Two, do not have enough seats for all the members. Make them crowd in and sit on one another's laps or on the floor, because, Mr. Churchill said, "it's much more democratic that way—and besides, it's much easier to speak to a crowded chamber."

In the early days of Castro, Harry made two visits to Cuba, reporting at length on changes that were rapidly taking place there. One night while Castro was delivering one of his five-hour harangues in a Havana public square, Harry called home. From the tone of the bearded one's voice in the background, I was afraid Harry was going to be forced to become a permanent resident of Cuba.

In all of his business operations Harry operates very informally and delegates responsibility. But he expects things to be run in a businesslike way. Before we were married I worked for him as society editor and we dated almost every night—but in the office I was *never* Gretchen, *always* Miss Thomson. It took me quite a while to adjust to this switch. After we were married, it took a while for *him* to call me anything in public except Miss Thomson.

As a businessman, he has the peculiarity of paying bills before they come due—and demands that sums owed his business enterprises be paid within a reasonable period after due date.

When Harry first took charge of the operations of the *Star,* a prominent local lawyer owed a large sum of money for legal advertising, some of it dating back twenty years. After six months of patiently attempting to collect the amount due, Harry was told by the attorney that there was no proof that the attorney had inserted the advertising. So Harry gathered together forty *Star* employees, gave each of them a bound file of the *Star,* marched the group single column to the lawyer's office and presented the lawyer with physical evidence. He received a check on the spot.

Except for being on the lookout for new methods of production, he takes only a modest interest in the mechanical side of the papers. His real love is the news operation, as he contends a newspaper must be what its name implies, a NEWS-paper.

He still likes to surround himself with newspapers, and he keeps my house cluttered. He now subscribes to forty-four daily newspapers, some of which he reads standing up, letting them drop through his fingers to the floor as he finishes them.

Besides being buried in newspapers, he likes to work with able newsmen. At each of his papers the general manager is an Associated Press "alumnus." D. Lathan Mims at Harrisonburg was Associated Press state news editor for the Carolinas and Jack F. Davis, at Winchester, was Associated Press chief of bureau in West Virginia before joining the *News-Record* and *Star.*

Both are given free rein in the news operation and both tell me that Harry's newspaper operations are not unlike the Associated Press's own well established objective presentation of the news. Neither newspaper crusades and neither tries to be absolute or dictatorial in its editorial policies. Both are heavy on news and the news hole of each often equals that of some of the metropolitan papers coming into our area of the Shenandoah Valley.

Turner Catledge, Managing Editor
The New York Times

By Mark F. Ethridge

G eorge Allen, everybody's friend (particularly Roosevelt's, Truman's and Eisenhower's), once explained why Mississippi turned a disproportionate share of newspapermen loose on the country: "It's a damned sight easier than plowing."

Turner Catledge has found it so. Although a part-time clerk in his younger days in his uncle's grocery that "furnished" most of the cotton planters and sharecroppers in Neshoba County, Mississippi, and although graduated from an agricultural college, Turner was too smart to let himself be caught between the plow-handles behind a mule. Indeed, he can boast "without fear of successful contradiction," as some of his beloved Capitol Hill friends would say, that as far as his hand and plow are concerned, all the acres of all the earth are virgin.

His agricultural education was not wholly lost; it got him a five-dollar raise from a formidable editor and gave him a leg up the newspaper ladder. Early in Turner's stay on the *Memphis Commercial Appeal,* the late great C. P. J. Mooney stormed into the city room and wanted to know right fast, "What do you call the fellow who's an expert on bugs?"

Mr. Mooney was giving the boll weevil hell and was looking for a synonym. Nobody answered.

"Doesn't anybody on this paper know anything?" demanded Mr. Mooney.

"The word you are looking for, Mr. Mooney, is entomologist," answered the rawest and youngest and at that moment the meekest of cubs.

"That's right, young man. Thank you. You'll have a five-dollar raise next

Ethridge was publisher of the *Courier-Journal and Louisville Times* when this article first appeared, in 1960.

34

pay day," Mr. Mooney threw over his shoulder as he walked back to the cubicle that served him as an office.

But that's getting ahead of the story. Turner's birth is not recorded in Mississippi, which was late getting around to vital statistics. But he was finally able to prove two years ago, to the satisfaction of a marriage license clerk in New Orleans—with the help of George Healy, Bill Minor of the *Times-Picayune* bureau at Jackson, his old friend Ben Hilburn, president of Turner's alma mater, Mississippi State—that he was born at Ackerman, Mississippi (population 1,463) on March 17, 1901. While he was still a baby his parents moved forty miles south to Philadelphia, the seat of the Turner clan with a Choctaw Indian reservation nearby. There is a story around Philadelphia that for three years after he started talking, Catledge spoke only Choctaw. At any rate he has always been fond of his hometown Indians and stories about them, and the only political idol that he ever confessed to having was Congressman Adam Byrd, part Choctaw.

One incident of his school days crops up in the Philadelphia paper every time there is an occasion to note another Catledge triumph. He and other town boys organized a Roman candle battle that got so hot that one of the boys ducked into a barbershop, his Roman candle going full blast. Unfortunately, one of the town's citizenry was having an inflammable hair tonic applied. It caught fire, of course, with pretty spectacular results and Turner and nine or ten other boys were rounded up by the town marshal. But the officer had not figured on dealing with Catledge, who was up before daybreak and at the mayor's house, where he put the "fix" for the whole crowd.

In 1918 he showed up at Mississippi A & M as what some of his classmates thought a mild, meek youngster with a "country boy wit." But four years later, when he was graduated with a B.S. degree and honors to go with it, he had about taken over the campus. The yearbook, which called him "Cat.", said of him that his "natural assertiveness, innate leadership, and applied 'winology' have molded him into a pre-eminent politician." He was president of the Gordians, varsity debater, member of the Dialectic and Demosthenian literary societies, and member of the student council—in fact, he belonged to everything that gave him a chance to talk. He was editor of *Reveille* and also made lieutenant in the cadet corps, but from a yearbook reference I judge that he was somewhat less successful as a soldier than Stonewall Jackson.

During the summer of 1921, while Turner was still in school, Clayton Rand, publisher of the *Neshoba Democrat,* wanted to raise the circulation price of the paper from a dollar a year to a dollar and a half. He made Turner rural correspondent; Turner's job was to go out and write up the people and the farms in the county, the most promising prospects being, of course, the most promising prospects for the dollar and a half, payable in cash or potatoes, beans, or even stovewood.

The next year, when Turner got out of A & M, Rand borrowed the money to buy the *Tunica Times,* over in the Delta. It was then printed on a Washington hand press, with hand-set type. Its subscription list totalled eighty-three. Turner was on the masthead as "editor and assistant publisher," which meant he did everything there was to do. Rand took his newspaper empire of three weeklies into a knock-down fight with the Ku Klux Klan, the only three Mississippi newspapers to do so. The Klan committee at Tunica, a plumber, a lawyer, and a druggist, called Rand to tell him that if he didn't quit the fight the *Tunica Times* "would go to hell." He didn't quit and, as Rand says, the paper went to hell fast.

Turner landed on the *Tupelo* (Mississippi) *Journal* and served for a few months as managing editor and mechanical superintendent.

Then, as he would say, came the call to Memphis, the real mecca of the Tri-States. It was from the *Memphis Press,* a Scripps-Howard paper struggling against the great *Commercial Appeal* and the *Scimitar.* Everybody knows the story of Turner calling all the coal, wood, and fuel people in Memphis when the city editor told him to "get up an add" on a snow storm that had Memphis tied up. His stay on the *Press* was brief because he had his eye on the *Commercial Appeal* and the chance to work under Mr. Mooney.

Three of the men who were on the *Commercial Appeal* when Turner showed up for work are still there. They remember the cub as a "gangling eager beaver who wore his hat and whistled while he worked" until they broke him of it. The entomologist incident drew Mr. Mooney's attention and he soon began assigning Catledge to policy stories. The Florida boom was going great guns and the Tri-State area was losing hundreds of people to the "binder boys" at Miami.

"This damned foolishness has got to stop!" roared the old rip snorter to the young reporter. "Go down there and expose it!"

Even then Catledge was one of the world's top reporters, but he never believed in developing varicose veins when he could use his head. He cased the situation in Miami for a few days and then holed up in his hotel room. From there, he called a telegram through the switchboard to Western Union. It was addressed to Sam Kahn in Memphis and said, "Advise syndicate my opinion we should invest a million at once." Turner had thirty cents of his own money in his pocket, but by morning the hallway outside his room and the lobby downstairs were filled with the binder boys waiting to take the sucker from Memphis. He let them all in, got their stories, and did a series for the *Commercial Appeal* that cooled off the get-rich-quick fever of people in the Tri-States. He had discovered that switchboard, telephone, and wire operators were tipsters for the "binder boys."

Covering politics in Memphis, Turner had made a friend of "Boss" Crump, a fellow Mississippian. Mr. Mooney had the notion that "Boss" Crump was voting repeaters and set Turner and several other reporters and photographers to catch him. Turner and a camera landed in the gutter at a polling place. Indignantly, Turner took himself to "Boss" Crump's office and met a smiling, benign "red rooster."

"What you mean, having your men beat me up?" sputtered Catledge.

"Tell me all about it, son," said Mr. Crump.

Turner did, reaching great heights of fury. When he had finished, Mr. Crump smiled the smile of an angel and observed, "Now listen, son, I can tell you how we will avoid such unfortunate things. You just keep your damned nose out of my business and I'll keep mine out of yours."

When the great Mississippi flood of 1927 came along, Turner was assigned to cover it and the trip that Herbert Hoover as secretary of commerce made down the river in preparation for recommendations on river control. Turner's coverage, partly by plane, so impressed Mr. Hoover that he wrote a letter to Adolph Ochs suggesting that he ought to take a look at the young fellow in Memphis. A good many years later, when Percy McDonald, a Memphis lawyer, organized a sort of This Is Your Life party for Turner, Mr. Hoover wrote him, "My picture of Turner Catlege is that of a boy reporter in 1927—just into his twenties, alert, industrious, droll. He had already demonstrated that fine intelligence which carried him to the top in journalism."

Turner didn't land on the *Times* immediately after the Hoover letter to Adolph Ochs, but Mr. Ochs didn't forget it and two years later drafted him from the *Baltimore Sun* for a period on the city staff in New York. He has been with the *Times* ever since, except for seventeen months as national correspondent and then editor of the *Chicago Sun.* That was a period of unhappiness for him because his tempo is that of the *New York Times,* not that of a brash Chicago paper clawing its way to recognition.

In 1930 Catledge was transferred to the Washington bureau of the *Times* where for six years he covered the White House, Capitol Hill, political conventions, and the revolution that was the New Deal. In 1936 Arthur Krock, then head of the bureau, made him chief Washington news correspondent. In his swings around the country, we in the provinces had a chance to see him at work as the pre-eminent political reporter. He could hit Louisville in the morning and by night, with a few phone calls and a few visits, tell you how Kentucky would go. He has a sure instinct for getting at the sources of power and knowledge. Politicians like and trust him because he falls in love with all of them. Russ Wiggins and I agree that he would never make a great crusader.

"I think he never had enough confidence in his own piety to be a peerless muckraker," Russ said of him. "Moreover, he has a disconcerting tendency to develop an affection for the objects of his muckraking. He just naturally likes politicans, good, bad, and indifferent. A lot of people think that the only way a newspaperman ought to look at a politician is down. Catledge looks at them with amusement, skepticism, doubt—and with sheer delight when their hypocrisy reaches the level of high art."

He did indeed develop an affection for such diverse characters as "Cotton Ed" Smith, whose walkout of the 1936 convention he has embalmed in the country's folklore; "Tawm" Heflin, whose verbal passages at the Federal Reserve Act led another of Turner's favorites, Carter Glass, to threaten to "e-vis-cer-ate him"; "Cactus Jack" Garner, who admitted him to membership in his "Board of Education" and with whom Turner "struck many a blow for liberty" (he played him in a famous Gridiron skit); Pat Harrison, a fellow Mississippian, who in the quiet hours after the Senate lights were out, gave him many a tip that made a page one story; and Jimmy Byrnes, for whom he has always had a really outgoing affection. Mr. Byrnes tried to lure him away to an assistant secretaryship of state, but Turner wouldn't lure.

Turner cultivated politicians because he liked them and because they were good news sources. But at the same time he was impressing his fellow newspapermen with that somewhat more sophisticated "country-boy wit" he took to Memphis and with the fact that he was indeed one hell of a newspaperman. His coverage of the Supreme Court–packing bill was a masterpiece of reporting. Lewis Wood once wrote of *The One Hundred Sixty-eight Days,* which Catledge and Joe Alsop put into a book:

> During the long, tense Supreme Court battle, Catledge would often lead off with something about a "clash," or a "conflict" or maybe even an "impasse." But after a conversation with the passionate senator from Arkansas, Joe Robinson, there would be a "tussle" where one could see rural characters in butternut clothes rolling in the dust, with shapeless wool hats flying into white cotton fields. Turner was skillful in getting such flavor into his pieces.

The Washington era lasted until 1941 and was resumed when Turner came back from Chicago on May 1, 1943, to become national correspondent working out of the Washington bureau. In 1945 he was made assistant managing editor of the *Times,* executive managing editor on January 10, 1951, and managing editor succeeding Eddie James on December 17 of that year.

What has the *Times* been under him? Of course I happen to think that it is the world's best newspaper, impatient as I have been at times with its studied stodginess. But it has moved, slowly, almost imperceptibly, under Catledge.

That deadly index is off the front page and in its place real news and pictures. The writing is better, the women's pages much improved, the feature sense surer, typography cleaner in spite of the narrower columns, and major news stories still blanketed under the complete coverage. There isn't much you have to look for in news magazines if you read the *Times*. What Catledge has contributed to all that I don't know, but I have an idea.

And what about Catledge himself? What sort of man is he? Along with other "pick-lock biographers," as Stephen Vincent Benet called the people who tried to pin Robert E. Lee down to a specimen board, I've tried to figure him out. Indeed, I've invoked help. I conducted a sort of Gallup survey among a good many people who have known him over a period of years.

"What makes Catledge tick?" was my question.

All I got in reply was a cliche. Almost without variation, newspapermen and women said to me, "Well, you know . . . You know . . . It's Catledge."

And indeed it is Catledge. One of his executives said that he has the "facade of simple, unalloyed innocence." He does indeed have that, plus an affection for all mankind, a tolerance that would have done Virginia proud in her better days, and a gentle cynicism toward the demagogic of the earth. But don't let that fool you. There are those members of the ASNE who remember an occasion upon which a noted lawyer rose to utter McCarthyisms from the rostrum of the convention. I wasn't there, but one who was told me that for the first and only time he had ever seen, that pink face turned white as Turner strewed the man's guts on the convention floor. As Carter Glass would have more elegantly put it, Turner e-vis-cer-ated him.

But that's rare. Again as Lewis Wood said of him, he has "a warmth, an unaffectedness close to the ingenuous, sincerity, high intelligence, and a capacity for gaiety. . . . It's not the slightest trouble for him to free your doubtful mind and melt your cold, cold heart."

Russ Wiggins, with whom Turner worked when Russ was assistant to the publisher of the *Times* and now again as Russ's ASNE vice-president, said that he has always been a little uncomfortable trying to keep one jump ahead of him mentally, the same feeling the whiting had in Alice in Wonderland:

Will you walk a little faster, said a whiting to a snail,
There's a porpoise close behind me, and he's treading on my tail.

George Chaplin, Editor in Chief
The Honolulu Advertiser

By Howard Chernoff

I f I were a sportswriter, I would describe George Chaplin as a man who can do it all.

Although his title is editor in chief of the *Honolulu Advertiser,* he is at once an excellent reporter, an award-winning writer and editor, an influential civic leader, and a good businessman. The 1976–77 president of the ASNE is also a devoted husband and father as well as a doting grandfather. And he has time for all.

George was no stranger to Hawaii when he joined the *Advertiser* in 1958. During World War II, as a captain in the United States Army, he was sent to the Islands to establish and edit the Pacific edition of *Stars and Stripes.* The paper was printed at the *Honolulu Advertiser,* and George came to know Lorrin Thurston, the then publisher. Thirteen years later, when Thurston sought to replace his retiring editor, Ray Coll, he remembered the young captain who had been so strongly pro-statehood and invited him to take over the editorial department. George and the publisher's nephew, Thurston Twigg-Smith, hit it off. Later, when Twigg took over as publisher and began to move the editorial budget to its present $2.5 million a year, he and George combined to form a capable operating team. George began to acquire stock in the *Advertiser* almost as soon as he had arrived in Honolulu and, today, the Chaplin family owns a little more than 10 percent.

The complexion of the *Advertiser* changed from ultraconservative to moderately liberal. It livened its typography. It expanded its staff and news hole. It began to engage in investigative reporting the way George had in New Orleans and San Diego. George became active in community affairs. The prestige which accrued to him as a result, also accrued to the *Advertiser.*

Chernoff was general manager of the *San Diego Journal* during the time Chaplin was managing editor of the *Journal.* This article first appeared in 1976.

When the paper began to go after hard-hitting environmental stories (many of which didn't sit too well with some members of the Establishment), Twigg-Smith offered encouragement and ideas. It was, and is, a fine relationship.

George was born in Columbia, South Carolina, in 1914. He went to Clemson College to study textile chemistry. Had he not been made editor of the *Clemson Tiger*, ASNE would have been inducting someone else as president in 1976.

After he led successful campaigns in the *Tiger* to get better boxing match judges, to abolish compulsory church attendance, and to permit student evaluation of faculty, textile chemistry offered little excitement to him. So, he got a job as a reporter on the *Greenville* (South Carolina) *Piedmont*. He soon conned Esta, a charming Charleston girl, into marrying him, became city editor, and in 1940, at age twenty-six, won a Nieman Fellowship at Harvard. George was on his way. (Clemson gave him a Distinguished Alumni Award in 1974.)

Following World War II, he became managing editor of the *Camden Courier-Post*, then managing editor of the *San Diego Journal*, and finally, editor of the *New Orleans Item* for nine years before going back to Honolulu.

But wherever he was, George was involved in the community, and the paper was pursuing causes for good. It was exciting to work on a Chaplin-edited paper, because he had imagination, ideas.

In San Diego, where George exposed quack psychologists and got the city council to pass a pioneering ordinance requiring exams for all seeking psychologist's licenses, he sent a reporter dressed as a Russian colonel forty miles north to Camp Pendleton to cover the annual amphibious maneuvers of the Marine Corps. The MPs arrested the reporter, but the story wound up on a happy note when George ran a page one editorial congratulating the marines on their excellent security. *Time, Life,* and *Newsweek* telephoned for pictures. It just happened George had sent a photographer to tail the reporter.

In New Orleans, the *Item* successfully proposed reforms at the state penitentiary, exposed vote fraud in the city, campaigned vigorously against leading lottery figures, fought police graft, exposed a divorce racket on the neighboring Mississippi Gulf Coast, uncovered poor conditions in New Orleans nursing homes, and fought many other battles as well.

Down deep, George Chaplin is and was a reporter. Esta tells about the time in New Orleans when the house next door caught fire one night. The Chaplin family was evacuating its home because of the proximity of the blaze. Esta had the children and the housekeeper rounded up but suddenly, George had disappeared. She found him out on the sun deck in his pajamas taking pictures of the fire for the next day's paper.

George is not only an activist but a good listener. Although his advice is often sought for many Honolulu endeavors, he probably does more listening than a lot of psychiatrists. After a Honolulu executive told George in 1960 about the need for an additional $250,000 to complete the *Arizona* memorial at Pearl Harbor, George wrote letters to seventeen hundred daily newspaper editors in the United States and contributions came in from all over the country.

Col. Tom Parker, Elvis Presley's manager, read an editorial based on George's letter, picked up the telephone and pledged Elvis to a charity performance at Pearl Harbor with all proceeds going to the *Arizona* memorial. In one night, more than sixty-seven thousand dollars was raised. It stimulated the Congress to provide the rest. George was given the U.S. Navy League's Meritorious Citation for finally getting the memorial built. In accepting the award he had warm words for Buck Buchwach, then managing editor and now executive editor, who worked with him on this and many other projects.

George is determined, not only in his work, but in his personal life as well. A few years ago he decided to stop smoking pipes and cigars after forty years. So he stopped. Period! When he decided he needed more exercise several years ago, he began to ride a stationary bicycle—five miles a day. These days he jogs instead and plays tennis almost every Saturday and Sunday. When he decided his clothes were too conservative, he went all out again. Out went the Brooks Brothers suits. In came some pretty far-out shirts, jackets, and slacks.

In 1967 George made a speech in which he called for a comprehensive study of Hawaii's assets in population, ethnic mix, industrial and agricultural capacity or, as he put it, "examining Hawaii's future economic, political, cultural, and social systems" for the purpose of "identifying the objectives we desire and the action necessary to reach those objectives."

No sooner had he put forth the idea than the late Gov. Jack Burns appointed George to head up the project. Within eighteen months, the Hawaii legislature had enacted bills authorizing and financing the Governor's Conference on the Year 2000. The conference, involving large numbers of laymen (some seven hundred in all), including task forces and other delegates, was held in August 1970, and the Hawaii Commission on the Year 2000 is an outgrowth.

Since its creation, the commission has become nationally and internationally recognized as the first publicly established in the world specifically to explore the alternative futures of a particular society. A major private sector project stimulated by the commission is entitled Alternative Futures for Hawaii. George is its co-chairman.

Again—never one to go into anything halfway—George steeped himself in futurism, began to attend meetings of the World Future Society, got to know the Alvin Tofflers, the Robert Theobalds, the John McHales, the Herman Kahns, the Robert Jungks, and others intimately. He is now recognized as an authority himself and is in demand as a speaker and writer on the subject.

George and Dr. Glenn Paige, a University of Hawaii political scientist, collaborated in assembling and editing the papers presented at the conference. The result is a handsome and fascinating book entitled, *Hawaii 2000: Continuing Experiment in Anticipatory Democracy.*

After a prominent Malaysian senator read the book, he was inspired to sponsor a Conference on the Year 2000 in Kuala Lumpur and, you guessed it, George Chaplin was one of the main speakers there last August. The Hawaii project also contributed to similar endeavors in the states of Washington, Iowa, and Minnesota, as well as in Puerto Rico.

The *Advertiser* has taken on organized crime, hammering at conflict of interests at city hall with in-depth reporting which brought the resignation of the city's managing director. The *Advertiser* went after state purchasing procedures after it learned and disclosed that some of Hawaii's elected representatives were furnishing their homes with rugs and other effects owned by the state. Under George's leadership the *Advertiser* always comes out smokin', to borrow Joe Frazier's expression. If it isn't attacking substandard conditions in nursing homes and leading a fight for a tougher city and state ethics code, then it's fighting for a new and needed hospital. Or persuading the city to build a separate concert hall instead of erecting a combination concert hall and sports arena.

It's difficult to do a profile on George. It would be easier to do a book. One chapter would have to be devoted to awards. They include: two citations from the Overseas Press Club for series on Southeast Asia, Japan, the People's Republic of China; two John Hancock Awards for economic reportage; national Headliner's Award; and a flock of others.

His lovely and supportive wife, Esta, is as proud of him as are his son and daughter, Steve and Jerri, and their spouses. Steve is a career foreign service officer stationed in Bucharest, married to a former attorney with the Securities and Exchange Commission; they have two children. Jerri is a free-lance writer and public relations counselor in Honolulu; her husband is in the hotel business there.

William Ewing, the retired editor of George's evening competitor, the *Honolulu Star-Bulletin,* once sized up the situation this way:

"Statehood, Henry J. Kaiser, jet airplanes, and George Chaplin hit Hawaii at about the same time. I'm not quite sure where to list them in order of importance."

The phrase "mover and shaker" might have been coined for George.

John H. Colburn, Managing Editor
Richmond Times-Dispatch

By J. Edward Murray

John H. Colburn, ASNE's 1961 Freedom of Information chairman at a time when the going looks even rougher than usual in that department, is well equipped for the job.

As managing editor of the *Richmond Times-Dispatch* for the past twelve years, and a Virginia gentleman by adoption, he has steeped himself in the colonial traditions and documents which led to the First Amendment. He has been close to the FoI fight for years, and also close to Washington, D. C., which amounts to almost the same thing.

He'll be much closer to both if the new administration persists in its current efforts to curb full and free information. Being Colburn, which is to say both organized and energetic to a fault, he will fight back.

Speaking of "being Colburn," John's wife, Angie, and I have bantered for years over whether his main problem is his excess energy or his overorganization.

She thinks it's excess energy, and can catalogue John's fabulous expenditure: a brisk twenty-minute walk every morning with Clem, a big, German short-haired pointer; lots of tennis; golf by fits and starts; midday volleyball at the downtown Commonwealth club; ten- and twelve-hour office days; numerous professional chores in editors' organizations; frequent speeches; enthusiastic social life; Episcopal church activity; etc., etc.

In fact, Angie acted seriously worried about the energy problem last November when John finished his APME presidency, a fairly respectable energy consumer. She pleaded with me, as his successor in the job, to give him something to work at.

"Harness him," she said, "so he doesn't burn himself up."

Murray was managing editor of the *Arizona Republic* when this article first appeared, in 1961.

Angie is Georgia Southern herself . . . languid, slow moving, an energy saver.

My claim that John is only slightly less programmed than the Cape Canaveral telemetry room is based on considerable evidence.

For instance, several hundred present and former APME editors, and a score of Associated Press executives, will testify that Colburn almost single-handedly turned the APME Continuing Study—once a mildly pleasant confusion of committees, correspondence, and criticism which came alive a few months each year just before convention time—into an efficient, continuous twelve-month production of fewer committees, mountainous correspondence, more criticism, and little or no confusion.

Not that Colburn didn't help the APME Continuing Study in a decade of revamping it. He did. And he overorganized it.

Next item: he has two copies of the *Times-Dispatch* delivered daily to his Arlington Circle home on the outskirts of Richmond, one for his wife and two daughters and one for his own use in marking tearsheets for the staff. That's organization.

Next item: he literally has two accents—one southern for Virginia and one midwestern for elsewhere, including Columbus, Ohio, where he was born in 1912. I say that's organization. John says it's an unconscious result of his imitative ear, which it probably is.

Final item: he's a switch-hitter at the bar, keeps both his bourbon and Scotch palates ready, just to make sure.

In other words, he leaves little to chance. In his newspapering, this adds up to serious, single-minded, conscientious dedication.

John has been working this way at his career for thirty-one of his forty-nine years.

As he tells it, here's how the twig was bent:

"In high school, my ambition was to be an architectural engineer. As a senior, I needed an elective credit in English, and selected journalism rather than dramatics. I was a sportswriter on the school paper and began submitting articles to the local afternoon paper on the school's crack relay team, which was setting national records. The paper paid me for the material, and I shifted my career sights from architecture to journalism."

That architectural virus is only latent, however, not dead. John took quite a hand in both the design and construction of the new house he and Angie just built on a big, woodsy lot next door to their old house. I suggested that John chose the new site next to the old one mainly to keep an eye on every detail. He said he liked the neighborhood. It is lovely with hills and slopes, a variety of trees, spacious lots, and even a live brook.

The new house is modern colonial, incidentally, and modernized to the nth degree. I have the word of one of John's friends that he showed him every detail of the kitchen—convenient, mechanized, and electrified within an inch of complete automation—twice in the same long, gay evening, once early and once late.

That's Colburn, too. Relaxed after hours, friendly, cheerful, charming, and just a wee bit determined.

But I digress.

John got his foot in the door, as a copyboy-cub reporter at the *Columbus Dispatch* the summer he was graduated from high school, and, Colburn fashion, he was on the way to the top.

In the fact department, he worked all the beats and the copydesk, and became an assistant city editor in four years, all the while taking a fairly heavy part-time schedule at Ohio State University.

In the legend department, the files show that he saved a man's life as a police reporter. The wife of the victim of a holdup-slaying told Colburn at the scene that she didn't see the killer because of a flashlight shining in her face. But later at the trial she identified a man as the slayer. The defense attorney called Colburn as a surprise witness and he confronted the woman with her earlier flashlight statement. The testimony resulted in an acquittal instead of the death penalty.

In January 1935, the twenty-three-year-old assistant city editor of the *Dispatch* joined the Columbus bureau of the Associated Press. And, with his foot in the door, he was again on his way. But unobtrusively at first. Even a Colburn makes haste cautiously in the Associated Press.

Both the fact and legend departments are silent until the wartime December of 1942 when Colburn transferred to Associated Press's foreign service and went to London where I first met him. I was an only slightly less overorganized minion in the less cautious United Press.

Colburn's war and postwar service in Europe included assignments in Stockholm, Helsinki, Paris, Brussels, Prague, and Vienna. Before the end of the war, he was named executive editor of Associated Press World Service and secretary of the Associated Press British affiliate.

Associated Press's executive editor, Alan Gould, remembers that John was quite proficient "at reporting information gleaned from the well known 'Swedish travelers.'"

"After the war," Gould adds, "John beat the Scandinavian bushes in behalf of our World Service expansion program, and built the foundations for a thriving segment of our overseas business."

Before returning to the United States in 1946, Colburn met one situation which he absolutely could not organize, then nor since. Her name was Florence Angier Jackson, an American girl working with the Red Cross in London. They were married there. And the line about John not organizing Angie is not just word play. It's none of my damned business, of course, but I'm going to say, anyway, that a lesser woman would have had trouble.

The contrast between John's kinetic and Angie's potential energy is replicated in their daughters. Karen, now ten and called K-cee, is the extrovert with explosive energy, and something of a swimming champion. Charlotte, fifteen, is calmer, more introspective, and, like her mother, gently haunted by the spiritual mysteries. She is also about to beat me at tennis.

Back in the United States with Associated Press, Colburn was chosen as one of six new general executives. John represented the Associated Press general manager on news and membership problems in a territory including the entire Eastern Seaboard west to Louisiana, Tennessee, West Virginia, and Pennsylvania.

In fact, General Manager Frank Starzel of Associated Press relayed to me a lovely story, probably true, of how well John represented Associated Press in one instance. It goes like this.

One of Colburn's regular ports of call was Richmond. Publisher Tennant Bryan and other executives were considering a number of candidates for the job of managing editor of the *Times-Dispatch.* As a friend and Associated Press counselor in the newspaper family circle, John was asked to look over a couple of the leading prospects who happened to be on his regular travel route. John did so, then reported back purely as a confidential favor, and went on his way.

The next time he was in Richmond on Associated Press business, Bryan & Co. again asked to see him. Bryan came to the point quickly, to wit:

"John, we think so highly of the thorough job of investigating you were generous enough to do in our behalf that we would like to have you take the job here as managing editor of the *Times-Dispatch.*"

John did in May 1949.

During his twelve years as managing editor, circulation has increased from 115,000 to 140,000. The editorial staff has grown by 50 percent, including the personnel in the ten new bureaus John set up around the state.

Asked for his own appraisal of his influence on the *Times-Dispatch,* Colburn said:

"We've aimed at the reestablishment of the *Times-Dispatch's* reputation as a fine news gatherer, as a fine news medium. I think we've made the paper once more a great organ of public opinion. And we dig up a lot of enterprise material."

His *modus operandi* is fairly standard: reads the paper carefully at home, making notes and marking tearsheets; reaches the office about ten o'clock, handles mail, dictates memos, confers with assistants, department heads and reporters; takes over in the newsroom between three and four o'clock, reading the cream of day's news from all sources, hammering out a consensus on top news and picture play with his desk chiefs, and planning page one. He goes home for dinner, then usually returns to the office several nights a week as the occasion demands.

In addition to his daily flow of memos and critiques, Colburn issues a monthly "T-D Topics," which is a bulletin on staff successes and fall-downs, on new ideas for improving the paper, on staff chitchat, on professional shoptalk. It's a good job and valuable not only to the *Times-Dispatch* staff, but also to a number of John's APME colleagues around the country.

To recharge his own supply of ideas for improving his own and other newspapers, Colburn is an indefatigable worker in the professional vineyards. He has done a prodigious amount of work on APME Continuing Study committees, and even now as retiring APME president, normally a position of rest and revival after the suffering, Colburn is heading up an interesting committee of elder statesmen who are trying to work out a set of newspaper criteria which will apply regardless of the size of the paper.

Colburn maintains better than average contacts with J-schools and with the American Press Institute. He is a member of the Comics Council, and once debated with Walt Kelly his (Colburn's) right to edit political opinion out of Pogo. He serves on the editor's advisory board for *This Week* magazine.

Colburn draws on all this professional give-and-take for frequent speeches on newspapering, including an eloquent and diligently documented pitch on Freedom of Information. On the chronic topic of interpretive reporting, he had this to say in his APME presidential address at colonial Williamsburg last November:

> Our reporting problems have become more complex and they will become even more complicated, but we now tend to overwhelm our readers with opinion, analysis, and interpretation. Certainly some of this is necessary, but in my humble opinion we need sharper, better illustrated, and more dramatic displays of basic facts. What I like to call penetrative reporting, rather than pontifical reporting and writing, will give us more hard news on which the public can base sound, solid judgments.

That's Colburn . . . serious, sound, solid.

Or, if you would rather close on a more human note, I give you Colburn's competing managing editor on the afternoon *Richmond News Leader*, Charles Hamilton, on the subject of Colburn:

"John is a two-hundred-pound, six-two, blue-eyed swaggering blond. Looks like an athlete, which just goes to show you that all is not gold that glitters.

"If he *were* an athlete, he'd be the playmaker of the basketball team—or he wouldn't play. He'd be the holler guy of the baseball team and without question he'd be the quarterback of the football team. He's what is known as the take-charge type in sports; I believe, from what I've seen, that the same characteristic also marks many managing editors. . . .

"What do I think of Colburn as a competitor, with the understanding that the remarks will be printed? You may use what is found in this space (_____)."

Jim Comstock, Editor
The West Virginia Hillbilly

By Dave Peyton

J im Comstock, editor of the *West Virginia Hillbilly,* sits in the second-floor
workroom of his Richwood, West Virginia, offices, watching the traffic
move slowly through the main street.

It is a sunny day in late April. The lower river valleys display spring
blossoms and greenery. But in Richwood, a town of about four thousand on
the Cherry River, cold mountain air keeps most buds in their winter cocoons.

Richwood is a mountain town filled with mountain people and mountain
memories. Comstock, who was born on nearby Hinkle Mountain, is the
editor of a weekly newspaper that has chronicled events in West Virginia for
nearly thirty years.

The *Hillbilly* has become a new tradition. Nearly everyone in the state has
heard of it, and it's quoted often. But its sagging circulation proves more
people quote it than subscribe to it.

Those who follow the *Hillbilly* read it primarily for the regular feature on
the last page of the tabloid—an outpouring of humor, pathos, and other
thoughts from the mind of its editor.

Sometimes Comstock writes with the plain-spoken beauty of a country
editor. On the death of Marilyn Monroe, he wrote:

> The girl who lived across the street from us all got tired and
> wanted to go to bed and sleep. I hope her dreams are all nice dreams,
> like maybe growing up in a little town with a mother to love her and
> teach her, and a father to worship her, and then to find a prince
> charming who, after they have planned and worked together, will
> get her a little two-bedroom castle and a baby or two, and share with
> her a nice, long, uneventful life of being a very, very happy nobody.

Sometimes the truth, according to Comstock, hurts too much to be

Peyton was on leave from the *Huntington* (West Virginia) *Advertiser* when this article first
appeared, in 1976.

funny. Once he told the story of a Richwood resident who visited his daughter, a schoolteacher, in another town. The daughter was apologetic, because on her tight budget she could not afford real butter. All she had was margarine.

"The fellow told her not to take it so hard," Comstock wrote. "He said all she had to do was find somebody who was on the surplus commodity list and trade him out of his butter, because butter is one thing that the government has a lot of, and usually a family gets more than it can use and they barter a bit with their butter."

Comstock pointed out to his readers that here was a family earning money but doing without butter so it could pay taxes to buy butter for people who weren't making money and therefore weren't paying taxes.

"He laughed . . . telling me about it," Comstock wrote, "and I laughed, too. And then we stopped laughing and just looked at each other, because suddenly, it wasn't funny any more."

Sometimes the entire last page is devoted to praising simple mountain joys. Who else but Comstock could write reams about the joys of hogslaughtering and make it sound poetic?

When Sharon Rockefeller (Mrs. John D. Rockefeller IV) came to West Virginia, Comstock devoted the last page of his newspaper to giving her friendly hints on how to be a mountain housewife.

He reminded her that "corn dodger isn't worth a rap without cracklins. Restaurants don't know that, and that's why corn dodger isn't fit for the hounds in restaurants."

He provided Mrs. Rockefeller with the secret for gathering the best poke greens and how to choose the best sassafras for tea. He reminded her that not all mountain people eat mountain cooking. "They'll tell you that 'possum is eaten only by white trash, and then go off to the Greenbrier and eat snails," he wrote.

Most of Comstock's life has been devoted to telling about mountain life as he sees it. Unashamedly, he has made fun of mountain people and the "outsiders" who come to West Virginia with missionary zeal. During the 1960 Kennedy-Humphrey presidential primary in West Virginia, he wrote about the two contenders and their use of West Virginia as a springboard to the presidency. He did it through a mythical family composed of Ma, Pa, Sis, and Fiddlin' Clyde. Making light of some of West Virginia's most infamous political shenanigans, he proudly proclaimed (with tongue in cheek) that Pa had decided he couldn't bring himself to sell his vote to a Catholic.

Comstock is intense about Appalachia, although he doesn't consider himself an expert on the people and culture (a trait which seems common among those who are best suited to be called experts).

Comstock says the old-style Appalachian culture is gone, leaving the mountains with a form of mutated Appalachian culture, not at all like the old, but still out of step with the rest of America in many, many ways.

"I grew up on Hinkle Mountain where people represented a certain subculture all their own. Well, one time an Austrian family moved in. We couldn't help but see the difference at first. But sooner or later they became assimilated. They attended our mountain wakes. They were Catholics, but they took their kids out of Catholic schools. Why? Because of what we were, I suppose. Appalachians were like the Chinese. We eventually conquered everybody we came in contact with."

That still holds true to a lesser extent, Comstock says. Is it because the Appalachian people are so strong, their culture so tenacious?

"No. I think it's because the Appalachian subculture is so basically good. In Appalachia, for instance, you seldom find people who take advantage of others. You take all the big deals—taking money and going off to Switzerland. That's not done by Appalachians," he says.

He surveys the quiet street outside his window again. "Just recently, it was reported that there was a murderer loose. Police reported he was on his way to Richwood. The authorities came around warning people to lock their doors. Can you imagine that? People having to be told to lock their doors at night? I leave my keys in the car frequently. I never lock it at night and never in this world have I lost anything in Richwood."

No matter how "basically good" the culture is, it's changing, due in large measure to television, Comstock believes.

"I had a girl come here and scrub the office the other day," he says. "Back in the old days, all one ever needed was a mop, a mop bucket, some water, and soap powders. Well, my Lord, she had a list of things she needed that came to forty-two dollars. And they were all brand names she knew from TV. She was speaking a strange language. Now her whole life is shaped, not by her family or the things she has heard from them, but from the tube in her living room. And she listens to commercials more than anything. And her children eat the no-good fun foods. Her corn flakes must sparkle and crackle. She has forgotten how to feed her family, if she ever knew."

Destruction of cultural differences by mass media is widespread, Comstock believes. "All cultures are being destroyed by the media. I suspect Brooklyn has lost most of its dialect, its old customs. Portnoy's complaint of the ages will be something else. It will be against the media."

Government runs a close second to the media in forcing change, Comstock says. If the government isn't forcing change, it keeps the culture in an uproar so that the culture changes by degrees.

"We have government experts that come down here and study us and want to change us, make us like everybody else. Then we have more government experts come right on their heels and want us to preserve our culture."

The leaders aren't all to blame for the demise of the culture. The people of Appalachia have wanted to be in the mainstream. In moving in that direction, they have abandoned old ways, Comstock says.

Comstock calls artifacts of the old culture the "tangibles," and in recent years, much of his work, outside the newspaper profession, has been to preserve the relics of days gone by. He was also a leading force behind the restoration of Pearl Buck's birthplace, a popular West Virginia tourist attraction.

The editor believes that by preserving the tangibles, generations of Appalachians to come can learn about the past and perhaps be persuaded to preserve some of the cultural intangibles.

The writer himself is part of the new wave of cultural awareness. He is constantly asked to speak before groups about Appalachian heritage. At each opportunity, Comstock impresses upon the audience the need to preserve the heritage through preservation of the old "things."

And yet, this wave of awareness bothers him. Unlike his mother and father who simply lived in the culture without being aware of it, the modern Appalachian is being bombarded with programs designed to make him aware of his cultural heritage. Comstock believes this forces the entire culture into a very critical stage.

"If you're aware of who you are, you start losing it or keeping it. It's a point of no return."

Virginius Dabney, Editor
Richmond Times-Dispatch

By Charles Henry Hamilton

T imes-Dispatch editor Virginius Dabney occupies an office on the northern side of the big building that houses Richmond Newspapers, Inc. That is a paradoxical situation for a man who has earned a reputation as a leading Southern editor.

But it is entirely in keeping with the man, for his life has been full of paradoxes.

He never went to school until he was thirteen years old, yet he earned two degrees from the University of Virginia, gained honorary degrees from three more colleges, and later lectured at Princeton and at Cambridge.

He failed when he tried out for the campus newspaper staff at Virginia, never gave it a passing thought, and went on to become a teacher upon graduation. After a year, he found himself making frequent trips to Richmond, home of the charming Douglas Chelf, who later was to become his wife.

"Why don't you just get a job in Richmond?" inquired his father one day. "Why not try the newspapers?"

"It sounds like a good idea," agreed V. Dabney.

Almost exactly thirty-five years later, V. Dabney looks back and sees no reason to change his original opinion. The years have been kind, even though he departed from a family tradition in becoming a newspaperman.

Everything indicated a professorial life for him. He was born on the campus of the University of Virginia. His father served on the Virginia faculty for forty-nine years as professor of history and as dean of the graduate school. His great-grandfather, who was murdered in a famous student riot on Virginia's lawn in 1840, was chairman of the faculty. It was not at all strange that V. went back to Episcopal High School, his prep school, as a teacher upon finishing college. It took romance to turn the key opening

---

Hamilton was managing editor of the *Richmond News Leader* when this article first appeared, in 1957.

into another world.

Sometimes he wonders just a bit about his early education.

"You see, I never studied grammar at all," he says.

As a lad, he was taught by his father and by an aunt. They taught him what they thought he should know. They must have done well, for he never encountered trouble at Episcopal and he went on to earn a Phi Beta Kappa key.

Now in his middle-fifties, he packs 190 well-distributed pounds on a six-two frame. There's a trace of gray at his temples. He rarely laughs loudly, nearly always is smiling. The years have etched pleasant little crinkles around brown eyes that peer out philosophically—and humorously—upon a changing world.

If he looks athletic, there's background. For many years, he has been a crack tennis player—even if a slightly frustrated one.

"Never a city championship, never even a club title," he says, "but I was runner-up so many times I lost track of it."

He still enjoys tennis, although he has abandoned all title hopes. These days, he is more serious about fishing. There's something about fly fishing that is fascinating, he readily admits. Beyond that, it's something one can share with a son.

Besides the son, he has two daughters and don't forget, he adds proudly, there are three grandchildren.

He has come a long way since he wrote his first story as a cub reporter on the *News Leader,* on July 1, 1922. He still remembers that it was about Hanover County cantaloupes. He went through the *News Leader's* training grind as a cub—he still shudders at news of lodge meetings. By 1926, he was firmly established as a talented Capitol Hill reporter. He liked political reporting, found editorial writing alluring if distant at that time.

In 1928, he joined the *Times-Dispatch* and began contributing columns to the editorial page. In 1934, he went to Europe on a six-month Oberlaender fellowship.

"While there, I got a letter from our publisher, asking if I'd like to become chief editorial writer," he recalls. He doesn't recall if he cabled or wrote his acceptance, but he took the job and two years later was made editor.

Succeeding years found him branching out as a writer. He wrote three books, scores of magazine articles, won spots in all the leading publications.

His friends considered it an overdue honor when he won the Pulitzer Prize for editorial writing in 1947.

He arrives at the office around nine-thirty, leaves about six-fifteen. If he happens to be working on outside writing, he will have started on that about seven o'clock at home.

"Writing early in the day doesn't seem to tire me," he says. "I can get up early and write, go to the office, and work full speed. But at the end of the day, I'm mentally dry; there's no room for more writing."

Hardest subjects for him, he says, are farm problems and economics. These days, one of his two editorial associates handles those chores. The favorite subjects? Naturally, politics; also, anything about Virginia history, or about racial problems, or foreign affairs.

And what does an editor need in the way of natural equipment?

"Well," says V. Dabney, the laugh-crinkles deepening around his eyes, "it goes without saying that the first need is for a rhinoceros skin. Beyond that, there is a constant need to keep learning about everything; you never know when a bit of stray knowledge will prove helpful. Even the comic strips help out, I've found. And, of course, back of it all should be a broad, liberal arts education."

And what about editors of the future?

"As I see it, the basic requirements will stay the same," he says. "But I will admit"—the little smile again—"it is a rapidly changing world. As the world shrinks in size, the complications multiply. It's astounding. And," his smile deepening, "it's fascinating, isn't it?"

He turned back to his desk, this writer noted for his logic, this editor-by-chance whose career was shaped by romance that flowered in the warm spring winds of an earlier Virginia.

He owes it all to his wife.

Jonathan Daniels, Editor
Raleigh (North Carolina) News and Observer

By Sylvan Meyer

A t the age of eight, Jonathan Daniels set a precedent in contrasts. His father Josephus, as secretary of the navy, was entertaining distinguished guests in his Washington home when Jonathan, clad in his dad's high silk hat and cane and nothing else, descended the stairway with calm dignity.

The editor of the *Raleigh News and Observer* still presents the contrast of cosmopolitan training and experience topping unshirted Tar Heel directness.

Jonathan Daniels insists he's a country editor running a country newspaper and calls himself a "newspaperman with the galluses showing." Of course, there's nothing bucolic about Raleigh now (pop. 73,996 ABC-CZ) and not much of the rustic in the *News and Observer* (circ. 125,752 daily; 138,104 Sunday). When Daniels says "country," he means close to the people of North Carolina and personal in approach.

Born in Raleigh in 1902, Daniels attended prep school in Washington, received his A.B. and M.A. at the University of North Carolina, his law degree at Columbia University. Not bashful in criticism of lawyers or courts, he's found that degree sort of puts a damper on comebacks. As a cub reporter on the *Louisville Times*, he started in newspaper work. He became Washington correspondent for the *News and Observer*. That high silk hat and cane aspect of his life included travel in Europe on a Guggenheim Fellowship won in 1930 by his first novel. He roamed the continent with a couple of other country boys from North Carolina, Thomas Wolfe and Paul Green. On his return he took an editorial job with *Fortune* magazine, returning to the *News and Observer* in 1931. He became editor in 1933 and

Meyer was editor of the *Gainesville* (Georgia) *Daily Times* when this article first appeared, in 1956.

stayed until World War II when he took a break to hold several key jobs in the wartime administrations of Roosevelt and Truman. Then he returned to his country job.

In the meantime, he's written biographies, a study of the South, served on a raft of councils, boards, and committees, and dabbled in politics as a national Democratic committeeman.

Top-hatting in the high councils of the nation, however, hasn't changed his basic idea that local news is the most important of all.

The *News and Observer* sports no fancy dress. It wears an almost grim editorial page layout relieved only by a few lightface heads. Recent redesigning has lightened the page's appearance, but Daniels still isn't satisfied with it. It needs little typographic sparkle. The content provides ample glitter for its readers, who have responded to aggressive editorials and intensive news coverage by giving the paper an inordinately large circulation in proportion to the population of Raleigh.

Daniels's understanding of what his paper should do for its readers and his firsthand knowledge of nation, state, and region combined with a lifetime of continued research for his outside writing, lends high effectiveness to *News and Observer* policy.

This policy is, in a name, Jonathan Daniels. Just to bear out that fact, the *News and Observer* prints texts of his speeches as edit page features. Day to day, though, he calls regularly on the counsel of Robert E. Williams, associate editor, and Sam Ragan, managing editor.

"We're too small to set policy in conference," says Daniels, "but we are in conference, shouting from desk to desk, throughout the day."

Daniels leaves his staff members alone, dealing through the managing editor on stories of particular concern. On weekends he goes carefully through the papers and criticizes and praises as he presides over the Monday staff meetings. When he has an idea for a story, he passes it on through the state or city desks.

When he attends some national or state affair of note, he files "editorial correspondence" on the event but leaves the coverage of spot news angles to reporters.

"Our main weakness," he says, "lies in the old joke about the farmer who wouldn't buy books on scientific agriculture because he warn't farming half as well as he knew how already."

Last June, the morning *News and Observer* came to the conclusion that Raleigh could not have a good afternoon paper without a consolidation with the evening *Times*. So the Daniels family bought out their competition and looked around for a strong editor who would be given the same independence of action Jonathan enjoys in the morning field. Mark Ethridge, Jr., got the assignment. Theoretically, Jonathan isn't convinced that a monopoly newspaper operation is best for Raleigh, but thinks the present arrangement works very well. Ethridge frequently has opinions differing greatly from those of his boss, competitor, colleague, or whatever designation fits such a situation.

Two major policy objectives currently dominate Daniels's direction of the *News and Observer*. One is simply to put out a better and more meaningful paper.

The other is the South itself. Staying close to the people doesn't mean pandering to their more reckless impulses. Here the silk-hat frosting only sets off the bare truth. When the Supreme Court desegregation decision ignited attempts to convert public schools to private schools in the region, the *News and Observer* talked in plain country language: no tampering with the public school system. With force and reason it faces those "who step promptly, confidently, and angrily forward with ruthless remedies."

"They urge something more than secession from the Union," Daniels writes. "What they urge is secession from civilization."

Daniels researches and writes constantly, working at home in the mornings, often doing editorials then, and coming down to the office for the rest of the day. But writing is a sideline activity. "I am more interested in the *News and Observer* than any other form of writing," he says.

Then, there's time for politicking. Daniels likes to tell a story about his father, also a loyal Democrat, perhaps because it reveals his own penchant for sharp editorial comment. At the turn of the century in the early days of the *News and Observer*, the elder Daniels had heckled fire out of the Republicans, who controlled the state government at the time. One became so angered he rose in the legislature to propose removal of the state capital and all state offices from Raleigh.

"That will leave here," shouted the GOP leader, "nothing except the state hospital for the insane, the state prison, and the *News and Observer*."

This was a good idea, editorialized the late Mr. Daniels. "These three institutions are all that we need to take care of the Republicans."

Graham M. Dean, Editor and Publisher
Ashland (Oregon) Daily Tidings

By Chilton R. Bush

Did you ever notice whether your boy was reading a book by George Morris, Arthur Northrup, Lyle Harper, Edwin Green, or Harris Patton?

Or whether your daughter was reading one by Ruth S. Wheeler or Janet Singer?

If so, you probably didn't know that the real author of all of these thirty-one juveniles is editor-publisher Graham M. Dean.

Nor that the male pseudonyms were borrowed from Graham's newspaper friends (with their permission) and the first female pseudonym was borrowed from his wife (with her permission?).

You probably do know that this former longtime editor and publisher of Speidel newspapers (*Iowa City Press-Citizen, Salinas Californian, Reno Gazette,* and *State Journal* plus the *Western Horseman*), who has written *Helen in the Editor's Chair, Cheer Leader, Janet Hardy in Hollywood, Janet Hardy in Radio City,* etc., is now the owner of the *Ashland* (Oregon) *Daily Tidings,* the *Yreka* (California) *Daily News,* and the *Artesia* (New Mexico) *Daily Press.*

When Graham was a student at the University of Iowa, he took courses in the short story and novel from John Towner Frederick and Frank Luther Mott. As a hobby, he began writing juvenile fiction, first selling shorts to Sunday school papers and later to *Open Road for Boys.*

John L. B. Williams, then an editor at Appleton's, saw a railroad series in the *Open Road* and encouraged Graham to do a full-length book based on the characters in that series. After this first book, Graham was off running.

Then came a connection with the Goldsmith Publishing Company of Chicago, which sold its books through chain stores. The Goldsmith editor

---

Bush was the executive head of the Department of Communication and Journalism at Stanford University when this article first appeared, in 1959.

would consider titles and outlines. If he liked the outline, he authorized the story. Although the Goldsmith editor had only three or four writers, the writers used pen names so that the editor appeared to have a stable of fifteen to eighteen writers.

A manuscript mailed to this editor on a Saturday night would bring a check for outright purchase within a week.

"I often wondered," Graham recalls, "whether he read the full manuscript.

"I once asked him for a royalty deal and he offered one, but my arithmetic was poor—I misplaced a decimal by a couple of points—and I decided to stay on the cash outright deal.

"Since then I have been very careful about decimals, for I denied myself some hundreds of dollars of income."

The reason Graham used the term "income" is because the juvenile has a long life. One of his books appeared in a trade edition; then as a Junior Literary Guild selection; then in a lower-priced hardcover reprint; again in a special *Parents'* magazine book-package deal; and finally in a paperbook pocket book edition.

Three of Graham's books have been selected by the Junior Literary Guild. Selection by the Junior Guild adds about eleven thousand copies to the sales.

A good juvenile requires good writing, good characterization, and good story line. Information and background must be factually correct; young readers will detect any careless errors.

"My experience with juvenile fiction editors, practically all of whom are women, is that they are alert and eager to get new material," Graham says. "They are constructively helpful in their criticism."

Almost all of Graham's books were written on an L. C. Smith, purchased secondhand for about twenty-five dollars, and several were written in the kitchen on an upended orange crate out of hearing of Mrs. Dean, who then was ill.

This writer may be the only member of the Society who has ever read one of these juveniles. It was done about a dozen years ago in preparation for emceeing a well-attended complimentary dinner for Graham.

The reading yielded little material for gags, but it turned up an interesting fact: the name of the hero was Jack Patton, which is the real name of the present managing editor of the *Salinas Californian* who, at the time of Graham's writing, was a reporter on the *Iowa City Press-Citizen*.

I intend to read another Dean book some time next year. It will be an adult western. From now on most of Graham's books are likely to be westerns.

Arthur C. Deck, Editor
Salt Lake Tribune

By Norman E. Isaacs

S ome of his old associates at the *Salt Lake Tribune* turn speculative when you ask them to describe Arthur Deck.

"Well," they usually start, "Art is a kind of enigma."

They go on to flounder about, trying to find the right words to describe this shy, tough, humorous, dignified, urbane, hard-working, high-quality, high-standards man. He grimaces over the thought of sitting for a photograph and his *Who's Who* biography runs a cryptic nine lines.

The old saw is that you have to go fishing with a man to get to know him. I've done that with Art Deck, and more. We've bounced around in a boat off the Oregon coast and he's been my traveling partner over what I guess must be twenty-five thousand miles of territory, including, of course, the Soviet Union and China. In the process, I cheerfully admit, we've tested some of the world's potables, and so maybe there are reasons why I don't think Art is any mystery man.

But then I suppose any tall, erect, austere-looking editor who comes to the company picnic wearing immaculate shirt, tie, and vest would instantly be enigma to most people on a staff. What they don't know is that Art's starchy formality in dress is something that has been the despair of his children. Son John, a researcher at St. Luke's Hospital on Columbia's Morningside Heights campus in New York, must have given Art eight or ten of the handsomest sport shirts made.

Art means well about them, but they are crammed into drawers. He simply can't bring himself to casual wear. It's a throwback to his boyhood. His father was a most formal man, his mother loving, but stern. Shirt-and-tie was so drilled into Art that it became a fixed part of his lifestyle.

Fixed, that is, for everything outside the garden. One of the classic Salt Lake City tales has to do with the time a new housewife to the Deck

---

Isaacs, a former executive editor of the *Courier-Journal and Louisville Times*, was a teacher at Columbia's Graduate School of Journalism when this article first appeared, in 1973.

neighborhood admired the springtime garden being so busily tended by the partly respectable, but ever-so-seedy looking handyman. She approached to say:

"My good man, when you're finished with this lady's garden, we'd like to hire you for our yard."

Art inclined his head to look over his spectacles and replied, "Ma'am, you'll have to talk to the lady who lives here. She has most of my time taken."

He hasn't been doing the gardening lately. He says Win (wife Winnifred) won't let him. Win says Art hasn't been following through on the garden the way he used to. So she's taken over to make sure it's done.

But follow through at the *Tribune* Art has been doing all along and continues to do — seven days a week. Ten hours at the office is standard, and the rest of the time he is either on the phone to the office or stewing why the office isn't calling him.

Most of us have been (or will be) victims of office-embellishment of fact. So with Arthur Clarence Deck. The office poop sheet says he graduated from the University of Utah trained as a civil mining engineer and turned newsman because there were no jobs for engineers. Some veteran staffers say Art was fearless editor of the student newspaper, the *Utah Chronicle*, and quit school six weeks before graduation rather than compromise on editorial judgment.

In his own calm, understated way, Art shoots down the legends. He did think of a career in mining engineering. He also worked part time for the old *Salt Lake Telegram*. The Depression set in and, as Art puts it, "being rather thankful that I had any kind of job, I stayed on in the newspaper business."

O. N. Malmquist, the *Tribune's* emeritus political writer and historian, comments that most if not all of the staff now working have known Art only as the "boss" all through their careers.

"My association with him goes back to 1929," writes Malmquist, "when he was a cub rewriting handouts for the now-defunct *Telegram*. I've never known a reporter who was his superior as a rewriteman. He could assemble more information from half a dozen legmen and put it together into a readable, comprehensive and accurate story better than anyone I have ever worked with."

Aside from a brief period with United Press in Los Angeles, Art has always been with his home-city *Telegram* or *Tribune*.

The *Telegram* was the *Tribune's* afternoon paper, clearly kept in the field as buffer to the Mormon Church's *Deseret News*. It was on this undernourished, skimpily staffed *Telegram* that Art started as reporter and worked his way up through rewrite, city desk, news desk, and managing editor. Veteran sports editor John Mooney says the *Tribune* "would have been third in any category, except that with Art driving us, we turned out a highly competitive paper. We weren't loved and maybe we weren't respected, but no one gazed on us in apathy."

Art was elevated to executive editor of both newspapers in 1950 serving under the then-publisher, John Fitzpatrick. (The *Telegram* was sold in the mid-fifties.) Malmquist in his history of the papers writes that Deck's competence was such that he could serve under "four such disparate personalities" as Fitzpatrick, A. L. Fish, Eugene MacKinnon, and Jack Gallivan "holding the confidence and approbation of each one." Malmquist notes that "with the exception of Gallivan, all of them had complex personalities which were sometimes difficult to fathom and to appease."

Looking over it all, Art doesn't think "we have as many real self-starters among the young we get these days, but I do find that the quality of the younger people is much improved over what it was twenty or more years ago, and for the most part they are eager to climb the ladder where it seems to me, years ago, a lot of them were content with staying in a niche."

Through every *Tribune* staffer's account of Life with Art, one word keeps bubbling up: Tough.

Some evidence:

Witness A: "In those [*Telegram*] days, Art treated us all the same — rough. [But] as I grew older I could look back and credit any success I may have had to his driving and his demands for perfection."

Witness B: "He was tough because he wanted to make the *Telegram* the best paper in the country. . . . He had every local name in the paper checked out and those which were incorrect became the subject of a terse memo like 'John C. Blow. How please?' And we were required to answer each one."

Witness C: "Once at a *Tribune* social affair, the staff was feeling no pain. A few were standing around in a group. Art came up holding a bourbon and with a smile on his face, said out of the blue, 'Lots of people think I'm a sonovabitch.' There was dead silence. Finally, columnist Dan Valentine said, 'Art, I'm not going to comment one way or another whether you are one. I'll just go on record as saying one thing, 'You are NOT a dumb sonovabitch.' "

Valentine tells of an episode about an argument with Deck about whether to run an item, finally saying on the phone, "Art, I've worked for you twenty years and I'll go along. All these years you've been right 97 percent of the time." Five minutes later Art walked into Valentine's office and with a straight face, asked, "What were the three times I've been wrong?"

There is no argument around the *Tribune* about Art being the one who was the driving force behind the paper's winning the Pulitzer Prize for its 1956 coverage on deadline of the midair crash of two airliners over the Grand Canyon.

Art has always liked to check wire machines. He saw a service message about a TWA plane being overdue on a Los Angeles–Chicago flight. He kept striding back to take other looks, kept repeating the information it was on a heading that would take it over northern Arizona or southern Utah. Deck got phone-calling started to law enforcement agencies in southern Utah. Two private pilots reported sighting smoke in the Grand Canyon area. Art's pacing increased in tempo. Then came a report a United plane hadn't been heard from either.

"Those two planes could have collided," he said. "Let's get going."

A reporter and photographer were rushed home to change into heavy-duty clothing, a small plane was chartered, distances to airstrips in the Canyon area checked, wirephoto equipment made ready. And off they went.

The crash site of this example of "distinguished local reporting" was 375 miles from home base, a story covered swiftly, thoroughly, and with total accuracy.

I'm not surprised one staffer wrote: "What I'll remember best and longest about Art Deck is the way he smelled that midair crash before anyone knew for certain that it had happened."

Another Salt Lake City colleague described Art as "no pushover." He won't be as ASNE president, as can be gathered from this note he wrote in early March:

"I am as adamant as anyone that we should have unqualified shield laws, both at national and state levels. But I am not persuaded that anything effective will emerge on a national level and efforts to set up an effective one already have been shot down in the Utah legislature as in other states, so I look upon this as a continuing effort that isn't going to be solved in the relatively near future."

I read this to say that while Deck isn't optimistic, he has not the slightest intention of budging one centimeter on this critical issue — or on any other affecting press freedom.

No, there isn't any doubt about Art Deck's competence as a newsman, his stubborn streak of perfectionism as an editor, his being a driver and a demander.

Yet all those who say he's an "enigma" also see right through him, even if they seem unaware of it.

One put it, "Underneath that gruffness there hides the biggest softy in the business." Another wrote, "He wears his vest like a shield which belies the sensitive guy he really is."

Win Deck says it even better. "Art's enormously shy. He's just built a little fence around himself."

She chuckles when describing Art's relationship with son John and daughter Stephanie. "Art's the most indulgent man who ever lived," says Win. "I literally never heard him raise his voice to the children — and he never ever spanked them. For that matter he's rarely raised his voice to me. He gets firm, but it's a quiet firm."

If Art was a little indulgent about son and daughter, he is even more so with Stephanie's two youngsters, Ethan, eleven, and Amy Jane, nine. Son-in-law John Churchill is a research analyst at the Walker Bank in Salt Lake City.

Art had a little eye trouble for a while, but is over it now, except that it has cut down a bit on his voracious reading. He had eye surgery at the hospital, showed up at the office the same day.

I've watched Art in action over a lot of years. My view of him is that of loyal, affectionate friend — quiet, but totally aware of what's going on all the time, keeping his counsel until he's prodded. If all editors took accountability as seriously, we'd have far less of a credibility problem.

When a mistake is made of more than trivial proportion, he personally digs in until he knows how it happened. Once the error is aired and corrective steps taken, he moves on to other matters and never reminds the offending staffer. He simply believes passionately in the oldest newspaper credo of all: Get it right.

It's at parties, big and little, that Art's reserve melts, be it picnic or black-tie affair.

He may come to the company picnic in shirt, tie, and vest, but he is quick to don an Uncle Sam hat, peer over his half-glasses and act the part in one of those terribly cornball office skits. Some youngster will come holding a frog caught in nearby puddle and Art will give full, respectful, and admiring attention to both frog and child.

The same warmth comes through at more formal affairs where Art will beam happily, and insist on pouring a second . . . a third . . . and a fourth.

I don't think I've ever seen Art taken aback. Take our most recent sortie through China. I've told friends about China's maotai and how Kentucky moonshine is a dairy product by comparison. Anyway, in some place we bought a can of the local maotai and Art gravely took the first slug. Both his contact lenses popped out.

After we'd recovered them and regained our balance, Art twinkled as he reached for the can. "This just proves that the people of this country have real fiber."

It seemed to me that his reaching again for the can proved that HE was the one with the real fiber.

John O. Emmerich, Editor and Publisher
McComb (Mississippi) Enterprise-Journal

By George W. Healy, Jr.

J ohn Oliver Emmerich is an articulate gentleman of many abilities and attainments.

On his record, with the exception of one mistake, he is a man of excellent judgment. He is positively brilliant in his thinking, and this may be proved easily. He and I agree on all things save one. He and Turner Catledge think that Mississippi State University, which was called Mississippi Agricultural and Mechanical College when they were undergraduates there, is the state's finest educational institution. I, of course, know that the older, more respected University of Mississippi (called Ole Miss by the sportswriters) is paramount.

Earlier, Oliver had the good judgment to be born in New Orleans. His father was an Illinois Central railroad conductor, and when Oliver was small the family moved to McComb, Mississippi.

After receiving all the education offered in McComb's public schools, Oliver obtained a Bachelor of Science degree at Mississippi A and M and a Master of Science degree at the University of Missouri. Then he returned to Pike County, of which McComb is the county seat, as county agricultural agent.

It wasn't long before he determined that the best way to tell farmers how to improve their farming was through the community newspaper. He quit his job as county agent and bought the *McComb Enterprise*, then a weekly.

Having the vision to realize that the then-biggest industry in the county, the Illinois Central repair shop, might not always provide jobs for most of

---

Healy was editor of the *New Orleans Times-Picayune* when this article first appeared, in 1959.

McComb's male workers, the new editor undertook a double-header program for getting new industries for his little city and for improving Pike County's farms. An annual "grass roots" farm progress program which he established and for which his paper puts up most of the awards has grown to be South Mississippi's most spirited agricultural competition.

Progressive Farmer magazine in 1950 named him "Mississippi Man of the Year" in recognition of the success of this program. In 1955 Freedom Foundation cited him for a series of editorials on American freedom. Millsaps College, in appreciation of his community leadership, awarded him its Doctor of Laws degree. Offices which he has held in the Mississippi Press Association, the National Editorial Association, Rotary International, and other organizations are myriad.

Those who may expect Oliver to look and act the part of a small-town yokel are in for a surprise. Handsome, athletic, always well groomed and well dressed, he can hold his own in debate or in repartee with the most erudite New Yorker.

He has traveled extensively, most recently in Russia, and his readers have received the benefit of his sage observations.

Now a daily, his *McComb Enterprise-Journal* is quoted widely. He purchased the *Journal* and merged it with the *Enterprise* in 1945.

In a way, Oliver is a paradox. He is an excellent public speaker, but there is no actor in him. His modesty is such that there could be no "ham" in his personality.

With Oliver, Jr., accepting more and more responsibility for the *Enterprise-Journal*, his father has taken on additional duties. Besides editing and publishing the McComb daily, he edits also the larger *Jackson State-Times* in the state capital. He and Mrs. Emmerich keep their home in McComb, commuting to Jackson.

When he is not busy editing one of the two newspapers or advising farmers how to better their lot, Oliver has found time to serve as a trustee of Mississippi's institutions of higher learning, to keep speaking dates in cities twenty times the size of his own, and to crusade for states' rights and the free enterprise system.

Regarding himself liberal in his political thinking, he believes that overcentralization of government is a major curse. He opposes dependence by individuals and by states on largess from Washington.

He insists there still is truth in the adage that the Lord helps those who help themselves. His own life is pretty good evidence.

Although positive in his opinions, he definitely does not subscribe to the theory that the two sides to every question are his side and the wrong side.

Frank Eyerly, Managing Editor
Des Moines Register and Tribune

By Kenneth MacDonald

F rank Eyerly, managing editor of the *Des Moines Register and Tribune* for the last fifteen years, might be described as an eighteenth century man hugely enjoying the twentieth century.

Perhaps the eighteenth century reference is an exaggeration, but it is true that he respects reason and is suspicious of sentiment, that he prefers the leisurely and well-ordered life, that he is skeptical about progress, and that he has a deep distrust of all mechanical devices.

This does not mean that there is anything slow-paced about life in the newsroom when he is present. During his working hours orders, suggestions and decisions issue from his office in rapid spurts.

Probably his greatest asset as an editor is the sharpness of his news judgment. With unusual speed and a minimum of error he can see the possibilities of a news story in its earliest stages, recognize a new political or social trend before it develops, or identify the one fact that makes an otherwise routine situation significant.

This quality, which all good editors have in some degree, is frequently called intuition, but I think intuition is a small part of it. It is the product, in Eyerly's case, of a far-ranging curiosity, an abnormal amount of reading, a quick mind, and an unusual—but highly selective—memory. (He can remember the details of a political incident thirty-five years ago, but he has been known to regale his wife with the same joke at dinner that she told him at breakfast.)

He is not much interested in formal definitions of news. If a story interests him, he assumes it will interest others. He likes a sense of immediacy

---

MacDonald was editor of the *Des Moines Register and Tribune* when this article first appeared, in 1961.

on page one but he is not a slave to time element. He once reprinted an article from a scholarly quarterly on the front page of the *Register*.

He thinks anything that's fit to print is appropriate on page one if it will interest enough readers. When "Peter Pan" was presented as one of the first television spectaculars, he used a review of it as a top head on page one the next morning.

He has a discerning eye for political developments and a keen sense of consumer news, but he gets his greatest satisfaction from policing local government and uncovering news which public officials have tried to conceal.

He makes decisions rapidly and acts on them quickly. In more than thirty years of close association, I have never seen him disconcerted under the pressure of a deadline. This doesn't mean he is even-tempered. He has a low boiling point and no reluctance about losing his temper.

As an administrator he delegates authority widely, because he wants a staff of strong individuals and he wants to save his own time, but he checks carefully on how authority is used. He frequently starts the day by reading last night's dead spike to see what was left out of the paper.

He demands a high standard of performance, but he is not a perfectionist about trivial details. He is impatient with stupidity, he is contemptuous of ignorance, and he is infuriated by carelessness. He can be harsh in his criticism of staff members, but he can be equally vigorous in their defense if he thinks they are wrongly accused.

He is much more interested in content than in form, and he doesn't care much about technicalities. He appreciates good writing, but he is realistic about deadlines, and he worries more about getting facts into print than about how they are written as long as they are understandable.

Eyerly grew up in Newton, Iowa, a small manufacturing city (washing machines) thirty miles from Des Moines. As a boy he sold newspapers and later he was a supervisor of carrier boys, a job which helped put him through college. He also sold advertising for a small city daily. Perhaps this combination of experience is responsible for his understanding of the arithmetic of publishing.

He went to the State University of Iowa for four years and completed the academic requirements, but he has no degree because he refused to take military training, a two-year course which was a required subject. He wrote a column for the student daily called "Chills and Fever," which produced a considerable amount of both among various faculty members, and he edited the student humor magazine. When he left college he went to work for the *Register and Tribune* as a reporter.

His catholic reading habits were developed long before he arrived on the campus and have continued since. He has few casual interests; he is either deeply interested or indifferent. The range of his dinner table conversation can be startling. He can discuss with equal enthusiasm the stature of T. S. Eliot, the early life of Marilyn Monroe, or the construction of a life insurance policy.

His ignorance of mechanical objects is monumental, and so is his distrust of them. He has not driven an automobile since the 1920s and he has never ridden in an airplane. Through practical necessity he does ride in automobiles, but he doesn't enjoy it.

Like many of his colleagues, he is a hypochondriac, and he freely admits it. However, unlike many hypochondriacs, he gets little comfort from consulting doctors, because he considers medical men as fallible as proofreaders.

He is an armchair outdoorsman with an expert knowledge of camping, hiking, and wilderness life, but he hasn't been on a camping trip since he was a boy. He owns a collection of high-priced, high-powered rifles, although he never hunts. He reads outdoor magazines regularly, and he could give sound advice to an expedition outfitting for the North country, but his only physical exercise is walking. Several years ago he marched his teenage daughters on a one-day twenty-mile hike in Jackson Hole.

He has no interest in competitive games of any kind—bridge, golf, or baseball—either as a participant or observer. He goes to a football game once a year, but this is for the companionship and the pageantry. He thinks the game itself is about one quarter too long.

He likes to live comfortably with touches of luxury balanced by bits of frugality. Most of his suits are special-order from Brooks Brothers or Chipps, but he has a sports jacket which he bought from a mail-order house.

His greatest interest outside of newspapers is art. He knows most of the major museums in the country, and he has a wide acquaintance among artists, dealers, and directors. He and his wife Jeannette, who is a free-lance writer, own an extensive collection of paintings, drawings, sculpture, and graphic works. The emphasis is on twentieth century Americans, including Prendergast, Glackens, Sloan, Marin, Weber, Bouche, Zorach, and Mattern, but it also contains works by Picasso, Miro, Matisse, Renoir, Braque, Klee, Rembrandt, and Rodin.

Perhaps the best way to conclude this sketch is with a fragment of Eyerly's journalistic philosophy quoted from a recent speech he made at the University of Nebraska:

> I know how difficult it is to articulate moral purpose. If it were not difficult, there would be no accumulated body of philosophy stemming from the Greeks and providing an endless battleground for every generation and century.

But for your generation and mine, the moral aspect of the newspaper can be seen; it can be smelled and felt and identified by all of us. It involves integrity in reporting and editing; it suggests probity in publishing; it implies responsibility in the advertising columns.

It bars the fast buck, the fixed quiz show, the conflict of interest, whether an elected public official makes private gain out of his public commitment or a corporation officer makes personal gain out of his custodianship of a large corporation.

It forecloses the double standard or reflecting the news in terms of racial, religious, or political bias.

Finally, the readers' assessment of this concept will be based on what we do and not what we say. Our words and our protestations will have to be balanced by performance.

J. Donald Ferguson, Editor
The Milwaukee Journal

By Robert W. Wells

O nce in a debate over the value of syndicated opinion columns before the ASNE in Washington, J. Donald Ferguson declared:

"We wouldn't trade one experienced reporter for all of the syndicated opinion columns we could crowd into the *Milwaukee Journal*."

It is his conviction that good reporting makes good newspapers.

Throughout his long career Ferguson has been the direct opposite of the Hollywood version of the newspaperman. Even under pressure, he never lost his politeness or composure. His dress was always immaculate, his white hair neatly brushed. No matter how many titles or honors came his way, he remained the kind of a man his employees called "Fergy" or "Don," not "Mr. Ferguson."

No stranger would take him for a small-town boy out of Nevada, Missouri, but his friends could recognize that one thing had not changed since then. A small-town boy is likely to look on life with a kind of friendly skepticism that recognizes that everyone, great or humble, has much in common with everyone else; that the differences between people are not as important as their fundamental similarities.

Ferguson was the son of a railroad train dispatcher. As a result, he did considerable traveling, attending grade schools in four states: Missouri, Kansas, Mississippi, and Louisiana. He came back to his birthplace in Nevada to graduate from high school.

By that time, Ferguson had already decided he wanted to be a newspaperman. That decision stemmed from a day when, as a senior, he was asked to help the local paper's only reporter cover a cyclone damage story. Interviewing the survivors gave him a taste for reporting that has never left

---

Wells was a reporter for the *Milwaukee Journal* when this article first appeared, in 1961.

him.

He determined to go to college. But first he had to earn the tuition money. He got a job at one dollar a day at the Railroad YMCA in his home town. For that pay, he was required to sweep out and scrub the rooms and distribute the hymn books at Sunday afternoon services.

He got fired when he failed to report to his superiors that some of the railroad men were smuggling beer into their rooms. Still determined to save up college money, he went to Dearing, Kansas, and got a job pushing wheelbarrows full of clay at a smelter.

The gang boss and the paymaster, he discovered, were withholding ten cents a day from each of the workmen's wages and pocketing the money. When they refused to stop the practice, Ferguson quit.

He moved over to the coal fields at Fleming, Kansas, and took a job as a switchman at $3.45 a day. But his father, fearing an accident to the youth, induced the Missouri Pacific railroad to fire him. Ferguson then came back home and worked as a $45 a month train and engine crew caller. Later, he became a clerk, timekeeper, and division accountant for the railroad superintendent's office there.

With the college money finally saved, Ferguson enrolled in the school of journalism at the University of Missouri. He was graduated in 1915. Twenty-seven years later, while he was vice-president and associate editor of the *Journal*, the school awarded him a medal of honor for distinguished service in journalism. His photograph is in the school's hall of honor.

The year he was graduated Ferguson married Anna Irene Crotty, whom he had known in high school, and went into partnership with his college roommate, Houston Harte, who later became editor and publisher of the *San Angelo* (Texas) *Standard-Times*. The two young men bought the *Boonville* (Missouri) weekly *Republican*, with Ferguson serving as editor and his friend as business manager.

They borrowed enough money to buy a linotype machine and Ferguson learned to operate it. The paper's office was above a saloon. The editor's most difficult duties were social—it was the custom for him to buy a beer for each reader who came in to pay for a subscription.

After a time, Ferguson got tired of having to go downstairs each time some farmer came in with his payment and a thirst, so he had a dumbwaiter rigged up. When beer was needed upstairs, Ferguson would pound on the wall. The barkeep would put the beer in the basket and Ferguson would haul it up.

The paper was forced to move out of the building after Ferguson came out editorially for a local option proposal which would have put the saloon out of business. The paper was having financial problems, too, and the partners decided that one of them had to get a job elsewhere for a while to accumulate money to pay off the mortgage on the linotype.

Each wrote ten letters of application. Ferguson got an offer from the *Kansas City Star* and took a job for eighty dollars a month as a reporter and copyreader. He never went back to Boonville.

After two years on the *Star*, he moved to the old *Sioux City* (Iowa) *Tribune* in 1917. He was telegraph editor, managing editor, and editorial writer on the paper before moving to the *Milwaukee Journal* in 1923.

Four years later, he became chief editorial writer, moved up to associate editor in 1938 and to president and editor in 1943.

It has long been the practice around the *Journal* for editorial writers to get out of the office and see things happening. Sometimes they act as reporters, covering an important story, as well as obtaining background information for their editorials.

It was in such a capacity that Ferguson covered many important political events, including national party conventions. In 1924, he was able to score a scoop on the hundreds of other topflight newsmen covering the Democratic convention in New York.

He went there with orders to keep an eye on John W. Davis of West Virginia, known in the press as "the barefoot lawyer on Wall Street." Ferguson got acquainted with Davis and the rest of the West Virginia delegation. There was plenty of time to do so while the convention sweated through one hundred ballots, with Al Smith and William Gibbs McAdoo deadlocked.

One day, a delegate tipped Ferguson to stand by a freight elevator in the hotel. After forty-five minutes, out stepped Davis, his arms linked with the campaign managers for Smith and McAdoo. Ferguson, sensing what had happened, stepped up to Davis.

"Congratulations," he said.

"Thank you," said Davis, and added, "All things come to him who waits."

Ferguson wired in a story that Davis would win the nomination as a dark horse compromise candidate. *Journal* readers were the first in the nation to learn whom the Democrats were going to nominate.

Every newsman has his store of memories of the men he's written about. Ferguson is no exception. He recalls watching Woodrow Wilson pecking out speeches on a typewriter with two fingers while Mrs. Wilson sat by knitting; the time Al Smith squeezed past in a train aisle and shook his head and said, "Gee, I'm getting fat"; the day that Wendell Willkie was told that if he came out for a draft in the 1940 campaign he would lose, and Willkie declared, "I'd rather lose the presidency than see this country unprepared for the war that is coming."

Then there was the time when Ferguson was asked on a White House visit with Franklin D. Roosevelt in 1935 what Wisconsin people thought of the New Deal reform measures. Ferguson said he thought the changes were coming along too fast for people to digest them.

"We only get a reform administration once every twenty years," President Roosevelt told him, "so we have to work fast."

A friendly man, who likes being with people, he avoided joining fraternal organizations in which members pledged themselves to loyalty to fellow members.

His first loyalty, he felt, was to the paper and its readers. He wanted to avoid a situation where loyalty to a brother lodge member might be inconsistent with an editor's obligations.

"So many of my old friends just couldn't understand that as editor I could not consent to suppress news about them or their relatives," he said once. "I would try to tell them that news happens and that neither a newspaper nor its editor has any control over the happening. Our duty is to print it."

And so Ferguson has limited his memberships to such professional journalism groups as Sigma Delta Chi, the Milwaukee Press Club, and the ASNE.

In writing this story, the reporter asked the editor if there were any special instructions. Ferguson's answer helps explain his philosophy of newspapering.

"Just keep it simple," he said.

William H. Fitzpatrick, Editor
Norfolk (Virginia) Ledger-Dispatch

By Carl Corbin

Fathers nervous about the future of their young sons who show spirited, uninhibited tendencies can draw comfort from a case study of William H. Fitzpatrick, the editor of the *Norfolk Ledger-Dispatch*.

The message which comes through loud and clear from that study is this:

Be of good cheer if your boy gets into scraps, takes not too well to formal education, relishes pranks, seems irresponsible, and generally doesn't conform.

With traits like that, your son classifies as the Fitzpatrick type, with a potential for a colorful newspaper career.

When he was a harum-scarum teenager growing up in his native New Orleans, nobody would have guessed that a future as a distinguished editor lay ahead for him—a future which would include a Pulitzer Prize and even his picture in the *Time* magazine press section.

Take, for instance, the observations of his lifelong buddy, Torrey Gomila, now a New Orleans business executive.

"Man, my mother wouldn't let me run around with that Fitzpatrick," says Gomila—no little Lord Fauntleroy himself.

"But whatever else is said about him, the main point is that he was never afraid of a damned thing, even as a boy.

"I remember one late afternoon when he and I were walking home from high school. We couldn't ride the streetcar because we had spent our carfare on something else. We were walking through a rough part of town and got into a hassle with an older fellow who stuck a gun in Billy's stomach.

Corbin was editor of the *New Orleans States-Item* when this article first appeared, in 1960.

"Do you know what that crazy Fitzpatrick did? He told the man, 'You don't have enough guts to pull the trigger.'

"And the man didn't have. Billy took the gun away from him and we went on home."

Another acquaintance from boyhood days, Charles L. "Pie" Dufour— now a columnist for the *New Orleans States-Item*—describes the youthful Fitzpatrick as "the fun-loving Rover with a wild streak, fearless to the point of foolish," whose only mentionable distinction was as a fast football player and four-letter man in high school.

When it came time for Billy to tackle the problem of higher education, the Depression era was in full bloom. He made a stab at trying to attend Tulane University, but gave it up after his sophomore year to go to work. (Now he is a member of Tulane's Board of Visitors.)

Financial problems had followed the death a few years earlier of his father, Harry W. Fitzpatrick, a developer of real estate who was widely known in New Orleans and was a delegate to the 1921 convention which drafted the present Louisiana Constitution.

Young Fitzpatrick's first newspaper job was with the *New Orleans Item* at $14.50 a week. James Thomson was the publisher. (In 1958 the *Item* became part of the *New Orleans States-Item*.)

This was the same Thomson who had been publisher of the *Norfolk Dispatch*, a predecessor of the *Ledger-Dispatch*, from 1900 to 1906. And his managing editor, Marshall Ballard, later was editor of the *Item* when Fitzpatrick worked there.

"Mr. Thomson had been a friend of my father's, though they differed politically pretty much," Billy recalls.

"I introduced myself to him after hearing him speak at a banquet. And Jim Thomson said that if I ever needed any advice or help he'd be glad to aid me.

"So, about nine months later, I went down and asked if there was a job and he gave me one on the city-side. Later I switched to sports."

Dufour, then also an *Item* employee, recalls that the Fitzpatrick of that period "always liked to read, and had a great flair for words."

In 1935 Billy left the *Item*—according to Dufour, because the *Item* wouldn't raise him from $18.75 a week to $22.50.

The competition, the *Times-Picayune*, hired him as a reporter. During the next five years he worked on up into handling special sections and later serving as picture editor.

In 1940 the Times-Picayune Publishing Company, then headed by the late L. K. Nicholson, switched Fitzpatrick to its afternoon publication, the *New Orleans States*, to fill a vacancy that had occurred in the city editor's position.

That was the year, too, that he married Francis Westfeldt of a prominent New Orleans family. Billy's friends attribute to her steadying influence a big share of the credit for his emergence from a fun-loving young newsman into a serious newspaper executive.

The transformation wasn't accomplished easily and immediately, however. In their early years the young wife, whom everyone calls by her nickname "Coo," had to put up with such difficulties as lively talkfests that went on in her front parlor into the late hours, climaxed by the host goading a guest into a wrestling match or some similar pugnacious demonstration.

Fitzpatrick progressed to managing editor of the *States* under the colorful old editor James Crown, before volunteering for navy duty in World War II.

As a lieutenant and a lieutenant-commander, he served on the *Enterprise*, the *Intrepid*, and the *Hancock* in the assault and capture of the Gilbert and Marshall Islands and of Okinawa, and in the raids on Wake, Truk, and Japan. He was awarded a commendation ribbon by Admiral Nimitz for courage under fire.

While Fitzpatrick was overseas, Editor Crown died. Fitzpatrick was named his successor, as editor in absentia.

Returning to his newspaper in 1945, Fitzpatrick took up the directing of a campaign Crown had started to oust from city hall Mayor Robert S. Maestri, a wheel in the state's unsavory political machine. For the success of that campaign the *New Orleans States* received a Sigma Delta Chi Courage-in-Journalism award.

About this time the mold of Fitzpatrick the editor—his personality and journalistic characteristics as they are today—began to set.

In appearance he is six-foot and skinny. His hair is brush-cut. He wears bow ties and conservative suits with vests, of the Brooks Brothers look.

Nobody would accuse him of being relaxed. His two-fingered typing is accompanied by a constant nervous bounce of one leg. The neat desk is not part of his makeup. At times he swears off cigarettes. He drinks coffee all day long.

When he is not making like a newspaperman, you are likely to find him duck hunting, or mulching camellias, or painting his own decoys, or tracing genealogical lines, or fishing, or reading things Irish, or just observing four sons who range from five to eighteen years old.

In point of view, Fitzpatrick is a conservative. As he puts it, "The less government the people have, the better." He looks skeptically at high-sounding ideas, wanting to be sure that they do not do violence to such concepts as the Bill of Rights, free enterprise, home rule, and states' rights.

His conservative outlook was reflected in the 1950 editorial series for which he was awarded a Pulitzer Prize.

Entitled "Government by Treaty," the series attacked the United Nations' Covenant on Human Rights as a doctrine likely to "endanger some of our precious heritages."

There are today members of the staff Fitzpatrick formerly headed in New Orleans who openly acknowledge that they could never bring themselves to read the series, but that doesn't lessen the respect and affection they held for the author.

They threw a party for him when he received the award and made a big thing of a mock scroll reproducing the five-hundred-dollar award check and concluding:

Therefore, be it resolved, that we, his co-workers and friends are proud of our long-nosed, spindle-legged, brush-haired Billy.

They gathered around to honor him again in 1952, when he decided to accept an offer to become an associate editor of the *Wall Street Journal* in New York. They sent him off with a mammoth cartoon by John Chase that included symbols of Billy's conservatism, his fishing, his awards, his interest in New Orleans' famed Bourbon Street, his coffee drinking.

For eight years he was happy at the *Wall Street Journal*, but not too happy in New York.

Here is what he says about the *Journal*:

The *Wall Street Journal* is a simply wonderful newspaper and its policies as regarding the employees are out of this world. Working with Mr. Grimes and Vermont Royster and Joe Evans and Jack Bridge and Ed Roberts was a pleasure and, professionally, quite profitable.

Here is what he says about New York:

I think that basically it all gets down to this: I love people, but not that much.

Also, it seemed to me that most of the people I met where we lived were just sort of marking time to retire and go back where they came from. I felt that New York, and the suburbs, were kind of like navy receiving stations: everybody just passing through.

I decided, and of course I was wrong from the viewpoint of other people but not my own, that it was a sort of rootless place and with four boys I didn't want them spread all over the place when they finished college.

So I began looking around for a place that I thought we might be happier living in, thinking that sooner or later one would pop up. Norfolk did.

The Norfolk development was described in the *Time* press section of September 5, 1960, and Fitzpatrick confirms that to his knowledge the piece was a correct appraisal of the situation.

In Norfolk, the Norfolk-Portsmouth Newspapers, Inc. is the sole publishing company. Frank Batten, thirty-three years old, is the publisher of the morning *Virginian-Pilot* and of the evening *Ledger-Dispatch* (and *Portsmouth Star,* a separate edition). His view as a publisher, as reported in *Time,* is this:

"When newspapers have a monopoly, they have an obligation to the community to give it a wide range of expression and a wide discussion of the topics of the times so that people will have both sides of important issues."

To implement that view, he encourages the two newspapers toward fierce competition and maintaining their separate identities. Traditionally, the morning product has been the less conservative, while the afternoon has tended toward the more conservative line.

"He would prefer his editors to express different views if the views are honestly arrived at, because he thinks a monopoly has a responsibility to explore both sides," says Fitzpatrick.

"He would not ask a man to change his view to conform to the particular paper he was to work for, but he would seek a man whose views did not clash with the paper.

"All he asks is that an editorial position be honestly believed and that it be argued effectively and as reasonably and convincingly as possible."

Against that background, Fitzpatrick, now fifty-two years old, accepted the *Ledger-Dispatch* editorship. He fills a spot left vacant by the retirement in 1959 of longtime editor Joseph Leslie, and by the return to the *Charlotte News* of Perry Morgan, who had come to the *Ledger-Dispatch* about a year ago to edit the editorial page.

It was a "desire for a paper to run again," Fitzpatrick admits, that had much to do with his decision to leave the *Wall Street Journal* berth which he liked—that and his lack of affection for New York as a place to live.

In contrast to New York, Norfolk appeals to him.

"It is much like New Orleans, and its environs," he says. "Water everywhere, just like the bayous. Hot—and I mean hot weather—in summer. Flatland. Camellias and azaleas and gardenias and—though the term has fallen into literary disrepute—even magnolias.

"I really felt at home when one day I crossed the street and my heels dug into the melting tar. I hadn't had that sensation of the streets running since I left New Orleans.

"Then there are the ducks. Norfolk is great duck country. Better than Long Island, where last year I rented a blind and didn't fire a shot."

Victor Free, Managing Editor
The Pittsburgh Press

By Sherley Uhl

About one hundred and fifty people gathered around his desk to say good-bye, but hundreds of thousands with whom he was as close could have been there. For in forty years of newspapering, Victor Free considered his job in terms of people: those who worked with him, and those countless unseen ones for whom he sweated out the truth and the news in stories and editions—the readers.

Vic's retirement as managing editor of the *Pittsburgh Press* was typically in character—the result of a tough-minded decision.

He did it practically at the stroke of sixty because he still had full health and vigor.

His own prescription for retirement was: "Some writing and some loafing, I'm not certain of the proportions."

If Hollywood were searching for a frenzied character for one of its city room roles, Vic would never fit, and couldn't care less.

Calm, reasonable, seldom ruffled, he frequently wore a bemused expression, was tolerant of the confusion around him, and sometimes leavened it with a touch of wry wit.

As managing editor, first in Indianapolis and later in Pittsburgh, he never had an office . . . didn't want one. He was a far-ranging executive who spent more time in motion than he did at his desk.

Within a matter of minutes he could supervise a Roto feature scheduled to appear weeks in the future, offer suggestions on a breaking story on the deadline, and then drop in on a policy discussion in the office of editor W. W. Forster.

Vic was mild-mannered, short on sermons and long on advice, and a

---

Uhl was a staff writer for the *Pittsburgh Press* when this article first appeared, in 1964.

man who was convinced firmly that a community needs strong leadership from its newspapers, and that newspapers need strong leadership from their executives.

He was a chain-of-command managing editor, one who delegated great authority to department chiefs and supported them in their decisions.

He could be determined, even grim, but he was soft on some subjects—especially children, and family life.

He disliked publicity-seekers, pettifoggers, and predators who harass a daily newspaper's search for truth.

Vic was convinced that television—limited by time segments to sketching the news in broad strokes—could never capture the personal touch, never project the warm details available in a good family newspaper.

And he realized newspapering is much more than reporting, rewriting, copyreading, and editing.

He was himself a superb craftsman and writer. His *Press* Sunday magazine interviews with leading industrialists—Richard K. Mellon, Roger Blough, Arthur Vining Davis—were classics . . . and exclusives.

But Vic was primarily a production man, one of the best in the business, and he devoted his career to knitting professional staffers into a cohesive team, on papers ranging in size from the *Conneaut* (Ohio) *News-Herald* (circulation 4,872) to the *Pittsburgh Press* (circulation 380,000 daily, 740,000 Sunday).

No department escaped his careful attention, neither the women's department nor the sports page, and he was especially sensitive to the latter, because he was a sports fan.

To him important sports news was worth page one, and he was bold enough to play it across the top if he believed hometown interest justified this prominence.

Because he was attentive to every section of the paper, he was one of those editors who insist on a complete and appealing "package"—a newspaper attractive to businessmen, educators, steelworkers, housewives.

He had the intuitive knack of selecting the right man for the right job, and under this tutelage many promising cubs became old pros in positions of prominence or leadership.

Earl Richert, now editor of the Scripps-Howard Newspaper Alliance in Washington, was one of his proteges; so was Walt Friedenberg, roving correspondent for Scripps-Howard, whom Vic sized up immediately as a talented and poised youth and hired as a summer replacement.

Vic was born into journalism at Titusville, Pennsylvania, where his father was editor of the *Titusville Herald* for ten years.

He was graduated from Ohio Wesleyan University in 1926 and was "mousetrapped" into the newspaper business when a fraternity brother taunted, "You're no athlete . . . do something."

After that, said Vic, "The virus became a disease."

He worked summers on small-town newspapers in northeastern Ohio and then became editor of the *Conneaut News-Herald,* where he remained until 1935.

He joined Scripps-Howard in that year, starting on the copydesk at the *Akron Times-Press.* He was news editor when that paper was sold in 1938, at which time he transferred to the *Indianapolis Times.*

Vic was news editor at Indianapolis from 1939 to 1943 and managing editor there during the turbulent war and postwar years.

During the war he kept up an active correspondence with all *Times* employees in the service, and with their families at home. Many of them returned to better jobs than they had when they left.

At Indianapolis he established a working agreement with Ed Heinke, then city editor, now Scripps-Howard bureau chief in Columbus.

Together, they put out a freewheeling, flexible newspaper, one that could be replated on a moment's notice and frequently was.

Sober by nature, Vic was never a hard drinker. But these were his salad days in the profession. On one occasion John Sorrells, then editor in chief of Scripps-Howard newspapers, had come to town as guest at a big party. It was a BIG party. And afterwards Vic somehow lost his uppers. This was disastrous, because the following day Sorrells visited the *Times* office for personal introductions.

As badly as he felt, Old Reliable, as some of his colleagues then called him, reported to work the next day. Sorrells walked in, and shook hands with Vic, who was never more dejected because he had lost (1) his teeth and (2) momentarily his grip on the situation. But if Sorrells noticed his discomfiture, he never dropped a hint.

It was in Indianapolis that Vic's makeup wizardry matured. He experimented with horizontal layouts, color, overprints, and generous art lash-ups that later became part of journalism's stock-in-trade.

On one Memorial Day, as World War II drew to a close, Vic converted the *Times* into a memorial for those local men who had died in service. The front page contained nothing but their names—hundreds of them—overprinted on red, white, and blue.

When he moved to the *Pittsburgh Press* in 1951 as editor of the paper's magazine, he was asked by *Press* editor Forster to brighten up that Sunday standby.

Vic removed the syndicated fiction it then featured and enlivened it with local copy and pictures. He slanted it slightly toward the women readers, because he realized that they—somewhat more than men—were interested in features and had the time to digest them.

Later as managing editor of the *Press* he was a planner who always seemed to be a few steps ahead of the opposition in preparing for major events.

He was demonstrably skilled at putting together special issues. His promotion and planning on the *Press's* bicentennial issue resulted in the advance sale of one hundred thousand extra copies.

Vic and his wife, Helen, are moving from Pittsburgh to a cottage on Lake Atwood, near Dellroy, Ohio, a cottage he constructed himself.

He's almost as handy with hammer and saw as he is with typewriter and pencil. Woodworking is his hobby.

He plans to keep a hand in, however, doing free-lance writing from Ohio and from Florida, where the Frees hope to spend their winters.

To say Vic Free was—and still is—a dedicated newspaperman's newspaperman, is to belabor the obvious. He knew the imperfections of the trade, but he realized progress is attainable, and he worked at it.

He insisted, with typical modesty, that he had achieved nothing "outstanding," but his forty-year career is a notable achievement, and his credo is straight to the point:

"The objective in the newspaper business has not changed: to get the most news—factual, interpretative, and understandable—to the most people, fastest; and to help train staffers to do the same."

Alfred Friendly, Managing Editor
The Washington Post

By Chalmers M. Roberts

S oon after Al Friendly became the *Post's* managing editor in 1955, a
sometime contributor in a foreign capital received a cable asking for a
story. The cable was signed "Friendly *Washington Post*." The contributor sent
the story, along with the comment that he was glad to know the paper was so
pleasant. Well, it is. And he is, too.

Nearly twenty-five years ago and fresh out of Amherst College, Al
Friendly was an overpaid New Deal junior bureaucrat living in Washington
with an underpaid *Post* reporter (who happens to be the gent writing this
piece). Somehow, the smell of ink got transferred to Friendly and before
long Al went to work as a copyboy at Scripps-Howard's *Washington News*.
That was in 1936.

Handy with words, as well as with ideas, Friendly's first love is writing.
This has caused the same sort of dichotomy which has plagued many
another editor who came up from the ranks. At first Al tried to keep on
writing in his "spare" time but the paperwork finally ended that, with the
exception of the annual Sunday-before-Christmas poem of greetings (a la
the *New Yorker's* Sullivan) to the great and small of Washington and the
world. This full-page effort now acts as the annual steam valve. Sample 1957
greeting:

> Let mistletoe sprigs be agreeably pinned on
> The senators laboring *under den Lyndon*.

Doubtless it was this waggish tendency which led Friendly at Amherst to
join the college humor magazine rather than the newspaper. At any rate, a

---

Roberts was foreign affairs reporter for the *Washington Post* when this article first appeared, in
1958.

sense of humor has come in handy since Al reached the eminence of managing editor. And it should be recorded that he was prematurely gray long years ago, though he is now but forty-six.

Friendly moved from copyboy to reporter to columnist in the federal government civil service field, a key assignment on every Washington newspaper. The *Post* hired him away from the *News* in 1939 to write its government column and he's been at the *Post* ever since with three exceptions: a year out in 1940 to be assistant to the trustee in the reorganization of Associated Gas and Electric Corp., three years in the Army Air Corps (first lieutenant to major in wartime intelligence), and a year as the Marshall Plan's press boss in Paris in 1948 and 1949.

Friendly has covered most of the Washington beats, ending up with economics and atomic energy before becoming assistant managing editor in 1952 and then m.e. Consequently, he knows what the staff is up to—or should be up to. But he's the low pressure type and can say it with a smile and the staff can, and does, argue back. The staffers do get little blue-paper notes if they turn in good pieces and contrary-wise on the bloopers.

Al may be an egghead—he won't let anyone else review the books on ancient civilizations and the latest archaeological dig—but most of the staff has never seen his Phi Beta Kappa key. Tennis has been his passion and Adlai Stevenson among his guests on his own court, but of late he's gone in for duck hunting.

A believer in the interpretive school of writing, Friendly was involved as a reporter in many a rough and tumble: with the late Senator McKellar over David Lilienthal and the TVA when Lilienthal was named to head the Atomic Energy Commission; with the late Senator McCarthy on more than one occasion; and with the AEC's Admiral Lewis Strauss over the extent and dangers of radioactive fallout.

If his colleagues in the working press had any complaint, it generally was that he worked too hard, off the job as well as on. For Friendly soon learned that the cocktail circuit in Washington can produce news tips and stories as well as ulcers and tired feet. Besides, his beauteous wife, Jean, sets a fancy table and many a good argument has been heard across it on the issues of the day by people who make the news.

Of Al's five children, Alfred, Jr., a Harvard student, already has had a summer try at newspapering and another son, Jonathan, an Amherst student, spent last summer working for a senator. A Salt Lake City boy, Friendly is now a voteless resident of the District of Columbia, which both limits his politics and increases his zeal for that hardy *Post* perennial, the campaign for home rule for the District.

Friendly's reportorial instincts show best when a big story breaks. Then he pops out of his glass m.e. cage and joins the desk in laying out the paper and needling his reporters to pour it on. His eye for the best way to handle a story was never better illustrated than when he printed the verbatim text of the secret testimony of unhappy Ambassador-designate Gluck before the Senate Foreign Relations Committee, with only a brief italic precede and the head, "An Ambassador Is Born," under a picture of Ike and his envoy to Ceylon.

But an m.e.'s life is not all big stories. Like his confreres, Friendly has to be father confessor to some staffers and there are the usual luncheon speaking chores. And like most m.e.'s Friendly's job is never done. He gets the first edition at home in early evening and is usually on the phone calling for a switch in play of this story or that.

Careful staff selection is a Friendly imperative, with accent on brains and youth. The copyboys (and copygirls) have a thorough training program, which means they either go up or out. And it doesn't hurt to be able to say to the kid who is having trouble adjusting from being editor of the *Harvard Crimson* to cranking the office ditto machine that "I used to be a copyboy once myself."

William Franklin Gaines, Editor
Greenville (South Carolina) Piedmont

By James Walker

W hen Bill Gaines asks his hostess at a dinner party for the recipe of the main dish, it is more than just a compliment. He is pursuing his almost academic interest in excellent cuisine.

On occasion, he will pick up a cookbook for light reading, like *Food in England,* which concerns itself with culinary matters before the Norman conquest.

His publisher once said that whenever Bill goes on a trip he is certain to bring back a "plate-by-plate account" of all the new foods he has tried.

His love for country ham once sent him and his wife off on one of their "working vacations" to discover for themselves the regional subtleties in the curing of ham. They ranged from Herman Talmadge's South Georgia farm through the Carolinas and Virginia and up into the Pennsylvania Dutch Country. The series Bill wrote made interesting copy for readers already somewhat addicted to country ham.

Those who have tried the four "dishes" he cooks—Swedish meat balls, beef stroganoff, beef pyramids, and flounder—say they give every indication of his having been potentially a great chef.

He attributes his affinity for fancy foods to a childhood dislike for "turnip greens, black-eyed peas, corn bread, buttermilk—I hated them." His appetite now has gone full circle; along with the exotic foods, his palate craves also the very dishes he once abhorred.

In Bill's editorials, as in anything he ever wrote, you will find a craftsman's work—lovingly, carefully, precisely put together. Yet there is nothing ever forced about his writing.

Walker was city editor of the *Greenville News* when this article first appeared, in 1963.

Bill and an unabridged dictionary were wedded many years ago, and the romance still continues; he often spends minutes pinning down the exact word he desires.

Years ago, he hesitated not a moment in editing for publication a list of rural roads paved by the county. For "Whorehouse Road," picturesquely and appropriately named, he substituted "Bordello Road" and there was never a complaint from the Bible Belt constituency.

William Franklin Gaines, born April 8, 1908, had an inauspicious beginning in the newspaper business, but he remembers it fondly. "I wrote meeting notices for troop five of Central Methodist Church for the *Spartanburg Herald*. God bless 'em, they ran a scout page on Monday mornings."

At the University of South Carolina, where admittedly he spent a pretty riotous two years before having to give up school because of Depression-year financial problems, a college professor recalls Bill as "an exuberant, intelligent student, with a great deal of curiosity." He added, "He was erratic as hell."

Any such tendency has since been honed thin. An associate, who has observed him under almost all conditions, labels him the "steadiest, most stable" newspaperman he knows.

On July 20, 1928, Bill started a full-time job at the *Spartanburg Herald*. Less than an hour later a worker at a grain mill went methodically down a loading platform axing everyone in sight. Before attempting to electrocute himself by throwing a trace chain over a power line, he had done away with an even half dozen. Bill didn't write the lead or even a principal sidebar, but it was an exciting first day, spent mostly at the county jail keeping check on the berserk man's condition.

Nine months later, Bill migrated to Greenville, where he has hung out his shingle at the News-Piedmont Company ever since—as a reporter until 1938, when he was made city editor on the *News* (morning), and since 1955 as editor of the afternoon *Piedmont*. Bill feels, with some justification, that, considering the small staff, theirs is as "fine an afternoon paper" as is published anywhere in America.

If there were any reservations when his publisher asked him eight years ago to move from the night side into the editor's chair dayside, he quickly resolved them and is happy in his role. But the personal adjustments he has never quite resolved. He still finds difficulty at times in getting to sleep before two or three in the morning, and even then he may wake up at five or six-thirty, to eat a "typical" Gaines breakfast of Polish ham, kosher pickle, and cheese.

As far back as when he was city editor of the A.M., he operated on the principle of giving his people their heads and, "assuming you know them well," they will produce ably and satisfactorily. One articulate member of the staff feels that Bill might get even more out of his staff by offering more specific direction. But the system apparently is working—and the proof in part is the number of state press association awards the staff has won in recent years.

"We are the only paper in America with six city editors," he boasts. Any of six members of the staff, including himself, can move in that hotseat if the need arises. Recently, all three key jobs of managing editor, city editor, and telegraph editor were being filled, because of illness and vacations, by someone else. This is part of his insistence that each member of the eighteen-man staff knows the job above him or her.

His city editor has won two state press awards for writing sports features and the sports editor has won an award for local reporting.

His editor's job is "completely rewarding," he feels, despite the frustration of fighting a "lost cause"—the afternoon daily must fight just to stay even. The *Piedmont* has managed to keep at about twenty-six thousand daily for the past seven years by offering a solid fare of local coverage, including heavy emphasis on city and county government; features often played heavily on page one; and the interpretative angle on stories the morning competitor may have handled from the news viewpoint alone.

While he applies himself to the editorial page to a great degree, he is never far away from the newsroom. His managing editor and he probably will confer at least several times a day. But pretty much, he leaves his key people to their good judgment.

"I read—or at least look at—every proof on material that goes into our paper," he says. At any moment, he may stroll out to the city room to point out a misspelled or poorly chosen word, or some error not obvious to some others on the staff with less than his thirty-seven years of background in Greenville.

Those thirty-seven years he considers a time of quiet progress for the South, interrupted, he feels strongly, by the 1954 desegregation ruling of the Supreme Court. But he is realistic enough to say of racial integration of public facilities, including schools: "It's not coming, it's here. And no matter how we may feel about it, we must live with it."

On his editorial page he has tried to foster what he calls a climate of good will, which he feels is manifesting itself once again despite the present racial strife. In the uneventful integration of Negro Harvey Gantt into previously all-white Clemson College, his editorials spoke forcefully for common sense and for law and order.

Sixteen years ago there occurred at Greenville a significant landmark on the road of racial progress in the South, in his opinion. He means the trial of thirty-one men at Greenville for the lynching of a Negro man over the fatal stabbing of a white taxi driver. And though they were acquitted, "Never again after that was there any doubt but that a mob might be brought to trial, and with a chance of conviction, for violence against a Negro."

At the trial, which he covered, he became a friend of Rebecca West, whom he considers "the greatest living reporter—man or woman," and their friendship has continued warmly through the years. He considers her writing of about eighteen thousand words on the lynch trial for the *New Yorker* magazine in "two or three days" a "magnificent (reportorial) achievement."

Bill Gaines is no slouch himself as a reporter. In 1953, a series he wrote on North Carolina's prison system helped bring about reforms in Greenville County and won him an honorable mention in the Heywood Broun awards that year. The Federal Bureau of Prisons reprinted for national distribution a series he did on the parole and probation system.

After newspapering and food, Bill's next most absorbing interests are (1) children and (2) animals. With no children of their own, the Gaineses have showered affection on several generations of children of neighbors and relatives. His love for animals accounts for his always having given strong editorial support to the local Humane Society.

He tells with a chuckle how his courage gave out on him on one reportorial assignment years ago. In a North Carolina town, he was covering the trial of a mountain man turned desperado. Outside the courthouse, the man's sister accosted Gaines, who had a borrowed camera, "You had better not shoot a picture of my brother, or I will cut your throat." Bill recalls vividly, "I believed that she meant every word she said, and I handed the camera back."

If his courage ever were in dispute, it is belied by the story that he risked his life saving the city's fire chief from a falling wall at the scene of a disastrous fire nearly twenty-five years ago. He denies, however, that it was as dramatic as that, and says, with characteristic modesty, that he merely "assisted the fire chief away from the scene."

The year 1934 was both the year of the general textile strike and the year he married his high school sweetheart, Marisue Turner, on Christmas Eve.

Recalling the textile strike, Bill remembers most the day two strikers threatened to turn over the automobile he was driving. He brought them back into the office to make statements; they claimed "we hadn't been giving them fair treatment." This was an example of Bill's persuasiveness.

A voracious reader all these years, he averages a book a day. He has such a literary acquaintance with Thomas Wolfe's work, that for the Club of 39—irreverently dubbed the French Academy of Greenville—he identified 250 references to actual places in Asheville to which Wolfe had given fictitious names.

Charles E. Gallagher, Managing Editor
Lynn (Massachusetts) Item

By William H. Heath

When I read the by-line, I couldn't believe my eyes as I perused in the August 1956 issue of the ASNE *Bulletin* the article that jarred Jenk Jones loose from his rich source of persuasive rhetoric.

But there it was—"By Charles E. Gallagher, Managing Editor, *Lynn* (Massachusetts) *Item*."

Imagine it! Quiet, gentle, shy Charlie Gallagher mobilizing argument, satire, and hyperbole to express the thinking of uncounted scores of ASNE members about the concentration in a minority of editorial bigwigs of the opportunities to work for their august organization.

What has happened to Charlie? I asked myself. When no evidence appeared to show that he had been suddenly transformed into a dramatic extrovert or that he had dropped the reins on his emotions, I began to wonder how well I knew him. Since I had known him for only twenty-five years, I had to admit that probably I didn't know him well; for a quarter of a century is too short a time for one New Englander to acquire intimate knowledge of another.

So I undertook to learn what makes him tick.

Charlie was the oldest of ten childen and 95 percent of his paychecks in the first years of his employment went to buy fuel to keep the family pot bubbling. I think this is an important fact, because the oldest child of a family, if he has any good qualities, has to develop a strong sense of responsibility.

An eighth grade teacher decided Charlie's course in life. She said one day that he excelled in English composition. So he decided to be a writer. He was nineteen when he became a reporter for the *Lowell Sun,* an evening

---

Heath was editor of the *Haverill* (Massachusetts) *Gazette* when this article first appeared, in 1957.

paper published in the city of his birth. He wished to learn to write because, of course, he was going to produce the Great American Novel. He had no intention of becoming a newspaperman. That was almost forty years ago. Charlie is still a newspaperman. The Great American Novel remains to be written. But Charlie is looking forward to retirement on Cape Cod—and writing, and writing.

Although he has worn the title of editor for many years, he always has been primarily a writer and a reporter. He never takes a trip without wiring back a story, and nine times out of ten he ferrets out a local angle, even when he goes to an ASNE convention. He doesn't think much of this convention business, however, looking on it as what the late, lamented H. L. Mencken would have called a sort of mass contemplation of editorial umbilici.

Charlie was so good a reporter that an opposition paper, the *Lowell Courier-Citizen,* hired him as night editor in 1922. He held this job for eleven years and then the publisher decided to revive an ailing afternoon edition, the *Leader.* Charlie was made managing editor.

This was in the early days of the New Deal and modern Democrats were multiplying and replenishing the earth. Charlie was given complete control of the paper and promptly made it loudly Democratic, to the perturbation of the Republican publisher. And so it continued until a day in 1941, when Charlie was attending a managing editors' meeting in Boston. Before the meeting was concluded, the announcement was made that the *Sun* had bought its Lowell opposition. Charlie went home, a newspaperman without a job. Ever since, to quote him, "his heart bleeds whenever he hears of another newspaper merger."

In 1942 he became managing editor of the *Lynn Item,* and there, although he prefers writing to editing, he finds pleasure in getting out a newsy, well-balanced paper. He can flare now and then into spectacular anger, but generally he is a leader instead of the boss and, to quote one of his associates, "the example of his own clarity of thought, colorfulness of style, and breadth in coverage prod younger newspapermen under him to expand their own vision and sharpen their power of expression." Leadership with Charlie isn't limited to newspaper work. He engages in about every civic activity that an editor can be induced to take part in because he thinks they are part of the editor's job, but often wonders if he isn't being taken for a sucker—as who doesn't?

His newspaper regularly awards the "bouquet of the week" to a distinguished person in Lynn. Two years ago, when Charlie was in a hospital, he got the award and there was not, to my knowledge, any suspicion that it was made to him because, with him absent from his desk, the publisher didn't know what to do with it.

Basically a peacemaker and a diplomat whose ear is always ready for the other side of the story, Charlie frequently provides the "voice of reason" that dissolves fancied grievances and oils community frictions. But he's capable of righteous indignation and then his editorials sparkle with epigrammatic rebuke and subtle irony. He hates autocracy and "close corporation" tactics.

Charlie is a two-hundred-pound six-footer. He and Mrs. Gallagher live in Swampscott, a delightful Lynn suburb. They have had three children: Charles E., Jr., who died at the age of six; Walter C., a lieutenant in the army; and Andrea. Charlie's hobby of the moment is an eleven-month-old grandson born to the lieutenant's wife during an Alaskan blizzard. The grandson is also his most strenuous hobby, for puttering about the grounds, driving over woodland ways, swimming at Cape Cod, and reading, reading, reading are the pastimes of the man who used to play golf six days a week. Charlie doesn't play as hard as he works. A friend aptly described him as a newspaperman of the old school, serious, hard-working, prolific, urged on by high ideals. Would that there were more like him.

Edward King Gaylord, Editor and Publisher
The Daily Oklahoman

By Charles L. Bennett

I f some future Izaak Walton of journalism writes a book on "The Compleat Editor," he'll be wise to consider E. K. Gaylord of Oklahoma City as his model.

There are writing editors, editing editors, city-building editors, and empire-building editors—and "E. K." answers all those descriptions.

There's a strange thing about "E. K." He's popularly known by those initials around the adopted city he has helped to grow from a mud–streeted frontier town to a booming metropolis of the Southwest.

But around our plant he's known—always—as "Mr. Gaylord." Even his son, Edward L. Gaylord, who's executive vice-president of the Oklahoma Publishing Co., frequently refers to his father that way. I think it's simply a habit of respect, from all of us.

No recital of past accomplishments really can tell the story of Mr. Gaylord. The reason is that he is so vitally a man of the present and the future.

Everything he does and says bears out his preoccupation with plans and possibilities for the future. When we were designing our new building, completed two years ago, it was Mr. Gaylord who continually reminded all of us: "Now we don't want to build just for five or ten years ahead. Make it big enough for twenty or thirty, at least."

Then, while explaining the completed facilities to some visitors, he remarked matter-of-factly, "Of course, much of this will be obsolete in five or ten years and we'll have to do it over."

That new building of ours is, in its way, a monument to the vigor and

---

Bennett was managing editor of the *Daily Oklahoman* and *Oklahoma City Times* when this article first appeared, in 1965.

vision of this man who started his career in Oklahoma in 1903—four years before Oklahoma territory became a state. When he arrived, he bought into what he has described as a "terribly inadequate" daily paper. It was published in a twenty-five-foot-wide storefront office, with two Linotypes and a flatbed press. He was to run the business side and one of his partners was the editor.

But very quickly, Mr. Gaylord's innate respect for the job of a newspaper exerted itself and the spirit of the *Daily Oklahoman* was really born then.

He'd been on the job only about a week when a soldier was killed in a frontier brawl on "Battle Row." He knew the news staff was aware of the shooting, so he was startled the next morning when he went through the paper, page by page, and found no story.

"I got madder and madder," he recalls. The showdown came quickly. He marched into the office and learned the story had been suppressed at the request of the town's business leaders because "it would look bad for the city." Pointing out that papers in Dallas and Wichita had carried the story, he emphasized the ridiculousness—as well as the newspaper failure—in holding back such a story. That afternoon, there was another murder and the next morning that story and the story of the previous day's shooting were duly reported.

The little staff soon learned that the new man meant business. A new press was ordered and when it arrived, headlines were printed in color. The red-haired young man's paper was known for years as "The Red-Headed Daily."

He contracted for Associated Press service and then, on a hunch, hired a telegrapher to work on Sundays and alerted his staff. Most papers didn't print on Mondays then, and the very next Sunday he scooped the territory. The Russo-Japanese war started and the *Daily Oklahoman's* "Extra" was the only paper carrying the story between Dallas and Kansas City. He sent hundreds of papers and his own newsboys into cities as far away as Wichita, to the chagrin of the publishers caught napping. The feat put the *Oklahoman* on the newspaper map.

His passion for accuracy has tripped up many a less-than-meticulous writer and even Webster's dictionary hasn't been exempted. He once gleefully told a group of educators, "In the last month, I've found two errors in Webster's unabridged dictionary." Another time he startled a collection of noted scientists by calmly informing them there was another correct name for a particular element they'd been discussing. They demurred, but as you might expect (or at least, we would), he was right.

Recalling that "inadequate" paper he started with, Mr. Gaylord says, "I was ambitious to make it the biggest and best newspaper in the state." He wasn't long in getting about the job.

The *Oklahoman* played a key role in achieving Oklahoma's statehood in 1907, successfully pushing for it to be one state, not split into two as some had proposed. Before long, he led another battle. Guthrie had been named the state capital, but Oklahoma City was growing faster and other cities wanted the capital too. Oklahoma City won the balloting elimination contest, hands down.

In 1916, the firm bought an evening paper at a sheriff's auction—the *Oklahoma City Times*. The young business manager overcame a personal crisis, a bout with tuberculosis. His recollection: "I decided I would live, and I did."

By 1918, the young Gaylord already had been president of his city's Chamber of Commerce and had been placed in complete charge of the papers. The previous editor's share was bought out.

In 1928, it was Mr. Gaylord's decision that put the company into radio, with station WKY, the state's first.

When the railroads started withdrawing trains, making newspaper deliveries difficult, he started his own truck fleet. Mistletoe Express Service, dating back to that 1931 episode, now services five states.

In 1949, the company brought television to Oklahoma with WKY-TV, which in 1954 became the nation's first independent station with live color programs. Television stations in Tampa–St. Petersburg and Dallas–Fort Worth were added later and purchase of a UHF channel in Houston is awaiting FCC approval.

Ideas for further expansion and improvement have an eager listener in this editor, publisher, and president—if anyone can beat him to having the idea. His ambition to make 1903's *Oklahoman* into the "biggest and best in the state" has produced the Southwest's largest newspaper enterprise, but he's still looking for new worlds to conquer.

On his ninetieth birthday, March 5, 1963, Mr. Gaylord's staff celebrated appropriately by presenting him with the first newspaper ever printed entirely from computer-justified tape. With interruptions only for re-programming and added machinery, the papers have been printing this way ever since. Mr. Gaylord's reaction: "We've only scratched the surface of these new methods; we're in the primitive stage."

His leadership in building this solid communications empire might have satisfied most men. But to Mr. Gaylord it has been only one facet of the duties of the complete editor.

When he came to town, he recalls, "All Oklahoma City had was a future." But he liked what he saw. Arriving in December of 1902, he set out to look over the town by walking its dirt streets from one end to the other. Settled only in 1889, Oklahoma City was a raw but growing city of ten thousand. He looked in the store windows to see what kind of merchandise was being offered. What he saw assured him that these were people who had come to stay. And when he saw a piano for sale, he was convinced there were people who wanted more than the bare essentials, and it would be a good place. His faith in the town, and his own time, money, and foresight have gone generously into assuring its present and future.

In the newspaper world, he has done it all—from being a director of the Associated Press to being the key figure in establishing the South's first newsprint plant, Southland Paper Mills Inc., at Lufkin, Texas. Fighting for pulp concessions, stock sales, and contracts for the paper to be produced, he led the effort that gave a new look to newspaper economy in the region.

In every civic enterprise, in helping his city grow through unprecedented steps to attract industry, in private philanthropy, in support of education, in encouraging the arts and cultural activities, his role has been one of leadership—and his investment has been going on for more than sixty years.

His publicly stated philosophy is simple. The Oklahoma Publishing Company always takes a stand as a leader. It never has opposed a bond issue, nor any other worthwhile project for the growth and development of the city or state.

He and Mrs. Gaylord—and that's a partnership that goes back to 1914—have special interest in the YMCA and YWCA—his stemming from college days and hers from her premarriage career as a YW executive in France and in the United States. Their efforts and strong financial support have been major factors in the achievements of these two organizations in Oklahoma City. Mrs. Gaylord is the former Inez Kinney, a graduate of Wooster College and a director and officer of the newspaper company. In addition to their son, Edward, the Gaylords have two daughters.

Mr. Gaylord was born on a farm near Muscotah, Kansas. Droughts and grasshopper invasions drove the family westward, first to Denver and then to Grand Junction, Colorado.

By the time he was eleven, Mr. Gaylord had a job on a truck farm, picking strawberries. At twelve, he left for a job in a secondhand store. By the time he was fifteen, he had shown so much ability a businessman offered to furnish him the money to buy out the owner and go into business for himself. But the future publisher declined, saying he intended to get a college education, whether it benefited him financially or not.

After two or three years working on fruit farms, for a railroad and a coal company, he set off for Colorado College with seventeen dollars in his pocket. The fare back to Grand Junction was over nineteen dollars, "so I knew I was there to stay." His job as houseman and gardener at his boardinghouse helped and he managed, meanwhile, to be president of the college YMCA, a member of the college debating club, and both editor and business manager of the college paper.

While he was still a college junior, he and his brother, Lewis, had a chance to buy controlling interest in the *Colorado Springs Telegram* for twelve thousand dollars. A Missouri banker, attracted by young Gaylord's ambition and character, lent him the necessary six thousand dollars and he was in the newspaper business for the first time.

Meanwhile, he became a deputy district court clerk and studied law at night. Later, he served in the mining frontier town of Cripple Creek as chief deputy court clerk. (Recently he pointed out the absurdity of an expression one of our reporters used in a court story.)

The brothers later sold the *Telegram* "at a favorable figure." Mr. Gaylord had worked on it as an advertising salesman and editorial writer and his brother urged him to join a new venture in a paper at St. Joseph, Missouri. Mr. Gaylord worked there for a time as business manager, but wasn't satisfied with the opportunity. So he moved on to Oklahoma City.

Down through the years, the editorial credo has been and still is that the papers take a stand. Popular or unpopular, accepted or unaccepted, the stand is always there—clear, forthright, forceful. Some of the most forceful appear on the front page of the *Daily Oklahoman*. Most Oklahomans know what this means—Mr. Gaylord, himself, is having his say. Even without the identifying position, these personal editorials would be unmistakable. They punch out a concise, direct message that no one can misunderstand.

In 1919, the editorial fight was against a corrupt governor. That one nearly led to actual shooting in the streets. The paper stood fast; the governor was impeached. It goes on: This year—without the shooting threat—there was rugged infighting over Oklahoma's Supreme Court scandal. Imprisonment of one former justice, the resignation of one current justice, and the impeachment of another were among the results.

A personal "dry" and nonsmoker, Mr. Gaylord works at his personal dedication to *"mens sana in corpore sano."* Trim and vigorous, he does his daily exercises faithfully, sets a walking pace that taxes his younger colleagues, and drives his own car "aggressively" (as one daughter put it). He gave up golf "when I was about seventy-five." A hiker, fisherman, and hunter in his younger days, his chief hobby in recent years has been his Guernsey farm. It has provided vast quantities of milk for Oklahoma City dwellers, foundation stock for many prize herds, and tough competition in the show ring for his fellow-breeders.

One of the brightest facets of his personality—but perhaps least known except among his close associates—is his gentle and ever-present sense of humor. A good joke or quip brings delighted laughter and, as often as not, a line to top the original.

A longtime newspaper associate once wrote, "In my opinion, he has never used the tremendous power within his grasp selfishly; he has never attempted to reward a friend or punish an enemy through his newspaper's editorial policies."

When he speaks out sharply, the motivation stems from his conviction of what is right and best for his city, state, and country. While his readers often disagree, there are few who doubt his sincerity and many who respect his independence and forthrightness—even while disagreeing.

Roy Roberts of Kansas City, at the fiftieth anniversary of the company, commented: "There are two words that sum him up—courage and integrity. He answers the description I once read of a good citizen: He has put more into his community than he has taken from it."

Last year, Mr. Gaylord's Oklahoma City neighbors honored him as the "father of the city." One speaker, a nationally known industrialist and longtime associate, said simply, "He is a magnificent man, with limitless courage and determination."

But perhaps some of Mr. Gaylord's own words sum him up best of all.

Recalling the fire that once devastated his plant (but the papers didn't miss an issue because he swiftly arranged for printing and got the papers out anyway) he said, "I've thought of this many times; it isn't easy work that gives you any satisfaction. It's the hard things that we overcome that make us and make our business."

Another time, he said, "We are chained to the country . . . and we have tried to build up the country and grow with the country. In fact, we try to keep a little bit ahead of it."

He often cites a line that represents another of his personal convictions: "No man has the right to be less of a man than he can be." Few men have come closer to realizing that ideal than E. K. Gaylord.

J. W. Gitt, Publisher
York (Pennsylvania) Gazette and Daily

By Robert C. Maynard

During Barry Goldwater's 1964 presidential campaign, local Republican workers in York, Pennsylvania, presented their cash and their advertising copy at the front counter of the struggling morning newspaper. They intended to buy thousands of dollars of space that fall.

To their astonishment, the Republicans were turned down flat. The publisher of the newspaper, the *Gazette and Daily,* declared that the name of the GOP presidential nominee any place in the ads rendered them unacceptable.

The furor in that conservative colonial town rose to the point where the action of the newspaper was an issue in the campaign.

J. W. Gitt, the octogenarian publisher, said he refused Goldwater advertising for the same reason he refused for a half century to carry ads for alcoholic beverages, patent medicines, and later, cigarettes. All of them, Gitt declared, were bad for the health and welfare of his readers and would not be advocated on his pages. He referred the GOP to the conservative *York Dispatch,* an afternoon paper and the *Gazette's* competition.

A newspaper, Gitt said he believed, ought to bear the mark and stand for the principles of its owner. He considered it his property and his voice.

After fifty-five years of practicing that very personal brand of journalism, J. W. Gitt has called it a day. The news was received with mixed feelings wherever the paper was known.

"The *York Gazette,*" said I. F. Stone, the Washington newsletter publisher, "was really unique in American journalism because this wonderful old Pennsylvania Dutchman, Jess Gitt, showed you could turn out a progressive—even radical—paper in a small town and make a go of it."

Charles M. Gitt, the son of the publisher, said the demise of the

---

Maynard was on the staff of the *Washington Post* when this story first appeared, in 1971.

newspaper means to him that "an honest, crusading newspaper that takes a stand on unpopular causes won't be allowed to survive in these times. It didn't used to be that way."

A smile crosses the face of a policeman in York's Continental Square when he is asked if he misses Gitt's controversial newspaper. "Yeah, in a way. See, if you want to get the party line now, you have to listen to Radio Moscow or Radio Peking or something like that." His colleagues were fond of calling the newspaper the *"Gazette and Daily Pravda."*

It began in 1915 when Jess Gitt put together a couple of bankrupt newspapers and fashioned a morning daily with a mission—to talk of peace and peaceful change. He was, a friend later said, "literally haunted by the specter of war."

By 1970, three wars later, his country more deeply divided than at any previous time in his publishing career, Gitt said he had had enough. He was eighty-six. The paper devoted to peace ceased publishing in an atmosphere of bitterness on the staff and in the town. Many members of the staff maintain the newspaper could have advocated all of its causes and survived if it had been better managed. Townspeople, some of them friends of the *Gazette* through the years, contended the newspaper toward the end lost contact with its readers, became sloppy in its reporting and writing, doctrinaire in some of its views, and unprofessional in its approach to the news.

Gitt sold the plant and the facilities to Harold N. Fitzkee, the York County district attorney, for $650,000, less than half of what the paper would have brought on the market. But he didn't sell the name. The new paper is called the *York Daily Record,* and Fitzkee promised his readers it would be as little as possible like the old *Gazette and Daily.* For one thing, he soon dropped Dick Gregory as a columnist and added Jeanne Dixon.

The old *Gazette and Daily* of 1964, the year of the Goldwater flop, was a tabloid newspaper with columns that were even and tidy and a carefully balanced layout that consistently won typographical awards.

Its approach to news handling was also consistent, and the edition of September 15, 1964, is typical:

RUSK WELCOMES / BETTER RELATIONS / WITH COMMU-NISTS was a single-column lead story in which the then secretary of state was quoted as warning against "the advice of those [Goldwater, to be specific] who would erect a solid wall between the United States and the Communist world."

SCRANTON PROCLAIMS / ANTI-SMOKING DRIVE was a box at the top of page one reporting on an action of William W. Scranton, then governor of Pennsylvania.

AGENCY PROPOSED TO DETERMINE / WATER QUALITY OF

AREA STREAMS was a heavy-type, two-column headline on page one over a story whose second paragraph quoted a health official as saying, "The streams can be as pure as they were when Indians roamed this part of the country or they can be open sewers."

CHURCHMAN SCORES / THOSE DISCREDITING / RIGHTS MOVEMENT was toward the bottom of the first page with a second paragraph quote from the new chairman of the Council of Churches Commission on Religion and Race: "Riots and demonstrations are not the same."

If the *Gazette's* approach to news attracted attention, its editorial pages were even more controversial. In that year, 1964, James Higgins, who ran the paper for the Gitts, was in the fourteenth year as assistant editor and editorial writer. He would stay on nearly six more years.

"One day in 1950," Higgins said, "the old man called me in and said that I would be the editorial writer from then on. I asked him how I should proceed. Should I hold periodic conferences with him? Should I draft them and submit them? What?"

The old man waved aside those suggestions and asked Higgins:

"Have you read the Declaration of Independence? Do you understand it? Have you read the Bill of Rights and do you understand that? Have you read the Sermon on the Mount and do you understand that?"

Higgins firmly confessed to a working knowledge of all three. "Then go ahead and write the editorials," Gitt said.

McKinley C. Olson, Higgins's friend, and protégé, remained on as the first editor of the *York Daily Record*. He does not expect that kind of freewheeling approach to the editorials from the new publisher, Fitzkee. "That was another era and another paper," Olson has said. Editorially, the newspaper opposed the very first U.S. action of sending advisers to South Vietnam and it opposed each succeeding step in the buildup.

In that September 15, 1964, edition, the *Gazette* headed its column-long editorial, "The Alternatives," and followed with a commentary on the situation in Vietnam a month after the Tonkin Gulf incident. It concluded: "We sincerely hope the principle of peaceful negotiation and the principle of democratic procedures will be respected by the United States as the South Vietnam problem demands decisions. And we hope, too, that these principles will animate U.S. foreign policy everywhere."

On the second editorial page, a York County reader could find himself face to face with the lay writing of scientists such as Linus Pauling and Ralph Lapp, commentators as varied as Art Buchwald and Russell Baker, Milton Mayer and I. F. Stone. The tradition of that page was founded on rank theft. The idea was for the editor in charge to read virtually every liberal journal published in English, steal the best of the lot, and pare them down to 1,000 or

1,500 words.

None of this was very appetizing to most York Countians, people of simple rural tastes and conservative politics, with a strong Fundamentalist streak in their religious and social outlook.

Because York is working class, it had in 1960 a Democratic registration majority of 15,000. But Richard Nixon carried the county by 16,300 votes. John F. Kennedy's Catholicism made the difference.

It is fair to say that the *Gazette* and York viewed each other with uneasy eyes. A right-wing local radio program operated by the Reverend Carl McIntire in the early 1960s—it was one of his first stations—devoted much of its probing attention to the editorial policies of the *Gazette*. The station's equal-time policies later became the subject of reporter Fred J. Cook's suit in the Supreme Court against the Red Lion Broadcasting Company.

On another station in York, a radio show on which the audience called the studio hummed with criticism of the newspaper on mornings when particularly distasteful stories or editorials were printed. Sometimes those stories were national and were beats for the *Gazette*. During the buildup in 1961 that led to the invasion of Cuba at the Bay of Pigs, the *York Gazette* was almost alone in reporting daily that such an invasion was imminent.

More than once, such reporting and editorializing caused the newspaper trouble in the community and with its local advertisers. It had trouble with a major food chain because it insisted on reporting on page one that the chain was in antitrust trouble with the Department of Justice. It did the same with a clothing chain. Both chains pulled out all of their advertising because of the newspaper's persistence in reporting all antitrust suits and stories that were critical of big business.

Charles Gitt, who was editor and a columnist, said he believes the paper's independent stand on the Middle East caused it to lose substantial amounts of advertising in the last couple of years.

"All we did," Gitt said, "was to say that Israel had a right to exist, a right to defend herself. But when she went out to defend herself, she had no right to come back with half of the other fellow's land." For saying that, Gitt said he believes, "some of the businessmen in town just looked for other ways to advertise their products."

But other factors weighed even more heavily on the *Gazette* in its last days. Fitzkee, the new publisher, said in an interview that he believes J. W. Gitt was plowing in twenty thousand dollars a month of his personal fortune to keep the paper afloat. Sources closer to Gitt say it was not quite that high, but that Gitt did lose one hundred thousand dollars on the paper in 1969.

The last straw came when Gitt told the typesetters, members of the International Typographical Union, that they would have to take a 10 percent pay cut for the paper to survive. Such talk had gone on for years, increasing in recent months, but when it finally happened, the union struck. Gitt, as he had often threatened to do in the face of previous labor problems, put the padlock on the door. The plant reopened as the *York Daily Record*.

Despite the loss of the *Gazette*, York will continue to be unique for a city of its size (fifty-five thousand in 1960) in having two independently owned, competing daily newspapers.

The *Dispatch* is in almost every respect the opposite of the *Gazette* of old. Its format is that of a standard size newspaper—eight columns across. It almost never uses a headline more than a single column in width. Its front page might on any given day contain as many as thirty-five short stories. It rarely uses pictures, in fact has no facilities for making photo plates on the premises.

Politically, the *Dispatch* stands 180 degrees away from the old *Gazette*. Both are products of the nineteenth century, but whereas the *Dispatch* is impersonal in tone, Gitt is a personal journalist who used his paper to crusade in the style of the pamphleteer of earlier days.

The *Dispatch* compares editorially with such other conservative newspapers as the *Manchester* (New Hampshire) *Union Leader*. It prides itself on its hard stand on foreign and domestic issues. It is a no-nonsense supporter of the Nixon administration.

The *Dispatch* outsold the *Gazette* by a narrow margin during most of the lives of the two newspapers. Toward the end of the *Gazette's* life, its circulation and advertising linage slipped badly.

The differences in the newspapers were pointed up sharply in the area of local reporting. The *Gazette* made a small investment in hiring reporters and giving them time and space to develop their subjects. The *Dispatch's* reporters, with a few exceptions, are older men who tend to report public business in a straight style befitting the cast of the newspaper.

The rivalry between the two newspapers had its ludicrous aspects. The *Dispatch* was not permitted as reading material in the newsroom of the *Gazette*. Local Republicans and conservative Democrats would go to great lengths to see that stories were broken in the morning to favor the *Dispatch* deadlines.

J. W. Gitt's *Gazette* prided itself in its heyday on its independent reporting style. As the story is told, a new reporter had turned in a story written with a traditional lead when the editors wanted a lead that stressed some "policy angle" of J. W. Gitt.

"Kid," the city editor said, "I know you've been told to write 'em with the five-W lead (who, what, where, when, and why). At the *Gazette*, there's just one W, and that's J. W. Don't ever forget it."

Mike Gorman, Editor
Flint (Michigan) Journal

By Carl E. Lindstrom

C ould he drive anything but a Buick—this editor in Flint?
Even if it weren't a matter of diplomacy, Mike Gorman's civic sense—it's his seventh one, news instinct being the sixth—is what puts Mike at the head of that great corps of editors who consider themselves civic-minded.

The country is full of editors who have boosted hospital drives, bridge building, traffic solutions and any one of a hundred municipal projects, but Mike Gorman literally put a university on the map of Michigan. It is a $13 million cultural development, with its campus in the heart of the city of Flint, tied in with the University of Michigan.

Broad-shouldered and thick-set, Mike is luxuriantly roofed with hair the color of undulant iron. His features suggest, in roughest outline, a triangle with dark eyebrows.

People don't do things in Flint without consulting Mike, and it is a suspicion that the auto tycoons consult him on matters of policy. But you can never get this from Mike. He is fearless where principles are concerned and didn't hesitate to tangle with the Red Cross on the issue of relief to the city when disaster struck. Mike won, but there again you'll have to get the details from somebody else.

To know Mike you have to know Club Calumet. That's the name of the street where he lives but the club, a part of his home, is a rendezvous unmatched for hospitality and the brilliance of its guest list.

With virtually no notice at all, the master of Club Calumet can dress up an attractive table of snacks of the rarest varieties using his own cocktail sauce and a dizzy variety of salads. Glassware with the emblems of many different colleges and universities is brought out on occasion to the delight of alumni guests.

Club Calumet is sometimes the scene of Gorman-arranged parties with

Lindstrom was executive editor of the *Hartford Times* when this article first appeared, in 1955.

the host unavoidably absent and some friend recruited to do the honor. An Atlantic ship-to-shore call once greeted his guests.

Aside from his natural artistry and bringing in flowers from the city market, Mike is not an around-the-house putterer. He once received a gift of a home owner's do-it-yourself kit containing screw drivers, pliers, drill bits, etc. This he examined in a bewildered sort of way and remarked, "Just what I need—what is it?"

Trying to get Mike to talk about himself is something of a problem. You might ask him about that encounter with the Red Cross and get some such comment as this:

"Flint was a city of 13,103 in the year 1900. It is the birthplace of General Motors. While the city has no geographical or resource advantages, it has been blessed with people of vision and courage."

"You're a friend of Engine Charlie Wilson, aren't you?"

"Eastern financial interests missed the boat entirely. They had no vision. The population of the city is now—."

"When you were chairman of the program committee of ASNE didn't you—?"

"Journalistically," Mike enthuses, "it is fascinating. Its industrial operations gives it metropolitan connections and aspects, yet it retains the neighborliness of a normal town of its size."

"Didn't the University of Michigan give you an honorary degree last June?"

"You interrupted me—."

No use. If you let Mike write his own story it goes like this:

"Because a move to obtain a Flint College of the University of Michigan became dormant, attention was directed to the development of Flint Junior College. C. S. Mott, a rich auto pioneer, gave a new campus, and the money for an arts and science building; bequests by the late W. S. Ballenger included endowment for faculty and funds toward a field house; the Board of Education put up the Harlow H. Curtice academic building. This, with a bond issue library, constituted about a $4,250,000 nucleus for the $13,000,000. Federal funds are providing a reserve army training center.

"In the meantime the university idea was revived, spurred by the projection that the college population of the United States, now 2,500,000, will be 5,000,000 by 1970. Why not, it was proposed, help meet this problem by launching the plan of state universities supplementing acceptable junior colleges with third and fourth year university branches?

"While this was progressing, the fundraising was well under way. Paradoxically, the $9 million additional to be solicited was too large to get in a great, ballyhoo campaign. Therefore, a self-expanding Committee of Sponsors was established. To qualify as a sponsor, an individual, a family, or a firm must pledge a minimum of twenty-five thousand dollars. It seemed fantastic and maybe it was, but it is working. Terrific impetus was provided by a $3 million grant by General Motors on the occasion of the fifty millionth car. What ordinarily would be a financial program requiring many years will be finished in a little more than twelve months."

That's Mike's version. But Bob Considine, in an INS article, attributed the idea and the drive behind it to an editor named Gorman.

Mike has only one hobby—making and developing friendships.

When a young reporter covering the theater in his home town of Saginaw, Michigan, he would occasionally be missing on Monday morning because he had followed some vaudeville act to the next town. When Mike now visits Chicago or New York or San Francisco, there's bound to be a reunion supper with Wayne King, the waltz king, Harlow Curtice, the president of General Motors, Tom Dewey, or some other old friend.

Mike's modest home is at 2008 Calumet Street, Flint. He lives there alone except for a cleaning woman, a cook, a yardman, and others who come when he needs them. And he needs them quite often. For Mike has so steeped himself in the business of making friends that he dislikes being alone.

Charles Edward Green, Editor
Austin American-Statesman

By Harry Provence

C harles Edward Green doesn't look like a balancing-act artist but that's what he has learned to be in more than thirty years as editor of the daily newspapers in Austin, the capital of Texas.

Charles Edward—Charlie to most folks and CEG to readers of his column—does his balancing on behalf of his beloved Austin. Sometimes it involves putting out fires at city hall, sometimes a coaching rhubarb at the burly, surging University of Texas, sometimes a state brannigan in which the imperious voices of Lyndon Johnson, Allan Shivers, Price Daniel and other political wheeler-dealers of the Lone Star State come at CEG from several sides at once.

With the deftness born of long practice and the conscience born of his ranch-country rearing, Charles Edward Green usually manages to carry forward in the *American* (morning), *Statesman* (evening), and *American-Statesman* (Sundays and holidays) the tide of progress with as little bloodshed as possible.

Austin has flourished as a boom city in these thirty years, mostly during the past sixteen. Charles E. Green has been a potent influence in most of the scoring plays. The state capital has two hundred thousand persons inside its metropolitan area, five times the number who were there when CEG arrived from Laredo. The *American-Statesman* has grown correspondingly, from a struggling daily put out by a roomful of round-the-clock toilers to a big-city combination with a payroll and linage to match.

In this hubbub of expansion, the shiny, bald head of Charles E. Green has continued to move as a marker of the eye of the storm, the calm center circled by cyclonic winds.

Provence was editor in chief of the *Waco Tribune Herald* when this article first appeared, in 1961.

Green, at the typewriter or on the golf course, is better on the green than off the tee. On his hot days at either pursuit, his touch borders on magic. When he flubs one, it also is a miracle of completeness.

His column is utterly unpredictable. Even its name, "The Ninth Column," baffles those who don't remember its christening when the newspapers' format was widened from eight columns to nine. City editor Fred Williams persuaded Green to resurrect his personal column, which Charlie had dropped years ago due to lack of time for writing. "We need something to fill that ninth column," Williams said. "OK," said Green, "I'll start writing again but just call it 'The Ninth Column.'"

One day, Charlie's column may consist of an agonizing self-appraisal, the next day a brilliant piece of light narrative, the next a mishmash of local personals. Some of his closing sentences would grace the Great Books and one day he signed off with, "I think I'll go home and eat worms."

Charlie uses all the tricks of the trade. He sprinkles Austin names in the column, even when writing from England or Washington or San Francisco. He goes in often for stories about pretty women. He spares no descriptive detail, since he writes as much for his own entertainment as for his readers.

Charlie Green likes to describe himself as a reporter who took up administrative newspapering because it paid better. His obvious skill at writing and his ability to impart writing skill to others has made the *Austin American* and *Statesman* renowned far and wide as well-written, interesting newspapers.

A few old-timers like Charlie Guy out at Lubbock and John Ellis of the *Fort Worth Star-Telegram* remember Charles Edward Green when his silhouette was slim and his scalp covered with plenty of black hair. Those days, he was a student at the University of Oklahoma, from which episode he bounced into the newspaper trade.

Still fewer remember Charles Edward Green as a wart-covered little boy at Mineral Wells, in rugged, rural Palo Pinto County. Charles Edward has no difficulty recalling those warts. A Campbellite preacher removed twenty-three warts in one day from Charlie's hands and soon thereafter the sprat was putting out his own newspaper as a schoolboy. How many editors, including Charles E. Green of Austin, would love to have a guaranteed method of getting warts off their hands—human warts, that is?

Charlie's first baptism of fire as a reporter came in Fort Worth where he learned the difference between libel and news and began to perfect his skill with words. He and another Fort Worth reporter, Buck Hood, went to Odessa, Texas, to starve. This was years before the oil boom brought steady eating into style in that far-off corner of the Staked Plains. Green and Hood soon retreated to a friendlier environment at Laredo and perhaps enjoyed that bilingual, sunny, border town more than any before or since. But it wasn't long before Green was moved to Austin and he brought Hood along. They have been a flashy newspaper team in Texas journalism and politics from that time to now: Green the writer and Hood the promotional and production genius.

Charlie Green remained a bachelor during his first decade in Austin. In the midst of leading the gay blades of the town during his off-duty hours he managed to launch the Bachelors' Club as an ornament of the social life of the capital. It was more a thing of the spirit than of club house and dues and by-laws. Its chief formal activity was an annual ball. Once the bachelors were thinned out by the Austin girls, the club went into eclipse, but in recent years Charles Edward and some of the other charter members have reinstated its mythical franchise and once again the annual bachelors' club ball is a highlight of the winter season.

Green's immortality in the club world, however, comes from his principal role in organizing and directing the Headliners Club of Austin. With Machiavellian skill, he so constructed the constitution and by-laws that newspapermen will always be in charge, despite the fact that the membership of several hundred men reaches across all the arts, trades, and professions of Texas. The Headliners, located in a portion of the ground floor of historic Driskill Hotel, is a beauty spot, a waterhole of wondrous taste, a rendezvous where the movers and shakers of Texas can be found in a talkative mood, and where women are not allowed until after lunch. In the Press Box, modelled after an old English inn and situated due north of the Headliners bar, no women ever are allowed.

More importantly, Charlie Green has led, directed, ooched, and maneuvered the Headliners Club into an annual newspaper awards ceremony that spotlights a Publisher of the Year and hands out to working reporters, photographers, and editorial writers the largest cash prizes given away in Texas for excellence in their work. At last count, over a five-year period, Charlie's Headliners Club has awarded nine thousand dollars to members of the newsrooms of the state.

Austin's most eligible bachelor showed one of his rarer streaks of good judgment just before World War II when he married—out of his own women's department—Floy Ross Robinson, a quiet and lovely brunette, a member of one of Austin's oldest, most prominent families. Floy Ross went to California with Lieutenant (jg) Green and came back home to sweat out his Pacific duty with the navy's air transport service. She took over the controls from the navy when they returned the editor to his typewriter and desk. She still presides on the Green quarterdeck, but so quietly and gracefully that even Charles Edward himself usually doesn't realize who is driving the boat.

Green bought a wooded ravine and built therein a stone two-story house of rugged charm before he married. The street cut into the woods by the city of Austin to reach his residence was named, of course, Verde Vista, which is Spanish for Green View. It was on the edge of town at its start, and was when Floy Ross came to take charge. While today the city has enveloped Verde Vista on all sides, it still remains shielded from traffic noise and the eyes of passersby. It plays a vital role in Green's balancing act because it affords his body and soul a quiet place of serene beauty for restoring the day's damage.

Green's talent for keeping his city on an even keel against the buffeting of circumstance was never better demonstrated than when, immediately after the 1954 Supreme Court decision on racial segregation in public schools, Austin's school board decided to carry out the mandate without waiting for the duress and strife of a local court action.

Green helped in the biracial conferences that preceded the start of school in September 1954, by which selected young Negro students were admitted to Austin High School. He personally handled the laconic newspaper coverage, treating the historic event as matter-of-factly as if it had been going on for generations.

To newshawks from the East who wanted to bring their cameras and pencils into Austin, Green said calmly, "When did it become news that people are obeying the law? Stay out of here and leave us alone." His advice prevailed. Today, Austin public schools are in their seventh year of nonsegregation and the University of Texas has achieved more equality of treatment for students of all races than any other state university below the Mason and Dixon Line.

There have been incidents at the University of Texas where impatient students have insisted on taking down racial barriers faster even than the regents wanted to do it, but the news coverage in the Austin dailies has been restrained and modulated so that the publicity-seekers involved found no mileage in their stunts. Behind the scenes, Green has moved calmly with advice and leadership to the authorities.

Austin's municipal problems, characteristic of all the booming cities since World War II, have tested Green's balancing talents from time to time. With the help of superb city hall reporters, and with the confidence reposed in him by most of the city's leaders, Green has used the *American* and *Statesman* as the situation required, by turns bulldozing, sheltering, teasing, and snookering the community into more and more progress. Battles there have been, but with one or two isolated exceptions the good guys have won them. Austin today is considered one of the foremost examples of sound, responsible city government in the Southwest, which is mostly what Green was getting at all the time.

Green's personal problems and quirks are about as well known to *Austin American* readers as are the features of the stately capital itself.

A couple of years ago, the stresses of his balancing virtuosity brought on

CEG a stomach ulcer. The diagnosis, treatment, and cure of that little ulcer received far more detailed coverage in Charlie's column than all of President Eisenhower's ailments combined got in the national news report.

A few months back, while Floy Ross Green and their daughter Beverly were out of town, Charles Edward clumsily let the family dog stray away from the lawn of Verde Vista. Hoo boy! Never was a dog pursued so relentlessly in print. Stories and photos. Stirring appeals and offers of cash rewards. Page one, section one, page one, section two, classified lost and found. The works, doubled and redoubled. The mutt, named Barnaby and of highly uncertain lineage, was found and returned just before Beverly came home. It was Green's closest shave in peace or war, in politics or high society. When it didn't bring on a recurrence of his ulcer, he knew he was cured.

Charles Green is a dyed-in-the-wool football fan, though his playing days ended in high school before it was discovered that you could play football on grass instead of packed clay and gravel. He covets his friendship with Darrell Royal, personable young coach of the University of Texas Longhorns, rides with Royal on auto trips to see other teams play and flies occasionally with the mighty Longhorns as a member of the official squad. Last year, the Steers took CEG to the University of Maryland, had him sit with the subs on the bench, gave him an autographed football. Charlie finds the relative simplicity of gridiron combat a refreshing release from the tensions of balancing Austin and its daily newspapers over one chasm after another.

CEG has been on a thousand hunting and fishing trips but he lusteth not for blood or meat. He carries a few paperbacked novels along to read in the boat or the deer blind. But when the sport is over and the chinfest starts around the fireplace or the bar, CEG moves in with his needle and his reporter-trained ear. He warms to conversation, knows how to stimulate it, remembers the good stories, and shows remarkable skill in cleaning them up for publication.

For several years, Charlie has been a director in one of Austin's banks. He dabbles lightly in the stock market. He enjoys talking about money and the ingenious, sometimes bizarre, ways in which Texans make it multiply. True to his talent and training, he makes news out of money. His major frustration is that it is not in the American tradition to make money out of news. Some day he may hit the formula, for the benefit of us all.

Brodie Griffith, Editor
The Charlotte News

By Cecil Prince

I n the land of magnolias and molasses, it is still de rigueur to list the sprightly *Charlotte News* as a "newspaperman's newspaper."

That's really a sly and studiously impersonal way of saying that editor–general manager Brodie Sheppard Griffith is a "newspaperman's newspaperman."

For, from one chair or another, Brodie Griffith has set the style and character of this lively North Carolina journal (largest evening paper in the two Carolinas) since the twenties. The briskness, brightness, and hungry competitive spirit he fashioned over the years have been continuing articles of faith in a newsroom that still cocks an anxious ear toward his cubicle for attitudes and inspiration.

If the *News* has the dash of youth, it's not surprising. So does Griffith, at sixty-one. So does his staff, where the average reporter is in his twenties, a product of the Griffith "Get-'Em-Young-And-Train-'Em-Right" policy.

The policy has been a huge success. A list of distinguished authors and journalists "brought up" by Griffith reads like a literary *Who's Who*.

At the head of the class is the late W. J. Cash, who took his first reportorial job with the *News* in the 1930s and pecked out his monumental *The Mind of the South* practically under Griffith's nose while serving as a *News* editorial writer.

There is Pulitzer Prize–winning Harry Ashmore *(Epitaph For Dixie* and *The Negro and the Schools)* of Little Rock fame, who was editor of the *News* at the tender age of thirty-one in 1947.

There was the *News's* Marion Hargrove, whose letters about pre–Pearl Harbor army life were so humorous that Griffith transformed them into a series of regular columns. Later they were collected in a book entitled *See Here, Private Hargrove*. It sold three and a half million copies.

There was Burke Davis, who has a Literary Guild selection now, *To*

Prince was associate editor of the *Charlotte News* when this article first appeared, in 1960.

Appomatox, plus half a dozen other books to his credit. Davis was a first-rate sports editor and reporter under Griffith and later was editor of the *News.*

There was Cameron Shipp of Hollywood, who has ghosted many books for movie stars (Fred Astaire's *Steps in Time,* Billie Burke's *With a Feather on My Nose, We Barrymores*). He, too, was a Griffith pupil.

There was John McKnight, author of *The Papacy,* for twenty years an Associated Press foreign correspondent and now assistant director of the United States Information Service.

News-Griffith alumni also include LeGette Blythe, author of *Bold Galilean* and thirteen other books; John Harden, author of *The Devil's Tramping Ground* and two other books; Tim Pridgen of Jonesville, Tennessee, three books.

Other outstanding products of Griffith's youth movement are Editor C. A. (Pete) McKnight of the *Charlotte Observer;* Miles Wolff, executive editor of the *Greensboro Daily News;* Reed Sarratt, assistant to the publisher of the *Winston-Salem Journal and Sentinel;* Ray Howe, Sunday editor of the *Chattanooga Times;* the great reporter, Tim Jimisen, whose *News* expose of North Carolina's mental institutions led to a complete reform of the system; Charles Kuralt, CBS news correspondent, who brought the Ernie Pyle Award to the *News* in 1957; Moravian Bishop Herbert Spaugh, who began a religious column in the *News* in 1933 which now appears in forty other newspapers; Victor Reinemer, executive secretary to Senator James Murray (Democrat-Montana), who brought the Sidney Hillman Award to the *News* in 1955; and many more.

Griffith was born in Saluda County, South Carolina, March 14, 1899. He attended Erskine College at Due West, South Carolina, leaving in the spring of 1917 to enlist in the army. He served overseas as a sergeant in the Thirtieth (Old Hickory) Division. A few old friends still call him "Sarge."

In 1920, he married Thelma Wilkinson of Greensboro. They have two daughters and three grandchildren.

Griffith began his newspaper career in 1919 as a reporter on the *Greensboro Record.* He moved to the *Greensboro Daily News* in 1921, where he was subsequently state editor and sports editor.

He came to the *Charlotte News* on October 8, 1923, serving first as state editor and later as managing editor and executive editor. He was elected vice-president, secretary, and a director of the Charlotte News Publishing Company in September 1955 and was named general manager in October 1955.

In April 1950, when the *News* was purchased by the Knight Publishing Company, Griffith was named editor and general manager.

Although the rival *Charlotte Observer* is also a Knight paper, competition is as ferocious as ever for news, circulation and local retail advertising in

Charlotte. That's the way Brodie Griffith likes it and he has one distinct advantage: He generally knows which way the *Observer's* editor, Pete McKnight, and managing editor, Tom Fesperman, are going to jump before they do themselves. He ought to. He trained them, too.

William Henry Grimes, Editor
The Wall Street Journal

By Vermont Royster

O ne day in the early 1920s a juicy murder in Los Angeles crowded all the other news off the United Press wire. The next day UP headquarters got a complaint from a customer because he hadn't received the Buffalo livestock market. The result of this contretemps was that William Henry Grimes became editor of the *Wall Street Journal* and won himself a Pulitzer Prize for distinguished editorial writing.

The sequence is a bit involved. The complaint prompted the UP to start a separate wire to carry market news and racing results. Bill Grimes was plucked out of the slot to be its first editor. In short order UP readers found they could make sense of both hogs and horses. Thereupon Casey Hogate, then managing editor of the *Wall Street Journal,* hired him to make sense out of Washington. Since then he has succeeded in making sense out of just about everything except his turkey farm.

But even explaining Washington, his colleagues have discovered, is easier than unraveling the mysteries of Bill Grimes himself.

For here is a fellow out of Bellevue, Ohio, who at Sandusky High and Western Reserve got only a smattering of economics and less of journalism. Yet today he is one of the shrewdest and most respected commentators on political economy. He is also editor of a newspaper that in his thirty years with it has revolutionized "business" news and done much to jolt journalism generally.

Personally he can be a puzzle too. He speaks so softly that you can hardly hear him across the desk. Yet his typewriter has been one of the loudest of the times.

Royster was the senior associate editor of the *Wall Street Journal* when this article first appeared, in 1957.

118

In conversation he can bewilder strangers and confuse even longtime associates because the ideas go hop-skip-and-jump so that the listener gets lost in the tangle. Yet when a piece of copy rolls out of that typewriter it is so orderly, clear, and lucid as to drive other craftsmen to despair.

Readers sometimes picture him as a big, opinionated fellow who would pontificate at length on business and finance. They find him in person a small, shy man who would much prefer to talk about golf but who if pushed into an argument shows real respect for contrary opinion—although he's not easy to budge from his own position.

But that shyness covers a volatile temperament. He's been known to throw his golf clubs up a tree, or after some news department peccadillo to jump up and down on a brand new hat. He can get awful impatient when an afternoon's idea isn't executed by nightfall. And in the *Journal's* worldwide bureaus a message with the initials WHG usually sets people jumping.

That volatile temperament, in turn, conceals a deep kindness. Though he can at times be impulsive to the point of exasperating those who have to execute his ideas, where a decision may hurt someone he will often put it off to the point of frustration, simply because he does not give pain readily.

This complicated fellow landed on the *Wall Street Journal* in 1923 in the days when it was strictly a financial sheet. In 1925 he became head of its Washington bureau, and when the New Deal rolled into town he was one of the few newsmen who understood what the economic experimenters were talking about.

In 1934 he became managing editor (and people started calling him Bill instead of Henry). He began the first of the *Journal's* experiments that in time were to boost it from a thirty-thousand-circulation stock market paper into the country's only national newspaper—it's published in five cities and its circulation is now nearly half a million.

Since 1941 he has been the *Journal's* editor. Until then its editorial page had been like many others, overloaded with "facts" and jargon—and dull. He just started talking about economics, politics, and foreign affairs the way an intelligent man might talk to a neighbor. Homely analogies, anecdotes from old newspaper days, anything that would illustrate a point became grist for his mill.

Also by temperament, he couldn't hide an opinion. There certainly were several sides to most questions, but if you thought one side made the most sense, why not say so straight-out? It's a dictum the *Journal's* page still follows, even though Grimes has become an elder statesman and rarely writes editorials any more.

He also put another imprint on the page. "I entertain a strong conviction," he says, "that people are a pretty good and decent lot and that they are pretty smart. So I think that by and large the individual is a better judge of his needs and of his conduct than government and that he can manage his affairs better than the government can manage them for him."

His instructions to the "younger fellows" who work with him are typical."Make no pretense of walking down the middle of the road. Oppose all infringements on individual rights whether they stem from attempts at private monopoly, labor union monopoly, or from an overgrowing government.

"People will say we are conservative or even reactionary. I'm not much interested in labels, but if we have to choose one let's say we are radical. Just as radical as the Christian doctrine."

His colleagues know that time has mellowed him in many ways. But they are sure of one thing that hasn't changed. He is sure to be found prowling around the editorial sanctums growling: "You can't win friends by silence or pussyfooting. If we've got enemies, don't placate them."

Charles A. Guy, Editor
Lubbock (Texas) Avalanche-Journal

By Thomas Thompson

A sk one of Charles Armor Guy's cronies what Charlie would have done if he were not a newsman and you receive frowns and expressions of perplexity.

Parker Prouty, who handles the business end of the *Lubbock Avalanche-Journal* and who has been Editor Guy's close associate for nearly thirty-seven years, thought the question preposterous.

"Charlie is a born newspaper editor. Why, he doesn't even have a hobby," Parker declared.

Owen McWhorter was Lubbock county attorney when Charlie hit town. He studied the question.

"It's Charlie's nature to take sides. He would have made a fine trial lawyer or a sales executive, like in insurance," McWhorter said.

Oddly, it was dignified Dr. Clifford Jones, banker and former Texas Tech president, who came up with the off-beat response. He had a deep frown, but it melted and he guffawed.

"Why," he said, "Charlie would have been a crap shooter."

Everybody has his own version of the Lubbock editor.

Other reactions: "Charlie would rib his sick grandmother. He would have to be in some racket where needling pays off." . . . "Charlie Guy doesn't need dark glasses. He feels at home in the limelight." . . . "If Lyndon Johnson or the governor come to town, we always call on Charlie to emcee. He's at his best in a room full of people when he has the floor." . . . "Charlie is always belittling TV in his column, but he would make a crack performer. Never at a loss for a comeback. Memory like an elephant."

Charlie Guy came to Lubbock in 1924, fresh from the University of

Thompson was editor of the *Amarillo Globe-Times* when this article first appeared, in 1963.

Oklahoma Journalism School. He had done stints of reporting on Sooner dailies, including his hometown paper, the *Tulsa World*.

Lubbock, at that time, had about sixty-five hundred people. It was a bleak West Texas town on the Yellow House River, a dryish tributary of the Brazos. There was no Texas Tech. There was no irrigation and the prosperity of the cotton farmers was modest in wet years and rock bottom in dry years.

On the occasion of his thirty-fifth anniversary in Lubbock, Charlie wrote, "I had no more idea of staying here for keeps than I had of spending my life on the moon."

The chesty young reporter had his future planned. He was headed for New York via the great circle route: El Paso, the metropolitan papers on the West Coast, Denver, and finally the East Coast. But something happened. Charlie became preoccupied and he stayed around for thirty-nine years to play nursemaid to a growing Texas town. It became his role to front for the paper, for Lubbock, sometimes for West Texas.

Now the frame buildings with the sheet iron roofs are gone. Lubbock looks like a big inland California town, without the mountains on the horizon. Close to 140,000 people reside on its corporate premises. Irrigation has taken over (more than five thousand wells in the county) and Lubbock has become the world's third-ranking cotton market. Tech's two-thousand-acre campus is the state's most spacious. Some consider it the most handsome.

Tech is the apple of Charlie's eye. It has been the big thing with Parker, too. Long ago they figured Tech to be Lubbock's greatest asset, the one thing that might put Lubbock ahead of Amarillo, 120 miles north. They worked it so they had a say about who was on the board of regents, and they pulled all of the strings down in Austin. It was a day of crowning glory when Tech was admitted to the Southwest Conference. There are fifty permanent buildings on the campus and enrollment this past September peaked out at eleven thousand students.

Somebody pulled a smoothie on Charlie when the new Tech library was conceived. It looks like something that architect Edward Durell Stone might have had a hand in. Anyhow, it is a departure from the Spanish Renaissance style of the main campus buildings. Modern interpretation? Mediterranean? Whatever it is, Charlie became ired. He hooted and heckled in "The Plainsman." He made it a running conversation piece for months. One editor can't win them all any more, and Charlie lost this one. But he never gave up. When the books were being moved from the old library, he jibed: "It [the new library] is crawling with hot and cold running maintenance men and automatic nose blowers. It has all the conveniences of a modern jail." As for the architect, Charlie said, "He was frightened by an egg crate."

In "The Plainsman"—the oldest daily newspaper column in the Southwest—Charlie covers the spectrum. Politics, social commentary, sports—it's all there. However, "The Plainsman" is male oriented. "The Girl on Broadway," whom he quotes almost daily, doesn't sound feminine to all ears. The housewife grazes the column to see if there is anything of interest to women or if friend or relative is mentioned. He likes to hang made-up titles on people, such as "Doctor of Grunts and Groans" for the Texas Tech coach. Once, when vexed, he referred to his friend Gov. Price Daniel as "What Price Daniel." He is credited with nicknaming Frank King, the former Associated Press executive, "General." He calls the Lubbock division manager of the telephone company "Maharajah." Managing editor Jay Harris he calls "Major." This goes back to when Harris was a sergeant in the air force. An ace staffer, Kenneth May, he calls "Genius." He likes to put people's projects in this "Department of Overwhelming Unimportance." When a committee was picking a new Chamber of Commerce manager, he kept saying, "We don't want a cheerleader."

Three years ago the *Avalanche-Journal* moved to a new plant. The lobby is larger than the newsroom in the old building. Charlie's office, on the second floor, also has elbow room. It's paneled and carpeted; sumptuous to a degree. In the anteroom where his secretary works is a sizeable replica of "The Plainsman"—the unshaven, Stetsoned cow poke that for years has adorned his column on the editorial page. The drawing is framed in barbed wire.

"The Plainsman" image is completely misleading. Intended, of course. Charlie is ruddy complexioned, stocky, bouncy. He's an immaculate dresser. His parents moved from Baltimore to Tulsa when it was a booming oil town, a city in fact. If he ever wore a ten-gallon hat, friends don't recall.

Charlie has a large desk—less cluttered than most working editors. His taste seems to run to statuary, etc. Looking over his left shoulder is a bust of Sam Houston. Grace Guy, who helped with the decor, says that Charlie is very fond of the foot-high miniature of Rodin's *The Thinker*. Why, she is not exactly sure. At the other end of the office is a leather sofa and matching chair. On the wall is a John Meigs water color, depicting an old Spanish-American cemetery in New Mexico. Charlie has a macabre fondness for Herman who stares vacantly at him the length of the office. Herman, a present from Congressman George Mahon, is the skull of a Yankee soldier boy plugged by a sharp shooting Reb. The sizable slug is still in the skull.

In his bachelor days Charlie was something of a Beau Brummell. He worked hard and he played hard. He was more of a joiner than most newsmen. He sang in barber shop quartets and he made speeches. Frank King said Charlie made a speech in "every one-room school house on the

South Plains." And he traveled around. In the thirties he went to Mexico City on an excursion train from the Panhandle. He turned out his column every day; he also went every place and participated in all activities, except sleep. "An iron man," one of his weary traveling companions recalled.

Well, things have changed. He and Grace still travel. After ASNE in Washington, they left for five weeks in Europe, but back home Charlie follows a pretty regular schedule. He arrives in the office at 8:30 and leaves at 4:40 to get the jump on the five o'clock traffic. After glancing through his morning mail he dictates and starts knocking out his column. Usually this takes an hour and a half, or more, depending on how things go and interruptions. If callers stay overlong, Charlie shows impatience. Promptly at 11:50 he leaves the office for the Lubbock Club, where he converses and lunches lightly at the Round Table, or "King-Makers Table," as some would have it.

Here Charlie gathers ammunition. He shapes his views. The atmosphere is jocular, relaxed, often argumentative. If anybody gets on his soap box he becomes a target, including Charlie. Usually present are the city manager, the superintendent of schools, president of the chamber of commerce, a lawyer-oil man, an MD, a general insurance man, occasionally somebody from Tech, and somebody in politics.

In recent years Charlie's political thinking has shifted to the right, but not altogether. He believes in private ownership, but as far as the home town is concerned, he is for local public power because the city-owned power plan nets Lubbock a million dollars a year. He is vocally anti–New Frontier, but he is vocally anti–John Birch. "I don't need to prove my patriotism by sending twelve bucks to Whotunket, Massachusetts," he said.

One of Charlie's warmest friends is Congressman George Mahon, who is chairman of that little old military subcommittee that doles billions out to the Defense Department. Mahon votes the administration line too much for Charlie, and he says so, but the two have ridden the river together. They don't try to boss each other around.

With the younger breed of politicos, Charlie is cagey and sometimes roughshod. They are cagey with him, too, for they know he will sound off, pro or con. State Sen. Doc Blanchard currently is in Charlie's favor, but Blanchard claims he is still smarting under a Guyian crack in "The Plainsman." Several years ago Blanchard was a candidate for a seat in the House and Charlie had him figured for a playboy. He said in his column that Doc Blanchard, if elected, probably would go to Austin and spend his time playing golf and gin rummy.

This was quite a cross for a freshman candidate, seeking office in a dry Bible Belt town like Lubbock.

In Texas politics, Charlie is in the midst of a blue-chip game now. Both newly elected Lt. Gov. Preston Smith and newly elected Attorney General Waggoner Carr are Lubbock men. Both jobs are stepping stones to the governor's office, and both men are ambitious and in need of Charlie's goodwill. It seems that Carr would have the nod at this time, but Charlie is vigilant for signs of strength, signs of overreaching, and fatal missteps.

Years ago, C. W. Ratcliff, a former *Avalanche-Journal* editor, coined a description of Charlie. You still hear it around. "Charlie Guy," C. W. said, "is the only man I ever knew who could strut sitting down."

Like all fetching description, Ratcliff's oversimplifies. In his own home Charlie is a gracious host and good listener.

"He is fine with children," said Owen McWhorter, who has observed the rearing of three sons and now three grandchildren. "He can't enter their world, so he brings them into his. He talks with them as equals." McWhorter regards Charlie as rank sentimentalist.

Charlie is fond of his home. He likes that hour or so before dinner when he and Grace are at the card table playing sol and talking about the happenings of the day and what letters came in the mail.

As Parker said, Charlie has no hobby. He doesn't play golf. He loathes the thought of going fishing or hunting. He is sold on Alcoholics Anonymous. Two nights a week he and city manager H. P. Clifton devote to the AAs. And, he never misses a meeting of the Texas Commission of Alcoholism in Austin. His idea of a good time is to slip out of town with Grace and spend a few days in a city where they can dine well and observe life from a swank hotel.

Incidentally, digging Charlie Guy in his own hometown isn't a pushover. One of his loyal, but humorless friends, flared up and said, "If someone is going to write about Charlie, why does he have to be from Amarillo?"

Grover Cleveland Hall, Jr., Editor
The Montgomery (Alabama) Advertiser

By Robert W. Brown

Archaeologists are pick-and-shoveling a hill twenty-five miles south of Tel Aviv to see if they can prove it is the site of the Biblical city of Gath. This might come as a surprise to some readers of the *Montgomery Advertiser* (circulation sixty-two thousand), published mornings in the first, best, and next Capital of the Confederacy. Since last February, they have read a convincing volume of reports that Goliath's old hometown is somewhere north of the Smith and Wesson line.

"Tell it not in Gath, publish it not in the streets of Askelon . . ." (2 Sam. 1:20) has been the pennant under which the *Advertiser* has paraded a series of articles to show that some of the journalistic brethren to de Nawth are color blind. The theme: The interregional character of racial discrimination blurs into a dull gray behind the lines of the Feds, but sharpens into a glaring black and white in the cornpone belt. The series has titillated Southern whites, angered, but still impressed, some Nawthen colleagues, tickled more than one Uncle Tom, and even pleased the National Association for the Advancement of Colored People.

Thus almost everybody should be happy and, despite the embarrassing simplicity to which the theme is reduced, happiest of all one Grover Cleveland Hall, Jr. The theme "You, too, are guilty" can come out only "We are guilty" when examined through the other end of the barrel. But though a Deep South editor, Hall is not abashed, fortified as he is by an intellectual detachment. He has lamented at once that the discrimination-in-the-North articles have given aid and comfort to the kluxist element; that out-region

---

Brown was editor of the *Columbus Ledger* when this article first appeared, in 1956.

journalists are sloppy for stumbling over a story without picking it up. The role is one of professional observer, unbeholdened, unaffiliated, and to hell with your thought patterns, buddy! Still if one knows Grover he can be sure that the Sage of Goat Hill is getting a terrific chuckle out of it all—grinning in his editorial lair like the fox with which there is some resemblance, a comparison not odiously intended for either.

So who is Grover Cleveland Hall?

Hall, a pompadourish, Danny Kayish dandy, forty-one years of age and blissfully unwed, is first, last, and always a newspaper editor. He began as a cub on the *Advertiser;* probably will end there. He ticks on the ambition to be a great editor like his father before him (Pulitzer Prize, 1928), the memory of whom is the mainspring. That's what makes Grover Hall run. A stylish writer and precisionist, Hall is more critical of and dissatisfied with Hall than any one else could be.

A couple of years back at a convention, a group of editors was swapping notes on expense account padding and deploring the disparity between their income and that of relatively unimportant people like nuclear physicists and bricklayers. Grover acknowledged the complaint but exclaimed: "Hell, I've got the most important gawddam job in the State of Alabama! There's nothing more important than a newspaper editor."

He really believes and lives on this evaluation, a facet of the Hall personality which should endear him to all colleagues without regard to region, or whether Gath is south of Tel Aviv or north of Chicago. This controls his habits. He is an omnivorous reader and insists that an editor cannot perform well unless he blocks out three or four evenings a week for heavy reading. On his schedule is the Bible, whence came the Gath-Askelon title without research.

Publisher Richard F. Hudson, Jr., is authority for the report that neither Editor Hall nor company President Hudson, Sr., could qualify as an apprentice printer, since a high school diploma is required in the composing room. Yet Hall is one of the most literate editors in the South, an articulate speaker, versed in the arts, and contrary probably to some impressions, a Southern liberal. He might challenge one so labeling him to a fast game of tennis or a fast drinking bout, or both, and win easily. But the *Advertiser,* affectionately known as "Ol' Grandma," has a record that bespeaks the classification.

An editor whose newspaper somewhat overlaps the *Advertiser's* circulation area once described Hall's editorial page as brilliant and Hall as "an astute journalist, a magnificent writer." His reading routine is reflected in the page, which might go for days without being topical. There's no compulsion to follow events, deploring or applauding daily occurrences; neither is there a rule not to be topical. The result is a provocative, saucy, pert, and sometimes impertinent product. And it speaks plainly. If the *Advertiser* regards a figure as a "sap" or a "boob," he is so called in those words. Still it manages not to be strident, and is not always unsubtle. For example, editorial reference to Alabama's Gov. "Big Jim" Folsom first was reduced to a capital "J," then his associates became known as "J-Birds." The derision has been effective, and the chief J-Bird has something on his back that will ride him out of politics, for sure.

Hall's unwed bliss has generated some impressions and tales hinted at when a colleague said that Hall worked as a "lone wolf" and that the ladyfolk could prove it. He insists that he is no bachelor, says no bachelor ever was worth a damn, and none could be happy; suggests that he should be allowed to reach fifty before being so condemned, and hints that, like Pres. Grover Cleveland, he is just waiting for his bride to grow up. But he has bachelor ways; finicky in taste. He demands whiskey by specific brand and steak in special cuts, will continue to drive a venerable car for years yet, and buys his suits from the same tailor in annual visits to Birmingham (at $170 per copy, incidentally!!!).

This latter practice (Practice, hell! That's an idiosyncrasy) has placed the slight-statured and nimble Hall among Montgomery's best-dressed males, a classification of which he is acutely and pleasantly aware. At one point in his career, he carried a cane and sported a daily carnation. The latter was a hallmark which delighted his publisher, a story goes, because it identified the writer of those editorials to the horsewhip-toting gentry who sometimes wander into newspaper offices. This probably is a canard, but Hall could carry cane and carnation as well as any editor, and better than most.

See how the fellow is? You start out on a chips-where-may sketch and wind up being complimentary.

Coleman Harwell, Executive Editor
The Nashville Tennessean

By Frank Eyerly

C olie Harwell is a meditative man.

One morning about two o'clock he and I were walking across midtown Manhattan. The heavy burden of APME work and a series of significant and far-reaching professional tasks had taken us to a play, *El Morocco,* and 21. We were exhausted. "Don't you think, Frank, we should slip over to Lexington and get some doughnuts and milk before we go to bed?" queried Colie after a long block of soul-searching.

Colie Harwell is a provident man.

After we completed our chore in a little hole-in-the-wall cafe on Lexington, Colie studied the counter. "Frank, don't you think it would be smart to buy a dozen doughnuts and take them with us?" said Colie, fixing the cashier with an inquiring eye.

Colie Harwell is a generous man.

When we reached our hotel Colie turned to the cab driver. "My good man, wouldn't you like some doughnuts?" said Colie, recalling the lonely and hungry nights of a laboring man in New York City.

When Coleman Harwell was graduated from the University of the South in 1926, the Fourth Estate nearly lost a wise and effective editor to the stage. As a young man he had a distinguished reputation as an actor in Nashville's Little Theater movement. He was invited to try out for a Broadway production. A longtime associate in Nashville recalls that he was hell-bent on being a newspaperman. Between 1927 and 1931 he climbed fast, from reporter to managing editor. Then he spent six years on the staff of the *New York World-Telegram* before he was recalled to Nashville as executive editor of the *Tennessean,* when Silliman Evans purchased the paper in 1937. Colie is a

---

Eyerly was managing editor of the *Des Moines Register and Tribune* when this article first appeared, in 1958.

perfectionist and a hard worker, and it is inevitable that his newspaper's enthusiasms are his enthusiasms and vice versa. His personality leaves a strong mark on the newspaper.

Harwell works in a partitioned cubicle at the front of the city room, within strategic distance of the city, state, and copydesks. Most of the day and often at night the light is on in his cubicle, evidence that Harwell is aboard and busy.

Occasionally each day Harwell circulates through the city room, but most of his instructions to the staff come in an afternoon editorial conference and in intra-office memoranda. These memos may deal with the misspelling of a word, a badly phrased headline, or they may deal with the newspaper's broad approach to a major news area. Sometimes these memos are businesslike in tone, sometimes sarcastic, sometimes complimentary, but always they reflect the measured thinking of a dedicated editor.

Despite his conservative dress, appearance, and speech (he is a past president of Nashville Rotary), Harwell is a "liberal" Democrat. His newspaper was one of only four major newspapers that supported Harry Truman for reelection in 1948.

During many years of close association in APME work, I have been impressed by Harwell's inexhaustible energies. The several hundred editors who make it an avocation to "edit" the Associated Press report over the shoulders (sometimes the bodies) of the Associated Press's managers generate many issues during the year. I can recall few questions about which Harwell did not have thoughtful but vigorous views.

Twice in his thirty years as a newspaperman Harwell has deserted the desk for short periods. Once he took out two years for military service. On another occasion, following the war, the death of his father and brother forced him to enter the mercantile firm of Neely-Harwell and Company with another brother. He stayed in "buttons and bows" for three years, until he returned to the *Tennessean* as vice-president and editor in 1948.

In his formative years young Colie was the slickest Charleston dancer in Sewanee. At a more mature stage he became an ardent golfer. It is characteristic of the man's progressive evolution that he should now be preoccupied with water skiing. He is building a country home on the shores of Old Hickory Lake just outside Nashville.

While swimming in Old Hickory last year, Harwell collided with a huge, slimy, greenish-gray mass of Bryozoa, a low form of harmless animal life.

"I didn't know whether to shake hands with it or swim as fast as I could," he related ruefully later.

The next day a reporter was assigned to interview this denizen of the lake. Harwell's attitude was, characteristically, "If it interests me it will interest a good many of our readers."

Last summer in San Francisco Harwell did something at the ASNE convention that reflects well his kindly manner and his generous heart. He felt that a panel devoted to organized labor was loaded heavily with sentiment unfriendly to labor. At the conclusion of the program he quietly picked up a microphone and spoke for the record a tolerant and enlightened statement on organized labor in the United States.

In Nashville, Harwell and the *Tennessean* play a part in every activity and public responsibility that mark the integration of honorable newspaper work and society.

There is another phase of the Harwell story that impresses me more.

Harwell is married to the former Ann McLemore of Johnson City, Tennessee. They have two daughters, Ann McClure Harwell, twenty-one, and Carolyn Harwell, eighteen.

Most of Harwell's professional life is well synchronized with a rewarding and inspiring family life. When Colie is conducting sociological research in a New York supper club, Ann usually is there. When a new restaurant is to be explored on Manhattan Island, a daughter is likely to turn up with the party. When Colie is managing a convention program, Ann is sharing both the burden and the fun.

Last month Ann accompanied Colie on a week's inspection of the North Atlantic Treaty Organization. It is doubtful that the Treaty Organization ever before had had such a gracious and personable inspection.

In brief, Colie Harwell, like the man of the Renaissance, is the complete man and the whole man. If this sounds like an uninhibited paean of praise, please remember that for many years this writer has put up with Harwell's almost perverse infatuation with Jack Daniels whiskey.

Howard H Hays, Jr., Editor
Riverside (California) Press-Enterprise

By J. Montgomery Curtis

T im Hays wears many hats, two of them daily and simultaneously. A third is donned for special occasions, usually late at night.

The daily hats are those of newspaper editor and owner. Tim never doffs either in favor of the other. He is as committed to enduring, worthy financial success as he is to the editorial excellence which produces it and, in turn, is made possible by it.

That is one reason why the Riverside (California) morning *Enterprise,* evening *Press,* and their Sunday edition rank with the giants in any list of the best. This Boswell so ranked them on an ABC television panel several years ago. It was a Sunday afternoon and the editor and co-publisher missed the show. The reason is revealing. He was reading at the time.

A man of grace, wisdom, and concentration on the job, Tim has long believed that one purpose of a newspaper life is to enjoy it. Which brings us to the third hat. It is an Indian headdress symbolizing Tim's induction into the Blackfoot Indian tribe in Montana's Glacier National Park. Tim was dubbed "Red Feather" as he entered the tribe with his two brothers under the sponsorship of the famous chief Two Guns White Calf.

Tim mastered the Blackfoot Indian war whoop. He erupts with it late at night when a party needs a lively touch. Those who have been deafened by his performance say that the yell melds the tone quality of a buzz saw with the wail of a tenor banshee and the volume of a rocket blast-off. Certainly it has exorcised the tedium from many a party.

Curtis was vice-president of development for Knight Newspapers when this article first appeared, in 1974.

Those youthful summers at Glacier started an interest in Indians. This may not have caused Tim's enthusiasm for a *Press-Enterprise* campaign many years later but it did not hurt. The first Pulitzer Prize listed for 1968 reads:

"Public Service: The *Riverside* (California) *Press-Enterprise* for its expose of corruption in connection with the handling of the property and estates of an Indian tribe in California, and its successful efforts to punish the culprits."

This was accomplished by the most dogged kind of reporting. The file contains well over one hundred exhaustive news stories and about twenty editorials which brought justice to the Agua Caliente Indians and shame to the conservators who had been handling their estates.

As with any man of many hats Tim's life varies. He is all concentration and dedication on the job but he is equally devoted to relaxation, especially on the road. If you would know a man, know him through his traveling companions. One is editor Whitley Austin of the *Salina* (Kansas) *Journal*. Confessing that "these recollections lack substance and there is a certain mythical quality to them," Whit writes:

> Thank you for the invitation to do in Tim Hays. The following is a kaboodle of scurrilous recollections.
>
> The important thing about Tim is that wherever he is he is about to be somewhere else and soon is. He always is wanted on the phone. I have traveled with him to parts of the world where AT&T has yet to reach and those calls still come. I suspect they often are from his beautiful and stylish wife, Helen, who merely wants to confirm a tennis date.
>
> Where you and I might pack a quart of scotch, Tim packs a tennis racket. He can locate a court at the damnedest places and at the damnedest times.
>
> In his earlier years, this propensity to be elsewhere has got him into trouble. For example, one time we were having drinks at the Mayflower Hotel when Tim suddenly became missing. I found him on the ballroom stage helping the Daughters of the American Revolution in the flag salute.
>
> Tim is always the perfect gentleman. I think he awakes with his pajamas pressed and a smile on his handsome mug. Although a Californian, he can order the proper wine at Lassarre's in Paris with aplomb and taste. This being from California has suckered him into throwing cocktail parties at the Shoreham for such unfortunate senatorial characters as Kuchel and Tunney. I know, because my being from Kansas qualifies me as a bartender, and that is the job Tim always gives me at those parties.

You are aware of the sterling services Tim has performed for ASNE and the remarkable job he has done at Riverside, the press council and all that. He has rendered yeoman service to the International Press Institute (IPI) in the past decade. He has been chairman of the American committee, a job he has just turned over to Bill Block, and as such he has commuted to Zurich and other foreign parts in the IPI interests.

Somehow, he always gravitates to the important posts and then delegates the work with the greatest of skill. This ability to push should stand him in good stead now that he is to be the chief keeper of the American editorial zoo.

I do hope, however, he buys a new suit for the occasion. To the best of my recollection he has worn the same one since I have known him; or perhaps they merely are of the same material and cut, a sort of security blanket, not that he needs one.

While Whit speaks in parables to tell the truth, none are needed for the newspaper job Tim Hays has been doing for a long time. Consider the wedding of business-editorial success with the launching of a Sunday newspaper. By the late 1940s the morning and evening editions were quality and financial successes, but Tim and his associates were not content. They believed that Riverside County needed a Sunday newspaper and they wanted to found one. Tim discussed it at one of his API Seminars (for publishers and editors) in 1953. Detailed planning proceeded for many months and the *Sunday Press-Enterprise* was born in 1956.

The timing was right. The planning was thorough. The *Sunday* was an immediate success in circulation and has been growing with the dailies ever since. The morning *Enterprise* circulation is 58,700, the evening *Press* 36,600, the combination 95,300 and the *Sunday Press-Enterprise* is 98,300. Those 3,000 *Sundays* above the combination are street-sale copies.

There are business, circulation, and advertising reasons for this success and, as always, they are accompanied by editorial excellence with the six clear section fronts, thorough reporting, lucid writing, and sparkling pictures. This biographer has shown this paper to other editors with the suggestion to "go thou and do likewise."

The energy which directs a staff in winning Pulitzers and launching a Sunday newspaper shows no signs of slackening as our new president ends his fifty-seventh year. Maybe the daily tennis, sometimes at noon on the home court, keeps him alert. Or it could be tending his orange groves. (Riverside had California's first Washington navel oranges.) Tim also relaxes when he is in his woodworking shop or reviewing his collection of graphic art.

A lively family life sustains this editor-publisher. There is the redoubtable Helen and two sons, Tom, thirteen, and Bill, twenty-two. The Hayses entertain with small but notable dinner parties, and the host is famous for letting the guests know when it is time to go home. "He's very discreet," says Helen. "Like he disappears and then reappears in his pajamas."

Born in Chicago and with childhood in the West, Tim was prepared for eminence. His father, the late Howard, Sr., was the Riverside publisher. He sent Tim through Stanford for a B.A. in 1939; and then through Harvard for his law degree in 1942. Tim served with the FBI from 1942 to 1945, reported a year on the *San Bernardino Sun,* and began his Riverside career in 1946, the same year he was admitted to the state bar.

Like his father, Tim never ran from a fight. In the Indian government case, a judge under investigation and incensed by an editorial ordered Tim arrested. Tim held his ground, stayed out of jail and his paper won the Pulitzer.

In February 1971, pressures came from many power sources to prevent publication of the truth about the dean of an unusual law school at Riverside University. The dean had a felony conviction, forced resignation from the Florida Bar, two years in a Florida mental institution in lieu of prison, among other interesting items. The story was published. The dean vamoosed and the school closed.

Past ASNE president Norman Isaacs says he was first "attracted to Tim because of his gutsy stand against the giant *Los Angeles Times,* which was doing the old trick of buying up all the features available, claiming broad territorial rights and then sticking them in a drawer to gather dust. Tim had no hesitation in going before federal agencies and saying his piece."

Tim is devoted to professional improvement. That took him to his first API Seminar in 1949 and led him to send forty-one other executives and writers. Tim is on the API board now.

The same urge took him through the ranks of ASNE, to the American committee chairmanship for IPI, to the Nieman fellowship selection committee, to posts with Claremont College, Stanford, Associated Press groups, and others.

Tim is rightfully proud of the *Press-Enterprise* series of journalism lectures at the University of California, Riverside. Tim has obtained the best, including Louis Lyons, Osborn Elliot, Denis Hamilton, Wes Gallagher, Katharine Graham, Tom Wicker, John Oakes, Howard K. Smith, and Elie Abel.

The facts do not always mirror the man completely. It remains for Norm Isaacs to provide a concise profile.

Tim is invariably calm, analytical, lucid. I've never known him to be guilty of the pop-off remark. He's been a gem at ASNE board meetings, listening calmly, weighing the various arguments, and then making up his mind without extended oratory. Hyperbole is not Tim's bag.

While he's calm, collected and poised at all times, Tim isn't at all anyone you can overlook. You are damned well aware he's around and that there is a strong input; it simply is that in a profession populated by noisy, strongly opinionated nuts, he stands out by being sane. In a way, he reminds me of Lee Hills: A tremendously able extremely bright guy who operates in well-oiled, ball-bearing smoothness.

I suppose that's as high a tribute as one of the more celebrated nuts can pay a colleague who clearly has never needed a shrink, or ever will.

Tim's feeling of, for, and about newspapers is inherited. His father's regard was expressed by a *Press-Enterprise* editorial writer in tribute to Mr. Hays upon his death in 1969. The editorial recalled that a man who was "buying up newspaper businesses all over the country with no thought of them as newspapers" was the subject of a magazine cover story. Mr. Hays suspected that this man was the client of a broker who had asked him about a sale. Mr. Hays resurrected the broker's letter and returned it with this note:

"Would you sell your wife? I thought not. That's the way I feel about these newspapers."

George W. Healy, Jr., Editor

New Orleans Times-Picayune

By Turner Catledge

W hat I shall relate about George W. Healy, Jr., I believe to be literally true. For in my researches I have run onto the amazing fact that every story about him is told by everyone in exactly the same way. And, further, it is told precisely as we have heard Healy tell it himself.

George's successful business and professional career had its solid start at the Baker Grand Theatre in his hometown of Natchez, Mississippi. He was employed there in his youth as a peddler of popcorn and peanuts. He was good at it. Too good, in fact. His aggressive salesmanship cost him his job. The theatre manager thought that quiet in the theatre, back there in the days of the silents, was more important than a sell-out for the popcorn concession. The manager faced the choice between Charlie Chaplin's cavortings on the screen and George Healy's shoutings in the aisle. Charlie won.

There is something a bit vague about George's early education. We will just have to assume that he had one. In my researches I ran into only one suggestion that he went to school in early life. He was, for a time, a day pupil at Stanton College, a girls boarding school at Natchez. Several episodes in his career indicate that females have been a considerable influence on him.

There is no such blackout on George's later education at the University of Mississippi. George had some interest in newspapering before he went to Ole Miss. He had caught the fever indirectly from his father, who used to tell him of his days as editor of the Fayette, Mississippi, weekly. Later, George had what he called a "triple-dipping" job with the *Natchez Democrat*. He worked for the news department as a prep-school and sports reporter; for the circulation department as a mailer; and for himself as a carrier. The only money in the deal came from the carrier's job.

Catledge was managing editor of the *New York Times* when this article first appeared, in 1958.

George learned very early the truth of a statement of another former Mississippian, George E. Allen. When asked why so many newspapermen and writers came from Mississippi, Allen replied, "It's better than plowing." George found it better than selling popcorn at the Grand Theatre in competition with the pretty puss of Mary Pickford.

At Ole Miss, Healy continued his newspaper career by organizing a news service with his roommate. They lined up fifteen or twenty papers, whom they served at space rates. Their efforts at first were largely in sports. But then came an event that really put them in the chips. Here again a woman was involved.

Frances Birkhead, who had been secretary to the late Lee Russell, governor of Mississippi, filed at Oxford a hundred-thousand-dollar seduction suit against the governor. George got more out of it than Miss Birkhead. The Healy news service made a killing, what with the trial, Governor Russell's court victory, the jailing of former Gov. Theodore Bilbo for failing to show up as a witness, and other sideshows incidental to the suit.

Writing for the daily papers, booking the college dance band, and editing the college humor magazine—subsequently suppressed—George continued his upward march. He prided himself as a picker of talent. William Faulkner wanted to write for the magazine, but George took a dim view of him as a writer. Instead, he hired Faulkner as a cartoonist.

George's experiences at Ole Miss set the stage beautifully for him when he got out. He had a rash of newspaper offers even before he was graduated. He was first hired by the *Birmingham Age-Herald,* where he remained briefly. He left Birmingham to become managing editor of the *Knoxville Sentinel,* at an increase of five dollars a week. Later, when the *Sentinel* was sold to Scripps-Howard, George had two offers the same day. He accepted one from the *Times-Picayune.* He expected to hold the job for six months and then to move on to the *New York Herald Tribune.* At the end of six months, however, he was in the midst of covering the 1927 Mississippi River flood. At the end of the year he was traveling with Huey Long. After eighteen months, when he thought he was able to take the *Herald Tribune* offer, the managing editor who had made it had gone on and his successor had other ideas.

The writer witnessed an adventure of George's during that flood. The scene was Melville, Louisiana, where there had been a break in the levee. George hired a scow at Opelousas and rigged it with two outboard motors. He beat everyone to the story, including Herbert Hoover, who had been stuck with his relief party at Baton Rouge. When Mr. Hoover finally arrived, it was to watch George Healy swim down the middle of Melville's main street to telephone his story through a switchboard that had been installed on a high scaffold.

George was soon moved inside, as happens all too frequently to good reporters. He became city editor of the *Times-Picayune* and a couple of years later managing editor. Six years ago he assumed the designation of editor. He never gave up the title of managing editor, which indicates significantly his direct hand in the gathering, writing, and editing of news for the *Picayune*.

In World War II George did a stint with the OWI at the personal request of President Roosevelt. During the waning months of the war he set out on a trip with other VIPs to the Pacific. The group was shepherded by George's good friend and fellow Natchez alumnus, Vice-Admiral Stanton Merrill. On the last leg of the trip the pilot of the plane became violently ill. George immediately diagnosed his case as acute appendicitis. The question then arose as to who was going to take the pilot's place on the flight deck. "Have no fear," George consoled. "I took the controls of a Piper Cub once. I'll get you home." The passengers had a desperate choice, to let George help fly the plane or watch him operate on the pilot. He was hell-bent on doing one or the other. George went forward and kept the copilot awake by telling him funny stories. A few hours later the plane was set down in an "eggshell" landing, as Admiral Merrill described it, in San Diego.

If you want to see life really lived and enjoyed, see George in "New Awlyns." He is to the Crescent City what Louis Seltzer is to Cleveland. Go with him to the Boston Club, to Bourbon Street, to the Fair Ground; go sailing with him in the Gulf of Mexico. If you are not good at bridge and don't have an even temper, have something else to do when he suggests a rubber. (He almost broke up a national tournament once when, having made an impossible contract, he yelled "bingo.") See him playing with his grandson, George Healy IV, better known as King George IV.

On the professional side George has made an outstanding success of the *Times-Picayune*. He has kept it in the forefront of journalism in the South. He has dressed it up with brighter leads, simpler headlines, more pictures, and more pep. There is a story that a veteran engraver of the "good, gray" *Picayune* almost quit when Healy first ordered a picture for column one of page one. Fortunately, the engraver, George, and the paper all survived.

George is active in many civic movements. He is now in his second term as chairman of the New Orleans chapter of the American Red Cross. He is also national vice-chairman under Gen. Lucius D. Clay of the Red Cross fund drive for 1958. He gives to every activity the same verve and enthusiasm that we see him giving to the affairs of the ASNE, whether we are in session, at the bar, or on the "Bloody Mary Special" to New York.

Hobbies keep him young and gay. Search, as you will, you won't find many gray hairs on his head. He says, however, his favorite hobby is playing Cupid. The writer can testify personally that he's good at it. He is aided in the Cupid role by Margaret. He met Margaret Alford at a dance at Tallulah,

Louisiana. At that time he was a junior at Ole Miss and she was attending All Saints College at Vicksburg. George says Margaret was so smitten she followed him. She denies this. The known facts are, however, that she enrolled at Ole Miss the next year, that she never finished, and that she married him soon after he left school. And aren't we glad!

J. N. Heiskell, Editor
Arkansas Gazette

By Harry S. Ashmore

My departure from the *Arkansas Gazette,* after twelve years as executive editor and three as the personal devil of Gov. Orval Faubus, was an occasion for considerable public celebration and, I like to think, some scattered private mourning.

Whether pleased or disconsolate, most subscribers assumed the newspaper would change in my absence. It hasn't, except in detail. It couldn't, possibly, so long as the slender, meticulous gentleman who has been its proprietor for more than sixty years arrives each morning on the clock's tick to take his place in the corner office.

At ninety-one, John Netherland Heiskell has made his own legend, and made it work for him. When he crossed over from Tennessee in 1902 to invest his family's modest fortune in Little Rock's venerable but shaky morning daily, he offered the usual announcement that he considered the newspaper a public trust. Two generations of assorted Arkansas demagogues have since discovered that this was not a self-serving advertisement, but an irrevocable statement of fact.

Over the years J. N. Heiskell (this is the official designation, softened to Mr. J. N. by his associates, and to Ned by his few intimates) has himself taken on an institutional character. This may be a part of the natural defenses of an essentially shy and sensitive man, but he has also applied it as a device to depersonalize the tides of human passion that have often run high against his newspaper. The *Gazette's* implacable concern, he insists, is public; its watchword is calm reason; it condemns the act, not the man.

We differed, sometimes, on this. His charity is greater than mine, and I have argued that public acts may be minimized if their perpetrators must assume that they will be struck with an editorial baseball bat as soon as they raise their heads. In some respects we differ, too, in our view of the wrenching social change that has afflicted our native region—but this is

---

Ashmore was chairman of the Fund for the Republic when this article first appeared, in 1963.

largely a sentimental divergence accounted for by the more than four decades of difference in our ages. Mr. J. N. lived the first half of his life in the vanished, feudal South I can know only by hearsay, and the sense of that romantic past is always with him.

Early in our association he shook me at our morning conference with the stern announcement that the *Gazette* had perpetrated an unforgivable error. The "Fifty Years Ago Today" column had carried an item to the effect that a river packet had gone down off Helena with the loss of all hands. "The next day," he said, "we found that eight men had gotten ashore. I remember it very well. I was city editor of the *Memphis Commercial Appeal* at the time."

This was one of many reminders that he belongs, not only in tradition but in fact, with the storied provincial titans who were his contemporaries, Henry Watterson, Josephus Daniels, and William Allen White. Less flamboyant and aggressive than any of these, he nevertheless flavors his own legend with the courtly manner, the social grace, and the calculated eccentricities of the era of personal journalism. And he brings down intact from that simpler time an impervious, old-fashioned integrity.

Editor is the only title he has ever employed, although for legal purposes he also is president of the Gazette Publishing Company. But the company is no corporate refuge; he is impatient with the mundane trappings of the business side, looks only at the totals on the balance sheet, and grudgingly spares a maximum of fifteen minutes of his time for the annual meeting of the board of directors, which is in fact a sort of abbreviated family reunion. He cheerfully shares the income and the glory that may accrue to the newspaper and freely delegates the details of management, but no one who works in the old, bay-windowed *Gazette* building has any doubt where final responsibility lies.

I had an acute sense of how heavy that burden is, and how long he has borne it, when, in 1957, I brought him the intelligence that Orval Faubus had decided to defy the integration orders of the federal courts and seize Central High School with state troops. Hugh Patterson, his son-in-law and publisher, and I had come from a weekend of scurrying, futile conferences and I could spell out the extent of the impending disaster.

The *Gazette* had been skirmishing with the militant segregationists for some years, but now we faced an outright guerrilla war. He had to realize, I told him, that we would stand alone; the politicians and civic leaders were already running for cover, and the opposition *Arkansas Democrat* would play it safe and grow fat on our blood.

Neither he nor I had any doubt what his answer would be; he reminded me that he had never been willing to stand aside while scoundrels and mountebanks took charge of his city and his state, and at eighty-five no one could reasonably expect him to change his mind, or the *Gazette's* stance.

In the bruising years that followed, Hugh Patterson and I could man the bridge and draw some of the shot and shell. But it was J. N. Heiskell who had to watch the substance he had gathered for his family drain away under boycott and bitter, constant abuse—well over $2 million irrevocably lost before circulation and advertising hit bottom and began the slow crawl back. He had to bear with prudent friends who came to warn him that he had passed beyond considerations of financial loss, and that his newspaper faced extinction. If he felt panic, or entertained doubt, we never knew it.

By the time I left Little Rock the *Gazette's* lonely stand had been vindicated. Governor Faubus had become a permanent resident of the statehouse but his racist maneuvers had been contained; the closed Little Rock schools had reopened and the local leadership was emerging from their storm shelters; the *Gazette* was again on sound footing. The inevitable first-person books and articles began to appear, in each of which the author seemed to have been the sole hero of the fateful time.

I told Mr. J. N.'s daughter, Elizabeth Cook, of my regret that her father's exemplary role would never be fully appreciated. "I suppose so," she said. "But, you know, if we knew the truth I suspect we would find he enjoyed it."

She is probably right. Mr. J. N.'s sense of history is complicated by a youthful, sometimes almost naive fascination with the disorders, and the scandals, of the contemporary world. He uses his institutional austerity as a foil for his sly humor and is delighted with the shock value of the contrast.

Those who have seen him in social action at the Washington meetings, fueled only by a single glass of sherry, will appreciate my astonishment when I first heard him unfurl a wonderfully bawdy story in a company of startled matrons. "You will note," he once told me primly, "that I never use a dirty word"—a semantic feat that clearly demonstrates the superfluity of Henry Miller's vocabulary.

Then there is his office, a bulwark of the Heiskell legend. He occupies this bizarre retreat even on Sunday mornings, probably I suspect, as a thin occupational excuse to escape the boredom of church without totally compromising his Presbyterian conscience. He has the magpie weakness of many editors, an inability to abandon any part of the relentless flow of paper that washes across his desk. So the old, unread newspapers and magazines and press releases rise in tottering stacks on the chairs and tables and around the walls until there is only a narrow passage to his ancient, slant-topped desk.

His wife, a gallant lady who has accompanied him across the years with a poise unruffled by public crisis or personal tragedy, tries to keep a safe distance from the untidy sanctuary. "When people ask me why Ned has never smoked," she has said, "I explain that the fire hazard is too great. When we were first married I used to complain about his office on esthetic grounds. I'm past that now, but I still insist it is unsanitary." Mr. J. N. agrees: "Of course the place is unhealthy. That's why I died so young."

But the boar's nest has a utility, too, beyond the unforgettable impression it leaves upon all who pass that way. In the old tradition, Mr. J. N. keeps his office door open in standing invitation to the lowest company minion or the most modest subscriber to bring his troubles to the seat of ultimate authority. But the residue of the postal system fills all the chairs and there is no place for the visitor to sit and dawdle. Mr. J. N. courteously arises, crosses his arms, and stands gently teetering as the conversation desperately lurches to an end. Even the most stalwart bore doesn't last long.

I suppose you would now have to go well into four figures to add up the journalists who have been exposed to his tutelage. They will recall him as a determined foe of the cliche, a comma chaser, and an unbending grammarian. I have gone many a round with him on usage and I think there were a few occasions when I won fair and square. But my victories were short-lived; if the big Webster and the Oxford sustained my point, he would reach into the ruck behind his desk for a multivolume dictionary that must have gone out of print around the time of Queen Anne and produce the citation that suited him.

Gazette alumni will recall, too, the occasional handwritten notes, unsigned but unmistakable, that appear on the bulletin board. (He has never used a typewriter, not, at least, in the modern epoch.) One such, in the middle of a crime wave, read: "I am appalled that the revolting acts of these sexual deviates continue to occur on the *Democrat's* time."

The ceremonial manner marks his rare excursions down the hall to the city room. He appeared one day before the desk of his nephew, Carroll McGaughey, in the company of a large matron vibrating with outrage. "Mrs. McConifer," he said, "may I present Mr. McGaughey. Mrs. McConifer is the president of the Federation of Garden Clubs. Mr. McGaughey is responsible for the article that has deeply offended the federation's membership. And may God have mercy on his soul."

Thus the legend has proliferated, blurring the true image as legends always do, but not, I think, losing the essence of the man. My own favorite summary anecdote goes back to 1948, not long after I came out from the Carolinas. I reminded him one morning that we had not yet formally declared in the presidential race and were now bracketed by the *Commercial Appeal,* the *Dallas Morning News,* the *Daily Oklahoman,* and even the *St. Louis Post-Dispatch,* all flying the banner of Thomas E. Dewey. He didn't, he said, entirely approve of Mr. Truman, but of course we would support the straight Democratic ticket. "I ought to know this, Mr. J. N.," I said, "but has the *Gazette* ever been anything but Democratic?" He peered out that open door to be sure he couldn't be overheard, leaned forward, and confided, "I don't like to talk about this, but the fact is we went Whig twice."

There is a tendency to assume the obituary tone in writing of a man of Mr. J. N.'s years and usually forgotten attainments. (He was, for example, appointed to the United States Senate in 1913 and must be the only former member of that body who has forbidden the use of the title—as for many years he forbade the publication of his picture in the *Gazette*, unless the circumstances were adverse.) To make certain that I have not so lapsed, I append these revealing notes on his current status and future plans:

A couple of years ago, inspecting his tail coat in preparation for a family wedding, he found it showing green with age and promptly had his tailor run up a new full-dress suit.

At about the same time he bought a Mercedes-Benz, which he drives daily to the office in the face of Mrs. J. N.'s frequently stated conviction that he constitutes Arkansas's greatest single traffic hazard.

Finally, he has one last commitment to me. He has promised to be my pallbearer. And I have no doubt he will meet that obligation, too.

John Herbert, Editor
Quincy (Massachusetts) Patriot Ledger

By Francis P. Murphy

O nce upon a time there was a meeting of obscure newspapermen upon a rusty Liberty ship for some now forgotten purpose.

The unhealthy harbor launch, which picked up our small group at the New London shore, died entirely in midchannel. But a navy launch, in the very best of health, served as a tug towing us the miles toward the Liberty standing in the Sound.

Somebody threw a Jacob's ladder over the rail and we mounted much like climbing the side of a four-story office building.

On deck commanding the operation was the flaming red head of Jack Herbert of the *Quincy Patriot Ledger*. He had brushed aside the deck crew, brushed aside the gleaming brass, to take personal charge of this new landing party.

Jack Herbert was born to command.

It is to be noted that at staff meetings Herbert sits at his desk, as editor, with jacket on and tie straight. He is in command. The other subeditors— and the "Man Who Merely Owns the Joint"—sit more comfortably in their short sleeves, at his feet.

As recently as 1930, he was a cub reporter on the *Patriot Ledger*. In three years, he was a city editor and in another three its managing editor.

Sixteen more years had passed before he became editor. They had to create the title and the job, to hold him, one imagines.

The man who owns the joint is G. Prescott Low. He and Jack arrived on the scene at the somnolent country daily at about the same time. They believe in the same things and work together as closely as brothers, perhaps more closely than most brothers.

Murphy was managing editor of the *Worcester* (Massachusetts) *Telegram* when this article first appeared, in 1960.

Their junction occurred at the same time as a beginning of the explosion into suburbia. Inhabitants of Boston were fleeing southward, throwing up ranch houses in the cow pastures. Quincy, once just a bead in a chain of communities, was becoming a part of the vast Main Street of America, which runs unbroken from Boston to Washington, D. C.

Herbert coined the slogan, "Cover the World and Don't Forget the South Shore." He had the firm conviction that the reader who was paying two cents for the *Patriot Ledger* should not be obliged to pay another two cents for a Boston newspaper to find out what else was going on.

The necessary suburban chit-chat is all in there. But Herbert's paper covers the world, too. That's one reason its circulation has gone from around eight thousand in 1930 to nearly fifty thousand today.

Taking advantage of the State Department's exchange program, Herbert has a staff of correspondents throughout the world which he calls the "poor man's New York Times service." After the State Department's exchangees have served a time in Quincy and return home, they maintain steady correspondence with Jack and he with them.

That paid off, for example, during the recent Japanese rioting. The *Patriot Ledger* had a beautiful special from a Japanese newspaperman, one-time exchangee. In addition, the *Patriot Ledger* has a large part-time staff of former Quincy and South Shore residents now living in foreign lands.

When he was city editor, Herbert began rebuilding the city staff from the ground up, hiring almost exclusively college graduates. He has also built, and this is highly necessary in a ship-building seacoast town like Quincy, a staff of maritime experts. His training school is so highly thought of by young college boys that he usually has a long list of likely candidates begging to go to work for him.

He encourages undergraduates to work for a summer or two. This gives him a chance to assess the green boughs and also tends to open up a pool of talent. (He has learned in this process that a Harvard Law School student is apt to make a damn fine reporter. The law training permits one to understand what evidence is and also to distinguish between fact and opinion.)

Like a number of editors, and unlike others, Jack (a name he dislikes; prefers John) bends to take a definite and active part in community "do good" causes. His reason is simple: "We will not stand by and see our city go to hell for the want of interest by those who should care."

Herbert travels more often and to more distant points than most. Seems to be—but isn't—away from the office as much as he is at home.

There are many reasons. When Jack is away the "Man Who Merely Owns the Joint" is apt to be home minding the store. If it so happens both are away at the same time nobody suffers. The story is organization; an operation so closely knit and carrying such knowledge of both Low's and Herbert's minds that decisions are automatic. And the organization is never scared to make the decisions. Nice healthy attitude.

Moreover, both Low—better known merely as Pres—and Herbert have close interests in foreign affairs and news about foreign affairs.

Herbert is an active member—it is not in his nature to be a passive anything—of the IPI, of the IAPA, and of the FIEJ. He is also president of the IAPA Research Center which has a fifteen-thousand-dollar Ford Foundation grant to study newspaper affairs in South America.

Don't get any ideas that Jack is so wrapped in his paper and its affairs he thinks of nought else.

He's a warm, friendly, human-type sort of being. His primary interest is in his wife—whom he, and I, and others call beautiful—and his two sons.

His second is the sea, chiefly that rough arm called the North Atlantic which batters the shores of Quincy when it wishes. And often enough tosses on land sea-going ships which are conned too close to the ledges and sands.

He has sailed in windjammers. Now prefers the softer comforts of a twenty-six-foot sea skiff. Which is not soft at all if the sea be running.

Another interest—this a necessary one—is his thoughtful busy-ness in the experimental phases (and practical phases) of newer newspaper techniques. These are basically photographic composition and wider uses of engravings instead of plate castings.

Again the organization fits into the picture. There are no rules against; no international headquarters to negotiate with or to say no. Jack is in a position to try anything or do anything which can lead to either better or merely cheaper newspaper printing.

I think both Pres and Jack are again of one mind there. What they actually want are better, simpler, and less expensive printing processes. The interesting thing is they don't want this just for themselves but for all newspapers especially in the underdeveloped countries. That's why a day rarely passes at the *Quincy Patriot Ledger* without a visitor—or visitors—from all over the world. Mecca in Quincy is the new processes department.

Dan Hicks, Editor
Monroe County (Tennessee) Democrat

By John Pennington

Dan Hicks is sitting at his cluttered desk when we arrive, left shoulder hunched against the telephone while he bangs away at a typewriter with two fingers. "Yeah? Yeah? Okay." He talks through a cigar with a jaunty upward tilt. Cradling the phone, he turns to meet his visitors, swinging heavy-rimmed glasses to the top of his head, so they're looking straight up. A smile lights his face as he says hello. He is personable, direct, outgoing, obviously turned on with living. Why would anybody want to run him out of town?

Hicks is editor of the *Monroe County Democrat,* circulation six thousand, which operates out of an aging crackerbox house just down a peaceful-looking, tree-lined street from the courthouse in Madisonville, Tennessee.

One new to the town, arriving on U.S. Route 411 from Atlanta, drives through a picturesque countryside, by rolling hills, past Indian craft shops, past establishments named Mountain View. At a glance Madisonville appears no different from a thousand other southern towns of twenty-five hundred population; the *Monroe County Democrat* appears no different from other country weekly newspapers. One feature catches the eye: A placard nailed to a porch post proclaims: "What the people *don't* know will hurt them."

Many newspapers have slogans. Some editors live up to them.

In trying to live up to his, Dan Hicks has found the editor's desk no ivory tower. He writes a column on the front page of the *Democrat* entitled, "From Where I Sit." From where he sits, he pointed out a year ago in a full page ad for National Newspaper Week, he was, during 1968 and 1969, "assaulted, shot at, threatened, robbed, and indicted." Followup research reveals that

---

Pennington was a reporter for the *Atlanta Journal-Constitution* when this article first appeared, in 1970.

149

since then he has been further intimidated and finally burned out, forced to move the newspaper to another building without the luxury of insurance coverage. No company would underwrite the risk of covering a crusading editor who made folks mad enough to unleash shotgun blasts at midnight and to set fires.

Still, Hicks was smiling and bustling around with optimism when photographer Floyd Jillson and I arrived. Things had quieted somewhat. He was no longer sleeping in his office, a .30-.30 Winchester across his desk.

"Do you still keep a gun around?" I asked.

"Oh, I keep one close," he says, sliding a stubby, worn .25 automatic pistol from his left front pocket. He flicked the safety off and back on again, fondled the weapon as though it were his best friend—and well it might be—shuffled his cigar to the other side of his mouth and slipped the pistol back into his pocket again.

In language rich with the flavor of the Tennessee hills, Hicks explains what it's like to be the object of violent disfavor in a small town. "After a while you get like an old hunting dog," he says. "Every time somebody points a gun, you lay down and cover up your ears."

He overstates his own reaction. Guns have been pointed at him more than once and, while he may duck occasionally and wonder at the nature of man, he persists in telling things as they are in Madisonville and Monroe County, and draws some comfort from the little pistol he carries in his pocket.

It's not that Hicks is an outsider riding a white charger into somebody else's business. He was born in Madisonville, played football on the high school football team. The newspaper he edits is a family tradition, having been started by his father's uncle in 1889. Dan Hicks, Sr., ran the paper for years. ("Never a better man lived than old Dan Hicks," former Mayor Henry Veal once said. "He approached news from a different angle from his son.") When "old Dan Hicks" died, one of his sons—the present editor's brother—took it over. The paper was sold out of the family for about three years, and in 1967 "young Dan Hicks" (forty-nine this October), bought it back and began to inject the front page and editorial page with vinegar and spice.

Hicks operates with a total disregard for favoritism. "I made a deal with my wife when we came here," he says. "We were going to run this thing right if we lost it the next day. We're going to operate this way as long as I'm physically able."

In one issue Hicks ran a front page story about a well-known local citizen who had engaged in a chase with police, had resisted arrest, and finally was booked on drunk and disorderly charges. His society editor never showed up for work again. The arrested man was her husband.

Hicks had been away for seventeen years when he came back to the *Democrat,* working on newspapers in Maryville, Tennessee; Virginia Beach, Virginia; Knoxville; and Clinton. But all of this only prepared him for coming back home. "Never wanted to do anything else," he says. "Never wanted to do anything but be a weekly newspaper editor. All my life I've been aiming to get back to my own newspaper, and it's taken me a long time."

It didn't take him long to ruffle some feathers. The story of his purchase of the *Monroe County Democrat* (with partners) appeared in the August 30, 1967, issue. On the following September 20, he wrote an editorial shaming fans at a high school football game in the nearby town of Vonore for harassing a black football player. "The owners of stores and restaurants in Vonore picked up our newspaper racks and threw them out in the street the day the editorial appeared," Hicks says.

This was mild stuff, a rumble before the storm. Hicks had begun to probe behind doors long closed, and the establishment had begun to resist.

"I got to riding some special interests pretty hard," Hicks says, "and somebody told me they had organized a company of thirty men who put two thousand dollars each into a pool to start another newspaper and run me out of town. That kind of shocks you when you're operating on a shoestring in the beginning and you're running scared already. But I had one ace in the hole. I know how hard it is to find somebody who knows how to run a newspaper. So I laid with it and didn't get excited and that threat faded away."

The pressure continued to build.

"There was a clique here that had ruled the county for years and years. I was a threat to their little empire. . . . The next thing that happened, some of them went to my partners and threatened to withdraw advertising from the newspaper if they didn't sit on me and get me to calm down. So one of my partners came and spent a day with me in prayer meeting trying to get me to go back to the old bland way of operating. But I wouldn't do it, and he put his part up for sale and got out."

Now Hicks has three partners, each, like himself, owning 25 percent of the paper. "They've never said a word to me. I do what I damn well please and they've been real good about it."

What Hicks damn well pleases has not gone over too well with some, and he gets most of his advertising from the nearby, and bigger, town of Sweetwater. His circulation blankets the county.

Hicks edited the *Democrat* vigorously for a year without getting beaten or shot at.

"When I first came back here," he recalls, "one of my friends told me that if I needed any automobile parts or accessories, not to pay retail price, to go to the county highway department. I could buy them real cheap out there.

Well, that sounded kind of funny, so I got to poking around. I went to the sheriff, whom I didn't know then, and told him. He said he'd investigate. He came back and told me there wasn't anything to it; everything was clean. But I poked around some more and found out there was a bootlegger working out there who every payday hauled a tremendous amount of moonshine in and sold it to the employees and they'd have a big orgy every payday, get roaring drunk. When people found out I was interested, they started calling and telling me things. It turned out the old boy running the department really had a deal going out there.

"In the petition filed to oust him from office later, he was charged with making long-distance personal telephone calls and charging them to the county; drawing an allowance of one hundred dollars a month for operating a car while he was driving a county car; he was buying automobile parts which the department never received; he never took bids on anything and paid high prices for everything. . . ."

On the day the department head was called into court for ouster proceedings, Hicks got his first taste of real retaliation. He walked from the courthouse to his office and saw two young men standing out front. He spoke to them. "That's the last thing I knew for ten or fifteen seconds," he says. "They both swung around and started hitting me in the face. They pulled my shirt off and knocked a tooth out and started kicking me in the ribs. And then they ran."

Hicks found out later, by offering a reward, that the two boys had been hired by "the head bootlegger in the county," for thirty dollars and a gallon of moonshine whisky each, to beat him up. He took warrants for them, they were apprehended, identified by witnesses, and convicted of assault.

A few days later more violence was aimed at Dan Hicks. "I was sitting in the office one night," he says, "writing an editorial about people who beat people up, when somebody shot at me two times. They rode by in a car and fired twice with a double-barrel shotgun. If they had hesitated a split second, instead of hitting the side of the building they would have hit me right in the face."

Hicks got a good look at the car and a few minutes later learned that a car matching the description had wrecked just outside of town. There were two men in it, and they had a shotgun with two spent shells in it. Hicks told a patrolman, "I believe you've got my boys." He took warrants for them charging attempted murder and the case went to court. A hung jury tied up the first trial and the case went to court again. Again the jury was deadlocked. "The third time they submitted to a small charge—throwing a missile—and I had no choice but to let them go on that."

A week later another shotgun blast was aimed at the *Monroe County Democrat*, blasting a hole alongside the closed front door at chest level. Again

Hicks saw the car. "I know who did it," he says. "But I've never been able to prove it. I had such a bad experience with the other one, I just didn't push it."

In the meantime, the road department supervisor who had been the object of ouster proceedings pleaded illness and won a delay. Two years later the case still had not been prosecuted.

But Hicks's problems continued. In addition to racial prejudice, bootleggers, improper conduct of government business, he editorialized against bad street conditions, the town's water department, the board of mayor and aldermen, a Ku Kluxer who came to town selling memberships and bedsheets, a drive-in theater that showed "filthy" movies, a teen nightclub that he thought improperly supervised. Hicks knew no sacred cows. He developed a sense of outrage at whatever appeared improper, and put the burden of the public spotlight on the community.

The community put the burden of loneliness on him and his family, and some tried to burden him with fear.

If he knew fear, Hicks did not let it show, either in his personal conduct or in the editorials that he continued to hammer out of his office typewriter with two fingers.

After the two shootings he got in his car one evening and drove off over a bed of tacks that somebody had laid out in welcome. The result was several flat tires.

Windows were smashed in his shop repeatedly. The telephone rang with harassment. Callers threatened his life. A letter to the editor, which Hicks printed, said, "Nobody ever shot at our other editor, when he was here. Wonder why? Why can't we have a quiet peaceful town like we once had?"

Hicks considered the peace and quiet "we once had" a veneer covering governmental sanction of corruption, mismanagement of the public trust. He felt that the violent reaction to his newspaper revelations corroborated this view. He kept on.

One morning in the winter of 1968 he found his office ransacked. "All my cameras and my typewriter and adding machine, everything that was close to the side door there, was gone," he says.

At first he thought it a routine robbery. And then he found the note, scribbled on a piece of "mirror paper" used in offset printing and hung on his negative line with a clothespin. "You stupid SOB," it said, "see how easy it would be to put you out of business? You let up and your equipment will be returned." Hicks did not let up and he never saw the equipment again.

Following that incident, he wrote in the *Democrat:*

"I've been beaten up, shot at, threatened repeatedly, and robbed since I took over as the editor of the *Democrat*. It appears that there is a group of people in this county who would like for me to go somewhere else."

The year 1969 brought Hicks honor from outside his circulation area, more violence at home. He became the first editor ever to be awarded simultaneously the Lovejoy Award for courage in reporting and the Golden Quill Award for editorial excellence, both national honors. He also won the Community Service Award of the University of Tennessee–Tennessee Press Association, and several other awards.

In late summer Hicks was embroiled anew in controversy with the board of mayor and aldermen of Madisonville. On one street, he says, were a teen nightclub with more beer cans around it every morning than around the local adult beer joint, an illicit establishment which sold beer and moonshine whisky to minors, and nearby an adult poker game with high stakes running twenty-four hours a day. Hicks labeled the thoroughfare "Sin Street," and when the board of mayor and aldermen failed to order the offensive beer joint closed on the recommendation of the county juvenile judge, he shamed them editorially. He criticized the teen club which, he says, caused more violence and disturbance in the town than anything else, until finally it was ordered closed. When Hicks attempted to photograph the closing, the manager's wife and a gang of youths threatened to beat him. He pulled his pistol and held them off. The woman charged him with carrying a pistol illegally. He was indicted on the charge, pleaded guilty to it, and paid a fifty-dollar fine and thirty-five-dollar court costs.

Tennessee law does not provide for a license to carry a pistol, Hicks says. But with the threat of assault always on him his .25 automatic is a constant companion. "I'm illegal," he says candidly. "Anybody wants to litigate me, they can get me."

In the winter of 1969, having experienced violence and the threat of violence, and confronted with telephone threats that his building on the town square would be burned, Hicks set up an office vigil. He slept in his office, sitting upright in the same chair he worked in, with a .30-.30 Winchester and his pistol on the desk in front of him.

One night a car stopped, an empty beer can broke through a front window, and a car sped away. The next night, another car stopped and Hicks got a direct view of its occupant, a teenager. The boy threw a beer can through a window and sped away. Although Hicks had convinced himself earlier that he was tired of one-way violence and would shoot his next assailant, he could not bring himself to raise the rifle against the young man. Instead he asked the owner of the building in which his office was located to talk with the boy's father.

"I slept in my office thirty-one nights in a row," Hicks recalls. "The night I went home was when it burned down."

At one o'clock one morning last December, somebody set fire to the office at a side door. A combination of fire and water damage drove Hicks and the *Monroe County Democrat* to another location—a nearby building the paper had occupied years before when his father was editor.

Last February the board of aldermen adopted a resolution asking Hicks to stay away from their meetings. It may have been at that time that Hicks decided to run for city alderman next time around. At any rate, the resolution said city officials "have come to the conclusion that it is in the best interest of our town, due to the unfavorable publicity brought out by the editorials by the editor of the *Democrat*, that we request that Mr. Hicks refrain from attending our meetings."

"I sat there and listened to the resolution," Hicks says. "When they got through they looked at me like they expected me to get up and walk out, and I just kept on taking notes. So they went on to other business."

When we visited Hicks in late summer, he told us he had offered as a candidate for the board of aldermen. He was not optimistic that he could be elected. To offer, he had to get voter signatures on a petition. "There's a colored man running who got sixty-seven names without a turndown," Hicks says. "I got turned down five times before I got ten names."

Hicks had learned already that the cost of conscience in a small town is great. An editor in a town of twenty-five hundred lives close to those who don't like him and what he is trying to do, and to others who are afraid to show friendship for fear of sharing in the retaliation against him. Social life is affected, as well as professional life.

Hicks relates, "One professional man here that I grew up with said to me one day, 'You'll forgive me if I don't associate with you, Dan. If I did, I'd lose all my clients.' "

"What is it like living in this kind of tension?" the visitors ask Hicks. "What does it do to you inside?"

"It doesn't do anything to me," he says, obviously indulging again in overstatement. "It worries my wife. She's spent a whole lot of money on tranquilizers."

"What about your children?"

"It's been rough on my kids. My boy has been threatened many times. But they agree with what I'm doing and they come and say, 'Daddy, you're doing the right thing and we don't care.' Well, I know they care. But they've been real good."

"What about your social life?"

"My wife and I don't have any social life. We're not invited anywhere. We know the animosity exists so we don't invite anybody, because it would be embarrassing to them to turn us down and embarrassing to us to be turned down. The friends who visit us are friends from other towns."

As this discussion ends, Hicks invites us to lunch with the Madisonville Kiwanis Club, of which, it turns out, he is president. A dozen professional men gather once a week for the meetings. His relationship with them is loose and easy, as is his relationship with many people on the street. People wave and communicate with him freely, it seems. But they don't invite him home to dinner.

We left Hicks with a cigar in his mouth, his glasses looking straight up, a big grin on his face, a slight bulge in his pocket, promising to call him after the city election on September 1 to see how badly he had got beaten in his race for the board of aldermen.

Dan Hicks answered his telephone the day after the election with greater than his usual exuberance, it seemed.

"How did you do, Dan?"

"I won!"

The crusading editor had made it. Not big, but he made it. Eight men had run for five aldermanic positions, and the top five won. Hicks was number five down the line, winning a position on the board that had invited him to stay away.

"We have a new mayor and an entirely new board of aldermen taking office on October 1," Hicks explained. "We're all nonpartisan, independent. We have one man on the board with a master's degree, three with bachelor degrees. Another is a professional with specialized training. This is the most educated group the city has ever had in office."

"How will you cover city government meetings now?"

"I don't know. It's not going to be easy. But I can tell you one thing: I'll jump on myself editorially as fast as I will anybody else if I do something stupid."

Even over the telephone, I can tell that Hicks has a cigar in his mouth, his glasses pushed to the top of his head. "How does your wife feel about your victory?"

"She feels a lot better now. She had been worried, had a fixation that everybody was down on us. She realizes now there are a lot of good people here. They don't come forward, but they're here, and they're behind us." He paused a moment and chuckled. "We have our own Silent Majority."

Dan Hicks sounded very pleased over the telephone from Madisonville, Tennessee.

Lee Hills, Executive Editor
Knight Newspapers

By Don Shoemaker

O nce upon a long ago as a kid in Ohio I knew a boy who played a mean amateur xylophone, a talent which is so rare that I have not met it since.

This dexterous chap—his name was Harvey—comes to mind when I see Knight Newspapers executive editor Lee Hills bending over his chores in the *Miami Herald* building.

One of these early days the *Herald* will go clattering into new quarters, where everyone will have a desk and Lee most certainly will have an office. An editor in perpetual transit between Detroit and Miami, he works for the most part standing at a long table in the quarters of *Herald* managing editor George Beebe.

There Lee paces and handles letters, reports and neat rows of office papers, passing from one to the other and back with the dexterity of a xylophonist hammering the bars.

This is not inappropriate, for the man who describes himself as a "frustrated musician" (everybody in his family played something, but he never had time to learn) obviously works from a score. As publisher John S. Knight once observed, "Lee never leaves anything to chance."

The presidency of ASNE gives him the third leg on journalism's president trophy, for he is a past national president of APME and of SDX.

This should not greatly burden a man who actually unwinds the harder he works.

In 1955 he won a Pulitzer Prize for spot reporting for the *Detroit Free Press* when he stepped out of his editor's role to birddog critical wage negotiations in the auto industry.

Shoemaker was editor of the *Miami Herald* when this article first appeared, in 1962.

He kept at the job day and night, putting together bits of information into a mosaic which correctly described the turn of labor-management talks. Often he slept in the office sending out for food and fresh shirts. When the negotiators reached the precise agreement Lee had predicted, they staggered red-eyed out of the bargaining room. Observers who covered the Hills coverage recall that he, by contrast, was bright-eyed and bushy-tailed at the finish.

Seven years later Lee remains at weight (155), eats everything in sight, drinks socially, and owns an updated medical report which says he has the blood pressure of a twenty-five-year-old. If you have him in for a steak of an evening, he is likely to beg the scraps, tote them home and eat them for breakfast.

Lee Hills came out of Granville, North Dakota, and broke into newspapering at Price, Utah, where he was editing the town's small paper weeks after he left high school.

As he remembers Utah, this was "one of many forks in the road. At nineteen I had a chance to buy two weeklies and build a hometown future. I decided instead to go back to school."

He had quit Brigham Young University to help support his family, and now he was off to the University of Missouri School of Journalism on a bank loan secured simply by his signature. Thirty years later, in 1959, he had entered Missouri's Hall of Honor, and in 1960 he delivered the thirty-first Don R. Mellett Lecture.

The text of that talk is a clue to the man. In the Carolinas, a small daily once bore the legend over its masthead, "The Only Paper In The World That Gives A Damn About Onslow County." The Hills dream of newspaper responsibility is just as specialized.

In the Mellett lecture he paid his respects to crusading journalism but he noted that "this is the time of specialists" who can root out facts and explain them understandably.

"I venture to predict," he said, "that before many years pass our major newspapers will be able to find and willing to pay bright young medical graduates who will write about medicine, educators who will quit the campus to write about education, physicists who will desert the laboratory for the city room, and down and along the lines of information, expertly dispensed and readable, for which a growingly intelligent public hungers."

This conclusion as to the future must have been the product of lengthy brooding over the present and the past. Certainly it reflects Lee Hills's experience.

His first big-time job with the *Oklahoma City Times* in 1929 led him from a beat to the copydesk to political writer and then to editorial writer. Meantime he managed to study law at night, and while city editor on the *Times's* competitor, the *Oklahoma News*, he got his law degree and was admitted to the Oklahoma bar in 1934.

Lee uses his high school shorthand to good advantage. It helped him along as reporter and news editor of the *Cleveland Press*, then to the executive level in 1936 as associate editor of the *Indianapolis Times*. In 1938 he was back at the *Oklahoma News* as editor—the youngest in the country.

Scripps-Howard service then being somewhat akin to shuttling from charge to charge in Methodism, Lee was transferred in 1939 to the *Memphis Press-Scimitar* as an associate editor, then back to Cleveland in 1940 as news editor of the *Press*.

In 1942 he joined the Knight organization in Miami, soon becoming managing editor of the *Herald*.

The rest is more modern history: European war correspondent (he can still get into his uniform) for the *Herald* and the *Chicago Daily News* in World War II; executive editor of the *Herald*; then executive editor of the *Free Press*, in 1951; and the executive editor of the Knight Newspapers in 1959.

With Lee's major responsibilities divided between Miami and Detroit, where he heads up the whole operation, this involves keeping a wardrobe in each town. Through some uncanny communication with fate he manages to attend all the hurricanes in Miami and to catch most of the blizzards in Detroit.

In Florida, where I see Lee most, you have to do everything fast—including, as Jim Knight is wont to point out, sleep.

Once when he was courting the lovely Eileen, who died of a heart attack last year, Lee ran a stop sign and met head-on with another Miami motorist who was legitimately claiming the same air space.

As Whitey Kelley of the *Charlotte Observer* and an old Miami hand recalls, Lee immediately buzzed the *Herald* and gave it the story. The paper was busy scourging the gamblers and feeling various public pressures. Lee ordered his mishap on the front page to show that the *Herald* played no favorites.

Not incidentally, Hills-directed pursuit of the racketeers brought the *Herald* a Pulitzer in 1951 and rid Dade (Miami) County of "the syndicate." The town can be accused of a lot of things, but no longer is it a haven for the rackets, which had flourished to such an extent that J. Edgar Hoover is supposed to have remarked: "If I could stretch a net over 23rd and Collins on Miami Beach, I could end crime in America."

The putative president of ASNE began to give the *Free Press* much of his attention and pulled it up from third to first place in Michigan circulation before the merger of Detroit's *News* and *Times*.

This was done, as it was done at the *Herald*, with revamped typography, tighter writing, more white space, and pursuit of excellence in staffing.

When Lee landed in Detroit as helmsman in 1951, he was regarded with some suspicion by the old hands. This attitude sharpened when the new editor criticized—wrongly, as the defendants knew—*Free Press* handling of a particular story.

So the editor took space on the bulletin board and abjectly retracted. All hands acknowledged that the new boy had an open mind as well as an open door.

In Detroit Lee Hills is conceded heft as a civic leader, although he cannot give that city all of his time. (Neither can the automobile tycoons, who have plants and responsibilities in several cities.)

At one point he held membership on sixteen or seventeen boards, all of them civic, since it is a Jack Knight-Lee Hills principle that Knight editors shy away from corporation board rooms. Now he is a member of a mere eight or nine, having delegated *Free Press* representation.

Among them is a directorship of the Detroit Athletic Club.

This is a kind of state of grace for the auto city's business community. Nominees actually campaign for board membership, rallying friends much as mothers rally the girls to get Gwendolyn into the Junior League. When Lee edged out a tycoon whose lineage is so famous that it is a (nice) four-letter household word, his friends figured he had arrived.

The range of Hills's activity as executive editor of Jack Knight's five-paper group has fringes which reach to Charlotte (*Observer* and *News*) and occasionally brush Akron (*Beacon Journal*).

When the Knights bought into Charlotte, Lee phrased the necessary announcements and supervised the revamping of the *Observer*. He also instilled a sense of purpose and an air of excitement into a stodgy but much loved old journalistic mishmash. There is a youthful legend in Charlotte that the Hills enthusiasm got people so much on their toes that the urinals in the gentlemen's walk had to be raised a clear foot.

The Hills enthusiasm for a job of work is a kind of trademark for a man who does not dramatize himself but delights in dramatizing other people.

When he hired C. A. "Pete" McKnight to edit the *Observer*, he first immured this scarcely shy character in a room with a typewriter and invited him to grind out a prospectus of what a new editor might do.

Pete did. And he was hired. And nobody could be happier with the consequent promotion of McKnight than Hills himself. It is the kind of vicarious satisfaction in somebody else's achievement that seems to please him most.

What about hobbies?

Well, Hills has a precious few of them. He will fish if asked, but he much prefers swimming, both in Detroit and in his own pool in Miami.

No gem polisher, he hones his head bone on better than half the best-seller novels each year and most of the prize nonfiction entries.

A reserved type, he can mix with the folk easily. On such occasions he may essay a faintly vocal—though not loud—sports coat on the theory that a newspaper editor need not resemble the director of a funeral parlor.

Long after that first fork in the road in Utah, Lee was led up on the mountaintop for a look at a special vista. To most of us in the profession who at best can only parlay the impecunious, it must have seemed like the Promised Land.

I'm not privy to any secrets, but I suspect that Lee's professional kinship with the Knights and a certain personal affection precluded any divorcement. At any rate, this was another fork in the road. Like back at the ranch, in Utah.

A personnel evaluation of Lee Hills once faulted him for a "tendency to be too optimistic about subordinates and too considerate of their welfare."

This could be true. But, as we know, personnel evaluators are hardly human. The question is whether any overevaluated subordinate ever let him down, and to this he says, no. As to the welfare state in the newspaper industry, probably it could stand heavier appropriations.

This is a miniature of a friend, who is also a boss. It is at times irreverent, which such pre-presidential profiles by precedent are supposed to be.

But it is also a synopsis of a career which, to date, involves the parceling out of Pulitzer Prize winnings to city room stars after deduction for taxes and more humility than any of us claim as a mere matter of privilege. This is quite a lot of newspaper guy, if I do say so myself.

Robert Melvin Hitt, Jr., Editor
Charleston (South Carolina) Post

By Frank R. Gilbreth

T he first time I saw Red Hitt was in 1936 when he started as a reporter for the *Charleston* (South Carolina) *News and Courier*, where I had been working for a couple of years.

The first thing you noticed about him was the mop of flaming red hair atop as raw-boned a body as ever was produced by the thriving municipality of Bamberg, South Carolina (population then about two thousand), where his mother and father ran the weekly paper. He weighed 160 pounds which barely covered his six-foot three-inch frame, and he walked with a slight stoop as if somewhat embarrassed by his height. His face was long and Lincolnesque, with dark brown eyes and bushy, almost black eyebrows.

After you had sized him up physically, there was his voice—a deep bass that you could hear all the way across the newsroom, even when he was whispering. When he wasn't whispering—when, for instance, he leaned back those long bones for a laugh—you couldn't hear yourself think. Don't tell me! I had a desk right next to him.

For the vital statistics, he was born Robert Melvin Hitt, Jr., June 12, 1914, and started working on the *Bamberg Herald* with his parents when he started grammar school. By the time he entered the Citadel in 1931, he had done everything there was to do on the paper. He wrote stories, put them into type on an ancient Model L Linotype, made up pages, and hand-fed an old flatbed press which had been purchased secondhand in 1892.

After graduating from the Citadel in 1935 he reported to his father for work but was refused a job. (Southern weeklies were in shaky condition in those Depression days.) He wrote letters to a number of dailies, seeking work. None too modestly he outlined his many qualifications, to the end that

Gilbreth was assistant publisher and vice-president of the *Charleston* (South Carolina) *Post-News and Courier* when this article first appeared, in 1966.

the letter he sent to the *Greenville* (South Carolina) *News* was posted on the bulletin board with an unkind legend blue-penciled across it saying, "You're too good for us, brother."

In desperation that fall he took a job as grammar school principal in the crossroads town of Smoaks, South Carolina. After five weeks he had raced sixth grade pupils through a history book that he learned was supposed to last all year and he knew then he was in the wrong business.

In October, he read a news story saying that $50 million had been appropriated to start the National Youth Administration. Being a youth, he figured he was eminently qualified to be a national director so he got off a letter to President Roosevelt saying so. The White House sent a letter back saying Aubrey Williams, a protégé of Eleanor, already had the job. He wrote Aubrey, offering to serve as state director, but a college professor had already been selected. Doggedly, he wrote the professor and got appointed a regional director to supervise the NYA in a nine-county area. So, January 2, 1936, found him at the age of twenty-one, in Charleston with a private secretary, three stenographers, and a New Deal function to perform with no directions except to see that some needy youths were employed doing something.

A couple of weeks passed and Red, upon emerging from a meeting of school superintendents, was told that Thomas R. Waring, then city editor and now editor, of the *News and Courier* wanted to see him. At NYA headquarters he got the same message. Visions of a front page splash about the new NYA chieftain and his plans for salvaging the youth of nine counties passed before his eyes.

"I thought I was a pretty big wheel," he recalls, "so I said hell, I'll play hard to get. Late that afternoon I figured Tom had sweated enough so I returned his call. He said could I drop by to see him."

This was something of a letdown, but Red went to his apartment, put on his new suit, slicked his hair just in case a photo was wanted and dropped by the newspaper plant after supper.

He was interviewed all right, but not for a page-one story. There was an opening on the city staff and the starting pay was fifteen dollars a week.

"I snapped it up before Tom could change his mind," Red says.

So that's when I first met him and he's been "working" on the Charleston papers ever since.

I put the word "working" in quotes because the fact is that he is one of those lucky people who can get more done with less effort than any character I have ever unforgettably met.

In a matter of weeks, he had news sources in Charleston eating out of his fairly mammoth and freckled hand. If he needed a ride to the police station to check a story, they'd send a squad car. If he was too busy to get to the station, they'd telephone and give him the dope. And sometimes, if he was too busy to be tied up on the phone, they'd write down the facts and send them to him.

I don't know how to describe the quality he has of attracting people and making them work for him—but he's a genius at it, and it explains why he's had the time to bring his golf handicap down to five and to take time off to make speeches all over the country.

The quality is part personality and part his looks. He towers above most people and that shock of red hair—now a distinguished silver-white, but still one hell of a shock—makes him stand out in a crowd. And that deep bass—he has sung for years in the St. Phillip's Protestant Episcopal church choir—attracts attention, even when he tries to mute it, which isn't always. He likes to talk, he's witty and he's—well—engaging! All in all, people simply don't forget him.

Jack Hornaday, a veteran syndicate man, told me that a few years ago he invited Red to play in the member-guest golf tournament at Sleepy Hollow, Tarrytown, New York.

"After a couple of hours in the clubhouse, everyone there knew Red," said Jack. "Damnedest thing I ever saw. And you know, people are still asking me, 'When are you going to bring that fellow Red Hitt up here to play again?'"

That's the kind of impact he makes. And he's such a good speaker that he could stay on the road all the time, if he wanted to. For instance, the Jack Tar Hotel organization flew him to San Francisco a few years ago to emcee the grand opening of its new $12 million hotel out there.

To get back to the chronology, though, in the spring of 1938, Red was hurrying back to Charleston after a weekend in North Carolina. Two flat tires caused him to be three hours late reporting in, and on his typewriter was a note from the boss saying, "See me at once." Braced for a stern lecture if not dismissal, he waited for Tom Waring to return from lunch. The two went into a corner of the city room and Tom said, "What do you know about sports?" Red replied, "Not much." And Tom said, "Well, you'd better start learning because you are now the sports editor."

The sports editor had quit in a huff over the weekend and Red had a new assignment. He had put out the sports page a few times on Sundays but he never had been a really ardent sports fan.

Fortunately he had friends in the composing room, including the foreman who appointed himself as a special committee to monitor and correct Red's headlines—until the new sports editor came to know that the Chicago Americans were the White Sox, not the Cubs, and that the Yankees ordinarily didn't clash with such teams as the St. Louis Braves or the Philadelphia Giants.

He began a daily sports column which, naturally, was labeled "Hitt's Runs and Errors," and within a few weeks the sports department was functioning with unprecedented smoothness. He boned up on baseball and football and things like that and his authoritative (well, at least he knew the teams' nicknames) column was deemed one of the best features in the paper.

Five years later, management of the Charleston newspapers decided that the *Evening Post* needed a reorganization. Hitt was offered the job of news editor and with it a free hand to do whatever he thought necessary to revitalize and improve the newspaper. The staff was composed of four old-timers, including the editor: two female reporters, a society editor, a police reporter-sports editor, and two male reporters.

Hitt took over the city desk on a Monday morning in an atmosphere icy with resentment. The old-timers didn't cotton to the idea of the lanky, young redhead from the "other" newspaper moving in. The reporters had been deliberately accumulating copy for days and they flooded his desk with more material than he could handle in a week.

"I wasn't very happy those first few months," he recalls. "I understood the resentment and I knew I just had to wear it down. It took a lot of time."

By the end of World War II, the old-timers had come around. The *Post* had a new look and Hitt was gently but firmly in control. His title changed to managing editor and he was given carte blanche to build up a staff. Circulation began to climb and it has done so ever since—from a little over twenty thousand when he moved in to more than forty thousand today, making the *Post* the largest afternoon paper in the state by a comfortable ten thousand margin.

Red was named editor in 1953 and a director of the publishing companies in 1963. He brought to the editorial page a positiveness the *Post* had not known for years. He has been active in all phases of civic life and it's doubtful if any small-town boy has ever been more successful at cracking Charleston's citadel of "high society." In 1948 he was president simultaneously of the Country Club of Charleston, the Lions Club, a vice-president of the Chamber of Commerce, and commodore of the Carolina Yacht Club. He was elected a director of the APME Association in 1950 and has just completed a term as president of the South Carolina Press Association. In 1963 the Citadel awarded him an honorary Doctor of Laws degree. He joined ASNE in 1946. He and Mrs. Hitt have five children, the youngest nine years old, and two sons-in-law.

His newsroom, like Red himself, is alert but relaxed and the turnover of personnel has been unusually small. He strongly believes in letting his key men have their heads. He doesn't remember ever issuing an order but his staffers say his booming voice carries with it a high degree of persuasiveness. The boys in the composing room who knew him "back when" still, for reasons he can't remember, call him "Joe."

All in all, his is a "stay loose" operation, especially when big news breaks on the deadline. And the loosest man in the shop is always Editor Hitt whose creed is that rules and policy must never get in the way of sound judgment. His golf handicap has risen to seven and his office is often vacant (he leaves as decoys a pair of glasses and a half-filled pipe on his desk and an old coat on his coatrack), but miraculously he gets the job done in spades and somehow manages to be on the scene when big news is breaking and he's needed.

William H. Hornby, Editor
The Denver Post

By Robert W. Chandler

William H. Hornby, editor of the *Denver Post*, is not your common, ordinary, garden-variety editor. He's more of a Rocky Mountain Renaissance man, with a variety of accomplishments and interests the breadth of which continually impresses friends and acquaintances.

There is, for example, Hornby the organization leader, who as a former chairman of the ASNE's FoI committee nurtured the continuing shift of the organization into a strongly activist role in FoI matters.

Then there is Hornby the readership man, who with others worked mightily and effectively to help make certain that editors retained a major voice in readership research matters as they became a subject of national interest in the newspaper business.

Hornby is the pourer of oil on troubled waters, the humorist who managed—while he served as the society's secretary—to make the minutes of board meetings interesting reading.

But there's another William Harry (not a physical description, obviously) Hornby who manages to find time for other activities almost staggering in their number and diversity.

Hornby is an editor—and former copyreader, slot man, and editorial writer—of the graphite pencil school who, given his lack of familiarity with most things mechanical, now contemplates uneasily the *Post's* scheduled conversion to an electronic newsroom.

He's a columnist who writes regularly for a small group of Montana newspapers which his family controls. He offers an erudite discussion of Montana history, the state's current social problems, and a variety of other subjects which come to his facile mind.

Chandler was editor and publisher of the *Bend* (Oregon) *Bulletin* when this article first appeared, in 1979.

(Over the years, an editor of the newspapers in which the columns appear says Hornby's column has attracted a "few" letters. A more recent addition to the newspapers' editorial pages, a potpourri written by Bill's wife, Helen, and edited by Bill to the tune of anguished cries from Helen, has drawn mail "by the bagful." So much for a Stanford degree in journalism cum laude, graduate study in London, and thirty years of experience.)

Hornby, the fly fisherman, reads everything written on the subject. (He reads constantly, in any event, on almost any subject ever written.) Fishing companions say he is more successful at reading about fly fishing than he is at catching fish.

Hornby, the historian, serves as president of the Colorado Historical Society and has written about the history of the Intermountain West.

Hornby, the public speaker, speaks any place, at any time, on any subject. He writes a new speech for each appearance, a rarity in these days of the canned discourse.

Hornby, the businessman, never has money in his pocket. If he does start the day with a few sous on hand, he's likely to drop them before the day ends. Janitors at the *Post* bid for the job of cleaning his office. His secretary draws extra pay because she must furnish him small sums, soon forgotten, for parking fees, traffic tickets, and cab fares. Yet he serves as president of a profitable small newspaper group and is a director of a successful bank in Wyoming.

Hornby comes equipped with the usual biographical data. He was born in Kalispell, Montana, on Bastille Day, 1923, and went to school in Missoula, where he attained note as a high school orator and thespian. He entered Stanford three months before Pearl Harbor.

He had a typical checkered college career, thanks to the United States Army, and eventually wound up in China in the Signal Corps. There's a story only perhaps apocryphal, that General Albert Wedemeyer's telephone refused to work for a week after Hornby hooked it up.

(The Chinese language he had learned, courtesy of an army training program, was so far in the past it was of little value when he returned to that country with ASNE's China I in 1972.)

Then it was back to Stanford for a master's degree. Hornby and a small group of early returning veterans made shambles of the school's grading system when they competed with the girls and 4-Fs with which the school had filled its student body during the war years. They also made shambles of a series of roadside bars to which they repaired after lunch to drink beer and solve the problems of the world. Much beer was consumed; the world's problems seem to have survived the onslaught.

Then it was off to London for graduate study, a series of jobs, and back to the West Coast before he returned to Montana to pay some attention to his family's lumber interests. That palled. Soon he joined the *Great Falls Tribune* and, later, shifted to the *Post*.

He and Helen have reared two children, John Sullivan, editor and publisher of the *Livingston* (Montana) *Enterprise,* and Mary Hornby, about ready to finish college and to attend graduate school in journalism. Life must not have been too hectic in the Hornby household in spite of Helen's claims to the contrary.

Reading and writing and newspapering and his family take up most of his time. He gave up golf after a disastrous experience in Kalispell. When his editor friends grab up their tennis racquets, he quietly heads for a book or a bar. If he's home he may pick up a shovel and pair of pruning shears and head for the rose garden, which is his pride and joy.

Josh Horne, Editor and Publisher
Rocky Mount (North Carolina) Telegram

By Miles H. Wolff

J osh Horne is a big man—bluff and hearty. He is easily one of the best-known newspapermen in North Carolina. Editors and publishers all over the country call him by his first name.

In one election for directors of the Associated Press, he came in second. The only person getting more votes was the eminent Robert McLean, longtime AP president and publisher of the *Philadelphia Bulletin.* An election of this kind is something of a popularity contest.

On the other hand, Josh's paper, the *Rocky Mount Telegram,* is *not* one of the best-known newspapers in the country. It could hardly be compared to the *Times* of either New York or London. That is not to say that it is not a respectable small-city daily. But it *is* small. Josh says it is in the tadpole class.

This situation makes for interesting meditation—how a small-town editor and publisher became so widely known. Two things could be mentioned as helping push him into the limelight.

The first is obvious. It is his disposition. He simply exudes good nature, laughs easily and loudly, and can more than hold his own when convention storytellers get together.

The other is not so obvious. It comes under the heading of fortuitous circumstance.

Back some forty-five years ago, there were eight newspapers in North Carolina wanting to obtain an Associated Press membership. That was long before the Supreme Court had forced a change in the rules and it was possible then for newspapers to have "protest rights." It happened that three

---

Wolff was executive editor of the *Greensboro* (North Carolina) *Daily News* when this article first appeared, in 1958.

newspapers in the larger towns had exerted their protest rights and prevented the eight newspapers from securing AP service.

Josh was selected to make the pitch for the "outs" at a New York meeting. He did, and was turned down.

When he left the meeting, Kent Cooper, then a secondary executive in AP, followed him outside. He told Josh not to be discouraged, that he had a plan. The plan was soon revealed. The newspapers holding to the "rights" were informed of an increased assessment to cover what the AP lost from withholding membership to the eight petitioners. It didn't take long for the three to reconsider and Josh won his fight.

As a result of this, Josh was made a second vice-president of the Associated Press the following year. This began a long association which later brought him a twelve-year term as director. At AP board meetings, Josh was the leader of tadpole row. Other members were Stuart Perry of Adrian, Michigan; Houston Harte of Texas; and Roy Roberts of Kansas City. Just how Roy rated this small-city lineup is not clear.

Josh founded his newspaper in 1911 because, to hear him tell it, he was hungry. Prior to that time, he had sold newspapers on the streets of Rocky Mount and had worked for a short period on a now-defunct journal there. He launched his own sheet with ten thousand dollars, of which seven thousand dollars was borrowed. When a fire ruined some of his equipment during the first year, he was convinced that the bank would call his loan. Not only did the bank not do this, but it and the three others in Rocky Mount offered to lend him money. To the outsider, this indicates the Rocky Mount banks must have had their eye on a promising young newspaper publisher. Josh was so pleased that he vowed never to leave Rocky Mount.

There is no question that the newspaper has been successful. Asked if he hadn't made "a pot of money," Josh burst into laughter and then replied, "It would have to be a small pot. But I ain't suffering."

The thing Josh is most proud of is his seventeen-year stint with the State Board of Conservation. He apparently really took charge at a time when nothing of the kind was being done in North Carolina. Some of the accomplishments were the erection of historical markers, rural electrification, and the beginning of a program of advertising.

And during those seventeen years, Josh says, he "never took the first nickel for travel, per diem or anything else." It was a labor of love.

There is another work dear to his heart. That is the YMCA. He has been vice-president of the Rocky Mount Y for thirty years and a member of the state board of directors for a like time.

"To get into heaven," he says, "if St. Peter misses the page on my work with the YMCA, I'm a goner."

This doesn't cover nearly all the Horne activities. For example, he's vice-president of a television station in Greenville, North Carolina, he's on the board of Press Wireless in New York, director of a bank and a motor club, president of the Rocky Mount Sanitarium, chairman of the airport commission, trustee of Duke University, and a member of the board of High Point College.

For some years, it was not unusual to see Josh squiring a newspaper lovely such as Hedda Hopper or Sheila Graham in New York or Washington. That is a thing of the past. He married an attractive widow this year.

For several years, Josh gradually has been turning the operation of his newspaper over to executives who have been with him for a long time. Not only that, he is giving stock in the paper to these same executives, as rapidly as he can do so without incurring a gift tax.

If he lives to be one hundred or maybe less, Josh probably won't own even a tadpole newspaper.

L. D. Hotchkiss, Editor
Los Angeles Times

By Richard F. Pourade

"Hotch" of the *Times*.

That generally is the way newspapermen refer to L. D. Hotchkiss, editor, as well as managing editor, of the *Los Angeles Times*. Hotch is a smallish man, with a questioning and rather disturbing owlish look.

In fact, he doesn't look like the prototype of an editor at all. But Hotch of the *Times* is an editor from the newsroom, one who shuns the White Tower of the world pundits, the speakers platform and, generally, the public pen. His platform is the newspaper. Expressions and opinions are institutional and not individual on the *Los Angeles Times*.

The *Los Angeles Times* has had three managing editors in its seventy-five years. For the last twenty-two—almost one-third of its existence—it has had just one, L. D. Hotchkiss.

When Hotchkiss became managing editor in 1934, the *Los Angeles Times* ranked third in Los Angeles in circulation. Today, the *Times* is first by more than 90,000 daily and more than 100,000 Sunday. It has grown from 180,000 daily in 1934 to more than 450,000 and from 250,000 on Sunday to more than 850,000.

The *Times* leads all newspapers in the country in volume of advertising and in total editorial content.

A check of his friends up and down the Pacific Coast is necessary to gather enough facts to get a picture of Hotch as an individual. He's certainly no talker, except among close friends. But be you friend or foe, all you have to do is ask him a question and you get your answer right now. Not always the answer you want, but an answer. Ask the syndicate salesmen, especially the one who has to explain why unusual but recognizable characters appear in Li'l Abner.

He doesn't work at his job, he breathes it. He lives it seven days a week around the clock, to the exclusion of all other interests. He has no hobbies.

Pourade was editor of the *San Diego Union* when this article first appeared, in 1957.

He sometimes tries to take his allotted four-weeks vacation, but a week and a half seems to be all he can stand of such frivolity.

In 1945 he also became editor of the *Times,* and in 1952, a director of the Times-Mirror Company, which publishes the *Times,* the *Mirror-News,* operates television station KTTV, the Times-Mirror Printing and Binding Company, and the Publishers Paper Company. In 1953 he was asked the difference between being managing editor and editor. His answer was, "About ten dollars a week."

Hotchkiss believes in the straight line. He has organized his staff on that principle, delegating full responsibility to the heads of his departments, including the hiring of their employees, and leaving the details of operations flexible. He can be devastating in his judgments. He has caused almost as many ulcers as he has had. As one of his assistants said, "All he needs to be a tiger is a set of stripes."

Hotchkiss does not believe in too many full-dress conferences. "I could hold one every hour," he says, "but how would I find out what we were really doing?" He has an editorial writers' conference every morning, promptly at 10:00, and a brief news conference at 4:50 P.M., followed immediately by a rehash of the first edition.

His other conferences are largely man-to-man—a few minutes with his city editor from time to time, a few minutes with his news editors at three o'clock at their desks, a few minutes once a week with Women's and Sunday editors. He keeps up a constant patrol, department by department, throughout the day. This keeps him accessible. Anyone can stop him in the third-floor corridors of the *Times* to ask his opinion. He welcomes direct questions but hates lengthy memos. He seems to feel that formal conferences and memos stifle clear thinking.

Hotchkiss was a fine reporter and a great city editor and he retains the working newspaperman's distaste for windbags and stuffed shirts. He is a master at the art of puncturing pretentiousness. His reports from political conventions—the only writing he does for the *Times* these days—tend to infuriate enthusiastic Democrats and to exasperate devout Republicans, and also to delight them both, depending upon whose convention he is reporting.

Hotchkiss has a passion for thoroughness. He will tolerate a long story if it assays high in facts, but the shortest flight of fancy writing irritates him. He commends clean makeup and was an early apostle of the impact of photography. He discourages stories of cheap crime and cheap divorce. He wants unusual crime covered adequately, but not for his front page.

He gives short shrift to bores, crackpots, zealots, or salesmen who have nothing that he wants. But a loyal staff insists he is patient with earnest men, regardless of their cause, and gentle with those in distress.

Hotchkiss insists he cares nothing for comics, yet he takes great care in trying to select the best of them for his newspaper. He will not confess a fondness for any of the arts, yet his knowledge of them continually astonishes his special writers in those fields. His greatest interest, aside from general news, is sports—particularly baseball, football, and boxing in that order. And despite the thirty-two years since he left Iowa he remains aggressively loyal to the Big Ten Conference.

Roy W. Howard, President
Scripps-Howard Newspapers

By Louis B. Seltzer

R oy Howard reminded me of a preacher. He used the same words usually delivered from the pulpit. He rearranged them, however, to suit his own purposes.

In one other respect Roy resembled the sky pilot. He invariably had both chapter and verse upon which he based his eloquent sermon.

I know. I was on the receiving end of many. They burned into my very journalistic soul. As they were intended to.

You don't talk back to the average minister. You could always talk back to Roy. If you didn't you lost stature with him.

My first meeting with Roy was in the *Cleveland Press* office. He came to town with E. W. Scripps, the founder of the Penny Press, from which ultimately the Scripps-Howard Newspapers blossomed.

To meet one was enough. To meet both of these celebrated journalists was more than a novitiate in the business could tolerate in a single working day. And both talked to me. It was like Jupiter and Thor descending from their ethereal altitude to talk to a mere mortal. Both asked me questions ordinarily reserved for a prosecuting attorney. They both looked sharply into my cerebral receptacle. I never did know what they found. They both wore poker faces. But I did have a feeling I was being "cased." It turned out I was right.

In the thirty-six years during which I have edited the *Cleveland Press* the number of occasions when Roy Howard and myself (as was true of virtually every other editor in the concern) stood toe to toe was infinite.

Allowing for prudent editing, out of consideration for the ineffably tender sensibilities of the readers, Roy would start out by inquiring, tenderly

Seltzer was editor of the *Cleveland Press* when this article first appeared, in 1965.

and solicitiously, "Have you suddenly taken complete leave of what might pass for your mind?"

That would start it. He would then document the initial assertion by citing either a questionable display, a trend in the paper's typography, some oversight, some journalistic inadvertence—something that his perspicacious mind had detected but which you and your associates had left uncovered. Like, for example, first base with the pitcher throwing the ball right at it.

You were lucky if you had a plausible explanation. You were out of luck if you didn't. If it was a matter of judgment and you stood up to it, he would, after he got off of his chest some language as brilliantly matched as his sartorial habiliments, listen attentively. If he felt you were right, he would say so, and say it with a broad smile. If not, he would stay hitched to his original premise.

What I am trying to say in the space allotted to me, and I wish it were much more, is that Roy Howard was a fighter for what he believed in, in or out of our profession, on big matters and small matters—an all-out, no-holds-barred fighter, and you had better be prepared for it.

When it was all over, and Roy had had his say, and you had had yours—as always you did—he called it quits, went on to another subject just as sweetly and serenely as if nothing untoward had happened at all. He never held a good fight or a good argument against you. He wanted to say what he had to say. He wanted you also to have that same opportunity.

Thus, what I really want to say in tribute to Roy Howard is that, I, like everybody else who ever worked alongside Roy, for, or with him, is the better for the experience. He brought out of you the utmost within you. He put something into you by that process—which I always suspected was the reason for employing it.

Roy Howard compelled me to reach way down inside myself for everything I had. I needed it. He did it often enough so that it became a lifetime habit.

Everybody who ever brushed with Roy could say the same thing. The RWH alumni, seared, scarred, goaded, is a fiercely loyal and proud alumni, because he strengthened, disciplined, put sand in your soul, and made you a better man for it.

John Hughes, Editor
The Christian Science Monitor

By Warren H. Phillips

J ohn Hughes is a rarity among newspaper editors: His talents and achievements are exceeded only by his modesty.

An amiable Welshman, he is admired by friends and colleagues as able and urbane, unhurried and unassuming. As befits the editor of the *Christian Science Monitor*, John is a nondrinker, nonsmoker, and noncusser—hardly from the same Welsh mold as Burton and Dylan Thomas. He also is a very private person, not given to talking about himself. Yet his heartiness and quiet wit make him a valued companion fully at ease with those assigning a higher priority to frivolity.

What few realize is that John also is deceptive. He appears not at all flamboyant. But his life has been colorful, even dangerous, at times. He is gentle of heart, soft of tongue—but tough of mind.

At age sixteen he was working as a reporter in South Africa, and has been at it ever since in other parts of Africa, Europe, the Far East, and America.

He never took time for college, but he has written respected books on Africa and Indonesia, been awarded a Nieman fellowship and a Pulitzer Prize, and impressed colleagues as an assiduous, practical accumulator of knowledge.

He has spent long night hours up to his chest in water in Vietnamese rice paddies, seeking out the Vietcong with U.S. troops. And he has faced a charging Indonesian mob that was shouting, "Kill him, kill him, he's an American."

He has been editor of the *Monitor* since 1970, and in 1976, he was given the additional title of manager, the equivalent of publisher, with responsibility for the production, advertising, circulation, and promotion departments. Still, he finds time and energy on the side to run a weekly

---

Phillips was president and chief executive officer of Dow Jones Company when this article first appeared, in 1978.

newspaper that he and his family bought on Cape Cod last year, and has also served as a board member and consultant to the Wilmington (Delaware) News-Journal Co.

"He's a workaholic," says his wife Libby. "Any leisure time is devoured by newspapers, by an all-consuming love of newspapers. It's what he knows and loves."

John was born forty-seven years ago in a little town called Neath, in South Wales. He was brought up in London, where he won a scholarship to a private school founded by one of the old guilds. The guild, prophetically, happened to be the Honorable and Worshipful Company of Stationers and Newspapermakers.

Many were the nights, starting at age ten, that were spent in air-raid shelters with his mother as London shuddered and burned during the blitz and later was subjected to bombardment by V-1s and V-2s. His father, who had had an auto sales and repair business, was away all those years with Montgomery's Eighth Army in North Africa.

John's father had become enchanted with South Africa during a six-week stopover there during the war. In 1946 he moved the family there. John immediately began work as a cub reporter on the fifty-thousand-circulation *Natal Mercury* in Durban. He spent three years there, then two in London with the *Daily Mirror,* Reuters, and a local news agency, then back to the *Natal Mercury* in the early fifties as bureau chief in the provincial (state) capital.

John, as a Christian Scientist, had read the *Monitor* over the years, admired it, and aspired to join its staff. He contributed articles from South Africa. In 1954 he wrote to then-editor Erwin Canham asking for a job. Canham wrote back that he didn't have an opening and couldn't promise anything. John packed up anyway, took a ship to New York and a Greyhound bus to Boston at his own expense, and after several weeks of waiting, was offered a job as a copyboy at *Monitor* headquarters there. Three months later he was editing overseas news. It was 1954 and John was twenty-four.

In 1955 he met and married Libby Pockman, an actress. She was at Boston University's new theater school after winning one of two scholarships for which six hundred others had auditioned at New York's Carnegie Hall. A week after they were married they left for Africa—John to be the *Monitor's* correspondent south of the Sahara until 1961, Libby to roam the continent with him with time out to act in professional companies in Nairobi and Cape Town.

Their first assignment was the Mau Mau campaign in Kenya. Their first home was a cottage rented from a former English Guards officer. After they had paid up and moved in, the Englishman remarked offhandedly that two of his cattle guards had had their throats slit by Mau Mau the week before in the ditch that ran behind the cottage.

The Hugheses rattled across more than six thousand miles of east, central, and southern Africa in their Volkswagen, the back seat laden with extra gas and water, a large Labrador retriever and a pile of documents attesting to the dog's identity, health, and right to transit various countries. "John is very meticulous, very thorough," says Libby. "Everything was in order for the dog."

Other animals were pressed upon them along the way. A tribal chief offered them the gift of a pig. John, with characteristic diplomacy and aplomb, suggested a sack of potatoes instead. In Nairobi, an Arab dignitary, smitten by Libby, offered them a pet cheetah. Libby was delighted. But John ruled that a cheetah and a Labrador together would overcrowd the back seat.

"To understand John Hughes properly you have to remember that he is Welsh and loves dogs," contends Tom Winship, whose *Boston Globe* is published across town from the *Monitor's* offices. "His Welshness has given him the capacity to look at the whole Anglo world with fresh eyes. And his passion for dogs has given him a convenient index for classifying the rest of humanity."

He may describe an investigative reporter as "a regular basset hound"—meaning methodical, a bit awkward, but ultimately getting his man. Or he may hint that a budget auditor is a Doberman—a characterization likely to keep correspondents' expense accounts in line. This canine imagery provides a convenient code for character summary—as long as the person on the other end of a Hughes communication knows the subtleties of the game. John once referred to a large, likable, true-blue type as a Saint Bernard, and his listener jumped to the mistaken conclusion that he was implying a fondness for the keg.

By the time John, Libby, and the Labrador returned to Boston in 1961, John had covered the growing oppression in South Africa (which shortly afterward prompted his parents to return to Wales) and the rush from colonial to independent status of much of the rest of Africa. He also had been arrested in Guinea, South Africa, and the Congo.

After a stay in Boston as a Nieman fellow and then assistant foreign editor of the *Monitor,* John was reassigned to Hong Kong in 1964 as the paper's Far Eastern correspondent. The business office noted an item on the expense estimate that called for flying the Hughes' Labrador retriever along with the family. John was called in.

"We don't want to see the Hughes family without a dog," the business-office man began with a broad smile. "So, couldn't you sell your dog here and buy another in Hong Kong?"

"All right," John replied, "if you'll sell one of your children and buy another."

Within a week of arriving in Hong Kong, John left Libby and their new daughter Wendy in a hotel room and was off to Vietnam, which he was to visit some twenty times over the next six years. It was early in that period that he became a United States citizen.

One of the highlights of those six years was John's coverage in 1965 and 1966 of the Indonesian army's smashing of an attempted Communist coup, the bloody purge of thousands of Communists that followed, and Sukarno's overthrow. This coverage won him the Pulitzer Prize for International Reporting in 1967.

John was the first American correspondent to reach Jakarta after the attempted coup in late 1965. Phone, cable, and radio circuits were blacked out, and Jakarta airport was closed, except for a few hours of daylight each day. Each dawn, as soon as the 6:00 P.M. to 6:00 A.M. curfew was lifted, John made a dash to the airport and to any airliner leaving Indonesia that day. He gave duplicate copies of his stories to pilots, passengers, diplomats—anybody who would agree to carry his copy out. At least one copy of each of these stories was successfully filed by these amateur "couriers" from cities where the planes stopped.

It was during this period, when Communist party youth groups burned the U.S. Information Services library and were rampaging through Jakarta, that John was caught in the streets as a mob surged toward him shouting, "Kill him, he's an American." He was saved by someone crying out, "How do we know? He could be Russian or British." The mob hesitated, then passed him by.

John wound up his Asian assignment with a five-month, around-the-world investigation of the flow of the international narcotics traffic. He worked himself into situations in which he was offered the chance to buy top-grade heroin in quantity. The resulting series won the Overseas Press Club's award in 1971 for "best daily newspaper or wire service reporting from abroad."

During their years in Asia, Libby had a second child, Mark, wrote a book on Bali that was published in Hong Kong and London, and gathered material on Chinese revolutionary theater for a book she completed after their return home.

John came back to Boston in 1970 to be managing editor of the *Monitor* and four months later became editor. "He's a very decisive editor," says one of his bureau chiefs. "He knows what he wants to do, where he wants to go."

Newsweek has credited him with instilling "a new sense of immediacy" in the *Monitor's* news coverage and adding "a new forcefulness" to its editorial page. Aggressive young reporters have been hired, some old-timers let go. The feature pages have been improved, the paper made brighter and more readable.

One goal has been to attract younger readers. A 1970 readership survey showed the average age in the upper fifties. The latest survey, taken two years ago, showed substantial growth in the twenty-five-to-thirty-four age bracket, with the average age down to fifty.

There have been stories one might not have expected to find in the *Monitor* in the past—on the Patty Hearst trial, the Manson trial, homosexual issues, drugs, the Pentagon Papers (in defiance of the government). "Nothing is off limits to us now," says John, "as long as we perceive a genuine social purpose to the examination of things that otherwise might seem tasteless or even abhorrent."

As television spot news coverage and all-news radio has pushed more newspapers into the interpretive journalism the *Monitor* has considered its specialty, John has been laying increasing emphasis on what he calls "problem-solving" journalism. The idea has been to take problems that concern broad segments of readers—problems ranging from urban decay to big government and big labor, from nuclear arms control to garbage disposal—and examine case histories of what has been done in labs, in experimental government programs abroad or here, or in other ways to probe for more knowledge and solutions.

John took the initiative in introducing high-speed facsimile transmission of *Monitor* pages to printing plants in New Jersey, Illinois, and California in 1974 to speed delivery to the paper's 195,000 readers. He organized syndication of *Monitor* material to some 180 papers with twenty million circulation, and introduced last year a radio service that now has nearly two hundred client stations.

In 1975 he converted the *Monitor* from broadsheet to tabloid format, to achieve major newsprint economies. In another economy move, he removed thirty-two people from the 170-member editorial department staff three years ago. Such steps have kept the *Monitor* from requiring any increase in the subsidy of about $5 million that it receives from the Christian Science Church.

Norman Isaacs, who was publisher of the Wilmington papers when he proposed John as a board member there, remembers that "the only question in the minds of the veteran Du Pont people on the board had to do with his running what they considered a not-for-profit enterprise.

"In John's comfortingly thoughtful, sympathetic, and slightly self-deprecating manner," Isaacs recalls, "he made it clear early that he had no taste for losing money. He captured them instantly when he made the point he was taking the *Monitor* to tabloid size to slash paper costs. It is a measure of John's wit and diplomacy that while he never said so, the oldliners convinced themselves that he thought losing money was a sin, and John may well have lost a great opportunity to convert all of them to Mary Baker Eddy then and there."

On John's office wall, behind his neat, almost-clear desk, is a small picture of Mrs. Eddy, who founded the Mother Church of Christ, Scientist, in 1892, and directed the founding of the *Monitor* in 1908. The other walls are lined with low bookshelves. Above them are photographs, many of Asia, by Gordon Converse, the *Monitor's* chief photographer. Sometimes a bizarre plaster of paris statue, sprayed with Woolworth gold paint, sits on top of one bookshelf; this is a trophy, the Editor-Artist Squash Hypogeum, for which John and the paper's political cartoonist, Guernsey LePelley, compete in their weekly game at the Harvard Club.

John's office is on the second floor of the forty-five-year-old, nine-story, neoclassical limestone building that houses the Christian Science Publishing Society. Upstairs on the eighth floor is the three-person board of trustees to whom John is responsible, and who in turn are responsible to the five directors of the Church.

The building is in the Back Bay section of Boston, between Symphony Hall and the Prudential Center. John can look out his window at linden trees and Symphony Hall beyond. Chances are that as he does so these days his mind wanders frequently to his two newest ventures.

One is the *Cape Cod Oracle*, the tabloid-size weekly he and his family purchased last year. Its circulation ranges between 7,500 in midwinter and 10,400 in summer. And it brings a close family even closer together.

In the summer months all work long hours there. Libby is there writing reviews or handling a delivery route; Mark, now twelve, will be working in the darkroom or as assistant pressman; Wendy, fourteen, will be taking classified ads, or stuffing the papers as they roll off the press, or helping with deliveries; John will be writing editorials or conferring with general manager Glen Dwinnells.

"The *Oracle* is great for my morale," John has told friends. "Whenever I get depressed about my failure to accomplish anything in the metropolitan newspaper bureaucracy, I head for the *Oracle*. Down there I can look at the front page, object to a headline, and go out into the back shop and set a new one myself. You have no idea how that restores one's ego."

The other project that must be on John's mind these days as he gazes out his window through the linden trees is his year as ASNE's 1978–79 president.

Those who have worked with him on the ASNE board share the conviction he will be among the society's distinguished presidents. Tim Hays, a former ASNE president himself, recalls that "when John came on the board, it was apparent from the first meeting that he was worth listening to. He's never talked much but he's always said a lot. He articulates his thoughts beautifully and, of course, this isn't just a matter of British erudition but reflects an organized mind."

Gene Patterson sums it up this way: "John Hughes elevates the image of us unwashed editors. In company that is renowned for being long of wind and short of temper, he is crisp and equable. This may be because he doesn't drink. It also could be that he's a gentleman."

Norman E. Isaacs, Executive Editor
Courier-Journal and *Louisville Times*

By Michael J. Ogden

T here was this night half a dozen years ago when I sat alone with Norm Isaacs in one of the sorry Columbia campus hotel rooms that the American Press Institute provides for the members of its seminars. We had argued with our fellows all day around the big table on the ground floor of the journalism building and now we two were still at it—exchanging notes on newspaper operations, comparing his budget at the *Courier-Journal* and *Louisville Times* with mine, debating the merits of chicken-supper coverage, discussing the two dozen other editors at the seminar with us.

We decided to broaden our field of investigation. We went through every reasonably sized city in every state in the union, discussing the quality of each paper and each editor.

We were very fair, very thorough, very keen, very analytical, very drunk. The conclusion we reached at three in the morning was inescapable: We were the two greatest editors in the country.

I can tell you part of it, like the first time I ever saw (and heard) him. You just don't "see" Norman; you're bound to hear him at the same time—whether he's only standing around in a hotel lobby or prowling though a newsroom or presiding on a platform before an audience of a thousand.

This first time was, coincidentally, my first attendance at an APME meeting. Norman was on the podium and roaring at his transfixed audience, "I wanted to be president of APME. I'm glad to be president of APME. I'm honored . . . but you bastards out there. . ."

Ogden was executive editor of the *Providence Journal-Bulletin* when this article first appeared, in 1969.

I don't remember what the issue was—maybe it had to do with interpretive writing or the Associated Press's handling of a story or the failings of publishers—but the bastards cheered him, anyway.

Norman never is diffident on any subject. Some of us, for example, will never be top-notch editorial writers, because we're always being swayed by the last argument we hear. Not Norman. His opinions are instant, articulate, verbose, profane, frequently cockeyed, but they're firmly held.

He doesn't write editorials any more. "I sit in on the daily editorial conferences," he says.

"Do you give your views?"

Incredulous stare.

Okay, ask a silly question. . . . So he's a character. Probably one of the most sought-after speakers in our craft; maybe, at that, one of the great editors, and he never finished high school, no less college, to say nothing of the fact that he didn't even know his own name until he was fourteen years old.

He is husband of a newspaperwoman (Dorothy Ritz, homemakers' column in twenty-six papers); father of a newspaperman (Stephen D., metropolitan editor of the *Washington Post*); and father-in-law of a newspaperman (John Mathews, staff of the *Washington Star*, married to Roberta Isaacs).

One thing at a time. Born Manchester, England, 1908, son of a music hall singer who used the stage name Rob Watson and who was somewhat related to a Lord Chief Justice of England, Lord Reading, né Rufus Isaacs. When his parents moved to Montreal, Norman went with them—he had scant choice, being but two and a half at the time. A dozen years later, by which time the family was living in Indianapolis, the youth learned he wasn't Norman Watson at all, but Norman Isaacs.

He also found out that the Canuck French he had spoken so fluently in Montreal wasn't anything like Parisian French and couldn't even get him through a language course at high school. He either flunked out, dropped out, was ushered out, or thrown out. It gets a little confusing here.

Son Stephen, who wasn't there, has a few things to say about it. But he may or may not be a reliable witness. After all, he's the kid who discovered some time before his ninth or tenth Christmas the present that his father was hiding from him in the hall closet. It was actually a miniature printing press, but Stephen didn't know that; he went around for some time hugging to his young bosom the gnawing suspicion that his dad was a counterfeiter.

Anyway, Stephen talks about his father being captain of the basketball and baseball teams, as well as a star 440 runner to the point of entering the Olympic trials. Norman kisses off his entire athletic career by simply saying in his own modest way, "I was a sensation as a catcher."

Why did he get into newspaper work? "I don't know. Maybe because I was fascinated by the presses in the windows of the *Montreal Star*."

When and where and how? "I was seventeen. The *Indianapolis Star* took me on as a sports department copyboy. I started out picking up bowling alley scores, but I got to writing pretty quickly because of a sports editor who was a little lazy about doing his own column. He foisted it off on me but kept his by-line on it."

Then there was a better offer (twenty-five dollars) from Scripps-Howard's *Indianapolis Times* to be assistant to one-armed sports editor Eddie Ash. "You want to know how I got this thing—this hangup on the need for virgin ethics in newspapermen? It started with Eddie, the most incorruptible man I ever knew. Wouldn't accept a cup of coffee—not even a cigarette—from a source. His idea of the worst thing that could happen to any newspaperman was to be under the slightest kind of obligation."

When the *Times* won a Pulitzer Prize for work on the Klan, Norm decided the world outside sports was bigger. He volunteered for the beat jobs. Like all newspapers everywhere, they were short on the desk and Norm was soon commandeered. Things began to pick up. At twenty-three he was city editor. At twenty-seven, managing editor. Then a fight with Scripps-Howard and he went over to the *News* as chief editorial writer. Somewhere in there, he married Dorothy, a secretary in an ad agency. "She proposed to me. She thought I needed help."

There was more help when he moved to the *St. Louis Star-Times* in 1945. "I really had to learn the business then. Working against the *Post-Dispatch* is one thing that educates you."

The *Post-Dispatch* tutored him until 1951, when it took over the *Star-Times* and folded it. Norman will tell you that he was the most unemployed managing editor in the United States at the time. What he doesn't tell you, but which his old staffers will, is of the battle he put up to get them jobs elsewhere. Said one of them, "You'd have had to see him sitting in that tomb of a place spending old Elzey Roberts's money on long-distance phone calls to get his men placed. The Guild even gave him a commendation then."

With that part of it over, Norm found his own job: managing editor of the *Louisville Times*. After ten years in that spot, he succeeded Jimmy Pope, who had reached retirement age, as executive editor of the works—with recently a slightly added fillip to the title—"Vice-President and Executive Editor."

And now, after all these years, what does Barry Bingham, number one at the papers, say of him? "Norm has a complete conviction that newspapers ought to be better and he wants to work on this every day of his life."

Quote this to Norm and he comments, "I *am* a wonderful editor and

Barry richly deserves me."

Barry also likes him for what he calls the qualities of his character, personality, and mind, because Norm likes to bring young people along, because he's many-faceted and because he's tough but cultured.

Now, take culture. If I had to choose among those facets, I doubt that culture is one I'd zero in on. And yet, what about an editor who comes into a new town, finds the Louisville Symphony tottering, moves in, and in no time is president and has the orchestra on its feet? Add to this, previous service on the boards of the Indianapolis and St. Louis orchestras.

Norm goes broader and deeper than that too. Back in 1937, in Indianapolis, he was on the board of Flanner House, a Negro settlement project. Later, he was a member of the mayor's Race Relations Commission. In Louisville he quickly became campaign chairman of the Urban League.

More facets: Served on the Committee on Foreign Relations in each of his three cities, now on the National Council's Edward R. Murrow Fellowship Committee, was chairman of Louisville Committee on Foreign Relations, spoke at the thirtieth annual conference of all the committees, and proceeded to blast the hell out of them—in this case because, he told them, they weren't representative of their communities, racially and professionally.

One more facet. As Norm puts it, "I'm sort of a half-assed expert on police and court affairs. And on penology. That's how come I've been longtime buddies with people like Chief Justice Warren, the police chiefs of Indianapolis and St. Louis, the ex-director of federal prisons." And he was on the board of the National Council on Crime and Delinquency.

About the only social facet that he won't dwell on is the entertainment he dreamed up as program chairman for ASNE in 1960. In case anyone who sat through the banquet speeches that night has forgotten, it was our Norm who dreamed up the idea of having not one but two U.S. ambassadors drone on through the night. "I do remember," he says, "that I was sitting with my guests and about the second or third hour I tried to get out by crawling under tables toward an exit but, do you know, that every damn editor and guest sitting in my path kicked me as I went by?"

But Norm is never down for long. Mention the ambassadors and he'll shrug them off. "I'm also a wonderful photographer." No one else may think so, but he does. What else is he wonderful at? Well, head writing, makeup (he pioneered in the six-column page), editorials, getting the most out of staffers.

On one of the old days when Norm was actively in the news end of the *Times*, a visitor stood by while he made up page one on a dummy pad. Norm lacked only a beret and a palette.

"There," he bellowed, "that goes as the off-lead." A sweep with his copy pencil and a shouted, "That's for the top of one. That four-column cut there. No, hold it. Make it a six." He flung copy about. "Cut that goddam story in half and take it away." He yanked from a pile the proof of a head and hurled it in the direction of the copydesk. "No, no, no. For chrissake, why does it always have to be 'Clash.' I know—it fits. Well, find something else that fits." More great slashes with the pencil. "And that there. That in column four. That at the bottom. There. There. And there!" He threw down the pencil and looked at his visitor. "That about the way you do it in your shop?"

Some of Norm's staffers looked up curiously. "Well, just about," said the visitor, "but not quite so noisily."

The staff promptly broke up.

At home, Norm reads. "No novels, but almost anything else and just about any book on journalism that comes out." He must have got his hands on most of them; they're all there in his den—stack after stack, row upon row.

It is possible that Norm reads quietly and to himself. But it couldn't be for long. The door to his den, which is adjacent to Dorothy's, is always open, as is hers. "We bang away at our typewriters," he says, "and in the pauses we yell at each other."

That's on the second floor. In the basement he keeps an Exercycle and once in a while Norm rides that—not stolidly, just pumping away. "Oh, no. While I'm riding I curse out loud, like against editors who tell me they'll write a piece for the ASNE *Bulletin* and don't come through."

He's gone a lot farther than just the cycle stand in the basement. There was a six-month trip to India for the State Department to talk to newspaper editors. And did he tell them off? "Oh, sure, but not as much as I sounded off to Dulles. I used to give him hell. The Commies were giving us the shaft."

Now, what about this constitutional inability to tread lightly? "Oh, all my noise doesn't mean anything. I'm just supercharged. It's when I'm quiet that something's wrong.

"I think my own greatest asset—and maybe my worst failing—is that I have a sense of mission. I'm an evangelist. I'm always preaching the way journalism ought to be. I try to instill things in the young guys. Whether I like a kid doesn't matter. I don't care if he's sassy or whatever, so long as he can produce. When I was on the firing line, I operated that way. I think I did things—for instance, that I changed the *Times* from a boisterous five-penny dreadful into a damn good, civic-minded, responsible operation.

"A lot more of us ought to make things happen. Instead, we stand around in bars talking about things that we never accomplish.

"I think I accomplished some things in the field generally and ethically, some things I used to holler about way back in '48 when the major leagues were paying the freight for a hell of a lot of papers. In twenty years there's been a remarkable cleanup and I take some of the credit for it. How? I embarrassed the sons-of-bitches, that's how."

That's something of what we have coming up. Maybe not the Norm of twenty years ago, but then he hasn't changed all that much. Grayer and thinner on the top, a little more pot in the middle, still wearing his trademark bow tie. Either going on the wagon for long periods or falling off with a crash—he thinks the very dry martini is an affectation, demands gin straight.

One who knew him way back when and now, says, "That patina of age has mellowed him just a bit, the edges smoothed a little but the language isn't any better. And he still whizzes back and forth, all brashness and exuberance, with a fiendish delight in tipping applecarts."

Ruth Lindsay, his secretary, accepts him with only a slight sigh. He doesn't like to dictate, bangs out his own stuff, and turns it over to her for retyping. "I guess it's hunt and peck, but I'm not even sure of that. He doesn't look, and he's almost a good speller." Nor does she know what he does with everything he grabs off her desk. He's an early riser and has the mail before she can get to it. He sequesters clips and files and she doesn't know what he does with them.

There's only about one thing left to say. If there's an investigating commission around or a study group working on some angle of the media, they'll want to hear from Norman. Unless the probers or the students know him, the odds are great that he'll bring them up short.

Last December the National Commission on the Causes and Prevention of Violence had three days of hearings. There were other witnesses, but it was probably difficult to remember what they said by the time Norman got through.

He was sweeping—"Americans not only don't believe what they read and hear, they don't believe what they see. I attribute a whole lot of this to our own [the press's] behavior."

He was personal—"My own views are anathema to most of the establishment in journalism."

He was specific—"Police reporting is dreadful on most newspapers in the United States with most of the police reporting being done by unlettered copyboys who prove to be PIOs for the police departments. Court reporting is equally as bad."

A member of the Commission, a Texas lawyer, leaned forward incredulously, "How did you ever get elected president of the APME?"

Said our Norman, "That's what amazes me."

President of APME, indeed! That Texas lawyer ain't seen nothing yet.

Vincent S. Jones, Executive Editor
Gannett Newspapers

By L. R. Blanchard

V incent Starbuck Jones, hereinafter called Vin, attained early eminence. He was six-five—give or take a few millimeters—before he was
twenty. With trifling adjustments he'd almost qualify as a national
monument.

Had he honed reflexes rather than brains he might have become famous
as a basketball star.

Graduated from Hamilton College, near his home town of Utica, New
York, he applied a Harvard glaze to his education with postgraduate study.
Hamilton may have shaped his career. It is the foster mother of a notable
pride of literary lions, a zoological happening worthy of noting. At any rate
he became a reporter on the *Utica Daily Press*—and a good one.

After the Gannett organization had purchased the two Utica newspapers, Vin became a managing editor, then executive editor of both the *Press*
and the *Observer-Dispatch*. When need arose for an executive editor in the
Rochester headquarters, he was tapped for that spot and has lived busily and
happily ever after. He is now a vice-president as well.

Vin is a bale of enthusiasms, not quickly burning infatuation, but
glowing and lasting devotion. He is traveler, photographer, railroad buff,
wordsmith, musician, and above all, dedicated newspaperman.

His chest bears the ribbons of a score of newspaper honors. He has
headed every New York state editorial society as well as the national APME.
Attending a photographic seminar, he compiled so glossy a record that he
was made a discussion leader. He has been a regular lecturer for the API,
covering every band of the newspaper spectrum, except possibly typesetting,

Blanchard had retired as executive editor of Gannett Newspapers when this article first
appeared, in 1968.

stereotyping, and press operation. In recent years he has thrown his vim and vigor into the IPI.

Such activities demand travel, but travel is one of his hobbies. He rides herd on editors of a vast triangle from Illinois to Connecticut and south, by way of New Jersey, to Florida. Other errands zip him around the world for stops in Europe and the Far East. Africa and Australia still are missing from his travelogue but, if they will be patient, he will be there.

As a managing editor Vin absorbed the rudiments of newspaper art. With characteristic dispatch he quickly stocked his desk with all the known gadgetry for fitting, sizing, and cropping prints. To learn more he set up a photographic lab in his home. To keep the lab busy he bought cameras enough to test the neck capacity of a giraffe.

Rail buff that he is, Vin wangled front-end passes on the New York Central and photographed every mile of track, practically every spike, between Grand Central and Rochester. He'd rather rock on the deck of a diesel than laze in the cushioned comfort of the lounge.

Like most good editors he is still a reporter. He can outlast the most boring speakers, waiting like a cat at a mousehole for one good phrase or idea to appear. Then he pounces and the world never knows that most of the audience had long since gone to the bar. His writing is plain and direct without a Spencerian flourish.

Vin's prose is Churchillian. Long words are shunted aside if short ones will carry the load. It is not that he lacks a vocabulary. His impressive private library features a battalion of dictionaries, captained by the three-volume Oxford, backed by troops of auxiliary lexicons and reference works.

His skills as photographer and reporter have been exhibited in the *Bulletin*. Readers may recall a series of candid shots in which the gullets and tonsils of some of our more eloquent editors were exposed.

In music his taste is ecumenical. Following his do-it-yourself course he developed an expertise at piano and organ far beyond the "Chop Sticks" and "Three Blind Mice" repertory. Small wonder he was tapped speedily as a board member of Rochester's famous Philharmonic Society.

One more facet is Vin's readiness to explore and pioneer. Set down in a strange city, he will spot unerringly the best steak house, the most comfortable hotel, and the fastest transportation.

In Fort Worth an editorial group was shown through the then mammoth of military planes. So big was it that travel between tail and cockpit was through a nose-skinning tunnel in which the passenger lay stretched out on a tiny flat car. Recollection is that Vin was one of the few among the 150 visitors to make the trip.

To his cabinet Vin will be a threat. It must produce or Vin may pick up the task himself.

Retirement, at present, is just a dirty word to Vin, one spelled in four letters. But it will come, of course. Then we will see Vin enjoying the placid sunset years with demonic activity. He's built that way.

A. H. Kirchhofer, Editor
The Buffalo Evening News

By Millard C. Browne

With Alfred H. Kirchhofer, the legend and the reality were always rather difficult to tell apart. I was first introduced to the legend right after I had first met the man.

It was on a Thursday in 1944 that Mr. Kirchhofer (many friends called him Kirk, but no staffer in my time ever called him to his face anything else but Mr. Kirchhofer) had interviewed and hired me, effective the next Monday. So I went happily off for a weekend visit with a friend at the *Cleveland Press*. When he introduced me to Louis Seltzer and told him I was about to go to work at the *News* in Buffalo, Seltzer's eyes lit up. He did a mock salaam, in awed tribute, he said, to the formidable figure I was about to work for.

If most legends are made of half-truths, the Kirchhofer legend in Buffalo is much more solid. It is built on a multitude of at least three-quarter truths, or even of whole truths twisted only slightly out of context. Thus Monty Curtis, a Kirchhofer protégé and fan of earlier vintage than I, bears solemn witness to the most famous Kirchhoferism of all—the visitor's chair, bolted to the newsroom floor beside the Kirchhofer desk so it could not be hitched forward. "Mr. Kirchhofer was and is a fastidious man," says Monty, "and he did not want a couple of the newsroom characters, who were anything but fastidious, to sit near him. I saw the bolting process late one afternoon and witnessed the discomfiture of the offenders next day."

But to this reality, Monty adds a morsel to the Kirchhofer legend for which only he can vouch. Being then young and vigorous, he recalls, he was an active pallbearer at the funeral of the city editor he succeeded. "The old boy had shivered and shook for ten years at home before he died. When we returned from the cemetery, I was called to Mr. Kirchhofer's office and told solemnly: 'I saw you help carry that casket down the aisle. I saw you help

Browne had retired as editorial page editor of the *Buffalo Evening News* when this article first appeared, in 1980.

plant poor Eddie out at the cemetery. There was one thing winding through my mind all the time: Exactly the same thing is going to happen to you and I have no replacement. Get back down there and train someone.'"

Well, fact is fact and legend is legend, and I have heard countless other anecdotes where I wasn't sure which was which. In one, an errant reporter being rebuked had made bold to stammer, "But, Mr. Kirchhofer, I think . . ." to which came the shattering reply, "You're not paid to think!"

All I know is that no editorial writer ever drew that particular rebuke. We *were* "paid to think" and expected not to take any holidays from doing it. I remember one of those famous AHK blue notes spelling out in some detail the particular kind of hell he would like to see visited on some local proposal. I not only wrote an editorial along the lines I thought he had in mind, but I made the egregious error of taking it for granted that his memo had its facts straight. It didn't, and when one of them blew up in my face, it was quickly made plain that I was not being paid to take for granted any facts cited in an AHK memo; the accuracy of any facts on which I based any future editorial comment were strictly *my* responsibility, not his.

Kirk was a thorough Republican partisan, but his partisanship had a special twist that always held the beneficiaries of *News* endorsements to an even higher moral standard than it did all lesser breeds. I got my most memorable instruction on this point one day when he called me in to say he had word that a grand jury was about to bring graft indictments against six city councilmen, three of them Democrats and three Republicans, and that we ought to have an editorial on it ready the next morning.

"About those three Democrats," he said, "it's no more than you'd expect of them. But as for the three Republicans, let's boil 'em in oil, because we supported them." There was a certain president a few years later about whom I had occasion to recall that lesson.

The Kirchhofer style rules were likewise legendary for their primness. But here, too, there was some reason to wonder where the real Kirchhofer primness left off and the staff's awe of his every dictum took over. Some rules he first intended only as suggestions got hardened into concrete, I suspect, by staffers treating them as rigid commands. A few absurdities resulted which I doubt Mr. Kirchhofer really intended. His ban on words like "abortion" and "rape," for example, led to such standard usages as "illegal operation" and "criminal assault," which became so frozen over the years that the *News* would even describe a therapeutic abortion as a "therapeutic illegal operation" and carry an occasional policy story about a woman who had been "savagely attacked but not criminally assaulted."

Two other famous Kirchhofer aversions were rats and snakes, which invariably appeared in the *News* as rodents and reptiles—and were never portrayed in pictures or cartoons. A *Time* magazine profile of Mr.

Kirchhofer during the Eisenhower era quoted him saying stiffly, "We don't use 'rat' on page one unless it bit Eisenhower and he bit it."

Would that Kirchhofer stylebook have withstood the assault of the lifestyle revolution and journalistic adaptations to it that he has seen since his 1966 retirement? I asked him recently if he would not relax some of those word taboos.

"Well, I wouldn't go overboard," he said. "I was raised on the tradition of E. H. Butler, Sr. [founder of the *News*], a stickler for keeping the paper clean. I always thought you have to have a feeling for restraint." On abortion, he added, of course he would accept its common usage as a public issue today. But he saw no good reason why "prostitution," "rape," "sexy," and such terms had to be bruited about on television and all over the press as much as they are now. He quoted William Randolph Hearst to the effect that you could tell any story without departing from good taste or discretion and that you didn't always have to be overly explicit.

In a journalistic age of swiftly expanding newspaper chains, Al Kirchhofer was basically a one-strong newspaperman throughout his professional lifetime. His only quests for other fields to conquer were pioneering ventures—and brilliantly successful ones, as they turned out—into both radio and television. But these were strictly related, in his mind, to the strengthening of the single newspaper property which was and always remained his first love, and to the providing of a fuller dimension of enlightenment to the community his newspaper served.

He was born in Buffalo (May 25, 1892) and raised there as the oldest of four sons of Robert and Elizabeth Boldt Kirchhofer. From his early boyhood memories, he regarded journalism as his vocation and, with that in mind, he attended night classes at the YMCA Institute while working full-time at the old Bank of Buffalo. At eighteen, he got his first newspaper job as a reporter on the *Buffalo Commercial*. Within three years, he had moved to the *Buffalo Times* and the *Buffalo Courier*.

He thrived on assignments where he could expand his knowledge. Covering the Advertising Club, for example, he learned so much about the basic elements of advertising and publicity that he organized his own agency as a sideline while working at the *Courier*. In 1913, he and a friend organized a regional paper, the *Western New York Post*, in nearby Lancaster. He sold this property the following year but not before forming another kind of partnership, with the paper's witty and charming secretary, Emma M. Schugardt, who became Mrs. Kirchhofer on January 27, 1914. That marriage endured for nearly sixty-five years until Mrs. Kirchhofer's death in 1978.

All this early experience with other entries in the competitively crowded Buffalo newspaper field was introductory to what was to be the last job-switch of Mr. Kirchhofer's career. In 1915, at age twenty-five, he joined the *Buffalo Evening News* as a church reporter. From there he went to city and county hall beats, then assistant city editor. In 1916 he got the call to cover the state legislature in Albany. There he quickly earned a reputation for eighteen-hour days. But after America's entry into World War I, he was borrowed from his newspaper to use his advertising and publicity expertise selling Liberty Bonds. His success at that led to another extra-duty assignment as publicity director for a $5 million endowment fund for the University of Buffalo.

The job opportunity which "Kirk" most cherished, and the one which probably most broadened his outlook and certainly began bringing him to national attention, came in 1921, when he was picked to open the *News's* first Washington bureau. He became a familiar figure at President Harding's press conferences, and quickly became a member of a group of correspondents (it included such leading colleagues as Roy Roberts of the *Kansas City Star* and Arthur Sinnott of the *Newark Evening News*) who got together for interviews with Cabinet members and other leading government lights. He thus developed close associations with Calvin Coolidge, Herbert Hoover, and others, which led later on to his being named by the Republican National Committee as assistant director for Hoover's successful 1928 presidential campaign, and as publicity director for Alfred M. Landon's not-so-successful 1936 campaign.

While in Washington, Mr. Kirchhofer typically became a leader in the drive to finance and construct the $11 million National Press Building and in 1927—just ten years before his presidency of ASNE—he became president of the National Press Club. In that same year, he was called back to Buffalo as managing editor, the title he held for more than twenty-eight years before becoming editor and executive vice-president of the *News* in 1956, following the death of Edward H. Butler, Jr., who had been editor and publisher since inheriting both titles from his father in 1914.

It was during his long managing editorship that Mr. Kirchhofer personally talked Mr. Butler into taking two pioneering plunges that were to prove the most commercially successful plunges the *News* ever took. The first was into radio, when it was in its infancy and most papers and wire services regarded it as a potential rival not to be aided in any way. Mr. Kirchhofer disagreed, and the *News* both prepared and sponsored regular newscasts and printed program logs in the late 1920s. Then, in a fight to break a local radio monopoly, Mr. Kirchhofer was instrumental in establishing the *News's* own station, WBEN, which rapidly became Buffalo's leader in both AM and FM, especially in public-service programming. Soon after World War II, the *News* and WBEN then led Buffalo into the television age by launching its first television station. All three WBENs—AM, FM, and TV—held unchallenged dominance of the western New York air at the time of Mr. Kirchhofer's retirement, and it was not until the sale of the *News* by the Butler heirs eleven years later that the paper's ties with the stations were severed.

It was also during his managing editorship that all the Kirchhofer legends took root. They were built of a mixture of awe and respect, sometime tinged with envy or bemusement, by staffers, community leaders, syndicate salesmen, publicity seekers, and practically all others who crossed his path. Both legends and reality composed a very complex portrait of a gruff exterior with a heart of gold, of an incredible glutton for work who expected only little less from those around him. It was a portrait well painted by Carl E. Lindstrom in an *Editor and Publisher* profile. To the casual visitor, or even a young staff member, wrote Lindstrom, AHK could seem "downright terrifying, less because of what he says than because of his disconcerting brevity and devastating silences." But for longtime friends there was a friendly but shy warmth, consideration, and a firm helping hand.

And the Lindstrom portrait also included an "intimate view of a quarter-century associate" to every word of which I, as a later-arriving third-of-a-century associate, would heartily subscribe.

". . .a born newspaperman of incredible competence and frequent brilliance, absolutely devoted to the highest standards of newspaper work; a perfectionist who is intolerant of everything but the best writing and editing; the possessor of an uncanny instinct for the hidden error (or the missed point or angle) . . . and a news and editorial writer of incredible speed and precision."

One early accolade—which "Kirk" deprecates today as "not merited" but still cherishes because of his own respect both for the man who said it and for the company it puts him in—came from John N. Wheeler, one-time editor of the old *Liberty* magazine and later head of Bell Syndicate.

"The three great managing editors I've known," said Wheeler, "were Carr Van Anda of the *New York Times*, O. K. Bovard of the *St. Louis Post-Dispatch,* and A. H. Kirchhofer of the *Buffalo Evening News.*"

That puts him and Mr. Kirchhofer in full agreement on at least one of the three: "Carr Van Anda," AHK told me, "was one of the greatest heroes in this business."

Herbert Klein, Editor
The San Diego Union

By Richard M. Nixon

I t has become a cliche to say that we live in an age of specialization that is gradually reducing the number of men knowledgeable and able in many callings. Nevertheless, the cliche contains the seeds of truth.

There are no more "triple threats" or "sixty-minute men who go both ways" on the professional football field, and they are a vanishing breed in college ball as well. The professional quarterback and passer who opts to run more than absolutely necessary will have a brief and unhappy career, while most running backs simply cannot throw well enough for professional football. As for the kickers, it is more often than not they can be identified by the cleanest uniform on the bench, having been sent in only when their speciality is needed.

The same is true in newspapering. Once the prince of reporters was the general assignment man, who would cover all major stories from fires, to elections, to crime, and even to war. Today the great papers have a medical editor, a science editor, a religion editor, and even lately, the *New York Times* can boast of an aerospace editor.

Being more than a casual observer of the press in recent years, it is my opinion that Herb Klein is among that vanishing breed of versatile men who could cover any beat or assignment on a newspaper and do it well.

Before I met him he was a sportswriter; when I met him he was a reporter. During his subsequent career, he wrote features, covered political stories, spent time on the desk, became a news editor, wrote editorials, and finally became the editor of the *San Diego Union*.

(As an insert I might add that I, too, toyed with the idea of sportswriting and eventually a column. But neither Herb nor I, as prognosticators, would threaten the position of a Red Smith or Shirley Povich, as we both—I recall—were in general agreement that Coach Lombardi's Packers were in for an unpleasant afternoon with the Kansas City Chiefs.)

This article first appeared in May, 1967.

When I first met Herb he was with the *Alhambra* (California) *Post-Advocate* as a reporter and since that day in 1946, when I was campaigning for political office for the first time, he has half a dozen times interrupted his professional career for a tour of duty as my press secretary. On his return to his typewriter, or desk as editor, he has scrupulously maintained that wall of separation that should exist between the news columns and politics, just as it should exist between the news columns and the editorial pages.

One of the tributes that should be made to Herb Klein as an editor is his perpetual vigilance against a persistent flirtation between news and editorials, which on some papers has become a scandalous and open affair.

I do not deny, however, that Herb's talents as a reporter served me well on a number of occasions.

I recall one occasion vividly when Herb showed himself to be a capable and persistent investigative reporter—to my subsequent relief. It was in Louisville in 1956. President Eisenhower had returned to good health, the tour was going well and the victory seemed more assured with each stop. From my hotel I saw a barber shop across the street and decided it was time for a haircut. With a complement of some fifty reporters I started across and waved to the barber closest to the window.

He took one look and bolted out the back door leaving an empty chair and a highly confused and embarrassed vice-president. I sat down in another chair while puzzled reporters and photographers milled about.

Not until Herb had tracked down the fleeing barber, questioned him, and returned did we learn that our barber had been moonlighting as a bookie and thought the vice-president of the United States was leading a posse of lawmen in a raid on his establishment.

On another occasion in 1960 Herb demonstrated that with a little experience he might make a fine medical reporter. When I injured my knee in the 1960 campaign and spent some time repairing at Walter Reed, Herb handled the medical bulletins splendidly—once Jim Hagerty and the doctors had drilled him in the pronunciation of "hemolytic staphylococcus aureus" infection.

One of the pitfalls against which young journalists are warned is "not to get involved in your story." This proscription was of course lifted when Herb took one of his leaves of absence to handle my press relations and Herb turned out to be an enthusiastic participant.

In 1956 in Alaska Herb and I each captained a dog sled on a trial run. With Mrs. Nixon as sole passenger, Herb succeeded in running his sled into a tree stump and capsizing the then second lady into the snow, where she remained until a rescue party had caught up with the sled and its errant driver.

In a more serious vein, Herb served his country and he served me well as press secretary. During the trip to Moscow in 1959, the Kitchen Debate was not the only memorable discussion. After that debate was over at the American Exhibit, Herb was informed by his Soviet counterpart that during our travels through Russia only twelve American press would be permitted to accompany us and their reports would have to be censored by Moscow.

On the spot Herb told the Soviets that if they intended to violate their agreements in this manner, our trip would stop then and there and we would start home, and he personally would relay to the outside world that the Russians would not keep their word even in a gentleman's agreement.

When Herb reported to me what he had said, Ambassador Thompson and I backed him completely, and four hours later the Soviets backed away from their bluff. The incident, as much as any other, indicates the confidence and trust that I had placed in Herb as a friend and adviser and participant in decisions which I made as vice-president.

In the wake of that 1960 campaign, a number of critics singled out Herb as partly responsible for what they felt was a lack of rapport with the press corps. I think these charges are wholly unjustified.

It is natural enough, in an election so desperately close, to point to this or that individual or to this or that statement or position, as responsible in itself for the loss. I am sure that had the critical twelve thousand votes in crucial states been reversed, the same sort of attacks would have been leveled against Senator Kennedy and his staff.

However, in my opinion Herb was a conscientious press secretary, who modeled the handling of his duties on the fine job done by Jim Hagerty. He felt himself to be the servant of the press as well as the vice-president, and a good measure of the job he has done for me in every campaign is that the reporters who covered us then and who cover me now invariably ask about Herb, and speak highly of him.

One final testament to the capabilities of Herb Klein is the tremendous success of the *San Diego Union* in recent years under his management—and with the support of one of the finest publishers in America, Jim Copley.

John S. Knight, Editor
Knight Newspapers

By John M. Johnston

Plutarch, a master biographer, almost invariably begins with a brief genealogy of his great men. The significance is not always apparent. In the case of John S. Knight a note or two on his parentage may explain a great deal.

His father was Charles Landon Knight, who became the advertising manager of the far-from-prosperous *Akron Beacon Journal* in 1900, its flamboyant editor in 1907, and its owner by 1915. It is beyond doubt that John Shively Knight's footsteps were thus guided away from a law career and into the newspaper business, which he learned all the way from the police beat to sorting type.

He is actually annoyed, however, by the suggestion that he fell into a velvet-lined cinch upon the death of his father in 1933. "All I inherited was an opportunity," he says. It was in the depths of the Great Depression and the paper was so short of cash that employees were paid partly in scrip.

He made the most of that opportunity. The *Beacon-Journal* absorbed its Scripps-Howard competitor, the *Times-Press,* in 1938, and became the foundation for a flourishing empire of seven dailies, as many weeklies, and interests in television and radio.

There was another, and an invaluable, bequest. His father was a "personal journalist" who sprouted political ambitions, served a term in Congress, and began a dream of the governor's chair.

This gave his son a clear demonstration of the natural incompatibility of objective journalism and a political career. Jack Knight chose detachment, and built his newspapers on a keystone of independence of thought and action.

Johnston was a retired member of ASNE doing contributing work for the *Chicago Daily News* when this article first appeared, in 1965.

It is another explanation for Knight's success that at seventy-one he still has a full reservoir of vigor and of enthusiasm about his undertakings.

This statement may surprise casual acquaintances. Their impression may be one of grave courtesy but guarded reserve, totally devoid of effusiveness. The description would positively dumbfound many an importuning politician, upon whom Knight can turn an eye as cold and uncommunicative as that of an aging flounder.

Edwin A. Lahey once described Knight's initial impression upon people as that of a "brittle" man, the sort "who counts his change twice before leaving the ticket window." Contributing to this impact is a directness of speech, an impatience with nice-nelly locutions, that many find startling upon first encounter. Typical of this bluntness were his comments after acquiring the *Chicago Daily News* in 1944.

Trustees of the Frank Knox estate had chosen Knight from the group of bidders, citing his record as businessman and editor as evidence that he "would preserve and strengthen the paper's character." As secretary of the navy in the Roosevelt cabinet, Colonel Knox had engaged in lusty feuding with Col. Robert R. McCormick, publisher of the *Chicago Tribune*. Knox's *Daily News* featured a lampoon of McCormick in a cartoon "Col. McCosmic," and its readers confidently expected Knight to escalate and improve the brawl with the conservative *Tribune*.

There was something akin to consternation when Knight calmly announced, "I bought a newspaper, not a feud." He startled hearers in private conversation with the blunt remark, "I am content to let God and Colonel McCormick fight it out for supremacy." The two remained on cordial terms until McCormick's death in 1955.

Under Colonel Knox, the *Daily News* had acquired a reputation for space devoted to foreign news. It is a matter of opinion whether this coverage was truly superior or merely voluminous and dull. Knight insisted that a story had to be read before it informed anybody, and therefore that his papers had first of all to be readable. This editing, admittedly not directed primarily at delegates to the United Nations, once got Knight bearded by a foreign policy dilettante who demanded to know why he didn't produce the kind of paper that Colonel Knox had published. Knight snapped, "If this paper had continued to be edited as it was under Colonel Knox, there wouldn't be any *Daily News*."

Nevertheless, many never forgave Knight for the insistence that the paper avoid the ponderous. Some such anger, for instance, was responsible for Carl Sandburg's curt rejection of a staffer's invitation to come over to his former haunts for a visit. "John Knight is guilty of so many little sins that they add up to one big one," said Sandburg.

Knight's newspaper ventures have been uniformly successful. After the

Beacon Journal's absorption of the *Times-Press* he enjoyed a monopoly situation, but he took it to be an obligation to expand both volume and points of view in new coverage.

In 1937, he bought the *Miami Herald* and the *Miami Tribune*, folding the latter into the *Herald*. To say that it has prospered is to say that Miami has grown, which is a massive understatement. Its latest achievement is a new multimillion-dollar building on Biscayne Bay, built for a million circulation in the future.

In 1940, he bought the *Detroit Free Press* from E. D. Stair for $3,200,000. The whole newspaper profession was goggle-eyed at his feat of paying off the debt and adding a hundred thousand circulation within three years.

In 1954, the Knight interests bought the *Charlotte* (North Carolina) *Observer,* and in 1959 acquired its afternoon competitor, the *Charlotte News.* It was understood that these papers were to be the particular responsibility of Knight's younger brother, James L., who is also president of the Herald Publishing Company.

John Knight has stayed conscientiously in the background of the Charlotte picture. He and his brother work profitably together, although they are of different temperament. On one occasion, after an all-day meeting, associates were mildly surprised to find James still around after his brother had caught a plane. Jim explained why he had deferred his departure. "Heck, he'd want to talk business all the way to Miami, and I'm tired."

The latest Knight acquisition earlier this year was the *Tallahassee Democrat.*

The formula for editing the Knight Newspapers is flexible. There is no "chain" operation and no canned "must" material. Executives of each paper enjoy a degree of autonomy that, some even confess, is uncomfortably heavy with responsibility.

Knight demands clear, forceful writing and is himself an omnivorous reader who goes rapidly through books, magazines, and newspapers, including his own. But he is calculatedly sparing with suggestions, knowing from experience that a word from him may carry more weight than he intended. "Sometimes it's hard to avoid stepping in with an elephant's foot," he says.

He looks the way a newspaperman likes to have his publisher look—jaw square, eyes challenging, well tailored, with the poise and polished language of a diplomat, and a flatteringly attentive interest to the remarks of others.

The years have etched more lines into his face, grayed and thinned his hair. But they find him erect, a fact which is a monument to his determination, reflecting the many hours at a rehabilitation center to overcome the effects of chronic back trouble.

The ailing back had threatened to interfere with his golf, which would have been a blow to a devotee of the game who still shoots in the eighties.

This score, too, is eloquent evidence of his streak of dogged application to a task. When his first wife, Katherine, died in 1929, he immersed himself in golf as an anodyne, going out almost daily with the pro, fixing his mind unwaveringly on the game.

His share of personal adversity has included the death of his eldest son, John S. Knight, Jr., killed in action with the Seventeenth Airborne Division in Germany in 1945; and the unexpected death of a son, Frank McLean Knight, from a cerebral hemorrhage, in 1958. Intimates say that on these occasions he became a tight-lipped stoic, plunging into work as therapy.

In 1932, he married Beryl Zoller Comstock. They have a winter home on La Gorce Island near Miami where they spend four months a year. His second son, Charles Landon Knight, is head of a Knight subsidiary, Portage Supply Company, and a grandson, John S. Knight III, of Columbus, Georgia, is a sophomore at Harvard.

For all his secure niche in the world—fifty-two lines in *Who's Who* to President Johnson's seventeen—few men work more conscientiously at good public relations. His "Notebook" generates a large volume of mail, growling, cheering, and suggesting. On a heavy day he may dictate two score answers, not stereotyped, but thoughtful and courteous, although never soft-soapy, and sometimes sharp.

Local autonomy is such that Knight newspapers have taken sharply differing views on important national issues. Once a professional liberal took after him as an "unprincipled opportunist" because "in liberal, labor Detroit" his paper had supported control of the rates of independent gas producers, while "for his conservative, Republican readers in Chicago" his paper took the opposite side.

The accusation was pure demagoguery, because the accuser knew very well that the explanation was simply that Knight had not told his editorial writers what to write. He seldom does. They get editorial guidance along broad lines, and a guide to Knight's thinking, from his weekly column of commentary, "The Editor's Notebook." This is the enduring love of his newspaper life. Every Thursday, wherever he may be, he latches the door, shucks his coat, and opens a folder of clippings, memos, and other material that he has accumulated. He sends out for a spartan lunch and often spends nearly the full day on his copy. "I'm a bleeder, and it doesn't come easy."

"The Notebook" ranges widely over politics, public affairs, and personages. It frequently displays an intimate knowledge of the thinking of the great and the near-great. This is not guesswork. His opinions have been solicited—all the way to the White House—and views exchanged in the process.

At year's end, he reviews his work of the twelvemonth, printing salient excerpts from the weekly columns, sitting in judgment on himself in footnotes. Often he can glow pridefully over an astonishing prescience, but occasionally he almost gaily concedes an egregious error. Such a one was his 1956 conclusion that President Eisenhower would not recover his old vigor and again head the Republican ticket.

His comment upon later review: "Isn't it wonderful to have been so wrong?"

Sometimes he quotes his own papers as impersonally as he does others and is unconcerned over the possibility that he might disagree. Once an editorial writer being interviewed for a job inquired what happened if "The Notebook" came along and contradicted some opinion already expressed by a Knight paper.

"If I'm willing to take that chance, why should it bother you?" inquired Knight.

In politics, Knight's instincts are conservative, but they are tempered by a conviction that the complexity of modern civilization requires an expanded role for government. He was among the earliest supporters of Adlai Stevenson for governor of Illinois, but he backed Eisenhower for the presidency. He took Nixon, although with somewhat mixed feelings, but he balked at Goldwater. In general he has spoken approvingly of the performance of President Johnson.

He is not a flag-waver, and one of the few bits of counsel he has given to his editors is: "Think twice before you declare war in Laos."

He knows about war firsthand. He was a junior in Cornell, with plans for going on to Harvard Law School, when World War I came along. His father pulled wires to get him a captain's commission, which he turned down to enlist as a private. He served eight months in France as a sergeant in motor transport, and was sent to infantry officers school and won a second lieutenancy. He fought through Alsace-Lorraine and the Argonne with the 113th Infantry, 29th Division, and returned home sickened by the carnage. "War is not my dish," he says. "I wouldn't shoot a quail, today."

In World War II, he worked through the London blitz as chief U. S. censorship liaison officer, then covered the final phases of the war in the Pacific for his newspapers.

Knight's firm determination to avoid even the risk of compromising the integrity of his papers or himself by involvement in politics extends also to outside corporate directorships. He believes that such a position could lead to a conflict of interest that clashed with the position an independent editor would take on an issue affecting the public.

Not that he avoids the company of tycoons. Being a man of big business himself, he naturally has many friends from that group. But he is under no illusion that virtue and business are synonymous. He raps knuckles here impartially. He seemed to enjoy needling the steel industry when he considered pricing policies to be short-sightedly selfish.

Several years ago when Harry Ashmore won a Pulitzer Prize for his civil rights editorial in Little Rock, Knight observed pointedly in his "Notebook" that somebody ought to bow in the direction of Publisher J. N. Heiskell, who, after all, was the one to take the punishment for unpopular editorials, which could be written by anybody. It was clear that Knight realizes that, without a courageous publisher, any paper's editorial independence would rate fewer posies.

In his independence, however, he does not shrink from leadership in his profession. He has been given the helm of the ASNE (twice) and of the IAPA. In Akron, which he continues to make his legal residence, he has led and supported assorted civic activities.

Next to newspapers and golf, Knight's favorite recreation is horse racing. With the late Marshall Field, he established the Fourth Estate Stable, and either luck or his business acumen has caused it to show a profit. His horses' names reflect his profession: "Editorialist" has done very well, and so would have "Etaoin Shrdlu" if anybody could yell it to urge the bearer toward the wire.

At seventy-one, Knight has no plans to retire. "If I quit and sat on the beach, I'd go crazy," he says. But an executive committee of the Knight Newspapers has been formed to meet monthly and relieve him of some executive drudgery.

Its members are John and James Knight; C. Blake McDowell, Sr., general counsel; Lee Hills, executive editor of the papers and publisher of the *Free Press*; and Alvah H. Chapman, Jr., general manager of the *Herald*. He says that the members specialize in different areas of management, and "I major in editorial work."

This specialty conforms to the impression left by one illuminating anecdote. At Charlotte, when titles were under discussion, one associate suggested a fancy handle for the editor of the *News*, which, as he puts it, "would imply somewhat broader responsibilities than just running the newspaper."

"Hell," said Knight, "there is no title higher than editor."

Robert Lasch, Editor
St. Louis Post-Dispatch

By Robert E. Kennedy

Robert Lasch is probably the only Rhodes scholar who can build a house, construct furniture, paint pictures, sculpt sculpture, operate a power cruiser, and guide it by shooting the stars. Oh yes, and write editorials, too, for the *St. Louis Post-Dispatch*, an activity that brought him a Pulitzer Prize this year.

Bob Lasch goes about his many interests in a quiet, efficient way, whether the job at hand be a commentary on the war in Vietnam—the subject of his main prize-winning editorial—or the putting together of the ingredients of a newly discovered recipe for a cocktail.

He views life as a serious piece of business and his political outlook is a strongly liberal one. This comes through in his writing. The Pulitzer piece was against Vietnam escalation and for negotiation. But the Bob Lasch you talk to is no argumentative pedagogue. Anyone meeting him for the first time as, say, a seatmate on a plane, would be impressed with his quiet studiousness, his innate sense of humor as he views the human comedy, and his broad range of interests.

Bob is the type of uninhibited but well-behaved person about whom anecdotes are rare. He is regarded highly by my wife Rosetta as a man who is a thoughtful husband; he once bought a Japanese cherry tree while attending an ASNE convention in Washington and lugged it back to St. Louis as a present for his wife, Zora. (The transplant took root, too.) He also built Zora a greenhouse. He experimented with various mechanical and electrical means of keeping squirrels out of their bird feeders. (All failed.)

Most people who know Lasch are impressed by his skill at his many hobbies. Those who know him well know that his newspaper work is his true and intense interest. He has been connected with the newspaper business in one way or another since he was thirteen and was a printer's devil. That would be 1920; he was fifty-nine last March 26. Lasch was born in Lincoln,

Kennedy was associate editor of the *Chicago Sun-Times* when this article first appeared, in 1966.

Nebraska, but grew up in Kansas City. When he was in high school in Kansas City, the schools operated on a double shift so he took on the printer's devil job on a part-time basis.

When he enrolled at the University of Nebraska, in Lincoln, he worked on the college daily but soon became a reporter for the *Lincoln Star* and covered the police beat between classes. After graduation in 1928 he was awarded a Rhodes Scholarship and for three years studied modern political history, philosophy, economics, and English literature at Oriel College, in Oxford. For the next ten years he rose from reporter to editorial writer of the *Omaha World-Herald*.

In 1941 Lasch was awarded a Nieman fellowship for a year's study at Harvard. Late that year, Marshall Field founded the *Chicago Sun* and when his Nieman term was up, Lasch signed on as an editorial writer with Field, whose liberal views were more congenial for Lasch than the *World-Herald's*.

During this period, and particularly after the merger of the *Sun* and the *Times*, for which I was editorial page editor, I became acquainted with the Lasch family.

In 1942, Lasch came to national attention when he won the one-thousand-dollar first prize for the best article submitted in a "Freedom of the Press" contest sponsored by the *Atlantic Monthly*. The press, he wrote, "needs a transfer of power from publishers as kings to publishers and editors as prime ministers." Referring to newspaper owners, he wrote:

> Theirs it is to decide whether they shall rise above selfishness or remain representatives of wealth and economic power; whether they shall fight the people's battles against special interests, or fight the people for the interests; whether they shall administer a trusteeship, or exploit a privilege.

In 1946 he won a *Sun* award for the best idea of the year—a "Voters Guide" that he planned and executed himself. During this period he was greatly interested in the problems of slum clearance and in public housing. He was the author of a book, *Breaking the Building Blockade,* that was published by the University of Chicago Press. He was an early advocate of urban renewal through public condemnation and purchase of blighted areas and selling the assembled land to private developers, a system since then used extensively in Chicago and elsewhere.

When Lasch wrote of housing, he knew the practical as well as the theoretical; he helped build his own suburban house.

When the founder of the *Chicago Sun* turned over the editorship to his son, the late Marshall Field, Jr., in 1950, Lasch correctly forecast a more conservative political policy and he moved to the *Post-Dispatch*. (His forecast was correct; the *Sun-Times* supported Dwight Eisenhower in 1952 and 1956;

the *Post-Dispatch* supported Adlai Stevenson. In 1960, the *Sun-Times* supported Richard Nixon; the *Post-Dispatch*, John F. Kennedy. In 1964 both supported Lyndon B. Johnson.) He became editor of the editorial page of the *Post-Dispatch* in 1957.

The Lasches soon became an important part of St. Louis. He took up residence on two acres in suburban Ladue where he could enjoy to the full his basement workhouse, where he filled the walls with oils and watercolors of still lifes and abstracts and where he could romp with his dachshund. Zora taught philosophy at Washington University and the University of Missouri St. Louis branch. Their son, Christopher, became a teacher of American history at the University of Iowa, and is author of a book, *The New Radicalism in America*. Their daughter Catherine is married to an engineer and lives in Libya.

With the children gone, the Lasches have now moved to a downtown apartment and turned their main hobby toward the Mississippi River. They own a power cruiser which they have manipulated through cruises of several hundred miles. Bob joined the U.S. Power Squadron and is taking its fourth course, in celestial navigation. (He can get a bearing only five miles off, a tolerable margin.) Fortunately Zora has become as much of a boating fan as he.

Lasch not only won a Pulitzer this year but in April he and James Lawrence, an editorial writer, received the annual award of the St. Louis Civil Liberties Committee. Specifically, they had denounced the denial of a state license to a doctor because of his pacifist views; a denial later reversed after the case was taken to court.

One of our fellows around the *Sun-Times* plant got to know Lasch well while working as the *Post-Dispatch's* editorial page cartoonist. He is Bill Mauldin, also a Pulitzer Prize–winner. This is what Mauldin says about Lasch:

"Bob Lasch is probably the smartest man I ever knew. The nice thing about him is that he lets you find this out. He doesn't rub your nose in it. He is even more remarkable to me because he combines brilliance of mind with a tidy desk and a sense of humor. He understands the anatomy of a cartoon, has a real appreciation of the art, or craft, or trade, or whatever it is, and was a real joy to work for in the years I was on the *Post-Dispatch*."

Cartoonist Burck, another Pulitzer winner, has similar high regard for Lasch, particularly for his originality. He is the only man Burck knows who papered his bathroom with front covers from the *New Yorker* magazine.

Carl E. Lindstrom,
Executive Editor
The Hartford Times

By Michael J. Ogden

I If you are a good, average, all-American, competent editor of a medium-sized afternoon paper, you probably were in the office today about ten minutes after you intended to get there . . . after a hurried breakfast, after a fair-to-middling night's sleep . . . after a day, an evening, or a lifetime of not quite getting around to doing all the things you wanted to do in that day, evening, or lifetime.

If, on the other hand, you are Carl E. Lindstrom, executive editor of the *Hartford Times* (circulation about 125,000), you were awake and breakfasting early enough to allow for half an hour at the piano playing Bach preludes and fugues.

You would have driven in a dark blue Jaguar from the smallish, English cottage in Windsor, Connecticut, where you have lived for the past quarter-century, to the *Times* office ten miles away.

In your glass-paneled cubicle at the end of the city room you'd have checked through the overnight proofs, the morning *Courant,* the *New York Times,* the *Wall Street Journal,* and the *Christian Science Monitor.* Additionally, there would have been on your desk tear sheets from other out-of-town papers, placed there by the theater editor, whose hobby is going through the out-of-towns, and during the day you would receive carbons of every piece of locally written copy.

In the early morning you'd meet with your picture and city editors and then attend to correspondence and the administrative chores involving a staff of about sixty including twenty-seven reporters. You would break only for an invariable lunchtime at the Hartford Club. At two every afternoon

Ogden was managing editor of the *Providence Journal and Bulletin* when this article first appeared, in 1959.

you'd plan for the future with the managing, city, picture, news, financial, makeup, sports, and state editors.

At four-thirty or so you'd return home to play Beethoven for about an hour. Then, a couple of bourbon highballs with Ethel, to whom you've been married for thirty-seven years, and on to dinner and an evening limited in variety.

Most often, you'd read—principally novels, and these written in Swedish, German, French, Italian, or Spanish. You'd keep a record of all your reading and tote up a total of seventy-five books for the past year. Among them, in 1958 you would have gone through *The Divine Comedy* in Italian and *Faust* in German.

Or you might play records—operatic or symphonic. Or you'd read Dickens aloud with Ethel, with *Our Mutual Friend* the current choice.

And, just before bedtime, you'd be certain to write in each of your six diaries a page of one hundred words or so in each of the six languages.

So you're not Carl. But Carl is. And if you want to know why he gets up early enough to play Bach each morning, and hurries home to Beethoven, it's because he enjoys it. As to what's in his multilingual diaries and why he keeps them, "It's mostly trivia, what someone said. It gives me exercise in the language. Sometimes, just to keep my hand in, I translate the weekly review in the *New York Times*, alternating among all the languages." He wishes he were better in French and Spanish. Of those he has only a reading and writing knowledge. He can converse as well in the others.

What might be overlooked in musing over this daily program is that it all represents Carl somewhat past his zenith—with Carl tossing in the air these days only eight or nine Indian clubs, where he used to keep aloft an even dozen.

For instance, he was advisory chairman of the ASNE *Bulletin* for five years and, during that period, thought nothing of writing five-hundred-word personal letters to each of some 550 editors—"I don't like mimeographed jobs; too easy to toss away." He is a founder and past president of the NESNE, helped launch and for the first two years was editor of the society's quarterly, the *American Editor*. He has been active in IPI and addressed its convention in Copenhagen in 1955. He has been a workhorse in the APME Association, a chairman of the NEAPNE Association, and for many years has been a member of the Pulitzer Prize screening juries. In the old, *old* days, not satisfied with Bach in the morning and Beethoven before dinner, he would dash during lunch hour to a nearby studio of a fellow pianist and play duets.

Until a couple of years ago, and for twelve years before that, he did five concert reviews a week for the *Times*, writing the reviews at home at midnight. Or, if it was too much for a day that then started at six o'clock, he would write the reviews on the bus going to work the next morning. Why? "I was born with a deep sense of original sin—other people's. This was the only real qualification I had for being a music critic."

The *Times* is not without musical criticism since he abdicated. Three staffers now alternate in his stead. He watches their output closely, disagrees with them occasionally, but gives each his head.

Then, there were the other labors of love. One involved regular trips to New York, accompanied by Ethel, to review Broadway plays. There were the five years during World War II when he taught Sunday school to teenage girls, and the two terms he served as president of the Greater Hartford Council of Churches, a job and an organization he describes as "creating a climate favorable for Christian living."

There were the twenty to twenty-five speeches a year delivered around the country to all sorts of professional and lay groups, the frequent calls to act as discussion leader at the American Press Institute, his contributions to musical and literary publications.

In the midst of all outside activities was still a dedicated newspaper editor.That's what the speeches were about.

He has spoken eloquently on the right of the people to know what is going on in their government. He has expressed the fear that the barriers to freedom of information may be going up faster than newspapers can break them down.

A topic equally dear to his heart is newswriting. How to make it clear or clearer. "I have this strong feeling against deadlines," he says. "The biggest events always cast shadows. We need more preparation, and failing in this is where newspapers put themselves at a disadvantage. A good story is always a good story. When it's told right."

It all begins somewhere. No doubt with his parents, who were born in Sweden; perhaps more specifically with his father who, after being the father of three, gave up a prosperous furniture business to enter a seminary and become a Lutheran minister in the Midwest. Eventually there were seven children, all of whom drifted east.

Carl was born in Wallace, Michigan, in 1896; he went to college at Beloit, Wisconsin, worked briefly for the *Davenport Democrat*, the *Beloit News*, and the *Waterbury Republican*, before joining the *Hartford Times* in 1917. He describes himself as copy editor and music critic for the next twenty-nine years. He was named managing editor in 1946, executive editor in 1953.

It adds up to forty-one years on the *Times* alone. In the office he strives to keep the *Times* an informative rather than a crusading paper. He is perhaps proudest of a long series on civic betterment started years ago and known as Go-Ahead Hartford, a project that is still going ahead in one form or another.

He doesn't like obstacles between him and the public, so he answers his own phone at all times. He will see anyone who walks into his office, and that applies to syndicate salesmen.

Carl is a stickler for the niceties. He is essentially serious-minded, and dignity suits him best. It extends to his person, to his habits.

He would like to play jazz, but he can't. "It's a gift. You have to be born to it," he says dolefully. He drinks with the boys, but never quite becomes hail-fellow. "I simply become loquacious."

If, seeking to appear jaunty in his sporty Jag, he seems at times more a misplaced country squire on a carousel horse, Carl feels that is vaguely the fault of the car. For Carl is sincere in what he tries to do, and it may well be the instrument or the author that is at fault.

He would like to play Beethoven's late sonatas as they should be played. He says, "If I'm not mature enough at the age of sixty-two to play 'em, I never will learn." All but Opus 106. He forgives himself on that one and blames Beethoven. "That damn thing's virtually unplayable."

There is little doubt that Carl would not have turned out as he did were it not for his and Ethel's thirty-seven years of constant companionship. It extends to all their activities, even to one of their current interests—sports cars. Carl drives the Jag, which he gave to her two years ago for her birthday. As a replacement, she received a Mercedes-Benz last winter.

Possibly reflecting a good newsman's curiosity, he drove the Jag early one recent Sunday morning to a nearby thruway and took it up to one hundred miles per hour. Satisfied, he returned proudly to report his feat to a rather irate Ethel at home. That's as close as their marriage has come to breaking up.

Ethel is a daughter of the late W. W. Swansbourne, who was for thirty years in the first violin section of the Boston Symphony. The Lindstroms have one son, Walter, on the staff of the *Denver Post*, and three grandchildren.

Asked the other day how he happened to meet Ethel, he appeared startled, as though it had never occurred to him there must have been a first encounter. "Let me see. I think it may have been at a concert of the old Hartford symphony orchestra."

Ethel, you can bet, would have a more precise idea. For she has not missed much, if anything, of what Carl has been up to all these years. If there's a convention, be it ASNE, APME, NEAPNEA, NESNE, or whatever, Ethel attends. And when the conventions are over, they return home and diet together.

If she is privy to all his doings, she is probably aware that he has seen all of Brigitte Bardot's movies to play over here. What she may not know is that after seeing the latest Bardot film, Carl arrived in his office one morning to remark to a female co-worker that he thought Brigitte was an actress, after all. The girl could only confide to a friend: "Mr. Lindstrom, of all people! I wonder what he was concentrating on in all her other pictures!"

Whatever Carl was concentrating on, he was probably a rapt student of it. In and out of the *Times* office, he is regarded as thorough.

He is proud of his wine cellar, which now contains between 150 and 200 bottles, with the red Burgundies favored. The bourbon and the wine are his concessions to vice. Unable to get cigarettes without queuing up back in the early war days, Carl, a chain smoker, decided he just didn't like queues. He gave up cigarettes forever.

Perhaps if he had not dislocated his right arm wrestling at the age of ten, the concert world might have been his career. Then, of course, he never would have met Ethel, the *Hartford Times* would have had a different executive editor, and someone else would be ASNE's second vice-president.

As it is, he intends to go on with what he's doing until he retires. Then he'll get those Indian clubs down to only two.

These'll be cooking and playing Beethoven sonatas. No baking, though. He doesn't like baking. And not Opus 106. That damn thing.

Walter Lister, Managing Editor
The Philadelphia Bulletin

By Carl E. Lindstrom

A New York newspaperman some years ago was walking along the street when something caused him to black out. The doctors told him that he had a heart condition. Instead of crushing him, the news gave him a fresh point of view and he said later: "It made me determine from then on to try to live my life every day as if it were to be my last."

Up to that time Walter Lister had been living what he considered an unplanned existence. He resolved that he would now do things that he had previously been putting off and that he would try to live by the golden rule instead of just thinking about it.

Although the doctors never did quite make up their mind about Walter's fainting spells, they came with decreasing frequency for several years and he now has no heart trouble, if indeed he ever did.

He learned how to play as well as work and became expert at any game he set his mind on. However, once he mastered it he dropped it for another. So with golf, so with badminton.

Bridge (he once wrote a bridge column for the *New York Post*) he continues. His skill persists at the sedentary sports such as matching dollars and poker. The day after election day he needs an accountant to untangle all the bets and hedges. People learn early to be careful betting with him.

That was quite a long time ago. His newspaper career began with a paper called the *Mirror* and was intended to serve the high school students of Twinsburg, Ohio (population two hundred). The *Mirror* lasted one issue and he has since worked on eight daily newspapers—as city editor of six and managing editor of three. He is now managing editor of the largest afternoon daily newspaper in the United States, the *Philadelphia Bulletin*.

Lindstrom was executive editor of the *Hartford Times* when this article first appeared, in 1958.

Perhaps it was the gambling urge that led him once, partnered by George S. Brooks, to write a play. It was called *Spread Eagle* and belonged to the vintage Broadway pressed in 1927.

Another joint enterprise—with a past president of ASNE—was an offer made for three hundred acres of beachfront land on the Dutch-French island of Saint Martin in the Caribbean. They had to deal with eight heirs—four of them legitimate—who couldn't get together and the offer was withdrawn.

Walter never mourned the failure of these excursions. He says, "Since my teens I have never held anything but a newspaper job."

Here they are: reporter for the *Batavia News*, 1921; *Cleveland Press*, 1922; city editor, then managing editor of the *Houston Press*, 1923-25; city editor, *Brooklyn Daily Times*, 1925-27; city editor and news editor, *New York Telegram*, 1927-30; city editor, *New York Post*, 1931-41; city editor, then managing editor, *Philadelphia Record*, 1941-47; since then, as nearly everybody in Philadelphia knows, with the *Bulletin*.

This silver-haired executive went to four colleges and, like Crecy, he included Poiters. It came about this way: He left Denison University to join up with the 135th Field Artillery, 37th Division, serving in France in World War I. After the war he stayed over and entered Université de Poitiers. Brown and Harvard followed. Ill of nostalgia, he went back to Poitiers in 1956.

Walter runs the news department of some 210 employees without ever raising his voice and without moving faster than the tempo allegro moderato. He likes a quiet shop and, mostly by example, he gets one. He sits at a flat top desk, the same dark blue of the rest of the newsroom furniture, in a glass cubicle near the main news desk. Besides the usual reference books, bound recent issues of his own and competing newspapers, he has a good radio with which on Saturday afternoon he checks football games for plays that can be pictured by sequence camera. His office door is always open and anyone on the staff can see him at any time.

He gets to work a little before nine, commuting from his home in St. David's where he lives half a block from the station. He is thirty minutes out on the main line.

His day follows the pattern of most managing editors—quick conferences for news rundown, an eagle-eye check of the first edition. He takes syndicate salesmen to lunch and picks up the tab. He likes a martini at noon and scotch before dinner. Lunch is usually at the Thirtieth Street Station lunchroom. In the afternoon more conferences.

William B. Dickinson, assistant managing editor, says: "If Walter finds it necessary to discuss poor performance with any of his people, he does it individually and privately. I have never heard him criticize anyone in the presence of another person. This is not to suggest that he has any tolerance for second-rate work. He can be a very rough customer to face across his desk if he detects sins of omission or commission. He has reasonable tolerance of the faults and foibles of newspapermen—nobody ever gets fired the first time he gets drunk and louses up a story as a result—but the second or third repeat performance brings the boom down quickly and quietly."

Lister resents nothing so much as any attempt by an advertiser—or anyone else—to influence coverage or play a story. One merchant first threatened and then tried to bribe a court reporter. Within an hour the merchant and his lawyers were in Walter Lister's office from which they departed half an hour later a much chastened group. When five Negro boys raped a white girl in a school yard, they were identified as Negroes and she as white. When the NAACP protested, Walter told them when five white boys rape a Negro girl we will report that too.

During the Army-McCarthy hearings, the paper ran sixteen to twenty columns a day. After the first week, the *Bulletin's* Washington correspondent called Walter and asked him how it was going.

"Great," he said. "We've lost ten thousand circulation. Pour it on."

Lister has made a great many changes in the paper but all have been accomplished so quietly that the public has hardly been conscious of them. The makeup has been streamlined little by little and the financial coverage beefed up.

He threw out the copydesk and put in a system whereby assistant city editors read and headline city copy, and assistant telegraph editors do the same for telegraph copy. Sports, financial, women's, and amusement departments handle their own copy. The result has been to give the people on these desks a feeling of greater personal responsibility and a sense of importance which has resulted in more interested and intelligent handling of copy.

Stanley G. Thompson, city editor of the *Bulletin*, says of his boss: "He is a real genius at delegation of authority, which means that he doesn't give up his own authority in the lazy fashion of some military men, but leaves the management of various departments to the people responsible, always keeping basic control. He is a stickler for protocol, and in some twenty years I haven't known him to butt in on anybody's operation. When the occasion arises he calls in the department head and says, in effect, 'I think we've had about enough of this and that,' or 'you don't have to keep covering that Levittown riot as if it were the third world war.'"

Walter never takes work home but spends the evening reading, watching television, going to an occasional movie with his wife, or playing bridge.

When his sons are home, there's usually a family bridge game going. Walter, Jr., his oldest son, is Chicago correspondent for the *New York Herald*

Tribune. His second son, John, is an attorney. His third son, Peter, is a talented artist. He now is painting in Sardinia on the second traveling scholarship he has won at the Academy in Philadelphia. Walter recently became a grandfather when a boy, Kevin, was born to the John Listers.

Kevin's grandfather drives a Cadillac sedan which he bought new in 1951, takes good care of and sees no need to replace it. For his wife, Dorothy, he bought a Thunderbird.

On completion of a course in advanced English composition with the late great Dean L. R. B. Briggs, at Harvard, Walter Lister asked the dean about his chances of being a writer. The answer: "You have mastered the mechanics of writing. It remains to be seen if you have anything to say."

To see, and to eke out a newspaper salary in the 1920s, Walter wrote for anyone who would pay anything. That included *Smart Set, American Mercury,* and *Pearson's* (where one piece got him an honorable mention in *Best Short Stories* and three copies of the magazine). For a couple of years he did a monthly feature, "Confessions of a Policewoman" for a thing called *Secrets.*

A decade later, when he was writing on bridge, he ghosted two articles for Ely Culbertson, but turned down the expert's repeated offers to collaborate on his biography. He was convinced it would be a colossal flop; actually it was a best seller.

Of the Broadway show he wrote with George S. Brooks, Lister says: "In the try-outs we had trouble killing an unwanted laugh. Finally Jed Harris solved the problem by telling Osgood Perkins (father of today's Tony), 'When you say that line, don't look at him—look off into space.' I brooded over that and decided that if the success of a play depended on where an actor looked when he spoke a line, the stage was a mighty risky business and I had better stick to newspapers.

"Since 1940 I have largely confined my literary work to office memos."

Wallace Lomoe, Executive Editor
The Milwaukee Journal

By Vi Lomoe

N ot long ago at a dinner party people got to talking about how they had met their spouses and who had chased whom.

"Vi made the first overtures in our case."

It was with some incredulity that I heard this statement issue from my husband. I asked for documentation. This was it:

"You were walking past my desk one day on the way to the composing room and you said, 'Hello.'"

Well, I had to admit it but in my own vindication let me describe the circumstances. The scene now shifts to the city room of the *Evening Telegram* in Superior, Wisconsin, late in 1927. I had been a reporter and feature writer since finishing high school that June and was then the state editor and an old hand in the newspaper business.

One day this man came in looking for a job as a reporter. Those were the halcyon days when you could walk into a newspaper office—anyway this one—fresh off the graveyard shift as a switchman for the Omaha railroad and say you wanted to be a reporter and they'd tell you to take off your hat and sit down at a typewriter. Of course the pay, fifteen dollars a week, wasn't as good as a switchman's but it was mostly inside work.

This man had a slim, sensitive face. And he wore a mustache! So after three—no four—weeks I felt this compulsion to say, "Hello." He said, "Hello," back and eventually his conversation grew less guarded. In fact it so enthralled me that I could listen for hours and pretty soon he suggested we be married so he could get some sleep.

He had been a fruit tramp in California, a harvest hand in the Dakotas, a gandy dancer on western railway construction crews, a teamster on the

This article first appeared in 1961.

Columbia River highway, a lumberjack in the big timber country of the far West. He was in Florida when the boom broke. During one winter he managed two oil company offices at International Falls, one on the Canadian side of the border, one on the Minnesota side, both cold.

He had held an awesome number of wildly assorted short-term jobs including sheepherding and grave digging.

And there was always railroading, to which he returned at irregular intervals determined by employment conditions in the hometown. Someone who knew his history once asked my husband to explain his success as a newspaperman. After a moment's thought he replied, "If you can keep body and soul together in Superior, the rest of the world is a pushover."

This answer is accurate but specious, with nuances typically Lomoe— wry humor and self-deprecation. During his years of rambling he traveled light but his packsack was heavy with books. He rarely refers to the intellectual obligation that accompanied his adventuring, preferring to describe funny and hazardous events and exotic or interesting characters. But he's a mine of information acquired through reading as well as "involvement" and observation.

His ambition then was to be a novelist and everything he had been doing was preparation for a writing career. His work on the *Telegram* was to be a few months' lab course.

He had holed up all the previous summer on an abandoned backwoods farm, planning to get a serious start on his novel. But characters followed him even there. One was an Indian priest who kept him supplied with out-of-season venison, congenial companionship, and Douglas County bourbon, widely acclaimed as the North's dauntless riposte to the Volstead Act.

This prologue would be incomplete without mentioning Wallace's impulses toward orthodox education. He dropped in at Grinnell College where he found the students pretty square. The compatible head cook, a man of the world, gave Wally a job as assistant vegetable cook which detoured him from the groves of academe.

However he did attend Superior Normal which years later, as the University of Wisconsin–Superior, invited him to give the commencement address. There he joined a fraternity whose principal activity was debating. Some members who became lawyers and judges are still his close friends.

Five months after joining the *Telegram* staff Wallace was made city editor. In that period of seasoning as a reporter he had experienced a rapid, melodramatic exposure to newspapering in the *Front Page* tradition.

He was thrown down two flights of stairs by the brother of a man who had just murdered his wife. Wallace had erred by beating the police to the scene.

He spent fourteen days covering a notorious bank robbery case in federal court, writing eight columns of copy daily including a Q. and A. account. He was also reporting this trial for the AP. So complete was his coverage that the district attorney used his stories in preparing final summaries.

Incidentally, covering this same court was one of my early educational experiences. Before that I had thought "Mann" was spelled "man."

Wallace occasionally eased items about prominent bootleggers onto the society page. When he wrote that they were vacationing in Milwaukee, the cognoscenti were tipped off that they had been sentenced to the house of correction.

He wrote a column in which the exploits of politicians and bootleggers were chronicled by a city hall sparrow. "Charley the Sparrow" was a confidante of Hank, the mayor's elderly Airedale, and the dog was his master's mouthpiece.

Superior deserved its reputation as a wide open town. Wallace witnessed the tableau in the mayor's office the day after an election the mayor had won by four votes: His opponent, a deputy sheriff, had the ballots impounded and had sent some deputies around to get them. The mayor lined up a phalanx of colossal cops to hold off the deputies while the city clerk threw the ballots into the mayor's safe. Wallace had been telephoning the story to the city desk when the mayor caught sight of him. "Where'd you come from, Charley?" he asked. Wallace said he'd been there all along and the story was already set up in twelve-point. And now a denouement to sear the souls of all newsmen:

The mayor called the *Telegram's* publisher, whom he persuaded to kill the story to avoid a scandal in what was about to become the nation's capital. President Coolidge had just announced his intention to spend the summer trout fishing on nearby Brule.

When Coolidge came to town Wallace found himself city editor of a paper gone suddenly metropolitan, with four editions to speed the increased news volume.

Wallace had already learned to value his work and travel background for its frame of reference in news writing. Now he utilized his office management experience to organize the staff. His years of railroading had schooled him in strict adherence to schedules and he found that meeting deadlines was somewhat like running the trains on time.

So the neophyte city editor was well equipped to handle the expanded job. He also wrote Coolidge stories for papers in New York, Boston, and Chicago and assisted the *Milwaukee Journal* staffmen covering the president.

At the end of the summer Wallace was asked to join the *Journal* staff. This he did against the advice of the late Gordon MacQuarrie, the *Telegram's* managing editor. Gordon felt it was better to be first in a little Iberian village than second in Rome and so on. Not too many years later Wallace brought MacQuarrie to the *Journal* as an outdoor writer.

Coming to the *Journal* September 24, 1928, Wallace's first work was on the state desk. Among the stories he did was one which exposed a Communist youth camp in Kenosha County. And his contacts in International Falls helped him get the complete story on the "Ranier Rebellion." The good folk of this Minnesota town petitioned President Hoover to send troops to fight what they claimed was a reign of terror by prohibition agents. The feds had killed a popular rum runner.

It was ten months after coming to the *Journal* that my husband became state editor. The state desk is a self-contained unit manned by four or five deskmen who directed a staff of two hundred correspondents and the Madison bureau where legislative and governmental news originates. Its comprehensive coverage makes Wisconsin and Michigan's upper peninsula the state editor's beat. This challenging assignment, in which he stayed for nine years, marked a permanent direction away from the writing which had first attracted Wallace to newspapering.

The early years on the *Journal* found him working evenings on the novel he still hoped to write. It had a railroad background and dealt with a segment of Americana which has never been treated adequately in fiction. The finished chapters had an authenticity, a precise narrative style, and a sensitivity to characterization that were very appealing. The concept was contemporary but with a backward glance that evoked nostalgic emotions in anyone who has never responded to the lonesome sound of a train whistle in the night.

As Wallace's responsibilities increased so did his absorption in being a newspaperman. Work on the novel faltered. Somewhere along in here the aspiring young novelist turned into an editor.

He has been successively the *Journal's* assistant news editor, news editor, and assistant managing editor. The last two slots he filled simultaneously during the late war years of acute manpower shortage. He became managing editor in November 1946 on the death of Waldo (Scoop) Arnold. Since late 1959 he has been executive editor.

Trying to profile my husband from this point on I get the eerie sensation that it's the *Journal* I'm describing. Both are painstakingly accurate, restrained, thorough, and devoted to objectivity.

Continuous expansion of staff and coverage has marked the paper since the wartime curtailment. A newspaperman's newspaper, it attracts men and women of talent and integrity. Fitting these gifted individuals into productive assignments has been a major concern. As managing editor Wallace initiated a men's section and a home section of magazine quality which have won national awards. He supervised the development of another Sunday supplement into the present *TV-Screen* magazine and broadened the coverage of art, music, and other cultural areas.

He has carried forward the paper's interest in conservation of natural resources and in the natural sciences. The sporting aspects of conservation have always fascinated him. As a boy he was a woodsman and trapper, as a man a duck hunter and muskie fisherman. But he is also of a more rarefied scientific turn of mind and found intense excitement in the seminar held in northern Minnesota last summer for a group of editors and eminent scientists.

Enumerating the subjects that interest my husband is like an attempt to list his gainful and not so gainful occupations, but all are reflected in his alter ego. He reads history, religion, and philosophy—all emphasized in the *Journal*. And to name just one of his more esoteric specialties: the American circus. The *Journal* helped to establish the Circus Museum at Baraboo, home of the Ringling Brothers.

Not a crusading paper in the tradition of personal journalism, the *Journal* is probably more effective with its strictly factual approach. It would be out of character for it to beat its breast and this too is a hauntingly familiar trait. Certainly it's formidable and relentless when it undertakes to support or oppose an issue or individual. The *Journal* had isolated and identified the McCarthy virus long before the rest of the country recognized the threat. Opposition to Joe was a viciously unpopular stand in Wisconsin but the editorial position was reinforced by revealing news stories which showed Joe as a devious charlatan even before he began his controversial anti-Communistic campaign. L'Affaire McCarthy had top priority with my husband and many able staffmen over a period of years.

Wallace and the paper to which he has given thirty-two years of his life share a conscience which dictates a standard of honesty rare in this time of easy compromise. It is a standard rigidly self-applied but lit by compassion toward people who need it.

When the *Journal* receives recognition as it did in a recent poll of editors who ranked it third nationally, after the *Times* and the *Monitor*, I privately award the honor to my husband. Perhaps I may be forgiven this foible since only I know his personal identification with this great newspaper and his dedication to it.

His extracurricular interests in recent years have been directed toward ASNE and APME. He served the managing editors as president in 1954 after holding other offices and working with their continuing studies committee.

Our children are Peter and Julie, a Radcliffe sophomore, both tremendously proud of their father and the *Journal*. They've always enjoyed the picaresque tales of his youth and early manhood but they never knew him before he became an editor. And this is sad because they've really missed something quite wonderful.

J. Curtis Lyons, Managing Editor
Petersburg (Virginia) Progress-Index

By Carl E. Lindstrom

I n the small hours of a certain morning the occupant of a room in the Hotel John Marshall in Richmond heard a knock at the door of a room down the corridor; then voices and a door closed not too gently. After a brief pause another knock at another door, the colloquy, and so on. The question which each occupant of that floor had to face was asked with a mixture of desolated anxiety and naivete.

"Have you seen a cricket I lost?"

This came from a rather slight, dark complexioned man whose distinguishing characteristic was a waxed moustache. His query produced a wide range of responses from fear to explosive anger—but no cricket.

This incident, which occurred during a meeting of the Virginia Press Association, was no practical joke. J. Curtis Lyons, at that time, had one of the best cricket collections south of the Potomac. Some of these he captured himself but he was always willing to pay neighborhood children five cents for a docile specimen of good habits and disposition. The fee was downgraded according to the cricket's condition.

The managing editor of the *Progress-Index* was born in Petersburg, went to school and has lived there all his life. He rose to his present executive job, which includes giving a supervisory eye to the *Fort Lee Traveller*, from the humble start of office boy. This steady climb would indicate a stable, plodding personality but nothing could be farther from the fact. Even longtime associates have learned to be surprised at nothing in the way of moods and personality facets since the only consistent phase is a boundless

---

Lindstrom was executive editor of the *Hartford Times* when this article first appeared, in 1956.

226

energy. He talks fast, writes fast, and his whole existence moves at a rapid pace. He is a practical newspaperman but has, as a friend once said, "no patience whatsoever with the highfalutin' talk about journalism ideals that one hears so much about at conventions." Realistic about the facts of journalistic life, he stands up adamantly against an advertiser or pressure artist.

He is a regular attendant at state and national newspaper conventions and I well remember at the New York APME meeting during a tour of the World's Fair in 1939 that he brought down the house with his imitation of Hitler.

Cricket collecting was a phase. Lyons later became interested in dogs—chiefly wire-haired and smooth fox terriers. He has had his own dogs in the top shows and is frequently consulted on the training and handling of show dogs. His services are in demand as a judge.

When he last passed through Hartford, he was the delighted possessor of a Reconstruction carpet bag which he had picked up at an auction in Athol, Massachusetts. He collects hats, too, and on that same occasion he had also acquired a particularly jaunty Tyrolean exhibit.

The man is superstitious. With his wife he was once returning from Richmond and at Colonial Heights, three miles from home, a black cat ran across the road. He immediately turned around and returned to Richmond where they spent the night. A hat must not be placed on a bed and if an umbrella is opened in the house he promptly throws it away. He picks up pins for good luck and always carries a rabbit's foot. It is, of course, a left hind foot of a graveyard rabbit.

"Between you and me," writes my informant, "I have one too, but black cats don't bother me!"

A friend one Christmas presented the Lyonses with a picture of Generals Jackson and Lee. Eva found a place for it in the dining room. That was as near as they ever came to a quarrel. Curtis declared that only the living room was a fit place for General Lee!

On the occasion of a testimonial dinner to a departing general during World War II, word got around that Curtis Lyons was dying. Upon hastening to the death bed in the Roosevelt Hotel a friend found a doctor in attendance. The patient was groaning. Asked what the trouble was, the doctor replied calmly, "I don't know; he won't let me examine him." Another friend arrived and, sizing up the situation, declared there was "a damyankee downstairs who says the Northerners won the battle of the Crater." At this Curtis jumped up and headed for the lobby.

That's how patriotic he is and he was also trained as a pilot during World War I. As a further mark of his devotion to the armed services he has commissioned some friends colonels in the Confederate Air Force.

Eva Lyons is the daughter of an old Virginia family from Claremont on the James River. Curtis's courtship was a whirlwind affair. They are charming as hostess and host and are gourmets of a high order.

He is a devoted husband who during school days was "most attractive to the girls and was known as cutey." During the busiest days he takes time to phone his wife and never lets a day go by without phoning his mother. He admired his father to the point of worship. He is especially attentive to old people and remembers unfailingly their interests and hobbies.

Lyons is a demanding boss but a considerate one. Anyone who is ailing in the slightest degree is promptly sent home. During a snowstorm he phoned a woman employee and told her not to attempt to come to work. When once a truculent visitor had dared Lyons to take his glasses off and the two joined battle, a loyal woman staff member by pulling the assailant's hair successfully terminated the engagement.

Curtis Lyons is active in church work and a member of the Petersburg Saints and Sinners. He received a certificate of commendation from the commanding general of Camp Lee for his outstanding services during World War II not only in the field of information but as a leader in army-community relations. He is interested in all major sports, particularly football and boxing.

Eva calls him Joe.

Ralph E. McGill, Editor
The Atlanta Constitution

By Bert Struby

"**M**ake mine a double order of turnips," said the big man with a kindly face, interrupting his discourse on the South's racial problem.

Turnips are a good Southern dish, but it's a sure bet few diners in Atlanta's swank Capital City Club eat them by the double.

It wasn't unusual for this particular gentleman, however, even though he be a gourmet of Dixie's finest cooking and has crusaded—if, indeed, he ever crusades—more vigorously in behalf of good food than any other cause.

Ralph Emerson McGill is as Southern as turnips, as corn pone and peas, as grits and gravy, as fluffy cotton bursting out of its boll in mid-August, as red clay soil baked dry in a hot summer sun.

He is soft-spoken, slow to anger, but has a firmness in his convictions comparable to the tough granite and marble dug out of North Georgia's mountains.

As editor of the *Atlanta Constitution*, Ralph McGill has grown during these troubled times into the likeness of a twentieth century Henry W. Grady, the eloquent and brilliant *Constitution* editor who so ably presented the South's cause to the nation in the post–Civil War years of the 1880s.

Widely quoted and recognized, McGill is, nevertheless, something of a paradox.

He is both beloved and strongly disliked by different groups of his fellow Georgians; his writings are read with a sort of religious fervor by his followers, particularly among the "intelligentsia," and at the same time are bitterly and vociferously resented by most of the state's well-known political demagogues.

He is a prophet both with and without honor in his own country—depending on which group of countrymen you are talking with.

Struby was editor of the *Macon Telegraph* when this article first appeared, in 1957.

To say that he is Georgia's and the South's most popular editor is a contradiction because many read him to disagree. But to say that he is the best read is a fact without dispute.

In a very real sense, Ralph McGill in his thinking, his outlook, his hopes, and his personality depicts the New South of the southern industrial-atomic era.

He is far ahead of many of his contemporaries in visualizing the future of this region. Yet he speaks the language of most Dixie leaders in the realms of economic, educational, and sociological progress.

A native of Tennessee, McGill grew up on a farm near Chattanooga, near a rural mountain community named Soddy, which hugs the southernmost of the Great Smokies where they tower over the rolling landscape of the Deep South. His student days at Vanderbilt University were interrupted by a one-year hitch in the United States Marine Corps during World War I. But he returned to graduate in 1922 and shortly thereafter became a reporter and sports editor for the *Nashville Banner*.

He moved to Atlanta as sports editor of the *Constitution* in 1931, was made executive editor in 1938, and has served as editor since 1942. He received a Rosenwald fellowship in 1937 to study Scandinavian small farm and co-operative practices. He has traveled Europe and the Middle East almost annually and watched firsthand when Hitler marched into Austria.

Now at fifty-eight, his appearance (only a wisp of gray in his black hair) and his young son, Ralph Emerson McGill, Jr. (age eleven), belie the vast experience and knowledge he has packed into the years.

For a purpose he has limited his affiliations.

"I belong to no organization committed to a cause," he once wrote in his daily column. "I like to think I may have served some causes. I have tried to put my shoulder to whatever worthy wheels seemed in need of pushing. I have joined to get a few oxen out of ditches. I like a fight, and I have had my share. I expect to have more."

Although he has restricted his memberships, lest he feel constrained in his freedom to express his opinion in some circumstance, McGill does not consider himself a crusader.

"I cannot be sure," he said on one occasion, "but admittedly I cannot be a good crusader because I have been cursed, all my life, with the ability to see both sides of things. This is fatal to a crusader. A burning crusader must be able to see only his side. I do not criticize this, because much of our progress has been brought about by crusaders. But, unfortunately, they often are rough fellows, and in their furious laying about they undo almost as much as they accomplish."

Today, in addition to his editorials in the *Constitution*, McGill's personal column appears in newspapers in Dayton and Springfield, Ohio; Miami; and

Ralph E. McGill

in the overseas edition of *Army Times*.

His reader mail bears postmarks from throughout the United States, from Italy, France and West Germany, and carries such signatures as Mrs. Eleanor Roosevelt and columnist Marquis Childs.

Through Editor McGill's conversation, as through his writings, runs a strong fiber of quiet, persevering patience. He is not of the troops which go shouting into battle; rather, he is the strategist and planner, directing a move here and calling a counterattack there.

The literary quality of his articles appearing in *Harper's, Atlantic Monthly, Saturday Evening Post,* and other publications and in his book, *The Fleas Come with the Dog,* has won him distinction. More acclaimed, however, is his depth of perception of events and trends on the Southern scene.

"There was a time when being a Southerner could be made into a pleasant, semi-official profession if one rehearsed it a bit," he wrote recently. "But not now. In May 1954, the trumpets of the nine black-robed justices in the Greek temple on the Potomac blew down the already weakened walls of political feudalism in the South."

Newspapers in this region, McGill believes, are doing a reasonably creditable job of covering the racial story—a definitely better job of it than they were a year ago.

"Northern editorialists may thunder at it and reason it away," McGill wrote last April (in the *Atlantic*) with reference to the South's fears of integration. "But the Southern newspaper editor or writer of any sensitivity, who knows his people, will not, though he disagrees with them, mock or denounce them. It is a part of his duty personally and professionally, since he knows the path his region has taken, to seek in every way to ameliorate the problem, knowing it cannot be 'solved.' Few great problems are solved. Persons of good will keep on ameliorating them until finally they cease to be major problems."

Perhaps McGill's guiding philosophy is best summarized in these words from the preface to his book:

"Great moral courage and force, and a true sense of spiritual values, are needed today more than ever before. As we strive up the path toward the atomic-age plateau of that great mass-man civilization the industrial revolution has brought us, we must find a way to make the great teachings of books, of minds, of religious truth, freely available along the way. We must learn to take the fleas with the dog—the bad with the good—and press on through faith in our selves, our country and our God. And, as always, there are signs that we will; that deep within us is some mysterious, indefinable element of God-given spirit which is a reservoir of strength in time of need; the great rock of promise in an often weary land."

Benjamin M. McKelway, Editor
The Washington Star

By John H. Cline

T here is an element of occupational hazard in undertaking to do a
candid profile on the boss, without his knowledge or consent. But Miles
Wolff (ASNE *Bulletin* chairman) has called and I am answering.

If I were writing this for the Sewing Circle Gazette there would be
nothing to it. I could say that Ben McKelway is nature's foremost nobleman,
that he is endowed with all the wisdom of the ages, that his concern for God's
smallest creature is as lively as his concern for the *Washington Star*, that he
goes to church on Sundays, and that he invariably is kind to widows and
orphans. The ladies of the sewing circle wouldn't know any better.
Unfortunately for me, the ASNE members do. They know Ben McKelway as
well as I do, if not better. So in writing this piece I am trapped between the
twin necessities of being reasonably truthful while also trying to stay on the
payroll.

As I look back on my first encounter with McKelway, I find it difficult to
believe that such a sober organization as the Associated Press really has
elected him as its president. This first encounter, as I recall, was in the
summer of 1926. Ben was a greatly harassed assistant city editor. And I was a
cub reporter—as green and as ignorant as they come. Not then having sense
enough to stay away from assistant city editors, I was lounging near the city
desk one day when the phone rang. Assistant City Editor McKelway was
trying to get rid of a piece of rush copy.

He picked up the receiver and shouted into the mouthpiece: "Copyboy!" Then he turned toward the bull pen and shouted: "Hello!"

This struck me as a strange way to run a newspaper, and I was beginning
to believe that all those things I had heard about newspaper people were

---

Cline was associate editor of the *Washington Star* when this article first appeared, in 1957.

true. I decided then and there that this fellow McKelway was an unpredictable character and nothing has happened since to change my mind.

But unpredictability is not without its virtues. At least, life around this shop is never monotonous when McKelway is on the scene. One day may bring forth nothing but charm and a twinkle in the eye. The next may witness a truly awesome display of righteous Presbyterian wrath. When he gets some misguided editorial or news treatment idea in his head, as he sometimes does, Editor McKelway can be incredibly stubborn and unreasonable. At other times one who has not learned the hard way to know this man may get the impression that he is dealing with a pushover. (If he gets such an impression he won't keep it long.)

This is *Star* shop talk, however, and I say enough of it. One of my extracurricular titles around here is "Associate Golfer." I would like to take all of you out to the course with Editor McKelway and let you hear him haggle for an unconscionable handicap, or have you listen to his purple language when he is deep in a trap and seemingly doomed to spend the afternoon there.

Some things should be left for the AP directors. They have elected their President McKelway. Let them experience for themselves the shock of getting to know McKelway, the golfer. That will toughen their hides for the harsher experience of getting to know McKelway, the boss.

C. A. (Pete) McKnight, Editor
The Charlotte Observer

By Kays Gary

At age four he had learned to read and write.

At twelve he had built a radio outfit and had shot his brother in the tail with a .22 rifle.

At twenty-two he had graduated summa cum laude from Davidson College.

At thirty-two he was editor of the Carolinas' largest afternoon newspaper.

At thirty-nine he was editor of the Carolinas' largest newspaper.

Today at forty-seven and still editor of the *Charlotte Observer*, C. A. (Pete) McKnight and his analytical brain have succeeded in mastering all challenges except two—golf and two-to-one martinis.

Associates call him a visionary who thrives on tackling broad, complex situations.

Perhaps the first complex situation was his name, Colbert Augustus.

By age six with the help of buddies who had trouble remembering that handle, he had become "Pete" to everyone except his mother.

It was that mother, the late Norva Proctor McKnight, who taught Pete, a sister and two brothers to read. A teacher and wife of J. S. McKnight, a wholesale grocer, she felt the family would be disgraced unless her children started school with something more than ABCs.

The acceleration paid off. Though the sister died in childhood, William A. McKnight became professor of Spanish at the University of North Carolina and John P. McKnight, veteran newsman and Associated Press bureau chief in Rome, became assistant to United States Information Agency chief Edward R. Murrow.

Gary was a staff writer for the *Charlotte Observer* when this article first appeared, in 1964.

But while Pete once labeled his childhood as "unspectacular," brother Bill of the scarred rear would beg to disagree.

"It was an accident. A pal had left the rifle in a barn. Pete picked it up, thought it was unloaded, and pulled the trigger. It hit me in what the local paper delicately referred to as 'the fleshy lower back.' Pete was terrified—so sick that he went to bed and asked Mother to give him a dose of castor oil."

To a nine-year-old it must have seemed the ultimate in penance.

In his hometown of Shelby, North Carolina, Pete was the backyard camper, tennis scrambler, swimming dervish, and everything but an introverted scholar.

"He just didn't have to hit the books too hard," recalls brother Bill. "He was always deep in other things. Played the piano and trumpet. Once I came home from school and didn't have any place to sleep. He'd taken over my room for his amateur radio station."

Graduating in 1933, "not at the top of his class but not at the bottom, either," Pete had his own ideas of something to do in that jobless Depression year.

He took off for Cuba where brother John was stationed with the Associated Press. Pete, at seventeen, figured he could get a job teaching English and learn Spanish at the same time.

It was a sizzling news summer. He arrived in Havana just as a roaring revolution broke. Trailing John around, he saw enough. Once when their hotel was under fire beardless Pete dived headlong over the counter of a Western Union booth in the lobby where he sat out the siege. On another occasion he watched from a balcony as troops fired into demonstrators, killing more than a score of them.

And on top of the revolution came the worst hurricane in Cuba's history. The McKnight brothers, in Cardenas near the beach, holed up in a stone house. It was the only one left standing in two city blocks when the storm had subsided.

By September Pete was back in Shelby and job hungry. He landed one as a clerk in a shoe department but his summer with John had given him newspaper fever. In January he connected at $12.50 per week with the triweekly *Shelby Star* and for nine months did everything from setting type to writing heads.

He decided to butt heads with the Depression to get on to college. He landed a small scholarship at Davidson for half tuition. He waited on tables and managed a boarding house. He represented a Charlotte department store, rounding up students for the store representative's visit with a line of clothing. He delivered the *Charlotte Observer*, worked in the library, graded papers as an English assistant for two years and as a Spanish assistant for one year.

His Phi Beta Kappa average at graduation: ninety-seven.

He had majored in Spanish, intending to teach. But realizing economic necessity would extend his graduate work over a long period, he decided to go to work.

It was back to the *Star* for the few months it took him to decide he was worth more than he was paid. Next Papa McKnight took him on in the wholesale grocery business, purposely gave him the meanest jobs, and got quick results.

In May 1939, Cameron Shipp, distinguished reporter and editorial writer for the *Charlotte News*, recommended young Pete for a job.

"'Total,' that's the word to describe him, then and now," says Brodie Griffith, who hired him and is now editor and general manager of the *News*.

"He was a digger. Time meant nothing to him. When he went after a story he wanted it all and he got it all, and not once was his accuracy ever questioned."

Griffith has other descriptive terms for the 1939 cub. "Excellent judgment" and "courage" are most prominent.

Both Griffith and J. E. Dowd, then editorial page editor and now general manager of Editor McKnight's *Charlotte Observer*, agree on his best reporting job. It was in covering hearings and the state's investigation of state hospitals for the mentally ill. The investigation had been triggered by a *News* exposé. It led to reforms and North Carolina's still-growing prominence in the care of mentally ill.

Griffith and Dowd still chafe because "we should have had a Pulitzer on that one."

McKnight hit all the beats with staff contemporaries like Harry Ashmore, Tom Fesperman, Ray Howe, Burke Davis, and W. J. Cash of the ivory tower. He also edited the book page, handled a record column, did reviews on drama and music.

The contemporaries agree that McKnight's powers of concentration were enormous.

"Good thing there was no railroad crossing between the office and the courthouse," says Fesperman, "or he wouldn't be with us."

But Ashmore wonders. He recalls the sight of skinny, black-haired McKnight, nose buried in the first edition of the *News* held in one hand as he crossed Independence Square in the heart of town.

"His eyes were on the paper in his left hand but he was holding up traffic with his right hand, just like a cop!"

"He always had to go take that second search in his stories," Fesperman says. "What I remember most about those stories were the numbered paragraphs—the lead and then one, two, three, four. No matter how complex the story he was going to make everybody understand."

He was a voracious reader of newspapers and books but he attacked hobbies with equal thoroughness.

No record player he could find would suit him. So he built one which Ashmore recalls "covered a wall in a cabinet big enough to hide a horse."

"Two blocks away you could hear that thing," Fesperman remembers. "Listening to the Philadelphia Symphony play Beethoven's Sixth wasn't enough. He had to hear Boston play Beethoven's Sixth and the New York Philharmonic play Beethoven's Sixth and Denver and San Francisco and anybody else. He had to hear all the best play the best, loud enough so he could tell whether the second violinist had waxed his bow."

By contrast McKnight played a mean saloon piano when weekend parties threatened to poop out at two o'clock.

In December 1942 with the nation at war, McKnight had to move. Twice rejected for military service for physical reasons, rejected again by the Office of Strategic Services for the same reasons (Pete lost an eye in childhood, following an accident with a .22 rifle), he accepted an offer to become managing editor of the *World Journal*, an English language daily in San Juan, Puerto Rico.

There he was also an accredited war correspondent for the Associated Press, wrote for the *New York Times, Baltimore Sun,* and *Business Week* magazine, and became editor, then executive editor of his paper.

In 1944 at age twenty-eight he returned to the *Charlotte News* as news editor, in two years became managing editor, and in two more the editor of the editorial page. That's where McKnight made his biggest mark.

"Whether the editorials concerned Charlotte or international affairs they were lucid . . . and at the same time like a learned speech," Fesperman says.

McKnight dominated awards of the North Carolina Press Association (NCPA). With entries limited to three editorials the usual results were "McKnight one-two" and sometimes "McKnight one-two-three."

Simultaneously, the thirst for challenge involved him in such things as development of zoning and planning and urban redevelopment commissions and cultural agencies.

Another change came, not surprisingly, in the wake of the Supreme Court's 1954 school desegregation decision.

With Peabody, Vanderbilt, and Fisk funds, a Southern Education Reporting Service (SERS) was being set up as a permanent means of objective, analytical tracking of the consequences of that decision.

A board of directors, including Harry Ashmore, worked up a list of men qualified to become executive director of SERS.

Ashmore phoned an old friend, McKnight, for his opinion on some of the potential candidates.

"There is one man you have forgotten," McKnight told him.

"Who?" Ashmore replied.

"Me!" said McKnight.

"You think you'd be the man for it?"

"Why," said McKnight, "I think I'd be ideal!"

That was it. McKnight organized SERS into an effective agency in 1954 and 1955.

In 1955 challenge and change came again when the Knight Publishing Company bought the *Charlotte Observer*, McKnight's big and rich old rival.

He sought out Lee Hills, executive editor of the Knight Newspapers. There was an interview before McKnight, like any cub reporter, was sent to a typewriter to put down all the reasons commanding his selection as editor of the *Observer*.

That did it.

He set out to make the *Observer* more than big. He wanted it to be a major force in the political, economic, and cultural future of the Carolinas. He wanted it to be an institution to be reckoned with.

He spent the first years building a staff of young intellectuals. More recent years have brought a turn to drawing on more experienced personnel. Many of the young ones, reacting much as McKnight had to challenge, would move on to bigger, quicker opportunities with national magazines, newspapers, foundations.

He went in for saturation coverage of major news events and startled old *Observer* hands by tossing a squad of reporters and photographers into planes and rented cars to intercept Hurricane Hazel in 1955.

McKnight tapped Don Oberdorfer, a Princeton lad, to handle the hurricane desk. The McKnight eye glistened when the young fellow headed for the public library on his day off to soak up everything he could find about hurricanes before the copy started. That was the kind of digging he liked.

McKnight brought Fesperman over from the *News* as his managing editor, and the two spent crowded months reorganizing the entire news department. They came out of it with a staff of specialists in medical, farm, human interest, sports reporting, community service, and photography. These specialists began winning regional and national awards.

The "visionary" and "challenge" hunger came on strong again from outside the *Observer's* walls. He saw Charlotte's community college as a someday great university years ago and has poured energy toward that goal, which now seems near.

He was deeply engrossed in attacking North Carolina's cycle of poverty long before Washington made it a household phrase and was a key man in Gov. Terry Sanford's campaign for support from Ford and other foundations in this attack. McKnight has become president of the resultant

North Carolina Fund and its studies.

McKnight has become similarly involved in Charlotte's United Arts Fund, holds memberships on a dozen high-level educational and cultural boards, has conducted fifteen or twenty different programs at American Press Institute seminars and frets for lack of time to write "my own share" of editorials.

But at home he's a relaxer with his wife and children. He married Margaret Henderson of Hickory in 1941. Son Peter, twenty, is a Charlotte College student; daughter Carson, eighteen, is a Salem College freshman; and son David, sixteen, is a brilliant young violinist of true professional promise.

He still takes a hot lick at the piano and is a great collector of jokes. A perspiring football and basketball fan with Davidson and the University of North Carolina as "his" teams, his friends often find him with two radios tuned to different games and a television set to a third.

"And the way his mind works," a friend said with a shrug, "he can give you a play-by-play recap of all three."

Felix R. McKnight, Executive Editor
Dallas Times Herald

By J. Q. Mahaffey

I t's rather like being married to Ruth. I can't remember when I wasn't. Neither can I remember when I didn't know Felix R. McKnight, executive editor of the *Dallas Times Herald*. So when they said, "Who will be the Boswell for McKnight," I threw away all of my many complexes and yelled at the top of my voice, "Let me go in coach, just this once."

It must have been twenty-five years ago when I was a stuttering cub growing up under the painstaking tutelage of Pete Hanes and Henry Humphrey that the McKnight by-line became something to conjure with in the news room of the *Gazette and Daily News*. He was with the Associated Press then.

"You don't have to look any further than Dallas if you want to learn to write," said Mr. Humphrey a long time ago as he dissected a McKnight lead. "Listen to it," he would say, "this boy feels a story and lets himself go."

In those days we all tried to write like McKnight. I can see myself now strutting across to the desk and pushing my copy across to the city editor. "How's that," I'd say, "a real McKnight lead, huh?"

Those were the days of Clyde Barrow and Bonnie Parker, when war was far away and bank robberies and the Oklahoma-Texas game were the biggest news we knew anything about in Texarkana.

Maybe it was later, maybe it was sooner (I get all mixed up on my chronology) but one day Cowboy Jack Crain, one of the greatest halfbacks in the history of the University of Texas, scored two seventy-five-yard touchdowns in the last four minutes to beat Oklahoma. We could hardly wait for McKnight's lead.

Mahaffey was editor of the *Texarkana* (Texas) *Gazette and Daily News* when this article first appeared, in 1961.

"Cowboy Jack Crain," he wrote, tensely, dramatically, "saddled up and twice clattered down shadow-swept sidelines when all seemed lost Saturday to give Texas an unbelievable 19–14 triumph over Oklahoma."

Felix was just a by-line to me until he came to Texarkana to cover the Texas Amateur Golf Championship. I didn't know then that he probably could have won the tournament. I wasn't interested in his golf. I wanted to watch him write about it. No one could write very fast on our old L. C. Smiths—we were all bleeders. But McKnight could. He was so damned big city you could hear the deadline screeching. Hunched over the Smith with the fastest hunt and peck I had ever seen, he spewed out the copy in takes to a waiting Western Union boy. "Gad," we said to one another. "He doesn't even take time to think."

The thing we didn't know is that McKnight had been thinking fast since he was a little boy. His mother was thinking fast when she named him Felix for a great-great-uncle and physician, Dr. Felix Johnson. The R stands for Roy, a World War I uncle and air ace of the old flying Jenny days. It was that war that brought on his first writing effort at the age of eight. Stretched out on the living room floor, he dashed off a letter to Gen. John J. Pershing, telling Black Jack how he could win the war—load up the single engine planes with homemade bombs and drop 'em on the Krauts. Give Uncle Roy a great big bomb. In the midst of the war and only a few weeks later, he got Pershing's reply: the plan had a few bugs in it but he liked hearing from young Americans.

Although born in Dallas, McKnight grew up in San Antonio, attending grammar and high schools in the Alamo City before going to Texas A&M on a semi-basketball scholarship.

His first actual newspaper job was on the *San Antonio Light* at age seventeen. You had to think fast and make every word count, because then as now the *San Antonio Light* is the most tightly edited paper in Texas. Working in a three-man sports department under the guidance of Harold Scherwitz, still sports editor of the *Light* and one of McKnight's many heroes, Felix covered high school sports and worked side by side with Gayle Talbot, who went on to become one of the famous sports by-liners of the Associated Press.

The Great Depression was having its way with bright young newspapermen in those days. After the third cut, McKnight was working sixty-five hours a week for $19.93. When he told me about it, I almost cried until I remembered that I was covering both sides of Texarkana for $18.50.

McKnight is something of a hypochondriac. I never saw him when he didn't have a cold or was just getting over one. It all started while he was working on the *Light*. The doc sawed into him and what did he find? Nothing so normal as appendicitis. This boy had an upside-down stomach, which was pretty hot news when everybody was thinking about stomachs and what to put into them. After two months in the hospital, the ambulance taking him home by prearrangement detoured by the *Light*. The ambulance stopped. They lifted him out on a stretcher and for four floors up employees hung out the windows and showered him with ticker tape and old newsprint. While traffic stacked up behind the ambulance, they presented him with a bassinet complete with baby, and put it in the ambulance. He had a relapse.

Golf and not fine writing got him his job with the Associated Press. The bureau chief at Dallas was an ardent golfer and McKnight had a one handicap. His sixty-nine made the Associated Press man drool and McKnight went to Dallas as a playing partner. Age and heavy responsibilities have now pushed his handicap up to four.

Starting as a pony editor with the Associated Press, he did occasional weekend sports and in 1935 was named southwestern sports editor for the Associated Press, covering the Rose, Sugar, and Cotton Bowls, National Open Golf, Davis Cup Tennis, major league training camps, and just about all the major sports events.

He continued covering some sports while also serving as state editor and later as acting bureau chief. After he left the Associated Press to go with the *Dallas Morning News*, he continued to cover some sports even after he had been named managing editor. He might still be in the press box if Bill Rives, sports editor of the *Dallas News*, had not suggested that he retire from that department so he might devote more time to being managing editor.

If I live to be one hundred, I'll never forget McKnight's coverage of the New London, Texas, school explosion of 1937 that took 297 lives. When the first flash came, I rushed up to the city editor and asked him if I could go in one of the ambulances taking off from Texarkana.

"Hell no," he said, "you'd just get in the way."

McKnight headed a seven-man all Texas Associated Press staff to the scene. They worked around the clock for five days with Felix writing general leads—about fourteen per day with the first two days—on both AM and PM cycles.

It was the greatest peacetime disaster involving children in history. Many writers let their emotions get the best of them and some of the stuff turned out was a kind of maudlin nothingness. If you will look back in your files, however, you'll find that McKnight and the staff he headed let the story tell itself. It was a tender, factual, restrained, fair, and objective account.

Felix has told me that for months after the assignment, he had great difficulty sleeping, dreaming almost nightly of the sight of those hundreds of children buried in the wreckage of the world's richest school. (It, as you recall, had scores of flowing oil wells right on the school grounds.)

Dumped out of the armed forces because of the aforementioned upside-down stomach, he served in various capacities with the War Department on loan from the *Dallas News*.

Ruth and I agree that the best job McKnight ever did in his life was in marrying a gal named Lib. They have been married twenty-seven years and have two charming daughters—Mrs. Don McIlyar and Anne, a senior student at the University of Texas. Felix likes to talk about having three women arrayed against him but to my subtle, reportorial ear they sound more like the SMU cheering section on a sunny Saturday afternoon.

McKnight thinks there is no city quite like Dallas and he has served the Central Texas metropolis with the same devotion he has given to newspaper assignments. He has been president of the Cotton Bowl Association and the Boy Scouts; chairman of the board of the Highland Park Methodist Church; vice-chairman of the Community Chest, etc.

Although McKnight is still a young man, a few years ago when he was much younger, he was named the Outstanding Young Man of Dallas and one of the five outstanding young men of Texas. He was nominated in the first fifteen outstanding young men in the nation.

Felix is a great ribber and he takes a lot of ribbing here in Texas. We started calling him St. Felix when he rewrote the Bible. Actually, however, that was the most rewarding work of his career. His mother gave him the assignment. Why, she said, shouldn't a newspaperman write the last eight days of Jesus as he would have seen it? McKnight went into three months of research with Catholic bishops, Protestant ministers, and even a Jewish rabbi who gave him access to a library that contained descriptive material that was almost not to be found. He wrote "The Immortal Story"—the eight days of Easter Week—for the *Dallas News*. The next year it was reproduced in series form in sixty-three American and foreign newspapers. Later, it was published as a four-color book by Henry Holt and Co. It is still being sold during the Lenten season.

Felix has never won a Pulitzer Prize but in 1944 he won the national Sigma Delta Chi award for his story on the Battle of the Bulge. It was a piece on the men of Bastogne and their Christmas Day which he did in editorial form.

In 1957, McKnight joined his old friend Jim Chambers on the *Dallas Times Herald* as vice-president and executive editor. He heads a staff of one hundred news and editorial people. Since he has been on the new job, they have gone through some freshening up, concentrating on the stories-in-depth stuff, which he thinks is essential to afternoon paper coverage.

"Today's newspaper," he says, "must tell the why of things. We have built, in three years, a staff that is backgrounding our readers on the 'why' of local, state, and national news."

About the only thing that Felix R. McKnight and I have in common is that we married well and both fell in love a long time ago with the newspaper business. We go up and down the land telling all the youngsters who will listen that they ought not to miss this exciting game. Who knows, maybe after we've grown old and grey and bald we'll form an evangelistic team. He's gonna do the preaching but I'm gonna lead the singing.

Holt McPherson, Editor
The High Point (North Carolina) Enterprise

By Miles H. Wolff

Holt McPherson is editor of the *High Point* (North Carolina) *Enterprise*. North Carolinians wonder if he has the time for this. In addition to being editor he currently is:

● General chairman of a campaign to raise $1,500,000 for expansion of the High Point Hospital;

● Chairman of the Board of Trustees of High Point College (nine hundred students) which last year dedicated five new buildings and has money for two more;

● Chairman of the Journalism Foundation seeking to raise a one-hundred-thousand-dollar endowment for the School of Journalism at the University of North Carolina;

● Vice-chairman of the American Council on Education for Journalism and chairman of the Southern Newspaper Publishers Association committee on journalism education;

● Director of the North Carolina Safety Council, a group appointed by Gov. Luther Hodges to promote highway safety;

● The lay member of the Committee on Medico-Legal Post-Mortem Examination, another appointment by Governor Hodges.

He also is chairman of the boards of two radio stations.

These are not all of McPherson's jobs but they illustrate the extent of his interests. But let's start at the beginning.

McPherson was born in High Point, started carrying newspapers for the *Enterprise* at the age of ten, did part-time work on the newspaper during high school and at college. After graduation from the University of North Carolina he returned to the *Enterprise* as a full-time reporter. In three years he was made editor. He was twenty-five at the time.

Wolff was executive editor of the *Greensboro* (North Carolina) *Daily News* when this article first appeared, in 1956.

After six years he was forced by his wife's illness to move to Florida. The real estate business lured him away from newspaper work. McPherson says of this interlude, "I made money so fast that I began to wonder if it was honest."

The story is told around Miami and Fort Lauderdale that he cleaned up a million dollars and bought a newspaper. He intimates that the million-dollar part is an exaggeration but he did buy part interest in the *Shelby* (North Carolina) *Star* in 1941 and became its managing editor.

Three years ago he returned to High Point and was welcomed at an enormous banquet with much speech-making.

For the benefit of those who live in far-away spots such as Hartford, Connecticut, and Spokane, Washington, it should be mentioned here that High Point has some forty thousand inhabitants and is a center of furniture-making and hosiery manufacture. The *Enterprise* has a circulation slightly under twenty-five thousand.

McPherson's chief responsibility is to get out the editorial page, which includes writing virtually all the editorials. He also supervises the news pages and the news personnel, although he does not handle directly the day-by-day news output.

McPherson shows up at the *Enterprise* around seven-thirty each morning and completes his editorial page chores by ten o'clock. He then is ready to turn to other work. And work he does.

An example of the way he operates can be seen in the campaign to raise money for the High Point Hospital. When he discovered that an old section of the hospital was to be condemned as unsafe, he turned his attention to the problem of a new building.

He knew of a wealthy resident of the city who was recovering from a heart attack. He presented his case before this wealthy gentleman and persuaded him to agree to contribute one hundred thousand dollars toward a heart center for the hospital if an additional nine hundred thousand could be raised.

In less than two months, the entire sum was raised and the goal has now been upped to $1,500,000.

The remarkable thing is that while McPherson was general chairman and really ran the campaign, readers of the *Enterprise* would hardly have known it. His name was conspicuous by its absence.

While this campaign was in progress, McPherson found that the contributions to the Journalism Foundation of the university were lagging. He took to the long-distance telephone and in a matter of a few days, every daily newspaper in North Carolina had contributed.

Incidentally, the Journalism Foundation was launched by McPherson in an effort to get supplementary money for the School of Journalism at the university. The one-hundred-thousand-dollar goal has not been reached as yet. Newspapers are notoriously niggardly. With the help of other industries, the goal might be said to be in sight.

It is almost impossible to count all the fingers McPherson has in many pies.

He has headed other campaigns to raise money, as for example the successful campaign to raise one million dollars for a new church building for the Wesley Memorial Methodist Church to which he belongs.

As president of the North Carolina Press Association he led the fight against last year's "secrecy law" which the North Carolina legislature proposed.

Last summer he was accredited to the United Nations for the Atoms for Peace gathering in Geneva. In 1951 he was delegate to the Ecumenical Conference of the Methodist church at Oxford, England, and in 1950 he took an extensive tour of South America.

He has nineteen years of unbroken attendance in the Rotary Club.

His publishers wanted an editor, and they got one in McPherson. They wanted someone to represent the newspaper in High Point and North Carolina. They got this in full measure.

His staff is fond of him and marvels at the way he gets around and the amount of ground he covers. They are particularly pleased at the way he stands up for them when the occasion arises.

There are a few other odds and ends that might be mentioned. Despite his 235 pounds, he is a determined tennis player and won the doubles championship and the senior doubles title of his country club last summer.

He is particularly fond of ice cream.

He has an air-conditioned Cadillac and a very sporty Packard.

He has made more than one hundred speeches since he returned from Geneva last summer.

One associate summed up McPherson this way:

"Holt is a fellow who will travel two hundred miles to speak to a small or a large group at night, return home, get a few hours sleep, and be down at his office writing editorials before the rest of the staff arrives. He will attend meetings during the day, play a few sets of tennis for all he is worth in the afternoon, then get back in his car and travel several hundred more miles to speak that night. He has boundless energy."

When he came to Greensboro at my invitation to talk about this profile, we had lunch at a downtown restaurant. As soon as he had finished eating, he excused himself. He had spotted at a nearby table a man known to be well heeled.

"You see," he explained, "we are just $160,000 short of getting the one million dollar endowment for High Point College."

J. Q. Mahaffey, Editor
Texarkana (Texas) Gazette and Daily News

By Maurice Moore

W ill Rogers probably never gave a second thought to the kindness and advice he imparted to a young Texarkana reporter who barely could make himself understood because he stuttered.

But J. Q. Mahaffey never forgot.

The kindness from Rogers, who was to die in a plane crash in Alaska a few years later, changed the course of the young man's life.

The story of the interview with Rogers is significant now because Mahaffey recently closed out a colorful newspaper career by retiring so he could take another job in a new field. He spent thirty-nine years with the *Texarkana Gazette and Daily News*—twenty-two of them as editor.

In recent months he has been pioneering the role of Citizens Participation Specialist for Texarkana's embryonic Model Cities program. He will try to help sell a new federal-local partnership program in an area known for its political conservatism.

The sixty-year-old Mahaffey still talks with a slight stutter. But long ago he turned his speech defect into an asset. Most of his addresses are spoken in a humorous vein. So he gets a lot of mileage out of something that once threatened to ruin his life.

When Mahaffey was seven years old, he was stricken with diphtheria and nearly died. He was given a massive dose of antitoxin to save his life. But the medicine affected his nervous system, and he became a stutterer.

The speech impediment made it hard for him to recite his lessons in school. He transferred to Columbia Military Academy at Columbia, Tennessee. The situation didn't show much improvement.

Since boyhood, Mahaffey had dreamed of studying law and going into partnership with his father, the head of a prominent firm. However, the

Moore was regional editor of the *Arkansas Democrat* when this article first appeared, in 1968.

speech defect prevented this. So his father suggested he go into the newspaper business. He received a bachelor's degree from Furman University in Greenville, South Carolina, in 1929.

On July 5, 1929, he went to work for the Texarkana newspapers on a voluntary basis. He received no pay.

When he applied for the job, he was given the admonition: "We don't need you, we don't want you, but when you are worth something we will begin to pay you."

Even though he was a college graduate, he could barely speak a whole sentence without hanging up badly.

It took him three months or so to get on the payroll at nine dollars a week. A story he had written about Negroes working on his father's river-bottom plantation had been reprinted in the *Denver Post*. So he told the Texarkana editor that if his work was good enough to appear in a big city paper, he certainly ought to be on the payroll of the Texarkana newspapers.

However, Mahaffey was still floundering on the day in 1931 when Will Rogers came to Texarkana for a benefit appearance in behalf of the drought victims of his native Oklahoma. His inferiority complex had dropped him to the depths of despair.

Mahaffey takes up the story from this point:

"There were no reporters available to cover Mr. Rogers's arrival. The city editor told me to get to the airport and get some good quotes from Rogers, come back, and give them to another reporter to write. As I left the office, he told me, 'Don't muff this assignment, because if you do, you are through.'

"So I grabbed a wad of copy paper and a pencil and took off for the airport. All the way out there, I practiced how I would approach him—I kept saying over and over to myself—'Mahaffey is my name, Mr. Rogers, and I'm a reporter for the *Gazette*, and I want to ask you a few questions.' But, I knew all the time, I wouldn't be able to say a thing when I got there.

"There was a tremendous crowd at the airport—over two thousand people. I wormed my way through and got right beside Mr. Rogers. But I blocked up and couldn't say a word. He looked at me with a quizzical expression on his face. I said to myself, 'He must think I'm the village idiot.' So I missed my first chance. However, I followed him to the McCartney Hotel in Texarkana and decided I would try to talk to him in his room. I picked up the house phone and called. He answered and I blocked up again. I couldn't say a word.

"So I was ready to give up. I couldn't be a lawyer because I couldn't talk. And I couldn't be a reporter for the same reason. I thought I would just go back to the office and tell the city editor I was no good and he wouldn't have to fire me because I was going to quit.

"Just as I started out of the hotel, the elevator came down and Mr. Rogers stepped out and walked into the hotel barber shop. I went in and sat among those waiting to be served. Mr. Rogers was getting a shave, and his face was full of lather, when another barber told me I was next. I tried to tell him I didn't want a haircut or shave—that I just wanted to interview Mr. Rogers. I was having a hard time making myself understood when Mr. Rogers raised up from the barber chair—lather all over his face—and said, 'Come here, old country boy.'

"He said, 'You've been following me around all day. Now what do you want?' Somehow or another, I managed to tell him that I was a reporter but I wasn't going to be one very long because I couldn't talk. He said, 'But you're talking okay now.' I told him that generally I couldn't talk at all."

Then, Will Rogers, the humorist, became Will Rogers, the philosopher.

Mahaffey remembers the next part of the conversation as if it were spoken yesterday.

Rogers said to the afflicted youth, "Let me tell you something about folks, old country boy. People who amount to anything in this world will know you stutter before you ever open your mouth. And they will be good to you; they will be kind to you, and they will do everything they can for you.

"Those that won't know you stutter—well, they ain't worth knowing anyway," he added. "So now I expect you will want to know what I'm doing in Texarkana, what I'm going to say tonight and everything like that."

Mahaffey explained, "What Mr. Rogers was saying to me was simply that people are generally kind and good and sympathetic, and I wouldn't have to worry about the few who are mean."

He continued the story: "Mr. Rogers told the shine boy to bring his stool over so I could interview him while he was getting his shave. This was one of the great moments of my life. Here I was, perched on that stool in a barber shop, interviewing this great man. And he gave me a great story. I went back to the office and wrote the story, and they printed it.

"From that day on, I knew the only way I could conquer this trouble was to bring it out into the open and let people know for sure that I stuttered before I ever started talking with them," he declared. "Afterwards, there was no trouble. I also knew that I had to begin making public speeches because I recognized that everytime I spoke, I would be knocking that old trouble a little bit further back into the corner."

What if Mahaffey had not received this fatherly consideration from Rogers?

"I think I would have retired into my shell and would have never come out," he replied. "It was just that desperate. You have no idea of the mental torture a stutterer goes through. Most are completely shattered by the experience and really aren't able to overcome it."

When he left the newspaper business he was put on retired status by ASNE and was elected a life member of the Texas Associated Press Association. He has served as president of both the Texas and Arkansas Associated Press Associations, and in 1963 was named Texas Newspaper Man of the Year by Sigma Delta Chi. He also has received the Baptist Press Award of the Baptist General Convention of Texas for outstanding service in Christian journalism.

Mahaffey numbers among his close friends a onetime Texas congressman who became president—Lyndon Johnson.

"I have known President Johnson for at least thirty years," he pointed out. "I have covered his campaigns for Congress and the Senate, and I was rather close to him when he was Senate majority leader. He relied on me to tell him the sentiment of northeast Texas on various issues. I visited his home in Washington when he was vice-president, and I visited his home in Texas when, as president, he entertained the president of Mexico."

A few years ago his daughter Prudence worked as a secretary on the White House staff.

Other close political friends included the late House Speaker Sam Rayburn and Congressman Wright Patman of Texarkana.

Memories! Mahaffey took hundreds of them with him when he retired as editor in March.

For instance, take the time Editor Mahaffey launched an editorial campaign against prostitution and attracted wrath rather than support.

"We used to have an old 'red light' district in Texarkana that I felt was a cancer in the city," he recalled. "I wanted to get rid of it, so I launched a campaign. Well, the businessmen accused me of running down the town. I received no support, so I finally had to drop the campaign. However, the 'red light' district did eventually close."

Mahaffey, a member of Texarkana's First Baptist Church, received considerable heat in the fall of 1964 when the Palmer Newspapers, of which Texarkana is a member, supported a proposed amendment to legalize casino gambling in Hot Springs. Here is an example:

"One Sunday morning, a television camera (the services are televised each week) caught me taking up the collection in church," he declared. "Well, I got a letter the next day from one of my irate subscribers asking me, 'Where do you old crapshooters go to shoot craps with the church money?' "

Mahaffey, like many reporters of the brawling 1920s and 1930s, cut his teeth on crime stories. The Bonnie and Clyde sensationalism of today brings back some haunting memories of yesteryear.

"Bonnie and Clyde were credited with robbing a number of banks in this area," he recalled. "We chased them at great lengths with tremendous headlines. I remember they used to rob the Guaranty Bond State Bank of

Redwater, Texas, almost every other month. Once I took my mother's brand new sedan on a bank robbery coverage trip. A posseman rammed his shotgun through a window while getting into the back seat. Come to think of it, the newspaper never did pay for the damage."

The most sensational story of his career was the phantom killings in 1946. Five persons were slain within a period of a few months, and the cases were never solved.

"The staff did such a good job of covering the story that we succeeded in creating one of the most tremendous cases of mass hysteria I've ever known. People were afraid to go to bed at night, and everybody kept their lights on. Some people thought the killings were done by the same man. Others thought they were slain by drifters who saw them in the lovers' lanes. I personally have no theories. But I don't think they were all done by the same person."

The veteran editor said he feels it is the responsibility of a small city newspaper, or any newspaper, to guide the community in which it serves.

"You've got to serve as the conscience of the community and at the same time be the gadfly," he said. "You must call attention to the deficiencies and encourage the people to correct them and improve."

Lester Markel,
Sunday Editor
The New York Times

By Helen Markel

T he genesis of this piece of nepotism lies in the simple fact that I am
Lester Markel's only and ostensibly unintimidated child. I place in
evidence the following letter I received recently from Mr. Fredric Gardner
Pitts:

"As editor of the *Bulletin*," Mr. Pitts started off stoutly, "I intend to
publish a profile of Lester Markel as one in a series of articles about
outstanding editors . . ."

By paragraph two Mr. Pitts's editorial resolve began to weaken. "Your
father is admired. He is respected. But he intimidates people," he confessed.
"Because of this, few of his fellow editors would dare write his story.
Therefore," Pitts wrote, bravely clearing his editorial throat, "I thought
perhaps you . . ."

By paragraph three my correspondent, obviously fearing reprisals,
suggested that the assignment be kept on a surprise basis, hurriedly tossed in
the fact that, although there was no fee involved, the *Bulletin* has had many
notable contributors (a variation on a theme I learned at my father's knee),
signed off with a sweat-beaded "Gosh . . . thanks!" and left me to surprise the
acclaimed, denounced, complex, sweat-producing, unsurprisable fellow
who happens to be my father.

I have spent years being Lester Markel's daughter. Whenever I am
introduced to a stranger, our glances hold a long moment while I brace for
the inevitable: "Any relation to Lester?" A few years back a young man met
my father for the first time and said, "Any relation to Helen?" and I married
him.

He's now working with my father and he's not intimidated by him either.

Markel was free-lancing when this article first appeared, in 1961.

By the end of the day he doesn't have the strength.

My father only frightens me when I am pressed into service as his bridge partner, a game to which he brings all of his considerable vigors, or when acting as his chauffeur, on which occasion he sits in splendid isolation in the back seat, simultaneously reading manuscripts and issuing route and speed directions.

What intimidates nonintimates is the towering institution called the *Sunday New York Times* which he has labored to build in his own image since a day in 1923 when Adolph Ochs asked the young man from the *Tribune* to move over and become his Sunday editor.

After thirty-seven years it is as difficult for people to think of the *Sunday Times* without thinking of Markel as it is for me to think of my father without the *Times*. My childhood image of him is a man in a red leather chair wearing a green eyeshade, the floor flung white with newspapers, magazines, and manuscripts-in-progress.

Unlike noneditorial offspring who go through paternal pockets each evening for candy or surprises, my particular joy at his return was to forage through his bulging briefcase, reading the vast reaches of barnacles, attached to the manuscripts therein. By the time I was ten I could recognize at ten paces an outline that hadn't been followed.

Perhaps this explains why I have seldom had to rewrite for him, although I understand that his penchant for revisions is so well known on both sides of the Iron Curtain that when the *New Yorker* ran a poem of his some years back without changing a comma, even Mr. Sulzberger was moved to verse in the *Times* house journal.

Ross didn't say 'Do it again,'
Or drive the author quite insane.
He merely sent the check with thanks
Which Lester split between his banks.

To which my father promptly issued a characteristically blazing rebuttal:

I resent all those dirty cracks about 'rewrite,'
And I ask the publisher, Do you want stuff to be or not to be right?
Such charges, I assert, are libel, slander, almost mayhem.
And I say to AHS, Shayem! Shayem! Shayem!
It's infernalism
In journalism!

I can testify at firsthand that as a writer he is even tougher on himself than he is on his contributors. When embarked on an article of his own, I have seen him agonize through six punishing rewrites, wear out three secretaries, and reduce the household to chaos before he finally considered his own piece fit to print.

When a *Time* researcher, at work on a piece celebrating his twenty-fifth anniversary with the *Times*, cautiously asked him about his reputation for rewrites, Markel produced a definitive answer.

"The good fellows say I'm a good editor. The bad ones think I'm a stinker. I'll settle for that."

On a recent birthday, however, he remarked with satisfaction that he feels the passage of time has made him softer in the heart, if not in the head. "I used to demand 100 percent perfection," he said. "Now I only ask for 99."

He is one of the last of that vanishing tribe of great personal journalists for whom newspapering is as much a passion as a profession. No detail in the four magazines he produces every Sunday under his eagle aegis is too small to escape notice.

His search for perfection is equally unbounded at home. He fiddles endlessly with his color TV set until he gets the perfect image, then switches to another channel. He directs the annual trimming of the family Christmas tree with the single-mindedness of Stengel directing his forces in the final inning of a World Series, and I have been benched more than once for throwing the tinsel on in handfuls rather than applying one fragile strand at a time.

He plots his garden with the same passion he fusses over a layout for the *Review*. One seed sown out of line is intolerable. When a blossom finally appears, his joy is as unconfined as Joyce Kilmer confronting his first tree.

On my fourteenth birthday he gave me a gold bracelet inscribed "ad aspera, ad astra!" which might well serve as his own epitaph. He works a six-day week: the magazine closes on Monday, the book review on Wednesday, drama on Thursday and the Review of the Week Saturday evening. To this end, he is up at six o'clock and fails to understand why the rest of the staff doesn't follow suit. By the time he arrives at the office at quarter to ten he has read all the morning papers, fired a fresh salvo of ideas into the dictaphone beside his bed, done twenty-five pushups, and eaten two breakfasts. By ten o'clock he is drowning a sea of secretaries in a tidal wave of memos, criticisms, cables, and occasional compliments to sleepy-eyed staffers who have just stumbled to their desks wondering if the man ever sleeps.

A dazed associate has clocked his idea rate at one every seven seconds. Any passing notion is recorded in the pocket notebook that always accompanies him. A second pad hangs on the hook outside his shower in case an idea strikes him underwater, and his night table is dominated by an electric pad that lights up when the pencil is removed for any quips that may pass in the night.

He lavished on me the same admixture of tough discipline and loving care which he brings to every other project he takes on. He saw to my physical well-being by taking me on long brisk walks during which he constantly exhorted me to inhale for twenty steps, exhale the next twenty. Between exhales I asked him endless questions. During one such outing I inquired about the word "prostitute," which I had just encountered in Mr. Luce's journal of opinion.

"A prostitute," my father said, barely breaking strides, "is a lady who shouldn't."

We spent long Sundays on the Asbury Park boardwalk, where he taught me how to rock a pinball machine without tilting it, and to throw a ski ball at the side of the alley rather than up the middle. Even now he cannot pass a penny arcade by and the apartment is cluttered with toasters and three-way heating pads that testify to the hand that has never lost its nontilting skill.

He is constitutionally unable to buy one of anything. His ten-room apartment currently houses four television sets, five radios, two phonographs, two electric shoeshiners, and six telephones, one of which is equipped with a gadget that plays "Time On My Hands" while you wait for your number. He has an unrequited passion for gadgets, which he orders sight unseen out of endless mail-order gift catalogues: an electric tie presser, a screw driver that lights up dark corners and a Venus Fly Trap house plant advertised "to eat insects and bits of meat and bear lovely white flowers." He is still waiting impatiently.

He plays with the same intensity with which he works. To celebrate my sixteenth birthday he asked Jack Gould, then nightclub editor, to take us on a guided tour of his beat. I still remember mother and Jack and me at the Savoy Ballroom in Harlem at four o'clock dropping with fatigue, while my father inquired what time the next show went on at the Cotton Club. Shortly after that Gould gave up the nightclub circuit.

In major crises, however, he is like a rock. I still remember the day a neighbor's pony kicked me when I attempted to tie him up to my go-cart and I went screaming home. "That will teach you," my father said, calmly wiping my bloody nose, "not to put the cart before the horse."

When a staffer came under investigation by the House Un-American Affairs Committee, he steadfastly refused to accept his resignation, instead ran his by-line in the magazine every week during the committee proceedings. The man is still there.

In minor crises, he tends to be more Vesuvian than Gibraltar-like. An overdone roast, a misplaced memo, an incompetent cab driver, a busy phone when he wants to reach someone, all become personal affronts.

He only sees movies at previews to avoid waiting for seats. His aversion to standing in line is so well known that one story, unquestionably apocryphal, has it that since there were to be no reserved seats for the preview of Marilyn Monroe's *Let's Make Love*, Columbia assigned two office boys to occupy a pair of seats in the Paramount loge from five o'clock until the time of Mr. Markel's scheduled arrival at eight-thirty. Miss Monroe, as all faithful readers of the *Bulletin* must know by now, is a great and good friend with whom the Sunday editor occasionally discusses the flow of the news at Sardi's and 21.

Once he makes up his mind, he is a man of unflinching conviction. He stoutly maintained for years that his favorite movie was something called *King of Burlesque* starring Warner Baxter. When he couldn't find anyone else who had seen it, he arranged a showing ten years later for a select group of friends who greeted it with minimum enthusiasm.

"That's the trouble with you intellectuals," he said glumly. "None of you has any real feelings."

A born New Yorker, he has been carrying on a long-term love affair with his city ever since. In an all-out effort to avoid entering the family banking business, he worked his way through the Columbia School of Journalism as a legman for the now-defunct *Bronx North Side News*. After graduating at nineteen, he went to the *Tribune*, stayed there nine years, moving inexorably from reporter to rewrite man, copyreader, telegraph editor, city editor, night editor, and finally assistant managing editor.

He came over to the *Times* via an Atlantic City wheelchair. On a winter day in 1923 Mr. Ochs invited him to Atlantic City and took him for a two-hour ride in a rolling chair along the boardwalk. At the end of that ride Ochs asked him to edit his Sunday paper.

At twenty-nine he was the youngest Sunday editor in America. The department he inherited consisted of a sixteen-page magazine, a grab-bag of a feature section, a staff of five, and a circulation of 563,740. Today the magazine averages 116 ad-fat pages, the feature section has been replaced by the Pulitzer Prize–winning Review of the Week, the staff numbers ninety-five, and the circulation stands at a whopping 1,400,000.

The only thing in the place that hasn't changed is Markel himself ("I came here as Sunday editor and I haven't advanced an inch"). After thirty-seven years at the same old stand, he is still relentlessly putting fact before fiction, conviction above comics, and running his taut ship on the same back-breaking schedule that has made the four sections he produces every Sunday the nearest thing to a national newspaper in the United States.

Fretting at growing attacks on press freedom, he persuaded the Ford and Rockefeller Foundations to finance a favorite crusade, the International Press Institute, to implement his residing conviction that the number one problem in the world today is a better-informed public opinion at home and abroad.

He edits to suit himself ("You can't scratch every man where he itches"), has no truck with public opinion polls, "key-hole kommentators," and the concept of a woman's angle ("There is news in sex, but there is no sex in news"). He often berates his editorial brethren who stress entertainment above enlightenment. "I have been impelled at times," he wrote in these same columns, "to inquire whether we should not properly be called the Froth Estate."

I often hear that my father is tough. He thinks tough, he sometimes acts tough, and he often sounds tough. But the fact of the matter is that underneath that mailed chest beats one of the most easily touched—and easily bruised—hearts in the business.

His first encounter with his grandchild, Mark L. Stewart, was pure Markel, deceptively brusque, deeply sentimental.

He picked up the child awkwardly, self-consciously casual, trying to hide his delight. We watched nervously as the baby's tiny head pitched forward.

"Mr. Markel," the nurse said, stepping toward him in alarm. "You have to support him."

"That's what I'm afraid of," said Mark's doting grandfather.

Dwight Marvin, Editor
The Troy (New York) Record

By Alice Fox Pitts

W hen Dwight Marvin—as ASNE director, treasurer, and president—contributed frequently to the *Bulletin*, his copy invariably sent the editor to the dictionary. Each time, the obscure word he had used was the right and only one to convey his precise meaning.

Once Webster was no help. Might the *Troy Record* editor have been in error? Replying to a query, he cited biblical chapter and verse for the word used, and added: "Suggest you spend less time with the dictionary and more reading the Bible."

Is his extraordinary command of English the result of continuous study, or is the right word transmitted effortlessly from brain to typewriter key?

Dwight denied the "extraordinary command" but evinced pleasure that it had been noticed. Endowed with practically total recall, he was reminded of a class in freshman English at Princeton in 1896 (Repeat: 1896).

Prof. Bliss Perry, later of Harvard, asked which of two descriptions of the London plague the class liked better. It was fifteen to one in favor of a starkly factual account against a more imaginative version.

Said Professor Perry to the one, "Defend your position!"

Mr. Marvin, age sixteen, was flustered only for a moment. The gist of his defense was that the first piece was prose; the second, in effect, poetry, "and to me that's the difference between noise and music."

The professor gave him the highest mark possible "for your eloquence although I do not agree with your arguments."

Dwight didn't do as well in other courses ("I was always on probation, always rebellious, and positive I'd be college president the year after next"). He transferred to Williams, earned his B.A. and A.M. there; and an LL.B. at Albany Law School, adding an honorary Litt.D. from Bates many years later.

While practicing law in his uncle's office, he wrote for any publication

---

Pitts was executive secretary of the ASNE and editor of the *Proceedings* when this article first appeared, in 1957.

that would take his contributions; when they wouldn't, he wrote anyway. After three years he quit law (no subsequent regrets) and got a job on the *Troy Times*. "But hold it open a few months," he pleaded, "I want to see Europe." He believed then that travel is highly educational and still does; he and Mrs. Marvin have booked passage, next spring, down the coast of South America and home by way of Africa.

In 1907 he moved to the *Troy Record* as exchange editor, associate editor a year later and, in jig time, he was editor.

An up-and-coming young man on a small newspaper was certain to receive an occasional big city offer. One was at twice his Troy salary.

"It's the most flattering thing that could happen to you," his wife said proudly, "but surely you won't take it?"

He and Troy were part and parcel of each other (fifth generation of the family in the area) and it was her opinion that he'd never be as useful or as happy elsewhere.

"Was she right?"

"Without a doubt. It's been a great deal of fun, with a lot of fights along the way—I've enjoyed them too. (Gleam in the eye implying 'even more.') In fact, I have another coming up this afternoon."

That one was about parking. Until the regulations are enforced, he said in an editorial, there's no knowing whether proposed municipal parking lots are needed. In Troy, cars are parked solidly beside "No Parking" signs. When a timorous tourist asked a policeman "Is it really all right to park here?" he replied, "Oh sure. Nobody pays any attention to those signs." This will be changed if the *Record* editor has his way, as he is prone to.

Dwight didn't have his way on August 12 of this year. When he reached his office (8:40 as usual), one of his reporters stepped in for an interview on "Fifty Years with the Record Newspapers."

He said no; a one-column cut and a stick or two was all, positively all.

"You've been boss long enough," was the answer. "Today *we're* telling *you.*"

The cut was four columns wide, the story two columns long, for the *Record* editor has packed a heap of service into fifty years. His organizational work, often on the board or as president, has been as varied as his interests: River and Harbor Congress, public library, country club, historical societies, church groups, musical groups (he has composed several hymns and college songs), alumni associations (both Princeton and Williams), fraternities, et al.

His longest association has been with the Emma Willard School, which his great-grandfather helped bring to Troy. His great-grandmother taught there; he is a past president and honorary trustee; and two grandsons attending the day school make the sixth generation connected with the institution.

In newspaper affairs (highlights only): Lecturer in journalism at Russell Sage College for six years; several as president of the American Council for Education in Journalism; past president of the State Society of Editors; ASNE president, 1941–42. That was the last time previous to San Francisco the society met out of Washington. He shares with William Allen White the distinction of being the only ASNE presidents from cities under seventy thousand population.

Lately he has cut down on outside activities, to give the youngsters a chance rather than of necessity, for the years have been kind. Either that or he's lived right, for he seems more like a man of seventy than the seventy-eight he'll be next March. Only his hearing has failed. "Deaf as a post!" he announces cheerfully and often as he readjusts his hearing aid. He seems not to have quite gotten the hang of the gadget and turns his head sideways for better hearing, then full-face for the square-in-the-eye look that always has been a marked characteristic. Conversationally, he's as quick on the uptake as ever, and that's plenty quick; nobody ever had to explain anything to him twice.

Dwight credits ASNE friends with the inspiration of *The Faith I Found*, a book he wrote in 1954.

"Between convention sessions," he told us, "over a scotch and soda—"

"You a Presbyterian elder *and* a drinking man?"

Like A. Lincoln, any casual remark reminds him "of a little story," this one about his grandfather, tried, in one of the last ecclesiastical courts in this country, for getting the minister drunk.

"My grandfather's defense was that the minister often stopped at his house on the way home from prayer meeting and he, being a gentleman, always offered his guest a drink. The minister, being a gentleman, drank but never got drunk; therefore there was no basis for the accusation. The verdict, in effect, was 'Innocent but don't do it again.' As for me, I never drink between drinks."

At the bar when ASNE met in the National Press Club, then the Willard and later at the Statler, Dwight noticed that the prime topics of conversation were business, politics, sex, and religion. Most of the editors knew how they felt about the first three and Dwight had firm convictions about the fourth. Spurred by the convention conversations, he wrote the book.

Again "a little story" and one that delights him. A clerk in the local bookshop told him she was surprised that she agreed with everything in *The Faith I Found*, since he is a Protestant and she a Catholic. At which a customer remarked, "I do too. And the surprising thing about that is, I am a Jew."

W. Donald Maxwell, Editor
Chicago Tribune

By Milburn P. Akers

I f William Donald Maxwell had been born fifty years earlier, he might now be the only surviving drummer boy of the Civil War. But an unkind chronological fate robbed him of that distinction, and he has had to settle for surviving as the only editorial member of the triumvirate that beats the drums in Tribune Tower.

Don Maxwell (he dropped the William years ago) is a gregarious Hoosier with an inordinate fondness for Dixieland jazz, a discriminating addiction to good cigars, and a connoisseur's appreciation of the bouquet of charcoal-ripened Kentucky dew.

He is not only the editor of the *Chicago Tribune*, but he is an editor who likes to write. This was proven to the satisfaction of the skeptics on his most recent trip to Europe. He armed himself with a bundle of ten-dollar traveler's checks, the signing of which kept him so busy that he developed writer's cramp, an ailment that seldom afflicts most editors. If this was a manifestation of tightfistedness on Don's part, it was true only in the physiological sense and does not reflect in any way on his generosity with a buck.

The bonuses he passes out to *Tribune* staffers for a job well done are almost legendary, and the natives of Taxco, Mexico, will tell you that Don Maxwell is a most generous man indeed. Colonial Taxco is the picturesque silver, art, and resort center where Maxwell often vacations, and Don in this case does not denote first-name familiarity with the gringo editor but is a Spanish title of respect usually reserved for those of noble lineage.

A few years back Don rendered financial first-aid to a temporarily straitened Taxco innkeeper of Hoosier antecedents. As such things go in Mexico, the story became public property and soon was distorted to

Akers was editor of the *Chicago Sun-Times* when this article first appeared, in 1959.

apocryphal proportions. It was widely bruited about that he had parted with his last peso to help a friend in distress, whereupon Don was richly rewarded by becoming the man's partner in several highly profitable Taxco hostels.

The truth is that the modest loan was quickly repaid and the incident promptly forgotten by the two principals, but taxi drivers and lowly peons will reverently tell you to this day that no greater philanthropist or benefactor of the poor ever lived than Don Maxwell.

Despite his broad travels and international repute, Don may be seen to best advantage in the therapeutic lair he has built for himself in his suburban Evanston home. In a basement recreation room, thirteen miles from the tensions of his editor's chair, Don happily pounds a massive array of drums and clangs his cymbals to the strains of Dixieland jazz emanating from a nearby record player.

He has been losing himself in that down-beat world ever since the days when he felt the need for occasionally escaping from the pressure of working for his boss and predecessor, the late Col. Robert R. McCormick. A stogie clenched in his teeth, a glass of corn ambrosia within handy reaching distance, and a Confederate forage cap perched rakishly on his noggin, Maxwell manipulates his percussion instruments with the skill of a George Wettling or a Zutty Singleton.

Don doesn't need an audience to enjoy this mental prophylaxis, but often enough he has one. It may range from such cronies as the governor, bank presidents, industrialists, and professors, on down to football coaches, reporters, or rival newspaper editors. Don and Basil (Stuffy) Walters, editor of the *Chicago Daily News*, are, as they modestly put it, "two poor boys from Indiana"—the implication being that they made good in the big city. It is a sort of charmed circle from which a financial giant from La Salle Street or a poor boy from Southern Illinois like myself are apt to feel excluded.

To go back to the beginning, the moon was shining brightly on the Wabash River that hot August night in 1900 when Don emerged upon the American scene in a state as mid-American as corn and hogs—a state of crafty politicians, songwriters, the Anti-Saloon League, evangelists, newspapermen, and literary lights. From the fields around Greencastle, Indiana, came the scent of new-mown hay. And there was corn: rich, succulent, yellow Indiana corn that marked the state's children as corn-fed Hoosiers.

Corn, corny, and corn-fed may be terms of derision in the Ivy League set, but not to Don.

"Corn?" Maxwell mused one day, in a moment of perceptive clarity. "Why, the *Tribune* was built on corn."

As one who knows firsthand what kind of a tough competitor the *Tribune* is, I must admit that it was built on much more than corn, and Don has done his full share to help bring our morning rival to its present heights of prominence. It was more than corn that enabled Don Maxwell, as city editor, to mastermind a beat on the Williams Heirens confession in the Suzanne Degnan murder case. Nor did corn account for his successful campaign to pry the Yalta papers loose from the State Department for the use of all newspapers after the documents had been "leaked" to the *New York Times*, edited by Don's bosom pal, Turner Catledge. The recent anti-inflation campaign that deluged Midwestern congressmen with mail against big federal spending was a piece of journalistic enterprise that any imaginative editor would envy. And agree with him or not, the recent series of editorials entitled "First Principles," seeking to reorient the Republican party to *Tribune* views, was a masterly job carried on under Don's direction. Anyone in Chicago will tell you, correctly, that without Maxwell's drive there wouldn't be a great exposition hall on the lakefront.

Equally at home with his hi-fi albums, the classical piano of his wife Marjory, the steady beat of Dixieland, or the back rooms of Chicago night clubs, Maxwell comes by his musical interests naturally. His father, Harry L., was a Methodist gospel singer and his mother, Grace Beck Maxwell, a high school English teacher, always joined the family singing group.

His interest in newspapering also developed at an early age when, as a lad, he delivered the *Banner* to Greencastle homes. The *Banner* later printed his stories while he was going through the local four-year high school course in three years. At DePauw University in Greencastle, where he spent three years, Don worked summers as assistant market editor for the *Indianapolis News* and assistant sports editor of the *Cleveland Press*. DePauw, which he now serves as a trustee, enriched his life in other ways. In 1920 he married Marjory Thomas, a DePauw co-ed, and in his junior year he became editor of the school paper. A young giant named Wilfred Smith held down the sports editor's chair and is now Maxwell's sports editor on the *Tribune*.

The year Don and Marjory married brought him to Chicago as a *Tribune* cub. The fact that his mother was an aunt of the late Edward Scott Beck, distinguished managing editor of the *Tribune*, and that they were Putnam County neighbors in childhood, may have had no bearing on Don's career, but it probably didn't hurt either. He was a copyreader in two years, and after a short sojourn with the *Vancouver* (British Columbia) *Sun*, he was back to the *Tribune*, earning his spurs as sports editor at twenty-five. He was given the job because Joseph Medill Patterson thought a man trained in general news would insist on making sports intelligible to ordinary readers. Among Don's contributions to the joy of mankind was the hiring of Westbrook Pegler. Maxwell became news editor in 1930, city editor in 1939, assistant managing editor in 1942, managing editor in 1951, and after the death of Colonel McCormick, editor in 1955.

The colonel's will also named Maxwell as a trustee of the McCormick-

Patterson trust which holds the controlling interest in the Tribune Company. He is a vice-president and director of the company and a director of most of its subsidiaries and affiliates. He is also trustee of the Robert R. McCormick Charitable Trust and the Cantigny Charitable Trust which administer the major portion of the McCormick estate. He is an Associated Press director and a member of the Pulitzer award committee, and he found time to serve as program chairman for an ASNE convention.

But Don still finds time to sit on the rim of the newsdesk doping out the early editions—and no one within range of a telephone anywhere in the world is ever safe from the Maxwell impulse to chat with old friends.

Tony Cole of Reuters may be roused from his sleep in Karachi, or Peking, or London. Forrest Tucker, playing the lead in the *Music Man,* was just finishing an interview with a local disk jockey at midnight when the telephone rang. It was Governor Stratton and Don, calling from the "drum side of Maxwell's house" to urge, "Come on out and help us have a party." Three other men earlier that night, answering an earlier Maxwell summons, had already arrived, bringing their own party guests. Any of them might have been Harry Moroni, restaurant owner and onetime immigrant boy who has been Maxwell's friend since the 1920s, or Col. Henry Crown, financier and industrialist, or George Halas, owner-coach of the Chicago Bears.

Some years ago Don's brother, Philip, returned to the old hometown of Greencastle for a visit. As promoter of the *Tribune's* annual music festival and other enterprises, Phil is widely known in the Midwest especially among musical groups. Phil encountered an old teacher of the Maxwell boys who discoursed at length on Phil's success, and then asked:

"By the way, whatever happened to that brother of yours, Don?"

Such is fame. But there is one last word. Don was a skinny bag of bones as a youth, weighing only 120 pounds on his wedding day. Some weeks later when Marjory was shopping in the neighborhood of their new home, the woman owner of the delicatessen, who had seen Don, shook her head and warned Marge: "You'd better take good care of that young man. I don't think he's going to make it."

Marge had had no experience taking care of young men but the result today, after painstaking study, is the robust trencherman who may some day even rival my own medieval bishop's girth.

Sylvan Meyer, Editor
Gainesville (Georgia) Daily Times

By Creed C. Black

Sylvan Meyer is not a displaced professional football player who wound up at the bottom of the pile once too often. He just looks that way.

What he is is editor of the *Gainesville Daily Times*, "Covering Busy, Scenic Lake Lanierland in North Georgia."

It is important to know that in all his thirty-nine years he has not been a gridiron gladiator, as they say on the sports pages, because that's why he's an editor. This, at least is the explanation offered by his lovely wife, Anne:

"When he was in high school (in Columbia, South Carolina) he had already reached his present height (six feet, two inches), was painfully skinny, and was still saddled with braces on his teeth. Since it was obvious he would never be a football hero or any kind of athlete (this was before the days of water skiing, of course), he turned to making his mark in journalism in self-defense. He earned his letter from high school for his work on the school paper and went on to the University of North Carolina at Chapel Hill, majoring in journalism, and became the first man since Thomas Wolfe to be elected editor of both the *Carolina Magazine* and the *Daily Tar Heel*. In those days, he carried the resemblance to Wolfe even further ,by having a real unkempt head of hair and generally sloppy appearance."

All that has changed now. The braces on his teeth are long gone, and there is some meat on his bones. His hair is not what you would call kempt, but there is less of it. And instead of looking sloppy he merely looks rumpled.

This is a multipurpose rumple which serves Sylvan well. It can pass for Casual Ivy at Harvard, where he was a Nieman Fellow a decade ago, or for the Folksy Look in Scenic Lake Lanierland. Sylvan is at home either place—or any other place. Gregarious, friendly, and easy to know, he can

---

Black was executive editor of the *Wilmington News and Journal* when this article first appeared, in 1960.

speak the language of either the eggheads of Cambridge or the egg producers of Gainesville. He speaks both tongues, by the way, in a husky voice which lacks the Southern accent that might be expected of a native of Atlanta.

Sylvan's personality, let it be understood, is not split or even slightly torn. As befits a man of his dimensions, it is simply expansive enough to accommodate a remarkable range of enthusiasms. (You can't say interests, for Sylvan does everything with gusto.)

He appreciates a drink of federal, for example, when the choice offered in legally dry Gainesville is between that and "local." But his keenest appreciation is reserved for the martini, which he studied at Harvard. He approaches a Lake Lanier cookout as though he invented the hamburger, but he also has a weakness for "some of the New York restaurants, especially the little ones where you can't hear the sound of those thousands of molars crunching together." And he gets excited about good music, good theater, and good bridge games wherever they may be found.

No project in Gainesville is too small to interest him, and he has conceived, led, promoted, sparked, or pushed enough of them to earn the town's Young Man of the Year Award. But his leadership, like his taste, is not provincial; he was instrumental in organizing the Southern Association of Nieman Fellows and, as president, in obtaining and administering a foundation grant which sent more than a score of Southern newspapermen off to see the world.

As for his newspapering, it has won enough local approval to lift the *Times's* daily circulation from zero less than fourteen years ago to almost ten thousand today and to line the walls of a new "Press-Radio Center" with Georgia Press Association awards. Appropriately, it has also brought Sylvan national recognition in the form of the Sigma Delta Chi Award for editorial writing, which he won in 1957.

The wonder of it all is not that Sylvan accomplishes much but that he accomplishes anything, for he could qualify as the original disorganization man. He majored in planning during his Nieman year, with astonishing results.

"He lives in a constant clutter," says Anne. "He finally bought a rolltop desk and though he tries to clean out his office periodically, it gets stacked up with *Congressional Records,* press releases, and assorted stuff that he can't throw away but never gets back to."

Sports editor Phil Jackson, who has been with Meyer (as he's known to his staff) since the birth of the *Times,* calls him "the busiest fella I know," and adds: "Always seems to have more to do than time allows . . . the rushing sometimes surrounds him with an air of disorganization, but he manages to win out over the confusion on almost every occasion."

Even at home, reports a recent house guest, "the whole household seems to run at a high pitch of excitability. Though this was a guest schedule I got the impression that in 'Mortgage Manor' there's a cheerful crisis every hour, even when they're alone."

These crises, both at work and play, often leave those around Sylvan considerably shaken. But though the skies may threaten to fall, Sylvan himself just plunges along with a supreme confidence that Everything Will Turn Out All Right.

And somehow, it does.

The aforementioned house guest reports, for example, that during his visit Sylvan was determined to conduct a boat tour of the man-made lake that has combined with the flourishing poultry industry to give Gainesville new life. The master planner encountered only three problems: one of the guests didn't like boats and chose not to go; the boat wouldn't start; and the whole schedule, designed to put the party home precisely at dinner time, was knocked back half an hour when Sylvan stopped to push a stalled car. In order, these crises were solved by:

1. A firm order from Sylvan that all guests would make the trip;
2. The discovery that the reluctant guest was sitting on the fuel line;
3. A wound suffered by Sylvan's son, who jumped out of the boat for a swim, cut his foot on a tin can, and necessitated an immediate return home—thus compensating for the time lost on car-pushing and getting the bleeding boy, the sulking guest, and the rest of the merry little band home right on time for dinner.

This example of the way Sylvan relaxes suggests something of the way he works, which is feverishly.

His daily stint includes writing three editorials and a local column, checking a regular beat list, supervising the news operation, receiving the inevitable callers and complaints, attending the equally inevitable civic meetings, marking the paper (at home in the evening), and handling anything else that comes along, which includes taking pictures of people who bring in big fish.

Unable to compete with the big dailies for experienced staffers, Sylvan looks for promising beginners and trains them himself. A visiting fireman who saw a paper he had marked says hardly a paragraph was untouched, but that instead of complaining Sylvan seemed pleased with what could be done in training bright youngsters. He laments his frequent fate in losing them to bigger papers just as they reach the postgraduate level in the Meyer School of Journalism, but he accepts this as inevitable.

When time threatens to run out, Sylvan just squeezes it that much harder. If he has a 2:00 P.M. meeting, he works at the office until 1:59. When each of the three little Meyers (Erica, 11½; David, 8½; Jason, 2½) was born, Sylvan deposited Anne at the hospital and told the doctor: "I'll be at the office. Call me when she's ready." And no one was surprised when he took a portable typewriter to the local bowling emporium one evening, held down his regular spot on the *Times* team, and knocked out the next day's editorial and columns between frames.

Sylvan travels often, though usually to make speeches or attend meetings. "I can remember only one ten-day trip to Mexico in the thirteen and a half years we've been married where we went on a vacation just for the sake of a vacation," says Anne. And not even when he's traveling does his typewriter rest. During the Democratic festivities in Los Angeles this year, he daily wrote his editorials and column, added three or four news stories, and then threw in a couple of broadcasts.

For all this, Life With Sylvan is much simpler now than it was when he started in Gainesville. That was in January 1947, shortly after he wound up thirty-eight months as a naval officer, twenty-six of which he spent aboard a destroyer in the Pacific. More specifically, it was three days after his marriage to Anne and three days before the *Gainesville Times* was to shift from weekly to daily publication.

Sylvan signed on as a reporter at $27.50 a week, which was $12.50 a week less than he and Anne were paying for a hotel room. (They have since erased the deficit by moving out of the hotel into a new dream house overlooking Scenic You-Know-What.)

When the managing editor resigned three months later with ulcers, Sylvan succeeded him and inherited not only the editorial responsibility but also supervision of the back shop, advertising, and circulation.

Ultimately a general manager was hired, and Sylvan shed half his duties and half his title, becoming editor. As a vice-president and owner of 20 percent of the stock, however, he still retains a lively interest in the paper's economic health; when this biographer asked to be put on the mailing list for a couple of weeks, Sylvan obliged with the papers—and promptly afterwards with a bill for eighty cents.

From the first, Sylvan has had a free hand editorially. The startled citizenry in the nine-county area covered by the *Times* was a little slow to adjust to his aggressive news policies, and his liberal causes have not always brought dancing in the streets. But fairness in the news columns and conviction in the editorials, plus a recognition that Sylvan is even right sometimes, have won acceptance for the paper, as its steady growth testifies.

On that most sensitive of all problems facing the South—the race question—it simply was not in Sylvan to join the stampede of politicians, many other editors, and the majority of his readers who roundly damned the Supreme Court and kept telling each other there would never be any integration in Georgia. But instead of remaining quiet while public opinion and the march of events could catch up with him, he stepped out in front to provide the moderate leadership that won him the Sigma Delta Chi award. Not only in his editorials but also on the public platform, he calmly stated the view that some integration was inevitable and that it would be the height of folly for Georgia to close its schools to avoid it. And he invited still further abuse by accepting appointment as chairman of Georgia's Advisory Committee to the federal Civil Rights Commission.

Fortunately, Sylvan has not only courage but thick skin, possibly developed during those early years when there was so little meat under it. He also has an abiding conviction about the responsibility of newspapers in general and small newspapers in particular.

"Maudlin as it may sound, I am convinced that the best newspapering will some day be done by the small papers. They are closer to the people, more flexible, more responsible. They lack only one thing: dough. A prosperous community newspaper can, or should, over the long haul be able to register on its community. It becomes, or should become, the dominant institution and, of course, a constructive one."

Sylvan frankly envies big city editors their anonymity ("Man, to write about somebody and then not have to bump into him every day at the drugstore!"), their staffs, and their resources. But his envy is not unbounded, for he adds:

"I look across that lake every morning and wonder what I could find somewhere else that I don't have here."

Greener looking grass, maybe, but not bluer water.

James E. Mills, Editor
Birmingham Post-Herald

By Grover C. Hall, Jr.

I issued from the Whig lowlands recently to lope up the pike a hundred miles to the Birmingham highlands, "to take dunner" with James Edward Mills, sixty-six, of the Scripps-Howard college of cardinals. A solid central impression was begotten by the reminiscences and that was of an apparently flawless *symmetry* in Mills's life, personal and professional, beginning to end.

Here and now, it becomes a *Bulletin* scoop to divulge that Jimmy will retire at the end of the year, concluding a harmonious forty-year relationship with Scripps-Howard. Jimmy looks like a boy, Mrs. Mills is in excellent health, their two sons have flourished (one in business, one sagging under the burden of M.I.T. degrees and lectures at Edinburgh).

Jimmy's role the past several years has been that of prophet and progenitor of the redemption of Birmingham from disaster and abulia. And in this ultimate year Jimmy has had the singular experience of having an editorial upheld by the United States Supreme Court.

Jimmy had had a good deal to do with electing Art Hanes mayor of Birmingham. Hanes, lawyer and former FBI agent, smelled sweet in everybody's dossier, but he went sour in office.

In the wake of the racial disturbances, Jimmy and other Birmingham leaders concluded that Birmingham could scour out its past and make a new beginning by a change from commission government to mayor-council and the proposition was initiated. Jimmy also felt it a duty to seek the ejection of Mayor Hanes.

On the eve of the 1962 referendum, there was some hanky-panky involving the incumbent commission and its blandishments to city employees and their families at a mass meeting, which was secretly taped.

Jimmy wrote a tart rebuke on the incident and the editorial appeared on election day. In a few days Jimmy was faced with a charge of violating

---

Hall was editor of the *Montgomery Advertiser* when this article first appeared, in 1966.

Alabama's Corrupt Practices Act: It forbids any kind of electioneering on election day.

Customarily, Alabama papers have ceased firing in the Sunday editions preceding Tuesday elections and it has not been inhibitive since a new issue rarely arises. Few citizens, including editors, know the contents of the law and many of its provisions are a nullity since even a vote-for billboard would violate it. The action against Jimmy may have been punitive, but it was resolute and Jimmy was not purged until the Supreme Court invalidated the restraint.

Jimmy was in the courtroom when the justices heard arguments. He quickly conjectured that he would be upheld, for the justices roused from a slumbrous consideration of another case to tendentious, firecracker questioning in his. I abstained from asking Jimmy if this subjective experience altered his judicial tyranny dogma.

In Jimmy's look and boxer's dance, one sees the high school quarterback that was in Little Rock. Next came War I and enlistment in the 1108th Aero Squadron and service over there.

Jimmy entered Princeton on a football scholarship, but marriage to Elise Austin, a Texan, became more important. He became a partner in a filling station at Pine Bluff and yearned to be a newspaperman.

The opportunity came from two directions: an interloper took most of his curbstone business by establishing the town's first drive-in station; and as he was walking down the main street there was a great explosion within a building.

Jimmy fell upon the story and the *Pine Bluff Commercial* was able to make an extra of it.

Jimmy was editor of the *Palm Beach Times* in 1927 when Florida blew up. He joined Scripps-Howard in Cleveland and presently became managing editor of the *Memphis Press-Scimitar*. He was made editor of the old *Birmingham Post* in 1930, when the city craved the sight of some new factory soot.

The *Post* was merged with the *Birmingham Age-Herald* in 1950 to become the *Post-Herald*. Newhouse subsequently purchased the *Birmingham News* from the Hansons and the *Post-Herald* and *News* papers were combined, though of course only symbiotically.

The *Post-Herald* is the largest of Alabama's morning papers (85,696) and is statewide. The bedizened, redundant-bosomed *Birmingham News* has twice the circulation, but not twice the influence.

To the editorial formula and righteousness of Scripps were fused, these thirty-six years in Birmingham, the steadfastness and high purpose of Mills, editor and president. The union makes a respectable and consequential organ. Its performance might sometimes disappoint, but never its motives.

I submit again, in this case all is symmetry. But hold. Jimmy resides in a chalet high above Birmingham in the alpine village of Mountain Brook. Mornings, he descends into Jones Valley, the city below, for the exertions under the sun. At eventide he ascends. Mountain and valley: symmetry all the way.

Warren Morrell, Editor
Rapid City (South Dakota) Journal

By E. L. Ingvalson

Three veteran, knowledgeable editors, waiting in line to register at an ASNE meeting, noticed the badge on a smilingly cheerful young man which read "Warren Morrell, *Rapid City Journal.*"

Where, they wondered, was Rapid City. Each made a wild guess. None was right.

But Rapid City and Warren Morrell are not unknown in far places. When P. Ratnaswami, native director of the YMCA in Madurai, India, arrived in New York, those in charge of his American tour asked what cities he wished to visit, suggesting Washington, Chicago, and Hollywood.

"I want to go to Rapid City and see Warren Morrell," the Indian answered. "I met him in Madurai."

Morrell probably has as many foreign visitors as anyone in the Northwest. Many, like Ratnaswami, are friends he made on trips abroad. Others just "drop in" on him because someone has told them about Morrell and the hospitable people of western South Dakota and eastern Wyoming, the territory served by his paper. The *Journal* editor is deeply concerned with winning friends for America and helping Americans to better understand people of other countries. On his trip to India in 1955, he spoke to eighty-five thousand people, trying, as he says, "to sell America to the Indians."

But Morrell has no Afghanistanism complex. As editor and columnist of the *Journal*, he hits hard on local and regional matters—so hard, in fact, that politicians he had opposed recently called him "Poison Pen Morrell" and tried to popularize the label in competing media. On occasion, irate readers have purchased large space in the *Journal* to answer some of his editorials

---

Ingvalson was managing editor of the *Rapid City Journal* when this article first appeared, in 1957.

and even have included personal attacks on Morrell himself.

"Makes money for the paper," is his unruffled comment.

A native of South Dakota and a graduate of the state college, Morrell worked for the Associated Press in Chicago, the *Dakota Farmer*, and being political-minded, wound up as press secretary for a governor and editor of the GOP state bulletin before going to Rapid City. Only last month, Governor Foss selected him as liaison representative between the governor's office and the state legislature. As Foss's representative, Morrell contacts not only the lawmakers but also the press to present the governor's views.

Now forty-one, he joined the *Journal* in 1946 after four and a half years in the infantry. He saw considerable service in the European theater and emerged from the army as a major. He is married to the daughter of his publisher and they have two sons, aged thirteen and fifteen. Among his personal exploits in the realm of hobbies:

● As an amateur deer hunter, he was lost for twenty-four hours in the rugged Black Hills.

● Seeking firsthand material for a skiing column, he suffered innumerable contusions.

● He lasted three days of a week-long pack trip although he had not ridden a horse for years.

The *Journal* was founded in 1878 and as a weekly did all right, recording gold claim legals plus occasional bits about the effrontery of gaudy ladies driving down Main Street in carriages while wives walked. This was two years after the famous Gold Rush to Deadwood, when Rapid City was called the "hay camp," being located neatly for supply trains, with water available and plenty of feed.

Rapid City is at the foothills of the Black Hills, which are not hills but mountains, with one peak rating as the highest point in the country east of the Rockies. The area has seen mining, tremendous cattle spreads, influx of homesteaders, and the subsequent dwindling of all of them.

Morrell believes Rapid City is the "last frontier" of the nation and that the surrounding territory justly deserves its label as the "richest one hundred miles square in the world." It boasts wheat and cattle and sheep ranches with two irrigated sections which produce sugar beets; several small packing plants, and a sugar factory. There is mining of nonmetallic minerals such as bentonite with processing plants and in the southern Hills a new million-dollar uranium processing plant for the carnotite extracted from the area. The only producing gold mine is the fabulous Homestead, largest in the United States.

An admitted extrovert, the young editor personally knows hundreds of people in his territory—the miners, the ranchers, the lumbermen, the shopkeepers, the fliers at the nearby air base. He knows them through speaking engagements, visits to their homes, their shops, their farms. This, he believes, is essential to learn the thinking of his readers, to get a glimpse of their dreams and ambitions, and to discover what they like and dislike in the *Journal*.

Apparently they like it pretty well. In the ten years Morrell has been with the paper, its circulation has more than doubled.

Marcellus Murdock, Editor
Wichita Eagle-Beacon

By Dolph Simons

B at Masterson, Wyatt Earp, Bill Hickok, and all the other gunslingers who roamed the dusty streets of Wichita less than a century ago were a bunch of softies compared to the present best-known resident of the town who roams the skies over Kansas and Oklahoma at least once a week.

The famed gunslingers were brave and daring, as long as they had a grip on ole Betsy and were only a step away from the saddle and a fast getaway, but anyone of them probably would have crawled for mercy before being required to do what comes naturally for our current celebrity.

Editor Marcellus Murdock, a seventy-nine-year-old native of the Kansas cowtown, probably is America's number one sports pilot and he apparently holds nearly every record in the book for longevity at a pilot's stick. In logging more than six thousand hours as a pilot, he has worn out five airplanes and now swirls over the midlands in his hottest ship yet, a 35-N Beech Bonanza.

It is right and proper that Murdock should fly a Beechcraft because it was in a Sedgwick County pasture, back in 1929, when he and barnstormer Walter Beech watched a plane land on the stubble and Murdock said, "I'd like to fly one of those things."

"What did you say?" scoffed Beech. "You're too old. Forget it."

"I'll show you who's too old," said the forty-six-year old editor. "Just get me a plane and an instructor and we'll start right now."

Beech found him an open cockpit biplane, became his mentor, even to the extent of unloosening him in the cockpit when the ship turned turtle in landing.

Simons was editor and publisher of the *Lawrence* (Kansas) *Journal-World* when this article first appeared, in 1962.

In nearly thirty-three years of flying, the vigorous, fast-moving *Eagle* editor has piloted nearly every type of aircraft including puddle-jumpers, trainers, tankers, and military jets. Last year he became a member of the elite "Mach Busters" when one of the Blue Angels gave him a 640-mph lift. At the age of seventy-two he received nationwide notice for passing the CAA instrument rating test with the highest grade ever recorded. His colleagues and flying associates have included Charles Lindbergh, Roscoe Turner, Amelia Earhart, Ruth Nichols, Art Goebel, Jimmy Doolittle, and Gen. Hap Arnold, who was a captain at Fort Riley when he gave Murdock a few pointers in handling latest military craft.

Today Wichita boasts of being the "Air Capital of the World," with a big share of the town's workmen employed at the Boeing, Cessna, and Beech plants. More than half the small planes built in the nation are turned out by Beech and Cessna who together claim 75 percent of the dollar value of all utility commercial planes produced in America.

Chairman of the Wichita aviation committee for ten years, when landing fields were being located and manufacturing plants were being lassoed, was the flying editor-publisher who passed the hat for purchase of the town's first airfield.

All the while, Marcellus Murdock has been a working newspaperman with the usual number of problems, frustrations, and rewards.

In the year of 1903 he was named managing editor of the *Eagle* and his tremendous desire to be regarded as a fearless crusader of the prairies soon was rewarded with knowledge that a bawdy house was operating successfully in the basement of the city hall. The exposé made good reading, but it likewise made a chief of police very angry and cantankerous. The offended chief was thinking of reprisals until a grand jury unexpectedly and pleasantly took young Mark off the hook by indicting the chief for robbery of a post office. The pleasure-cave in the city hall was turned back to the checker players and the crusade was a great success.

The principal irritant in the progressive and active life of Murdock came in 1928 when the Levand brothers purchased the *Wichita Beacon* from Sen. Henry Allen and came to Kansas with ungentle intentions of running the owner of the *Eagle* out of town. The dirty infighting which ensued made the early-day Denver scrap seem like sissy stuff. No holds were barred and tactics were rough. Each side fought not just to win, but to kill.

Bitter rivalry continued for thirty-two years; something had to give.

In August 1960 the Levands gave up and Marcellus Murdock had his hour of triumph. Today he runs the whole show in Wichita and the combination seems to be doing quite well under the direction of a seventy-nine-year-old native who lives life to the hilt and who proffers that the view from upstairs helps to keep a man young and active.

J. Edward Murray, Associate Editor
Detroit Free Press

By William Dickinson

In Khrushchev's famed Science City, outside Novosibirsk in far Siberia, an American newspaper editor uses some of about five thousand Russian words he's learned for this trip to discuss with a Russian thermophysicist the asymptotic curve . . .

At an agricultural experimental station, he reveals considerable understanding of botany, of beekeeping, of sheepherding, of farming, and of lumbering . . .

In Minsk, the same editor, when a political argument with Russian journalists waxes really hot, relaxes the tension by pulling off his shoe and pounding the table with it . . .

In a Moscow airport, when the schedule breaks down and our group of editors have to spend a night on scantily padded benches, he calmly does his morning yoga exercises, including a five-minute headstand, while Muscovites look on in amazement . . .

"What's with this guy Murray?" our interpreter finally asks. "How'd he get this way?"

"Murray," I reply, "is our Renaissance Man."

J. (for James) Edward Murray was born April 16, 1915, at Buffalo, South Dakota, which is just about as far northwest as one can get and still be in South Dakota.

Half Irish, half Czech. A lonely boyhood. Poverty. An apostate Catholic at fourteen. Valedictorian of his elementary and high schools at Lead, South Dakota. Off in 1934 to the University of Nebraska, hoping to get an education.

Dickinson was executive editor of the *Philadelphia Bulletin* when this article first appeared, in 1972.

"I didn't get one," he wrote years later. "I got a Phi Beta Kappa key instead."

Summers working for the Homestake Mining Company in Lead, first at manual labor, then as a civil engineer's helper. He left that in 1937, and on an application for employment somewhat later gave as his reason, "Wrong kind of work."

Editor in his senior year of the college paper, at sixty dollars a month.

He joined the United Press at twenty-five dollars a week; by 1942 was day bureau manager in Chicago. Then to New York and quickly on to London, arriving there in January 1943.

I was running the London desk then and that's when I first saw him: a tall stringbean of a man, unsmiling but not tense, with a habit of pushing his ever-sliding glasses back up the bridge of his nose.

"Dickinson," he said, "your relief has arrived." He was twenty-seven.

The blitz was long past, the buzz bombs were still to come, but life in London was anything but sybaritic—and the London news desk of United Press was a tough assignment. Just about every bit of war news except that from the far Pacific funneled through London. The deskman on duty had constantly to decide whether a given item was worth cabling—costly but fairly certain to move quickly—or waiting for the frequently fouled up radio transmission.

Murray took the job in stride. The United Press brass soon found out that if he okayed a story you could hang your hat on it.

Paris next, early in 1945, for a brief stay—and then on to Rome as manager for Italy.

Earl J. Johnson, then vice-president and editor of United Press, recalls visiting Murray in the Rome bureau about 1946. He complimented him on his command of the Italian language.

"I learned it on the plane coming down here," he quotes Murray as tersely replying.

Harry Ferguson, then Johnson's second in command, was another visitor to Rome. He tells it this way:

"At 8:30 A.M. Ed phoned us [Virgil Pinkley, then United Press manager for Europe, was with Ferguson] at the hotel and said the three of us had a private audience with Pope Pius XII if we could get to the Vatican in forty minutes.

"We made it, and on the way I was busy thinking up questions for my blockbuster interview with the Pope. He received us in his library, and started talking Italian to Ed. Neither Pinkley nor I had enough Italian to know what was going on, but Ed and the Pope were going at it hammer and tongs.

"The only thing for me to do was case the joint. I remember there were two phones on the Pope's desk, one white and one black. It occurred to me that the white one went to heaven and the black one to hell.

"Ed and the Pope were really going to town now, waving their arms and bombarding each other in Italian. Pinkley and I hadn't said a word. Then a functionary came in and signaled the end of the audience.

"Outside I asked Murray what had been going on. He said the Pope kept asking him about the upcoming Italian elections and especially how he thought the Communists would do.

"No blockbuster interview for me. No interview, period. Lots of people probably have interviewed lots of popes. But to my knowledge Murray is the only newspaperman who ever was interviewed *by* a pope."

In 1948 there were four daily newspapers in Los Angeles — Manchester Boddy's tabloid *Daily News* and Hearst's *Herald and Express* in the afternoon; Hearst's *Examiner* and the prestigious *Los Angeles Times* in the morning. The *Times* led in circulation and had a corner on roughly two-thirds of the advertising in the entire market.

Norman Chandler, *Times* publisher, was convinced that a new afternoon tabloid could be a big winner. As publisher of his new paper he picked Virgil Pinkley, the United Press manager for Europe. And Pinkley, in turn, chose J. Edward Murray as his managing editor. Murray knew almost nothing about the mechanics of putting out a daily newspaper. Nor, for that matter, did Pinkley.

But they resigned from the United Press in the spring, assembled a metropolitan newspaper staff, hammered out a racy tabloid format, conducted trial runs, and produced their first issue on October 11, 1948. The date was not propitious for big city newspapers. Their number was about to shrink sharply in face of the rising new television medium and other competitive factors.

"The *Mirror* was a catastrophe all its colorful life," says a former deskman who lived through about ten years of it. "But Murray tried mighty hard."

The paper started as a tabloid with page one printed sideways, so that on newsstands it looked like a standard-size paper but was only half as deep.

This innovation signally failed to impress Los Angeles newspaper readers. So the *Mirror* became a regular five-column tabloid, straining for attention and circulation with a lot of gimmicks as well as legitimate enterprise, sharp writing, good columnists, and some serious investigative reporting.

One of the first stunts was to incorporate the name "Mirror" into news stories on almost any pretext. Staffers were Mirrormen or Mirrorgals. Telephone interviews had cuts of telephones dropped in them, and were labeled Mirrorfone Interviews.

The final edition each day carried an over-the-mast banner printed in red. The fudge boxes with late racing results were red too.

The circulation came quickly, pushing beyond the 200,000 mark in less than five years. It eventually peaked at 320,000. But the advertisers, because they didn't like the product or didn't want to give Norman Chandler a bigger stranglehold on the market, held back. So the deficits mounted.

And the Mirrormen tried even harder. In fact, they brought off some stunts that had the managing editor talking to himself.

When Margaret Truman Daniel gave birth to her first son, one news service quoted her as saying he looked like his grandfather. Lacking any really sensational art, a news editor had an artist draw a baby bonnet on a picture of President Truman, and captioned it:

"We haven't got Baby's picture, but does he look like this?"

It ran in only one edition. It was too much even for Mirror Murray.

The tabloid *Mirror* wasn't all froth. Local news coverage improved. There were serious crusades against smog and political corruption. The makeup was sharp enough to win two N. W. Ayer typographical awards as the nation's bestlooking tabloid. But the ad linage continued to lag.

So the Chandlers killed the tabloid in favor of a much quieter eight-column format, dropping hard-earned circulation in the process. The advertisers yawned. The parent Times-Mirror Co. bought out the rival *Daily News*, and the paper became the *Mirror-News*. Still later, the name was changed again to the *Los Angeles Mirror*.

"The masthead changed so fast the readers never knew what to expect," a former employee says now.

Murray lasted almost twelve years. He left in 1960, about a year and a half before the *Mirror* folded. The *Examiner* went under simultaneously, leaving only the morning *Times* and the afternoon *Herald-Examiner* in a field where there had been five dailies.

"It's not a bit cold outside," Ed told me a few days after he had been separated from the *Los Angeles Mirror*.

He had offers from radio and television, from journalism schools, from magazines, and from several newspapers.

He was intrigued by the offers of teaching positions, doubtful about the radio and television proposals. He inclined toward another newspaper job, partly because he wanted the experience of working on a solid, sane paper for a change and partly because he was about to become president of the APME Association.

To the surprise of many, Murray took the job as managing editor of the *Arizona Republic*, at Phoenix, an ultraconservative Republican newspaper owned and published by Eugene C. Pulliam.

"You call yourself a liberal Democrat," a friend said. "How come?"

"He knows my politics, and he doesn't care," Ed replied. "He wants someone to put out a complete newspaper. He'll keep his opinions on the editorial page. This is going to work for both of us."

Work it did, for close to eleven years.

These were years when the job itself was not too demanding. There was time for leisurely living with Miriam and their two children in the typical Phoenix ranch house complete with orange trees and heated pool. There was time to read—philosophy, psychology, religion—and to travel. And there was time, too, to take tennis lessons, to do exercises of many kinds, and to play a tough game of bridge.

There was time to serve as APME president, and see through a cherished project, a listing of the criteria for an ethical newspaper. There was time to join the battle to moderate the Reardon Report, and help fend off other and repeated attempts to do violence to the First Amendment.

Here are a few words from one of his many excellent speeches—this one delivered in 1969, when he received the John Peter Zenger Award:

> I am not saying that there isn't a problem of fair selection and presentation of the news. I know there is. The record of the press is pockmarked with editors' mistakes. And there may be American publishers who think freedom of the press belongs to the man who owns one.
>
> The whole point, however, is that the editor, fallible as he is, can still do his job better than anyone else in a free society. And he cannot be compelled by judges, lawyers, policemen, or politicians without doing more damage than good.
>
> But once this constitutional pillar is reestablished, and with it as a starting point, then there should be vigorous criticism of the editor and his decisions. This can be done with good results from both inside and outside the profession. And it is being done.

There was time for solid ASNE slugging as head of the Freedom of Information and Press-Bar committee for two years, and as chairman for the program and the *Bulletin.*

The paper rolled along. This was a monopoly situation, and the two efforts to challenge it got nowhere. But Murray was an activist managing editor anyway, strengthening the staff and the news coverage, adding the two big supplemental news services, convincing the publisher to make room for a full page of liberal columns, redressing the paper to give it a modern look, and stirring up the readership with a half dozen big campaigns a year.

Murray and Pulliam gradually got farther apart in their thinking. Last spring the end came, with a brief announcement that Murray was out as managing editor. Murray's only comment regarding his departure was that "it was friendly."

"Don't worry about me," Murray told me when I called him in Phoenix while he was emptying his desk at the paper.

"I'll be okay. I'm good for ten years anywhere, as the record plainly shows. Ten years of UP. More than ten years of the *Mirror*. Ten years of Phoenix. The next ten will wind me up."

Within a few weeks, Murray was hired as associate editor of the *Detroit Free Press* and editor of the Knight Newspaper Wire.

A chronology, such as the above, tells something about a man. But often his own words, written or uttered, perhaps, in a more or less unguarded moment, tell more.

In June 1969, when he was chairman of the editorial board of the ASNE *Bulletin*, Murray read a *Saturday Review* article by Archibald MacLeish in which the poet suggested that the technological revolution is diminishing man, and that a new humanism is needed.

Murray wrote to MacLeish asking him to do a *Bulletin* piece on how newspapers "have helped to diminish man, if they have." MacLeish replied that he was too busy to write such an article.

Meanwhile, Murray wrote to Jim Bellows, who had called his attention to the MacLeish article.

> MacLeish piece profoundly great . . . . Having dug Joyce, exited Catholicism, gagged on Babbittry, tried the existential route and been introduced to Samuel Beckett by our [son] Jim, I decided about ten years ago that man needed a new ethic, and after I had worked out the ethic, I decided that man needed a new myth to make the ethic work. This is essentially what MacL is saying when he talks of the need for a new humanism.
>
> The thing that stumped me was how to get motivation, i.e., faith, for the new myth in an age still stewing in Comte's stinking positivism. MacL has given me an idea: the knowledge explosion itself diminishes man, showing him how ignorant he is.
>
> Ergo, as the amount of knowledge asymptotically approaches the infinite as far as any individual man is concerned, man turns again to the irrational and the superstitious and the speculative and the conditions for the birth of myth, for a new Genesis, come into being.
>
> I guess I've already told you that I had two boyhood ambitions: (1) to make a hundred dollars a week for *Time* mag in some far-off halcyon future, and (2) to rewrite Genesis to make it plausible as the basis for a new humanism which would wipe out the degradation of man's diminishment by a faithless age of small-bore rationalism,

affluence and technology.

Genesis is not all that long, you know.

That's J. Edward Murray. Never satisfied. Always looking for more answers. Our Renaissance Man.

Scott Newhall, Executive Editor
San Francisco Chronicle

By Ruth Newhall

S cott was planning to buy two motorcycles so that the two of us could ride north to the Yukon in the summer of 1935. He was already negotiating for one old Indian and a Harley-Davidson when I accepted the offer of a summer job (money looked better than motorcycles). Scott came to the reluctant conclusion that he would have to get a job, too, to span the summer interval between his junior and senior years at college.

That is how Scott Newhall became a newspaperman.

I remember the day well. It was about noon on a Saturday morning in late May. Our finals had ended the week before, and I was on the job at an effete Oriental art store on Union Square in San Francisco. From the balcony over the rear of the store I saw Scott burst through the front door. He ignored the owner, who was displaying rare Han dynasty sculptures to a customer.

He looked up and shouted: "I got the job! I'm a photographer! A hundred dollars a month!" Then, as he walked past a table of carved jade, his elation vanished. "The only trouble is, they think I can develop my own pictures. I go to work Monday."

The lone customer, distracted from ancient China, entered the conversation. "You've never developed a picture, young man? Where's your job?"

"At the *Chronicle*."

"Wait right here. Don't move. And don't worry." He hurried out the door. The owner, somewhat shaken, explained that the customer was Albert Bender, a name we recognized as the source of countless institutional and artistic philanthropies. In about fifteen minutes Mr. Bender was back again,

This article first appeared in 1960.

staggering under his latest philanthropy, a stack of seven books. They bore such titles as *How to Make Your Photographs Effective, Darkroom Techniques, Photography for Beginners*, and so on.

"Study these tomorrow," the philanthropist said. "Copy the formulas. You can do it. Knew your father when he was president of the Chamber of Commerce."

Scott's sole background in applying for the job was that two months earlier he had bought a twenty-dollar camera, and had been pleased with his snapshots.

He was sweating with nervousness when he set out for work Monday morning. About eleven o'clock he called me, and in a low, guarded voice gave me the flash bulletin. "I just took a picture of Johnny Weismuller and Lupe Velez and it came out!"

Scott was then twenty-one. It was nearly two years since we had eloped to Reno in a chartered plane (with his mother along to give her consent since he was under age).

Scott's great-grandfather came to San Francisco in the 1849 Gold Rush, and had been a good enough businessman to provide three prolific generations of Newhalls with comfortable lives in well-staffed homes. Scott prepared for college at San Rafael Military Academy, Webb School, Lawrenceville (New Jersey), and San Rafael High School. This variety had little to do with scholarship. The year he got an A in chemistry he was invited to leave school because his unassigned laboratory project had consisted of distilling grain alcohol from tincture of iodine, and bootlegging the product. Another requested change came when he promoted an after-hours prizefight between two houseboys, collecting admissions and running a heavy book. At one point during this cataclysmic educational period the Stewart Edward Whites took him on their steam yacht for an Alaskan cruise, which developed in him an inordinate fondness for the sea.

His plan had been to go to Yale, buy a yacht, and retire. But the crash and Depression, and his father's death at its lowest point, left just enough money to finance a bargain-variety college education. He entered the University of California to major in art, and that is where we met. Our mutual fascination began the day we found a piano and I played, "You're an Old Smoothie" and he came back with a pretty good "Chloe."

In the first two years of our married life we painted, sketched, and played on the fringes of Bohemia. We also ground a telescope lens and looked at the craters of the moon. The first summer we toured Europe by motorbicycle. Day after day Scott tirelessly sought more paintings by Giotto and El Greco; nights we spent in French, Italian, and Austrian courtyards and basements, while he tore the motors apart and reassembled them and I learned how to ask for gaskets and magneto parts in three languages.

The second summer he bought an ancient baby Austin, and although the Pan-American highway lay largely in the realm of future construction, we made it to Mexico City. We earned our meals and lived high, thanks to the roulette tables, until the day Scott's system failed. Then we headed the bantam car westward over donkey trails. The Austin eventually bogged down in quicksand and had to be rescued by two teams of oxen. Scott's salesmanship reached an all-time high when he sold the little car to the owner of the oxen. The buyer had twelve children and couldn't drive. Scott forthwith bought two horses, on which we rode to the coast in ten sore-making days.

My husband explained his choice of the newspaper business by saying it would give him a chance to look at the working world and decide what he wanted to do. At the end of the summer, however, he decided not to go back to college. He had other educational plans.

He let me in on those plans one day in November. "Surprise!" he said. The surprise was the ketch *Mermaid,* forty-two feet long, broad of beam, thirty years old, but (he said) seaworthy. Ideal for the trip around the world for the two of us. The remnants of his educational fund served to buy it and fit it out with water tanks and other necessities, including an enormous stock of photographic equipment (he now regarded himself as an expert).

He sent me to a twice-weekly course in navigation, and bought me a book, *Cooking Afloat.* He made a deal to write articles, with photos, for the *Chronicle* in return for a small income. One early morning in May 1936, while his tearful mother waved a towel from Land's End, and I lay flat on my stomach in the scuppers losing my breakfast, we pitched our way out of the Golden Gate. My navigation was still uncertain, and he had decided to go coastwise for a while until I could get my bearings on the trackless deep.

We stopped in big, busy ports and on deserted offshore islands. We went aground in Baja California, and got lost off Mazatlan. We scratched the backs of whales, sharks, sea elephants, sea lions, giant turtles, and porpoises. We were touched by the strange bird which landed in our cockpit and refused to leave, until we discovered, after our sails had been blown to shreds, that he was a stormy petrel. In mid-July we anchored in the small port of Manzanillo, Mexico, and the port captain refused to let us leave because the hurricane season was on. Friendly Scott, who had rapidly become fluent in Spanish, picked up a cagey old Mexican who volunteered to lead us to some unrevealed great stone idols on top of a distant mountain. We bought horses and spent two months swimming them across flooded rivers, leading them over freezing mountain peaks, sleeping with dozens of Indians in thatched huts, and wading through mangrove swamps. We never found the idols.

Back in Manzanillo, thirty pounds lighter, we refitted the *Mermaid* with new masts and sails. Scott decided to try out the new rig on a run to Acapulco, three hundred miles south, and then start from there across three thousand miles of ocean to the Marquesas. But as we dropped anchor in Acapulco harbor, Scott threw himself on his bunk with a fever. Local doctors were baffled. Thanks to the lucky arrival in town of an old prep-school classmate with a new Cord, Scott was driven to a hospital in Mexico City.

There his illness was diagnosed as osteomyelitis (abscess of the bone) of the right thigh. He was nearly dead of blood-poisoning, and when the doctors in Mexico had saved his life, they thought he should go home. The prep-school classmate bought the *Mermaid*, and a succession of planes and ambulances delivered Scott to a San Francisco hospital. After four months of blinding pain, he had his leg amputated.

He went back to the *Chronicle* on crutches, as a library assistant, where he clipped and filed while his strength came back. Then he joined the staff of a new Sunday tabloid news-summary magazine section called *This World.*

About a year later, he got his first wooden leg. It took a month of constant pacing back and forth across the living room, in front of a long mirror, to master it. He threw away his crutches just in time to be able to pick up the other new addition to the family—our first son.

After a year of writing for *This World*, he became its editor, heading a staff of eight who wrote the weekly news review. That was in 1938, and in the decade which followed world events were his concern. His other activities during these years included lecturing in journalism at the University of California, being a radio news commentator, serving as seaman second-class in the Coast Guard Temporary Reserve Afloat (the only service which would have him). He put on the uniform of a war correspondent in 1943 and went to England with the British navy. During the war years we had three more children—twin boys and a girl.

The year the war ended he left his editorial duties briefly to become a reporter at the United Nations Conference, where he used his Spanish to get exclusive stories from the flattered delegate from Honduras.

In 1948 he made a round-the-world trip as a guest of the navy on the big carrier U.S.S. *Valley Forge*, and got a quick look at the changing postwar world. The following year he was promoted to Sunday editor.

Three years later the great upheaval came to the *Chronicle*. Editor Paul C. Smith, who had revivified the *Chronicle's* staff and stature in the seventeen years that he had headed its operation, resigned. Scott was given the equivocal title of operations manager to help cope with some of the pressing problems. The *Chronicle* was the third paper in an overcompetitive four-paper city, and had only two-thirds the circulation of its morning rival. Its prestige was considerable; its cash position regrettable.

The first task was survival, which involved staff cutbacks. More than forty members of the editorial staff were given their severance in a bleak few weeks. It was an unhappy time. Then, as the cutbacks ended, the time of buildup began. Scott was named executive editor.

Scott believes in dealing with severe problems by putting them firmly in the back of his mind after office hours, where he is sure they will be properly worked over. Meanwhile, he occupies the front end of his mind, and his hands, with some other project. He bought an ancient army ambulance, and with machine tools and welding torch rebuilt it, complete with camping gear, elevated seats, and a plexiglas vistadome. In it he took the boys through the untracked fastnesses of high mountains and deep desert canyons in the western states. They saw every scenic wonder in the Southwest. After three years he added a military jeep to the caravan so that our daughter and I could come, too.

His most intense hobby over the past three years has been restoring "classic" cars. I am writing this in Santa Monica, where we have come to display our gleaming 1930 Packard roadster, which he restored from a wreck to a thing of beauty. He has rejuvenated four old cars; three others await his attentions. From time to time we take weekends off in the new jeep to gather arrowheads in the Nevada desert. He is also a frantic baseball fan. Every time the lights go on in Candlestick Park we are there to share the misfortunes of the San Francisco Giants.

Scott is a director of two family companies—a farming company and an investment company. He is also managing director of the Irrawaddy Steam Navigation Company, which sends out Christmas cards to our friends every year. The I.S.N. Co. (founded 1806, its seal says) has properties consisting of a model of its first ship, the *Burmah Queen*, a small antique safe, a large seventeenth century Malayan cannon, a Great Seal, and a portrait of its founder, all of which are in Scott's *Chronicle* office. In the downtown office which bears the company name on the door, the interior is simply a janitor's broom closet.

Scott is extremely excitable about matters which strike others as inconsequential—a bad plating job on one of his antique headlights; aphids on the shrubs; a vocalist who sings flat. But in major crises he is a rock. And he has had his share of such crises: the loss of his leg, a child with polio, the personal pain of staff upheavals, and—most shattering of all—the loss of his twelve-year-old daughter, killed by a runaway truck a few days before Christmas in 1955.

Over the past two-year period the *Chronicle* has shown considerable circulation gains. Policy, direction, and innovations are developed in daily conferences between Scott and editor-publisher Charles Thieriot, grandson of the newspaper's founder. They are contemporaries, and work with mutual respect. Both give a large share of credit for the paper's performance to a superb staff of executives, columnists, and leg-men.

Scott's basic premise, I believe, is that a newspaper must have a strongly flavored personality of its own. It must be well loved and respected by its readers, and yet occasionally irritate them. It must treat them to the recurrent chuckle, the intermittent challenge, the occasional belly-laugh. Its readers are learning that a controversial and sexy beauty column is not incompatible with examination of space-age problems or firm seriousness on civil rights.

Every now and then I get a strange feeling when the *Chronicle* suddenly reveals a new facet of its personality. It reminds me of someone I know very well.

If my feeling has any basis in fact, there is one thing certain: it will never be dull.

Everett Norlander, Managing Editor
Chicago Daily News

By Milburn P. Akers

E verett Norlander, the tall, white-thatched, sometimes dour but always courtly Chicago-born Swede who became managing editor of the *Chicago Daily News* in 1944, has brought to a conclusion the Windy City newspaper career he began in 1919.

Ev, after several "decompression" periods during the past year, retired last month, as he had long planned.

Ed Lahey, the distinguished Washington correspondent, spent many of his years working with and for the "handsome and youthful looking Mr. Norlander," as a woman reporter writing in the *American Swedish Monthly* recently described him.

Lahey was asked for a few anecdotes and impressions about the tall, quiet Swede.

"How can you write a profile of Ev without making it a profile of the 'Quiet Man'?" he queried.

"Everything about Ev as a reporter, an editor, and a person is a direct contradiction of the traditional devil-may-care, blithe-spirited reporter.

"Ev is the only man I know for whom the grand jury test of 'probable cause' is insufficient in tooling a fact for print. Whereas a grand jury will indict you on 'probable cause,' Ev would submit a fact to the test of 'proof beyond a reasonable doubt.'

"That, I think, has been his essential characteristic, from a professional standpoint. I remember once being very impatient with him (privately) because he was on top of the Bob Sweitzer story and even when it started to crack all over town, Ev took each development as cautiously as if it were still in the preliminary investigative stage. The impulse of a more irresponsible

---

Akers was editor of the *Chicago Sun-Times* when this article first appeared, in 1960.

---

journalist, like myself, is to let fly with everything once the gates are down on a story. That incident always characterized for me the basic conservatism of Ev as a newspaperman. And I might say that same deep need to have a fact filed off square at all its edges is one of the reasons why people in public life have always had such a deep and affectionate respect for Ev.

"The other reason is his personal, low pressure charm. I've never heard him raise his voice. I've never heard him be uncharitable or unkind. And I don't think he ever packed a knife in his entire career, which is more than can be said of most of us."

Norlander (this is Akers again, not Lahey, if you chanced to miss the closing quotes) is one of those steady, dependable characters who always knows exactly what he wants to do, and does it.

When he was ten years old he met a girl, Anna Hall, in Sunday School. He liked her then. He still does. It might be imposing upon your credulity somewhat to say that Norlander decided at ten to marry Anna. Maybe he did. That would surprise none of us who have long marveled at his well-charted life. Anyway, marry her some years later he did. But not until he had finished the public schools, attended Lake Forest College and the University of Missouri, and had served as a corporal in the 149th Field Artillery, 42nd (Rainbow) Division, overseas in World War I.

In fact, it wasn't until 1923 that he and Anna got married, a union which produced two stalwart sons, Everett and John, neither of whom emulated their illustrious father by becoming a newspaperman.

Ev, after the war and college, went to work for the Chicago City News Bureau, a cooperative maintained by Chicago dailies. After his cub days there, he switched to the long since defunct *Chicago Journal*.

He had determined back in high school to be a newspaperman, as he had determined in Sunday School to marry Anna.

In 1924, having done both, he got a job on the *Chicago Daily News* and there he has been for the past thirty-six years.

Reporter, political editor, news editor, and managing editor—that, briefly, is his history on the *Daily News*.

He became a member of the executive committee of the newspaper division of Field Enterprises, Inc., after Marshall Field, Jr., purchased the *Daily News*.

Earlier, much earlier, he had become president of the Chicago City News Bureau, where he had started his newspaper career. From cub on the CNB to president of CNB—Norlander gets a lot of quiet satisfaction from that span.

Ev has always been a creative newspaperman. Some of the finest and most successful *Daily News* features were originated by him. And many of its journalistic triumphs are attributable to him. Keen, discerning, knowledgeable, Norlander has quietly and effectively moved steadily ahead, along with his newspaper—always a newspaperman's newspaperman, always possessed of an impeccable integrity and the courage to do and print that which he determined was right.

Now, forty years after he first cubbed on the CNB, Ev and Anna are set to do some more of the traveling they had always enjoyed. In between trips, he plans to paint, an art at which one of his friendliest critics describes him as something of "an amateur Pa Moses."

Norlander, after forty years in the business, or profession, if you prefer, says:

"I am grateful for so wonderful and busy a life, and wholeheartedly recommend the career of a newspaperman to anyone who has the qualifications, stamina, and ability. He may not get rich financially but he certainly will become rich in experience and in the rewards of life. I have found that reporting recharges the brain cells, and supplies an inexhaustible fount of ideas—and endorse it enthusiastically."

Robert C. Notson, Executive Editor
The (Portland) Oregonian

By Dee Notson and Edward M. Miller

R obert Carver Notson became an editor and publisher at the age of twelve years. He resided in one of the original American tank towns, Heppner, a dusty crossroads in semi-arid eastern Oregon.

Significant happenings were seldom in Heppner. There was little to disturb the peaceful transfer of wheat from horse-drawn wagons to the tired cars of the stub line Union Pacific.

Young Robert, unaware of the unimportance of affairs in Heppner, commenced a typed newsletter for the exclusive benefit of an older brother who had reversed the western thrust to work for an uncle on an Iowa farm. Neighbors asked for copies. Robert, flattered and willing, increased production via an old jelly-bodied ditto device called a hectograph.

All this was in 1915. As circulation of the *Heppner Budget* increased, Robert began searching for a means to automate his laborious printing plant. Virtue and ambition had their reward when he found a discarded job press which was rusting behind a local print shop. Robert hauled the press, bit by bit, to the Notson family establishment and started banging the platen in the basement, supplying power by foot pedal.

When the amiable lender of the press, the town printer, appeared belatedly to assist in reassembling the machine, he found Robert running off the first real type edition of the *Budget*. The paper contained the kind of news that is dear to small towns and small boys. There were features, too, and sober statements of the determined boy's ideas of things.

During this period Bob attempted his first printed exposé. He encountered resistance, known to adults as censorship. The roof had burned from Heppner's Home Theatre. The young editor observed inept and

Dee Notson was married to Robert Notson and Miller was managing editor of the *Oregonian* when this article first appeared, in 1966.

disorganized efforts of volunteer firemen, leaking connections and bursting hose. Robert wrote and printed the story in stark terms and concluded with a prediction that Heppner would face a lot worse, if the firemen couldn't do better. Robert's father surmised correctly that townspeople would figure that Notson Senior had inspired the piece. Father confiscated the edition.

Three years later a Fourth of July fire laid waste three business blocks. Bob left a copy of the expurgated edition by his father's luncheon plate. Subsequently, he started a successful campaign for a fire truck and a department trained adequately.

Truly great news touched Bob all too closely when an infant. It was the one time Heppner made headline news in every paper in the nation. The event was the tragic Heppner flood of June 14, 1903, Oregon's worst catastrophe. Some 250 lives were lost in the Willow Creek valley that Sunday afternoon.

As a babe, Robert was carried to safety by his parents, as they fled to the hills. The Notson family home in Lexington, a small community near Heppner, was washed away.

Robert was then six months old, having been born December 28, 1902, the third son of Samuel E. and Mary Ann Notson.

The flood closed the schools, of which Bob's father was superintendent, and forced the family to start anew. The father tried homesteading and then the law, moving the family to Heppner. He served long terms as county school superintendent and district attorney.

Young Bob sat through many court cases, gaining an understanding of court processes and argumentation. Here was laid many of the foundations of his later ideas on bar-press relationships.

In 1916 the family councils sent Bob to Salem, Oregon's capital, where good schools and jobs were available. The young man matriculated at Salem High School, earning his way delivering groceries, newspapers, and milk, and juggling clay and stuff in a brick and tile factory.

He continued his journalistic proclivities as editor of the *Clarion*, the school paper, and bossed the *Clarion Annual*. Those who know Bob will regard this statement as superfluous: His debate squad won the district honors and came within one judge's ballot (a hanky-panky judge, no doubt) of winning the state debate tournament.

In 1920 Bob registered at Willamette University in Salem. Thus commenced a very happy association for Bob that continues to this day. For thirty-five years Bob has been a trustee of Willamette, a private Methodist-sponsored college that is the oldest institution of higher learning west of the Rocky Mountains. He has found the Willamette association rewarding, if at times wearying.

Bob was graduated in 1924. His out-of-classroom activities clue the usual industry and persistence: forensics, editorship of the yearbook, and campus reporter for the *Oregonian*. Bob's teams won twenty-five out of twenty-eight debates, including victories over Michigan State and the University of Arizona.

Perhaps the most important reason why Bob thinks well of Willamette University has nothing to do with journalism. While there he met Adelia (Dee) White, a pretty and cheerful coed, who soon was thinking more of Bob than her books.

Dee became vice-president of the student body and president of her sorority, then marked time until they could afford marriage two years after Bob was graduated. On June 5 they will celebrate the fortieth anniversary of a very happy marriage.

Bob decided newspapering was his dish, although then as now he was more serious of vein and outlook than most men who follow his route. One imagines he might well have chosen the law or education, but he liked the smell of ink.

Bob spent the summer following graduation as news editor of the *Oregon Statesman* in Salem, but he felt the need of further training.

That fall, 1924, he drove a 1917 Ford to New York via the tortuous roads of that time. His companions were two college friends. Bob enrolled in the Columbia Graduate School of Journalism.

He still regards fondly some yellowed papers across which are written in gaudy color, "Red Apple." That was the high approbation of greatly esteemed Prof. Charles Cooper, the Mr. Chips of the J-School in that era.

In the spring of 1925 he crossed the East River and took a job on the night staff of the late lamented *Brooklyn Eagle*. Bob worked for twenty-five cents a column inch. Not much money, but a start.

Returning to Oregon, the youthful unsophisticate approached the *Oregonian* which then, as now, was the oldest commercial establishment in the American Pacific Northwest. The *Oregonian* was seventy-four years old and if stuffy at times, was highly regarded as a leading American regional publication.

Bob made the grade, strictly uphill, by getting a job with termination date, one week. He worked for three weeks without a day off for fear the city editor would discover his week was up. The aspirant never did receive official word he was hired permanently.

Bob handled most of the beats with a major turn to Oregon politics, including legislative sessions. In time he was given the job of night city editor with its ghostly hours, then city editor for five years and, in 1941, managing editor. He held the post for nearly twenty-four years. In January 1965, he became executive editor with management responsibilities.

The forty years which encompass Bob's tenure on the *Oregonian* have been anything but dull. At times they have produced bitter worries, most of them fortunately resolved.

The broad scene brought wars, New Deals, New Frontiers, and Great Societies. The local scene brought hard times, good times, strikes and violence. And always there was the problem of adjusting newspaper content to a world that grew ever busier and to a community that grew from a rather small city to a metropolitan community. Out of his beliefs and challenges Bob has evolved his working philosophies.

His policies are represented in the promotional slogan "First of all a NEWSpaper." He has believed that ultimate success of a newspaper against modern competition lies in fair, thorough, and understandable presentation of the news. The makeup of the paper is conservative but not dull, the content well organized and authoritative.

Notson was one of the first editors to advocate reporting in depth, the setting of stories in perspective, the development of significance to the reader. He is proud of the degree to which subscribers rely on the *Oregonian* and take proprietary interest in its quality.

He believes in assigning capable men to tasks and letting them perform without undue second-guessing. He stresses improvement of techniques rather than blame for past sins. He welcomes ideas from others, although he may want to be convinced.

"The paper is read by many kinds of persons," he has said, "and we need many different ideas to make it universally interesting. Certainly 110 brains ought to produce more and better things than one brain. I want my men to decide what is the best idea, not what the boss is thinking."

He believes that if the public gets the facts and understands them, it will react in a constructive way. The *Oregonian* regularly presents reports on issues that require much digging.

Although not fundamentally a crusader, Notson has been willing to tackle some extremely difficult situations. In 1956 the *Oregonian*, under his careful supervision, exposed a politico-union-rackets ring. The powerful Teamsters union was the chief target. Suffice it to say that this exposé triggered the Senate rackets investigation with its many national reverberations. The *Oregonian* was awarded the three top prizes in journalism—Pulitzer, Heywood Broun, and Sigma Delta Chi.

At one time the *Oregonian*—and Notson—were being sued for four million dollars. "After the first million I stopped worrying," Notson remarked with wry humor. The cases were all eventually dismissed with payment of nothing.

Bob never stopped to debate whether or not civic activities made sense for a newspaperman. He has participated as a matter of simple obligation throughout most of his newspaper career. He served on the boards of the

Community Chest, USO, CARE, Salvation Army, Polio, Oregon Colleges Foundation, and others. He was chairman of the Salvation Army board for two years, and taught newswriting at Portland's Lewis and Clark College for five years.

All this was in addition to his first and last civic love, Willamette University, for which he has raised money through the years. Currently he is vice-president of the board.

He is a Methodist, a teetotaler by preference and uses profanity sparingly in gentlemanly wrath, but not in jest. He is respected greatly by his associates, enjoys their affection, and scares nobody very long. He is extremely tolerant of other people's shortcomings. He is teased by his fellow workers, particularly for his puns, and enjoys it.

Bob has been active in the APME Association, serving on the board two terms, and was a chairman of several study committees. He has been twice chairman of the Associated Press Oregon members and active on the Bar-Press Committee. He lent a strong hand in the formulation of the Oregon voluntary bar-press "Statement of Principles," which has become a national signpost toward responsible journalism in reference to police and court matters.

He joined the ASNE in 1953 and is serving his third term on the board. He was twice membership chairman and has been successively treasurer, secretary, second vice-president, and first vice-president. He collaborated with Lee Hills in revamping and codifying the membership procedures of the society.

The Notsons, Bob and Dee, share a "vice." It is gardening. Their idea of painting the town is to plant a new breed of dahlias and their idea of really roughing it is to cut the grass of their suburban Portland home with the electric lawnmower. Their shrubs and flowers are legion both at the Portland home and at an oceanside house they own and enjoy over weekends at Cannon Beach, Oregon.

Bob's associates can take a hint to stop, look, and admire color pictures of the pretty stuff he grows at the beach (as the shore is known in Oregon).

The Notsons, logically, have no sons. They do cherish two daughters and four granddaughters.

Bob Notson is quite content to be known as a family man. He has come to the point where he enjoys slippers, but he looks forward with zest to the next forty years. Meanwhile, he pretends to have given up golf because it took him from his family. The affirmation is a logical derivation from the fact that he never intimidated Hogan.

Dee is happy, too. Her measure of affection is a massive collection of scrapbooks of every printed or photographed incident of their shared career. They are companions, always.

Newbold Noyes, Editor
The Washington Star

By Norman E. Isaacs

I 've built quite a career out of being a troublesome character. Hence it will delight any number of people to learn that I've had an equally troublesome renegade to deal with myself. He is Newbold Noyes, a bundle of the damnedest contradictions ever encountered.

Puffing away at a big cigar, looking starchy, and declaiming, "No, sir, by God!" Newby Noyes can look every bit the stuffy old-Yale prototype of the Herbert Hoover school of charm.

But that's just one of the Newby Noyeses I know.

There is another one. This is when he's being one of the most fun-loving of men, singing up a storm, full of wit and a courtly grace.

Then there is the sentimental Noyes. A score of us at an API session recall his weeping openly when Monty Curtis read a beautiful, sensitive piece Newby had written from Italy during World War II.

It's all very well to quip, "Will the real Newbold Noyes please stand up," but it won't do. All the versions are true. There are several characters wrapped in that one square, sometimes sturdy, sometimes slightly flabby, form.

All the bluff nay-saying isn't window dressing. It's a trait common among the Noyeses. They are a disputatious lot. Sometimes they apparently love to argue just for the hell of it.

But it runs a little deeper with Newby. As past resident headshrink of the society, I figure Newby to be a little shy and so overcompensates a bit.

He tends to be uptight about his family owning a piece of the *Washington Star*. He wouldn't be if he ever heard the lovely, talented Mary McGrory rave about Newbold Noyes as a line editor.

"Best one I ever worked for," she exclaims ecstatically. "Absolutely out of sight! He was the most sensitive, perceptive editor I ever ran into—respect-

Isaacs was executive editor of the *Courier-Journal and Louisville Times* when this article first appeared, in 1970.

ful of other people's thoughts and ideas. Pure magic! So help me, a genius at it."

How is he now? Well, they don't get that close to Newby these days. There's that shy streak again. As boss editor of the *Star's* news and editorial pages, he doesn't think he ought to be ruining anybody else's act. Maybe he should get into the act more because veteran staffers can recite episodes where Newby was practically prescient.

He demonstrated it once when the late Joe McCarthy hired J. B. Matthews for his staff. Newby's nose twitched. He turned the entire national staff loose to examine Matthews's record. The story of that fellow's early radical years popped forth and, bingo, there was a new chief counsel for the senator's committee.

Figuring Newby out, you have to admit it's not easy for a man to adjust easily to being a fourth-generation member of one of the oldest newspaper families in the nation. Let's skim over it.

It all dates back to great-grandfather Crosby S. Noyes, who came to Washington in 1852, the year the *Star* was founded, and went to work for the paper, doing everything. President Lincoln, for instance, handed the young Noyes the script of his first inaugural address at the end of the speech and Crosby ran it back to the *Star* to have it set for that day's edition. Among a lot of other things, he covered the hanging of John Brown.

Great-grandfather Noyes also had foresight. In 1867, he and a couple of friends named Kauffmann and Adams bought the paper for one hundred thousand dollars. The three families still own it and the affiliated companies.

Grandfather Frank Noyes was the *Star's* boss for many years and first, longtime president of the modern Associated Press. Father Newbold was associate editor when he died in 1941, at fifty.

That was the year in which, after graduating from Yale, Newby came on the paper.

He was a cub for about a year, then took off for the war zones. He was ruled fit only for limited military service, but in typical Noyes fashion reacted in the "No, sir, by God!" pattern and joined up as a volunteer ambulance driver with the American Field Service. He served in the Middle East and Italy.

His year's duty up, he wrote Ben McKelway an eloquent plea for a crack at war correspondence. Always a shrewd judge, Ben gave him a chance—thus the story mentioned earlier, among many others.

He thinks he's different, but the fact is he's part of a vast club—all of us who believe so devoutly we were really cast to be great writing reporters and were thwarted.

He thinks he's different, too, in describing himself, "by the book, at least, a lousy administrator."

All the rest of us are lousy administrators, too, but who else can run a news operation but a newspaperman? Look what happens to newspapers when the business side tries to do the thinking!

He must be a miserable cardplayer, too, because he's so lucky in love. He tumbled for the beautiful "Beppie" (Beatrice is her legal name) on the first date he ever was on. She was fifteen and lived nearby in Maine.

Those were the days when Newby used to write and sing songs which he played on the piano and they put on their own musical comedies in the summer. Newby still plays some of these songs at ASNE board meetings (and other liquid occasions), and he and Beppie invariably stop the show.

Newby's still in great voice, as anyone can testify who has seen him perform on the Gridiron stage in Washington.

Anyway, he and Beppie live in Potomac, where Beppie has gone "thatta way" over horses and is even now trying to make the Olympic riding team. (The Potomac menage includes seven horses, five cats, four dogs, and two children; the two oldest are Howard, 27, and Newbold III (called Terry), 24; Alexandra (Axie), 21, and Elizabeth (Lisa), 14, are at home.) Newby's the one who taught her to ride, but he pulled a typical stunt by pretending to be sick of cleaning stalls, and giving it all up for jogging.

His jogging is better than either his golf or his bridge. Actually, I'm the one who presented him with his first (and maybe only) golf victory. It was at Greensboro. He was suffering total frustration. Beppie beat him every time. So did everyone else. He badgered me into playing—me, who hadn't touched a golf club in more than twenty-five years. One reason I hadn't was because my baseball swing wasn't intended for golf. So you can see what a pigeon he had—but, oh, how happy it made him!

On his fiftieth birthday (he'll be fifty-two come August 18), he won a bet by jogging 6.2 miles in less than an hour (fifty-eight minutes, forty seconds). That's about nine and a half minutes per mile. But any good jogger can do a mile in about eight minutes so you can see what flab can do to a great athlete.

Speaking of tub, every other year Newby has what he calls "a fat year." This is a fat year. A gourmet, he takes an arrogant pride in knowing what wine to have with dinner. You should have seen his eyes light up when he got his first look at Simpson's wine list in London!

He has an enormous silver bowl in the Potomac house which was won in a sailing race by the America's Cup yacht, *Vanitie*, owned by a maternal great-uncle. Every year he tries to fill the bowl with wine corks. They made it last year.

Newby claims to be a "lucky reporter."

"Things happen where I am," he says.

They sure do. He went around the world not long ago. In Japan, they started rioting over American carriers visiting Sasebo. The day he arrived in

Korea, there was an assassination plot on President Park. The day he left, North Korea seized the *Pueblo*. The day he was scheduled to fly into Saigon, the Tet offensive started. He went to Khesan and got a story because it was the night the camp commander had to turn away from the gates hundreds of friendly troops driven from their own base and seeking refuge.

Some of us have shared these "happenings" with Newby—like the fall board meeting in Bermuda three years ago. We arrived in gorgeous weather. But as soon as the Noyeses unpacked, the skies opened up with a record-smashing downpour—something like thirteen inches in seven hours.

Luck sure runs with him. He came to the Kentucky Derby for the first time a month ago. The Derby over, he held up two ten-dollar tickets on Dust Commander. He came away from the window clutching $326, saying, "Hey, why didn't somebody tell me this was so easy!"

The most typical of all Noyes stories reveals all of the many Newbolds in one big sweep.

It happened last summer. The Washington Newspaper Guild set up a large meeting in which black leaders of the community were to tell what was wrong with the newspapers.

"Awful idea!" barked Newby. "I won't go. Absolutely, no, by God!"

The meeting day came. Newby went. It was an all-day session in a steamy church basement. A welfare mother, Mrs. Etta Horne, said: "I know what happens on the *Star*. A reporter goes out and gets the story, and then some racist bastard edits it to say what the *Star* wants to say."

Newbold flushed. He growled that he didn't like being called a racist bastard, that the *Star* made mistakes, but that nobody edited the stories to slant them, and if anyone knew any different, get up and say so. Nobody did.

But a charismatic ghetto dweller, Marion Barry, chided Newby.

"You shouldn't get uptight at a meeting like this when you're called a bastard or a mother, or something like that," he said. "If we can't talk plainly to each other, what are we here for?"

Michael J. Ogden, Editor
Providence Journal and Bulletin

By Norman E. Isaacs

S omebody once described genius as the infinite capacity for taking pains—and for giving them.

Which in one manner of speaking can describe Michael Joseph Ogden of the *Providence Journal and Bulletin*. Just one, though. For Ogden can't actually be described. He has to be experienced.

He has incredible energy, great versatility, and unmitigated gall, a trait he gets away with because he also possesses—and practices artfully—a completely beguiling charm.

He is probably one of the world's loudest listeners . . . one of the most energetic loafers . . . a procrastinator obsessive about getting everything done . . . an untidy man who insists on cleaning off not only his own desk when he leaves at night, but everybody else's desk within range. A venture with Mike instantly becomes adventure. He is hectic, explosive, hilarious. Within the space of minutes, you can find him alternately obdurate, truculent, defiant, conciliatory, and docile. In short, he is an implausible character.

Yet behind this smokescreen is one of the steadiest of editors, one who believes in both reform and tradition at the same time; and who has guided for years what so many of us have considered New England's most distinguished daily newspapers.

I first met Mike in the early fifties. Our old colleague, David Patten, then Providence's managing editor, sometimes called "the Rhode Island roarer," was stepping out of ASNE and asked me to "take care" of Ogden. What Dave should have said, of course, was, "Take care of yourself!"

Anyway, from that moment to this, I have often felt what it was like to be in orbit with Ogden.

So far as I can see, our Michael fell short of full appreciation in only one

Isaacs was executive editor of the *Courier-Journal and Louisville Times* when this article first appeared, in 1967.

undertaking—service with the air force from 1942 to 1946. While fledglings who could barely grow *anything* on their chins were sporting eagles on their shoulders, Ogden could talk himself only as far as captain. But, then, you realize that generals have not been distinguished for their tolerance of the Ogden-type of free flight.

Mike was born in New York City, May 24, 1911. He went to Fordham, then to CCNY; got his master's in journalism at Columbia in 1932. He worked on the *New York American,* switched over to City News Association, went to Providence as a copyreader in 1935.

Washington beckoned—through the managing editorship of *Pathfinder* magazine—and Mike spent almost four years there. Then, in 1940, it was back to Providence for good (except for that air force humiliation). From 1946 on, Mike went through the Providence chairs like a rocket.

We're all familiar with Ogden, the conventioneer. He shows up, loudly proclaiming complete disinterest in the meetings. He's come for the fun and games. Then he sits through some speech, looking half-asleep. The speaker done, Mike springs up to fire off the day's most provocative question.

Put on a program, he is apt to start out: "In the first place, let me say I have no use for my portion of this program. I am far more interested in Vin Jones's assignment. Inasmuch as I'm on the program before Vin, I shall take his topic. He can then tell you, 'Why some newspaper editors irritate other newspaper editors.'"

That's pure Ogden.

He goes home from conventions, deploring the strains of all the cocktail parties, dinners, and excursions. Total waste, he proclaims. But he puts into operation the best ideas of the meeting, probably faster than anyone else. He explodes over finding a dinner date on the calendar, complains that he is worn out and must catch up on things. But he goes to the party, tells the best stories, dances with all the pretty girls, and leads the singing.

Over his morning coffee and on his way to the office, he scribbles on scraps of paper, the inside of book matches, on strips of stories or heads ripped from the paper. At the office, the batch is emptied onto his desk. And so starts one of the day's great logistic problems: deciphering. Everyone who passes through the office is pressed into this service.

Generally, about 90 percent get translated and passed on as criticism, praise, suggestion, but there are always a few defying the laws of gravity. If by day's end, it has not been determined what they say, they get discarded.

By day's end, too, MJO has answered everything—one way or another. Some stuff is marked FYI and sent off to someone else's desk. But off it goes. Then comes the custodian in chief act. A colleague not there to defend himself may find that the neat stack of papers saved for leisurely examination has been swept away.

So the Ogden entourage has learned to store anything important out of sight. They do leave old newspapers around as decoys. Even with all this patroling, however, it isn't uncommon in Providence to find an Ogden associate almost upended in a wastebasket, trying to retrieve precious clutter.

For a time there was a theory Mike was gathering fuel for his fires. He'd light up a cigar and flip the match into the basket. The moment anyone smelled smoke, they darted for Mike's office. There he would be, one leg in the basket, stamping out his blaze. Deciding he was risking immolating himself, the thoughtful at the *Journal and Bulletin* replaced one of his oil paintings with a fire extinguisher. He retaliated with a typical Ogden ploy: He gave up smoking.

He plays the role of morning grouch, wandering about, reading the gossip columns, checking the pinup pictures in the New York tabloids. Along the way, he drops on the city desk or telegraph desk the day's best story idea.

He is a fervent advocate of democracy—so long as it doesn't impede progress. When a staff meeting votes against his view, fourteen to two, he decides that the two win anyway, "because I'm older than you guys."

"What is going to come from this younger generation?" he asks. "How can a fellow manage to graduate from Yale without learning he has to keep his hair cut, shave regularly, and keep his pants pressed?"

This from the man who has a perfect record of being the only department head who never has worn a jacket to the weekly staff meeting, and who has never worked a day without loosening his tie, usually in the most careless way imaginable.

This informality extends to confusion over titles. He is never sure whether it should be Your Honor, Your Excellency, or Your Eminence. But get some third-rate wardheeler's middle initial wrong and Mike is out of his chair like a shot with a correction.

"Why can't people remember simple little fundamentals?" he thunders. But he never knows what he's done with his car keys—or his laundry check.

One of Mike's old associates says you've never heard the blues until you've listened to Ogden moan about a whole gang going off for a good time and leaving him with all the work. Later, says he, you learn it was Mike who rigged up the trip in the first place.

ASNE veterans have all heard Ogden, the tennis devotee—and of his scorn for those who waste time hitting a little white ball with a stick and chasing it over some pasture. "Better you should stay home reading dirty books," is Mike's dictum. Well, this is the man who can put in seventy-two holes on a weekend and from nine to eighteen holes when snow is on the ground. A red ball, thermal underwear, and loud amazement that there are not more people on the course. That's Mike.

Mike loves travel. Not just travel—but seeing the local sights and trying all the local customs. And in restaurants, always the specialty of the house. Except the salads. East, west, north, south, he wants his salad with dinner—not just eaten with dinner, but served with dinner. If it comes ahead of time, he sends it back. Mike!

He can hold forth on the new automated process, but he has trouble pushing the "hold" button on the phone without losing the call. The last time his portable typewriter needed replacing, he decided to go modern with an electric. The hum disturbed his train of thought. If he flipped off the switch, he forgot to flip back on. Result: Stubbed fingers. He finally surrendered, exchanging the electric monster for a manual.

The same mechanical ingenuity extends to other matters. Mike holds to a theory that goes, "When all else fails, read the directions." In the instance of his swimming pool the theory was disastrous. He waved away the directions, pulled the plug, and undermined the backyard by eight inches.

As ASNE *Bulletin* chairman, Mike was both prolific and ingenious. Once, he kept after me for months for a piece. He chided, turned provocative, then nasty. I just tuned him out until a note so plaintive came that I felt guilty of betraying an old pal. So I sent out almost one hundred letters to editors, seeking information to help me, and opening myself to all manner of criticism. Then I picked up a *Bulletin* and read—with astonishment and infuriation—a series of Ogden letters to Alfred Friendly. I had been tricked by a flock of lousy form letters! Ogden!!

Which brings up his yearning for "the good old days"—when reporters never forgot a fact, never overlooked an angle, never wasted an effort. Then he tours Russia and, on the way home, leaves all notes, plus several completed articles, in a Paris taxicab. If the cabby is bilingual, he is probably still in trauma!

Mike first wrote from memory, but the episode, naturally, gave him perfect ammunition for wheedling several *Bulletin* pieces from his traveling companions. ("You know I lost all my notes. What do you remember about such-and-such?")

Ah, yes, the good old days—"when a newspaper guy thought about the paper first and then about his family and friends." Only later does it come out that Mike had quietly checked a staffer's family to make sure an out-of-town assignment wasn't going to disrupt things at home.

And colors! He says he's color-blind and this seems reasonable, since his socks sometimes don't match and his ties tend to be dreadful. "But who the hell hired that new dictation girl? You know, the one in the hot pink sweater?"

It all seems topsy-turvy. Yet years of "taking care" of Ogden has disclosed that he always knows the precise circulation in Newport, East Providence, Pawtucket, or Woonsocket, and how so-and-so is doing over there; and what the news hole was last week; and what the papers did with that story or this one.

He telephones to trace the trend of some new development; then it develops he is only casually interested; what he really called about was trying to find out what might be available somewhere for some old pal who is momentarily displaced.

Lowell had it right all the time: "Three-fifths of him genius and two-fifths sheer fudge."

Michael J. O'Neill, Editor
New York Daily News

By William J. Brink

T he year was 1947. The place was Brewster's East Side gym in Detroit, an ancient fight palace where, in those days, you could stop by and, if you were lucky, catch a glimpse of a bronze demigod named Joe Louis working out on the big bag.

Walking into Brewster's was like getting hit in the face with a mop wrung out in human sweat and the overflow from the brass spittoons. The odor seemed to be embedded in the walls of the joint. And the air? I doubt if it was changed more than once a year. Apart from the fighters earnestly sharpening their skills, the place seemed to be peopled by fat guys with wide-brimmed hats and dead cigars in their teeth.

Maybe that's why the small band of young men and women—the men in the short haircuts of that day, the girls in their bright clothes—looked so out of place one quiet Sunday afternoon when they filed into Brewster's and took seats around the big ring.

In one corner, up under the glare of the ring lights, was a tall, black-haired Irishman with the words KILLER O'NEILL hand-sewn across the back of his yellow terry-cloth robe in bright blue grosgrain ribbon. Across the way, glowering under bushy blond brows, was a hulking, barrel-chested Swede.

A bit of background here. These guys were not fighters, as anyone could tell from their smooth, unmarked skins, white as milk under the lights. No, they were fugitives from rewrite desks at the United Press bureau in Detroit, where it seems that sparks were flying between them.

Both were young and feisty and ambitious, and there was a lot of noisy talk and even some shoving that was disturbing the more elderly and fragile

Brink had retired as managing editor of the *New York Daily News* when this article first appeared, in 1981.

writers. Cooler heads finally prevailed, suggesting that their differences be settled in the only gentlemanly way, with the eight-ounce gloves (or was it ten?). A Detroit old-timer who covered fights for the UP on a string basis offered to arrange the whole thing.

"I'll even getcha Joe Louis's gym," he promised.

And so he did. And so there they were, each with his gaggle of supporters from the young, postwar Detroit newspaper crop, ready to square off in three one-minute rounds (the outside limit, so medical experts said, for newsmen).

It would be fun to tell you that Killer O'Neill, aka Michael J. O'Neill, Jr., editor of the *New York Daily News,* got knocked on his keester.

Alas, no. O'Neill's first blow, a mighty right (or was it a left?) sent the Swede's mouthpiece flying ten rows back in the seats. The poor guy never had a chance against this incredibly smooth fighting machine. O'Neill won going away, and since this was really all in fun, everybody went off to a spaghetti dinner.

I guess the point of all this is that Mike O'Neill always has been a battler, whether it was in the ring, getting a story, fighting for the First Amendment, or putting out a helluva good newspaper.

O'Neill loves to fight his own battles in court, any chance he can get. When it comes to lawyers, he seems to side with that character in *You Can't Take It With You* who kept saying: "All lawyers should be taken out and shot down like dogs." The most memorable of his courtroom heroics, perhaps, occurred when O'Neill was dissatisfied with some landscape work performed at a home he owned in Bethesda, Maryland, and refused to pay the bill. When the landscaper took him to court, Mike trotted off to the state capitol at Annapolis and dug into some old statutes. Rising to defend himself when the case was called, Mike shot a hard question at the gardener: Did he have a current license to practice landscape gardening, as required by state law? Consternation in the plaintiff's camp! They didn't know anything about a license. Case dismissed, and as the gardener's lawyer walked out alongside Mike, he remarked: "I guess I learned some law today."

Born in Detroit in November 1922, Mike O'Neill was graduated from the University of Detroit in 1946 (he returned in 1977 to receive an honorary doctorate) and also took graduate studies at Fordham in the Bronx. As a freshman at Detroit, Mike met a pretty Irish lass named Mary Jane Kilcoyne in the chemistry library. Romance, as they say, blossomed, and they were married in 1948. At the time, Mary Jane was women's club editor of the *Detroit Free Press.* Although she bore five children (one of whom, Maureen, grew up to be a lawyer yet), she has pursued her own career and is today a highly successful executive in New York. She also was a solid professional backstop to Mike in his career, as we shall see.

O'Neill moved on to Chicago and Milwaukee with the United Press, finally ending up in the Washington bureau where he specialized in covering foreign affairs at the White House and State Department. It was about this time that Mike's talents as newspaperman began to come to the attention of the Washington press establishment. Ted Lewis, then the bureau chief of the *New York Daily News*, heard about him and lured him to his shop.

That was in 1956, and Mike's career began to take off. His assignments were the best: the Mideast crisis of 1956–57, the Berlin crisis of 1959, and Eisenhower's summit conference with Macmillan and Khrushchev. He also traveled with Ike on his tours of Europe, Latin America, and Asia, and went to Tokyo to report the security treaty riots that blocked Ike's trip to Japan.

In 1961, Mike accompanied then-vice-president Lyndon Johnson on his fact-finding trip to Vietnam, Thailand, India, and Pakistan. He made a profound impression on LBJ, who told the National Press Club after his return that the last guy still pestering him for news at the end of each day was Mike O'Neill. Years later, when LBJ was president, there was a hot rumor in Washington that he would appoint Mike his press secretary.

Paul Healy, then of the *News's* Washington bureau, went to White House aide Bill Moyers to ask him what was up. LBJ would like to have Mike, said Moyers, but was "afraid Mike would turn him down." O'Neill himself told one close friend: "I'd never be able to do what I thought best; I'd never be my own man."

Not everybody who knows Mike O'Neill knows that all the while he was covering Washington for the UP and the *News*, he was engaged in a totally separate and distinct career as a medical reporter and writer.

In the mid-fifties he began free-lancing (or moonlighting), for a new biweekly called *Medical News*. Its managing editor was Bill White, now a publishing tycoon in New York. White's early staff included Matt Clark, now medicine editor of *Newsweek*, and Howard Simons, managing editor of the *Washington Post*. As Bill White remembers, O'Neill turned out a "truly unbelievable" amount of copy for the publication, all the while carrying on his newspaper job.

"He produced the first stories I ever published with such words as open-heart surgery, heart-lung machine, interferon, DNA, chemotherapy, genetic code, and antidepressant drugs," says White.

Characteristically, Mike read thirty scientific publications a month to master his new domain, and when he was called away on long newspaper assignments, Mary Jane backstopped for him. His knowledge of medicine and acquaintanceship among physicians is so extensive today that he often is called upon by ailing staffers for medical advice.

"How could he do it all?" asks White. "The answer lies in a mixture of many things. First, Mike has an inner drive that I've seldom seen matched.

He rarely tires physically. He has an unquenchable thirst for new knowledge and an uncommon ability to assimilate diverse concepts—all the time remembering bits and pieces from the far corners of his mind. Outwardly, he appears cluttered and disorganized. And in a sense he is. But inwardly, he has that rare ability to shut out all distractions and bring forward an incredible degree of concentration and thought that explodes in one nonstop effort on the typewriter."

As a result of his medical labors, which branched out to a new magazine called *Medical World News* and a medical newsletter, O'Neill was making enough money to buy the light of his life, the thirty-five-foot sloop *Moonlighter*, named for the source of the purchase price. For aficionados, it's an Alberg 35, built by Pearson and carrying an Atomic 30 gasoline auxiliary, and it rides the waves of Long Island Sound.

So what do we know about Mike O'Neill so far? He is, obviously, a man of prodigious energy. "Tired me out just to watch him," remembers Ted Lewis. This translates into boundless enthusiasm, for his work, certainly, but also anything that catches his fancy—be it an El Greco, a poem by Yeats, Gilbert and Sullivan, grand opera, the Chinese language, celestial navigation, or whatever.

Mike likes peanut butter and raisin sandwiches and shredded wheat at home and gourmet meals out. He seldom exercises, except for sailing and an occasional tennis game. He is a skilled woodworker, currently turning out the dining room table he has been promising Mary Jane for years. He likes to read the Sunday papers while listening to a symphony on the stereo at stirring volume. Music, in fact, absorbs him. Unable to restrain himself, O'Neill has been known to burst into song along with the opera singers on stage, much to the annoyance of patrons in the nearby seats. Opinion about the caliber of his singing, or his taste in music, appears to be divided. Some find his baritone pleasing. But John Chapman, the late drama critic of the *News* who was an opera buff, referred to him sourly as "Old Tin Ear."

Mike has been known to sweep up a group of White House correspondents (while covering LBJ) and drive from Austin to San Antonio, a round-trip of three hundred miles or so, just to sample what was billed as the best Mexican restaurant in Texas.

But his enthusiasm is most in evidence when it comes to sailing—whether he is talking about sailing, thinking about sailing, or actually sailing. Characteristically, Mike loves to sail in a blow, putting the lee rail of the *Moonlighter* under as he battles the storm. This, I might add, is an enthusiasm not necessarily shared by others aboard, particularly Mary Jane. "It scares the life out of me," she says. "I go along because I'm afraid of what he might do if I weren't there."

As might be expected, Mike is devoted to things Irish, be it folk songs or history. He takes considerable pride in being descended from the High Kings of Ireland. Flying from the starboard spreader of the *Moonlighter* is a pennant bearing the O'Neill coat of arms. It features the "bloody hand of O'Neill," for one of the High Kings who lost a hand in battle. A proud moment came in 1978, at a glittering dinner in New York, when the American Irish Historical Society awarded him its annual medal as the American of Irish extraction who had made outstanding contributions to American life.

Mike's intense devotion to whatever he is doing inevitably has meant lapses in other areas. He is chronically late for appointments, largely owing to the fact that he is either too busy doing something else or can't remember the time of the engagement. Once, en route to Jack Howard's home for dinner, he drove frantically around Manhattan trying to remember where Jack lived.

In the view of some, O'Neill's preoccupation also has led to a certain sartorial carelessness. There is a story, possibly apocryphal, that when he worked at the *News* bureau in Washington a copyboy was detailed to conduct "sock inspection," i.e., check to see that he was wearing matching socks.

Mike's Washington experience ended abruptly in 1965 when the *News* summoned him to greater heights in New York, first as assistant managing editor and finally, today, as editor and executive vice-president.

As a reporter, O'Neill always was both tireless and resourceful, always looking for an angle to pounce upon ("angle-shooting," he calls it). As an editor he comes to work earlier and leaves later than many of his staffers. He can do any job in the shop, usually better than those holding the job. He loves to stroll into the city room, ask what's the latest, and maybe lend a hand with a lead at the VDT. He did that on January 19 this year, and out came these two paragraphs:

> Two Algerian jetliners revved up at Tehran airport today to fly fifty-two Americans to a freedom they had not known for 443 days and feared they would never see again.
>
> Anxious, disbelieving, the fifty-two moved into the final act of a terrible personal ordeal—including repeated death threats—and a dangerous and humiliating crisis for the United States.

Then he walked away, remarking to national editor David Oestreicher, "I think you can improve on that." Nobody tried.

"His exuberance and excitement over a good story are absolutely infectious," says Oestreicher.

Dick Oliver, an assistant managing editor of the *News*, recalls another occasion when O'Neill's zeal to defend press freedoms coincided with his reporter's instinct. This occurred in 1973 when Oliver and O'Neill journeyed to Baltimore to support William Sherman, a Pulitzer Prize–winner at the *News* who was one of nine reporters under subpoena to reveal their sources in the case of *U.S.* v. *Spiro Agnew*. As Oliver tells it:

"About 1:30 P.M., the doors of the fifth-floor courtroom opened, and it soon became apparent that something—something bigger than reporters going to jail—was in the works. Elliot Richardson, attorney general of the United States, and a long line of pinstripes carrying briefcases, marched into the courtroom at 2:00 sharp. "Bet Spiro's coming," O'Neill murmured.

"At 2:04 P.M., Agnew walked in and took his place at the defense table. Judge Walter Hoffman took his seat on the bench and announced that no one would be permitted to leave after the proceedings began.

"Of course, no one left. But when it was over, O'Neill was one of the first out the door. I looked up from my notebook and saw him, scampering like a wire service reporter at a 1930s execution, dashing down the hallway. He raced five floors to the street and sprinted some four blocks to Sherman's hotel room. There, after Sherman and I caught up to him, O'Neill assigned Sherman to work the phone to New York and Washington, ordered me to write a color story and he sat down at a typewriter. This was his lead:

> Baltimore, Oct. 10—In one of the great dramas of American history, Spiro T. Agnew abruptly resigned as Vice President today, pleaded no contest to income tax evasion charges and ended his 11-year career as a public official with a $10,000 fine and three years' probation.

Inevitably, however, Mike's role at the *News* began to move him in the direction of top-level management ("I never seem to do any real newspaper work anymore," he has lamented often in recent years). The truth is that Mike was shrewdly converting the *News* from an old-time *Front Page* tabloid to a modern, multifaceted metropolitan newspaper. He infused new ideas into the paper, brought in new top talent (e.g., Jimmy Breslin, Clay Felker).

He also has become a strong editorial force in New York, consulted by mayors, governors, and senators for his views and for his support of what the Big Apple needs to survive. Says New York mayor Ed Koch: "He represents the Fourth Estate at its best."

A gregarious man who loves to attend civic affairs and banquets in New York, O'Neill also is a friend of the nonpolitical great from Barbara Walters to Michael DeBakey. At the same time, he likes to lift a beer or two with his staffers—particularly young staffers—at Costello's bar.

No one knows better than Mike O'Neill, however, that the years just ahead may be the toughest. As anybody who has read the news magazines and other national journals knows, the *News* has embarked on a challenging course, entering the highly competitive afternoon field in New York with a new paper, *Tonight*, and launching five new daily themed sections.

Those who know him have no doubt that battler O'Neill will more than meet that challenge. For, as he himself likes to point out, he is still the undefeated champion of the Detroit United Press.

Eugene C. Patterson,
Editor
St. Petersburg Times

By Creed C. Black

I t was fifty-three years ago when that noise was first heard down in Adel, Georgia. There has been too much of it since then for one person to record, much less interpret. Happily, however, the impressions of a number of auditors who have come within earshot are at hand. So let's glue them together in the hope that a picture of Eugene C. Patterson will emerge.

First, to help you recognize him in Honolulu, he'll be the one in the bar surrounded by a group of admirers holding their breath as he courageously—and sometimes even successfully—attacks the final high notes of "Danny Boy."

In case you stumble on him at some other time, however, a description is in order.

"Patterson," *New York Times* man Martin Arnold wrote not long ago, "is stocky, of medium height, barrel-chested and walks with the roll and gait of early James Cagney, whom he resembles in style and shape."

The only part of that which might be challenged is "medium height." When Gene led an ASNE delegation through China two years ago, Acting Premier Teng Hsiao-ping thought he was tall. But then, Teng stands only five feet.

Fellow Georgian Joe Parham, on the other hand, has written, "Let's face it—he is sawed off, standing five feet, seven inches, with all hackles raised."

And therein lies a story, which Joe told in an earlier *Bulletin* profile:

"Gene's brother Bill, a surgeon, got the height and the dark wavy hair in the family. When Gene flew down from New York, where he was night bureau manager, to marry Sue Carter in Richmond, Bill accompanied him. Sue's Aunt May met them, glanced admiringly at the tall, wavy-haired fellow,

Black was publisher of the *Lexington* (Kentucky) *Herald and Ledger* when this article first appeared, in 1977.

and said, 'Son, I would have known you anywhere,' and hugged the wrong brother. 'It was,' Gene remembers, 'a black wedding day.'"

For all of that, Gene does have a commanding presence—a legacy, perhaps, of his military career.

It would be pleasing to write that the 1977–78 president of ASNE never wanted to be anything but a newspaperman. But it would be wrong.

True, as a boy he wandered off the family farm to read proofs and run errands at the *Adel News*, a country weekly in the county seat. And he went on to get a journalism degree at the University of Georgia. But then he became a soldier.

So did a lot of other people in 1943, of course. But after service as a tank commander and then as a tank platoon leader in George Patton's charge across Europe—winning a Silver Star and a Bronze Star with oak leaf cluster—our hero decided he wanted to learn to fly. He reenlisted in the regular army, transferred to the air corps, and became a pilot.

Fortunately for American journalism, that didn't last. Shortly after winning his captain's commission in 1947, he resigned, drove down the road from his base in Texas, and got a job on the *Temple Daily Telegram*.

From there he returned to Georgia to the *Macon Telegraph*, then joined United Press in Atlanta. Soon he was UP manager for South Carolina— where he met Sue, a reporter for the *Columbia Record*—and not long afterwards the UP transferred him to New York.

That was a learning experience, recalls Bill Landrey, a UP colleague of those days who is now Gene's foreign editor in St. Petersburg.

"Arriving in the big city," Bill's account goes, "Patterson headed straight for the places where strong beverages were served and young ladies congregated. It left a mark that some believe has remained with him to this day when one of the first beauties he was pursuing suddenly removed one of the bosoms from her low-cut gown and began practicing her basketball dribble. At least, the youngster from Georgia learned how to spell transvestite."

Either that or some other searing experience apparently gave Gene some second thoughts—again—about newspapering.

"The work was hard," says Bill Landrey, "and the guys on the New York desk tried to introduce him to strong drink after hours for relaxation. What happened early one morning at a place known as the 'Weenie Club' is still remembered.

"The Weenie remained open after the Third Avenue bars had shut down, and it was inevitable that one morning Patterson and his mentors would show up there. But the Weenie had one rule—you had to have a membership and to get it you had to affix your signature. To the consternation of everyone present, Patterson assumed a stern mein and refused. It would look bad on his record, he said, if he ever wanted to return home and run for governor of Georgia."

But he didn't. Instead, he went to London as UP's bureau chief. He is best remembered there for the lead he moved when Ernest Hemingway staggered out of the Uganda jungles after having been lost for three days. "Ernest Hemingway came out of the jungle today, carrying a bunch of bananas in one hand and a bottle of gin in the other."

Patterson's version of that is that he had the good judgment to pluck this gem out of the middle of a stringer's cable. Others have it that the stringer put it at the top to begin with and Gene was smart enough to leave it alone. Bill Landrey says it's nothing to be proud of either way, because anyone knows that Hemingway never would have preserved a bottle of gin for three days and the aspersion cast shame on a great writer.

Ultimately, Gene did return to Georgia—but not to run for governor. While in London, he caught the eye of vacationing George Biggers, Sr., president of the Atlanta papers, and in 1956 became executive editor of the *Constitution and Journal.*

Then in 1960 he became editor of the *Constitution* when Ralph McGill was named publisher. That, said Jack Tarver, who had succeeded Biggers as president of the Atlanta papers, was "like playing right field after Babe Ruth."

Gene admitted to being scared, but he didn't play that way. McGill continued his column, but Gene wrote six a week of his own on the editorial page. They won him a Pulitzer Prize in 1966, a role as a spokesman for the enlightened South, and the first of seven honorary degrees he now holds from such institutions as Harvard, Emory, and Mercer Universities and Tuskegee Institute.

He also won the respect and affection of his staff. "I'd be lively and mean about Gene if I could," Celestine Sibley responded when asked to contribute to this piece, "but I'm handicapped. I choke up over him. I am just so overwhelmed by this man's goodness and generosity I don't know how to be funny about him."

Not so Harold Martin, who was not only another Atlanta co-worker but a neighbor.

"They were good neighbors," he recalls. "If you needed a cup of whiskey, they were always glad to oblige and if they needed a cup they knew they were free to call. Nearly every weekend we would gather at one house or the other to share a cup of kindness together. My warmest memories of the Pattersons is of those evenings. We all loved to sing, though none of us could—except Gene.

"There was a fine old song called 'The Wild Goose Grasses' that he loved to sing and it was beautiful. But the one I remember the best was 'Git Along

Little Doggies'—with that line, 'Whoopee ti-yi-yo, get along little doggie for you know Wyoming will be your new home.' When we got to that line everybody would hush, and Gene would rare back and take a deep breath and shut his eyes and the muscles in his neck would swell and his vocal cords would quiver and when he hit the 'ti-yi-yo' crescendo, steers miles away on the west side of town would head for Wyoming."

The vocalist himself headed for Washington, where in 1968 he became managing editor of the *Post*. The *New York Times* reported he left Atlanta because of differences with Tarver. Gene denied the story, put Georgia behind him, and tackled his new job at the *Post* with his customary vigor and enthusiasm.

Again he endeared himself to his staff. "He is one of the few men in high authority that I have worked for who could bind people to him with love not fear," says Nick von Hoffman. "This isn't anecdote, but it is the most powerful thing about Patterson, the news executive. People who work for him adore him, not only because he is a good and kind person, as well as one who never lies, never strings you on, but also because—O rara avis!—he can change his mind."

The three years Gene spent at the *Post*, however, weren't his happiest professionally, and he resigned in 1968 to become a professor of political science at Duke University.

Looking back on his *Post* days, Gene told a recent interviewer that executive editor Ben Bradlee needs a managing editor like a boar needs tits.

"That is not quite right," says Bradlee. "Any editor with brains needs Patterson . . . if only to tell him that the South will rise again, that Agnew had something when he carped about eastern effetes, and that we northern boys can't sing worth a goddam."

Nelson Poynter's explanation of Gene's restlessness at the *Post* is that "he needed to be editor of his own paper and enunciate its editorial policy."

It was Poynter who gave Gene that opportunity again, after only a year at Duke, by tapping him to be his own successor as editor and president of the *St. Petersburg Times* and editor and president of *Congressional Quarterly*. "I was terribly jealous of that job," says Poynter. "Gene was the only writing editor I felt could make the most of the freedom and independence I could offer."

In that job, Gene is probably the only editor in the country whose publisher reports to him. He has total responsibility for the whole operation but takes his title as editor seriously.

He conducts the editorial conference every morning, drops in on the news conference most afternoons, and on Friday closes his doors for two hours—the only time it is ever closed—to turn out a Sunday column which reads as if he had spent all week crafting it. He does his writing on a video terminal, having been the first *Times* executive to educate himself in the mysteries of electronic editing.

Executive editor Bob Haiman reports that Patterson "unflaggingly pushes his staff to write better—'to restore literary quality to newspapers.'" Haiman says his boss is also a bear about professional ethics, conflicts of interest, and conducting the affairs of the newspaper with the openness it demands of public officials. "When Gene was arrested for DWI last year," Bob recalls, "he insisted that a story appear on page one, despite the fact that we don't publish those stories about anyone anymore—and local news almost never appears on the front page of the highly departmentalized *St. Petersburg Times*."

It all pays off. The *Times* and its sister paper, the afternoon *Independent*, are not only commercial successes, but *Time* magazine last year named the *Times* as one of the five best dailies in the South.

Gene spends six days a week to make it so, but he is no workaholic. There is still time for personal life he shares with Sue, daughter Mary (who was married last year), and his legions of friends.

"Patterson," as Joe Parham wrote, "is a go-go-go man, a grounded astronaut living life fully and savoring every sweet moment. . . . A proud-of-his-home, his wife, his child, his dog man. . . . A gregarious man and a come-by-for-a-nightcap-and-don't-leave sort of guy."

When the spring gets too tightly wound, he takes off for a Florida lake or river or the Gulf to do some fishing. How relaxing that really is, though, is questionable.

Harold Martin, who has been a companion on some of these expeditions, says that although Gene is "by nature a gentle, soft-spoken person, he lacks patience with those who do not carry out the roles expected of them, even fish. Patterson has no patience with a reluctant pompano. Fishing off the Florida coast, he flogs the waters with such fierce haste and vigor that the waters foam. More skillful and patient fishermen are sometimes startled when he actually catches something."

It would be less startling if he simply talked the fish out of the water. For Gene has a silver tongue which produces speeches as eloquent as his writing and late-night stories which have earned him a reputation as one of the great raconteurs of our time.

His oratorical skill never served him better than when at the last minute he succeeded an ailing Tim Hays as chairman of the ASNE China II delegation.

Tim and interpreter John Haeger had already collaborated on a series of simple toasts, which Gene inherited. But under some needling from his companions after the repetition grew rather tiresome as the trip wore on, the eloquent chairman began to improvise and soon was soaring to dizzying rhetorical heights. Haeger, of course, simply continued to use the old toasts in his interpretation. This mystified the Chinese, who couldn't understand the disparity in the time it took Gene to say something and the time it took Haeger to interpret it, but it left the chairman happily convinced he had knocked 'em dead.

For a man who relishes every moment that passes and looks forward incessantly to a future which he is determined to help shape, Gene is also sentimental about the past. His auld acquaintances can never be forgot.

One of these was Jimmy Flood, who had fought under Gene in the tank corps and then came home to become a Bronx policeman. They visited each other often over the years, and not long before Flood died he was in Atlanta. The jug, Harold Martin recalls, was going around, and Flood's Irish humor came to the fore.

"Gene," he said, "if you'd have thought to make an honest living—instead of becoming an editor—you'd have made a good Bronx cop."

Martin insists Gene thought it was the nicest thing anybody ever said about him.

But that was before he heard what Jack Knight—himself a former ASNE president—said when I asked for his impressions of his seatmate on the presidential mission to Vietnam in 1967.

"Gene Patterson," he wrote, "is my kind of man, who fears neither the truth nor his adversaries. He is a great editor, a staunch friend, a formidable adversary, and excellent company. I greatly value his friendship."

John D. Pennekamp, Associate Editor
The Miami Herald

By Luther Voltz

J ohn D. Pennekamp boasts that he's a better weather prophet than the men at the Weather Bureau.

The forecast may be: Fair with smooth seas.

But Pennekamp won't take that for granted. He'll glance at a palm tree growing beside his bedroom. If the fronds are being agitated too wildly by the wind, he'll turn over and go back to sleep.

There will be no fishing this day because he knows the Gulf Stream will be rough and Biscayne Bay choppy.

Pennekamp doesn't like rough seas. That is, Fisherman Pennekamp.

Journalist Pennekamp, associate editor of the *Miami Herald*, never fears to steer dead ahead into the roughest of seas.

Not one to boast of achievements, other than forecasting weather, Pennekamp in his own mind might give top place to his part in a famous contempt case in which the United States Supreme Court clearly established the right of a newspaper:

To inform its readers of what is going on in the courts without fear that an annoyed judge will use his contempt power to silence the newspaper or its editor.

Or, he might list his major part in establishment of Everglades National Park.

Reserved to the public forever is a lush tropical wonderland at the tip of the mainland of the United States. He can laugh when his two sons call it, "Dad's snake farm."

Pennekamp can take it as well as dish it out.

He was dishing it out when the contempt case arose. The *Herald* hit with

---

Voltz was an editorial writer for the *Miami Herald* when this article first appeared, in 1957.

two caustic editorials and a cartoon about criminal cases that were being dismissed in the Dade County (Miami) courts on technicalities.

One of the editorials said:

> Every accused person has a right to his day in court. But when judicial instance and interpretive procedure recognize and accept, even go out to find, every possible technicality of the law to protect the defendant, to block, thwart, hinder, embarrass and nullify prosecution, then the people's rights are jeopardized and the basic reasons for the courts stultified.

The *Herald* and Pennekamp were cited for contempt. Two circuit judges who issued the contempt citation rendered a verdict of guilty. They fined the *Herald* $1,000 and Pennekamp $250.

The decision was upheld by the Florida Supreme Court.

In fighting the issue, the *Herald* and Pennekamp scrupulously avoided technicalities and pointing out of clear errors of fact in court opinions.

It took the case to the United States Supreme Court solely on a definition of the rights of newspapers and free men under the Constitution.

The Supreme Court answered the question affirmatively and unanimously in reversing the Florida courts.

Justice Stanley Reed wrote the opinion handed down on June 3, 1946. Three justices thought the case so important they wrote concurring opinions. They were Justices Frank Murphy, Wiley Rutledge, and Felix Frankfurter.

Now, eleven years later, the *Herald* and Pennekamp are in another struggle involving the judiciary.

This one is a case in which a grand jury severely criticized two judges and two attorneys over the handling of curatorships. It suggested removal from the bench and disbarment without bringing indictments.

The state attorney sought to suppress the jury's report.

Pennekamp and the *Herald* were quick to surge into the choppy seas again. The basic issue was that the state attorney was blocking the people's right to know what was going on in their courts. The report was released, then expunged by the Florida Supreme Court.

The state attorney was beaten for reelection. The senior circuit judge, named in the report, faces impeachment. The *Herald*, with Pennekamp as the director of editorial page opinion, faces a sizable libel suit filed by the ex–state attorney.

Again, no technicalities, which Pennekamp hates, will be raised.

Pennekamp has spent thirty-two of his sixty years on the *Herald*.

He saw Miami first in 1925 when he was sent by the *Cincinnati Post* to do a series on the booming place. *Herald* managing editor Olin Kennedy, an old

Scripps man, asked him to return to organize the city staff of the *Herald*, which was changing from a country to a metropolitan daily.

Pennekamp accepted.

He has been a controversial part of the *Herald*, Miami, and Florida ever since.

On the newspaper he has been city editor, managing editor, and associate editor.

In the community he has been chary of joining civic organizations and movements.

"I believe an editor's independence is on the line when he is a joiner," Pennekamp says.

Yet, he has served on unpaid commissions under five Florida governors. He was the first chairman of the State Park Board.

He calls himself a "synthetic conservationist." Yet he has a citation signed by Douglas McKay, former secretary of the interior, for service on a commission which modernized the Fish and Wildlife Service.

An expert typist, more often than not, he will write his daily column, "Behind The Front Page," with a fountain pen on the back of a couple of envelopes or a restaurant menu.

Columns calling for merger of school districts (which came to pass), or for modernized metropolitan government (which has been approved by Dade County voters) might be written in longhand on an airplane while returning from a Park Board meeting or a congressional hearing on the Florida East Coast Railway.

"My thinking cadence is more in harmony with my handwriting than my typing," Pennekamp says.

The guy pushes a pen awfully fast.

Warren H. Phillips, Chief Editorial Director
The Wall Street Journal

By Vermont Royster

B ack in 1958 the United States Junior Chamber of Commerce picked Warren Henry Phillips as one of the Outstanding Young Men in America and predicted great things for him.

Warren has done a few other things besides become president of ASNE, such as serving as managing editor of the *Wall Street Journal*, executive editor of all Dow Jones publications, and has even been tapped as president of that estimable publishing house. He's also collected a few awards, such as a Doctor of Laws degree from the University of Portland.

Add to all this impeccable professional credentials as copyreader, reporter, foreign correspondent, and editor.

You'd never have thought all this in the beginning.

Warren is one of those rarities, a native New Yorker. He graduated cum laude from Queens College in 1947, his earlier educational efforts having been interrupted by the United States Army. In the army he worked on *Stars and Stripes*, at college he was an editor of the campus newspaper and a weekend copyboy for the *Herald Tribune*. He also did some stringer chores for that other New York paper, the *Times*.

After graduation he applied to Columbia Journalism School. He was turned down. Then he tried for a job at the *Times, Journal-American, Herald Tribune, World-Telegram, Sun, Post* and *Daily News*. Nobody was impressed.

So in 1947 he showed up as a copyreader on the *Wall Street Journal*, a lanky young fellow with tousled hair and a lean, dark face. It turned out to be a short stay, for in 1949 he went to Germany for *Stars and Stripes*. He lasted an even shorter time at that job. By the end of 1949 he talked himself back on the *Wall Street Journal* staff as a full-time correspondent in Germany.

Royster had retired as editor of the *Wall Street Journal* when this article first appeared, in 1975.

There he covered the lifting of the Berlin blockade, the end of military government, and the establishment at Bonn of the first freely elected German government since the early 1930s.

By this time he had learned to drink schnapps and order a proper meal in an international cafe, so the *Journal* made him chief of its London bureau.

This was the period when Europe generally, and Britain in particular, was just recovering from the Hitler adventures, and Warren was one of that band of correspondents who wore their overcoats in the office and learned to type with gloves on. On the testimony of contemporaries, he also learned to be a bit of a man-about-town.

Indeed, it was while he was being the suave foreign correspondent that he met Barbara Ann Thomas, a comely blonde from Cape Charles, Virginia. Barbara was working at the U.S. Office of Naval Research, and soon propinquity did its work. She must have been as prescient as the Junior Chamber of Commerce, for she yielded to his wiles and they were married.

Meanwhile, back at the home office the *Journal* was in need of a foreign editor. Largely because William H. Grimes, then the *Journal's* editor, had been charmed by Barbara—or so I suspect—Warren was brought back to New York, first as foreign editor and then as editor of those *Wall Street Journal* page one depth stories.

After that, things moved pretty fast for the youngster from Brooklyn. A year later he was named editor in charge of the *Journal's* Midwest news coverage and manager of its Midwest publishing plant in Chicago. By 1957 he was back in New York as the paper's managing editor, age thirty-one.

An impressive young man, without a doubt, especially since he grew his moustache. You can easily spot him now striding through the convention hotel corridors. Put a homburg on him and he looks like Anthony Eden. Put a burnoose on him and he looks like a delegate from OPEC. With Barbara on his arm, he has that distingué air of a jet-setter out on the town.

In fact, he's a very businesslike chap, not the kind around whom anecdotes collect. He makes some pretense of being a sailor, but though I taught him the rudiments of tacking many years ago, he's been known to miss mooring buoys in Bermuda harbor to the delight of a press-gang crew from the *Wall Street Journal* staff.

His main out-of-the-office interest is his family. He and Barbara have three daughters. Barbara, incidentally, is no idler herself. In addition to raising the daughters and spoiling Warren, she went back to school some years ago and got her master's degree in education. Withal she manages to be a lovely hostess in their East Side apartment in New York.

On the corporate roster Warren is now president and chief executive officer of Dow Jones. But in a tradition that goes back to Charles Dow, the *Wall Street Journal* founder, he is also the chief editorial director of the company's publications, which now also include *Barron's* and the *National Observer*, as well as the Dow Jones News Service. His is the ultimate responsibility for the editorial quality.

Warren himself never forgets that he is a newspaperman first, a managing executive second. In 1972 he spent three and a half weeks in mainland China with the ASNE delegation, and the result was a series of perceptive dispatches to the *Journal* which were subsequently published in book form.

As if all that weren't enough to keep a young man busy—he's several months short of his fiftieth birthday—Warren is also a director of Richard D. Irwin Company, textbook publishers, and a trustee of the Brooklyn Institute of Arts and Sciences.

But then everybody who's worked with him in ASNE knows that he's a prodigious worker. In addition to all the various Society chores as he worked his way up the fabled ladder, he's found time to be a trustee of the Freedom of Information Foundation and, from 1971 to 1973, to be president of the American Council on Education for Journalism.

Roy Pinkerton, Editor
Ventura County (California)
Star-Free Press

By Julius Gius

E ven his best friends find it hard to believe that Roy Pinkerton has been in newspapering for more than half a century. His zest for living and working belies his age and the breadth of his experience. At seventy-two he is making more plans for the future, exhibiting more intellectual curiosity, and reflecting more enthusiasm about his work than most men half his age.

The foremost beneficiaries of these attributes are the people of oil-, lemon-, and tourist-rich Ventura County, California, who read the *Ventura County Star-Free Press*, of which Pinkerton is founder, president, and editor. He performs collateral duty as editorial director of the John P. Scripps Newspapers, which has five other dailies (Ventura's 21,300 circulation is the largest) on the Pacific Coast.

If Pinkerton's pace has slackened from the old days, his associates aren't aware of it. He reaches his desk at 8:15 A.M. with such precision that the office clock could be set by his arrival. Between conferences with his news staff and front-office associates, he spends the morning carefully going through a stack of newspapers from all over the country. It is his custom to order assorted dailies from widely separated parts of the nation for a month or two; when the subscriptions expire, he takes on a new batch. As a consequence, Pinkerton can freely discuss the editorial notions and viewpoints of papers large and small in every part of the land, and he enlivens each of his own editorial pages with reprints of three to a dozen pieces clipped from, and credited to, the exchanges.

He spends the afternoon composing his editorials. He writes fast, clearly, and decisively, has few second thoughts and a remarkable ability to cut through any mass of material to the idea, paragraph, or plan that he wants.

Gius was editor of the *Bremerton* (Washington) *Sun* when this article first appeared, in 1958.

Pinkerton's mind is flexible, retentive, capable of encompassing technical details and hanging on to them. When his paper was spearheading a campaign for the Casitas Dam, to solve a part of the county's ever-present water shortage problem, one of the engineers confided: "That Pinkerton knows more about this project than I do—and I helped to design it."

His curiosity is unbounded. Roy saw some unidentified white birds near his home one day and, although he's no kind of bird-watcher or nature student, went thoroughly into the history of whooping cranes, on the chance these might be some. He knows how highways are built, cattle raised, and oil drilled, how champagne is made in France and fondue in Switzerland. He's flown around the world, explored Europe and Asia, ridden a jet on a Korean war mission, slept in a foxhole.

For all his venturesome spirit, Pinkerton is no hail-fellow-well-met. He is naturally reserved, almost stand-offish. But those at his own level, notably newspaper people, find him warm, gracious, a stimulating conversationalist, and all-around good company at bar, football game, or musicale.

His readers either idolize or hate him; few people in Ventura County are neutral about Pinkerton or his paper's outspoken advocacy of political liberalism. The epitome of flattery, however, is evidenced by the ardent Republican in nearby Fillmore who has been a subscriber for thirty years. The story goes that every evening he picks up his *Star-Free Press,* carefully tears off and discards the back page (which happens to be the editorial page), and then sits down to enjoy the balance of the paper.

His county's respect for Pinkerton was best exemplified a short time ago when the aforementioned Casitas Dam federal reclamation project was ratified by the electorate by a thirty-to-one ratio. It was the realization of a goal Pinkerton had advocated thirty years. A month later at a community testimonial dinner he received a plaque inscribed with a tribute to him as "the greatest single factor in solution of the area's water problem," and expressing appreciation for his "insight, unselfishness, public service and leadership."

With typical focus on the future, he told them the job wasn't done—just well started. And now he's begun promoting more dams, and more water lines, to serve other sectors of a county growing speedily richer in bodies and steadily poorer in water.

Like almost everybody else in California, Pinkerton is a transplant. Also like almost everyone else in California, he now has a fiery devotion to the state except for some lapsation during the football season. He was graduated from the University of Washington in 1911 and he loyally (but often hopelessly, alas!) roots for his school on its regular invasions of USC or UCLA domain. At all other times he is faithful to the Golden State, all that it is, and all that it pretends or expects to be.

Roy David Pinkerton was born June 28, 1885, in Crookston, Minnesota. He began newspaper work in 1905 in Tacoma, Washington, acquired his degree six years later and headed for Los Angeles. After working on the copydesks of the old *Tribune* and *Express*, he went back to the Pacific Northwest and ultimately became editor of the *Tacoma Times* (1915–21) and *Seattle Star* (1921–23), Scripps-affiliated papers which since have folded.

In 1924, Pinkerton was editor of the editorial page of the *Cleveland Press*. He worked closely with an eager city hall and political reporter, name of Louis Seltzer.

A year away from the Pacific was enough, and Pinkerton drew assignment as editor of the old Scripps-Howard *Sun* in San Diego. By this time he had the urge to be the proprietor of the paper on which he functioned: the future of Ventura, on the ocean sixty miles north of Los Angeles, looked especially promising since a new oil strike had just been made. True, there already were two dailies in the town of only six thousand population and three others in the county, but Pinkerton and a partner, the late W. H. Porterfield, resolved to risk it anyway.

It proved a *buena ventura*. They rang doorbells to work up a creditable circulation of eleven hundred for the *Star's* first issue June 15, 1925. Eleven years later the paper was alone in the Ventura field. Today it is among the fastest growing of California's non-mets.

As editorial director of the John P. Scripps Newspapers, Pinkerton gives his editors free hand on every issue—national, state, or local—but demands firm opinion, clearly stated. He evangelizes for political independence, disdains editorial platitudes and hokum.

Mrs. Pinkerton is the former Airdrie Kincaid, also a University of Washington graduate. As a reporter and its women's editor, she shared with her husband the labor pains of the *Ventura Star's* birth and the trials of its early years. She also has shared much of his travel experience, is a match for him in intellectual curiosity and wit, the librarian of his vast book collection, and a sparkling hostess at their expansive, modern new home at Ojai that looks out on one of the most breathtaking vistas in Southern California.

Yes, they have just built a brand new home. Cost a pretty penny. Their comfortable, beloved old ranch, you see, was inundated by the waters of Casitas Dam. That's right, the dam that Pinkerton plumped for for thirty years.

Alvin Meade Piper, Editor
Council Bluffs (Iowa) Nonpareil

By Harry Mauck, Jr.

A t eighty-three, Alvin Meade Piper has made one concession to age. No longer will he drive an automobile.

For the balance of modern life, count him in.

On a Thursday, this last mid-May, the willowy, gray-thatched gentleman who has directed the editorial page of the *Council Bluffs Nonpareil* for more than a quarter of a century announced he planned to marry on Sunday. Mr. Piper had been a widower for thirteen years.

His lovely bride, Susan Brinsmaid of San Francisco—formerly of Des Moines—and her late husband had been friends of the Pipers for thirty-five years.

Would we help with some of the details?

Had he arranged for blood tests, required by Iowa law? Taken care of, he replied. The minister? All set.

How about the marriage license? He'd get it tomorrow.

He was reminded that Iowa law requires a three-day waiting period between application and issuance—and he was bucking a courthouse that closed on Saturday. He thought for a moment.

"I guess they've fixed it so I can't be impetuous."

He was married—on Monday.

This is a man of many facets, but impetuosity is not one of them. This is a man of inherent integrity and built-in dignity. He can, and does, change. He is firm, but not immovable.

For years he was an ardent prohibitionist. Yet he was one of the state's

Mauck was managing editor of the *Council Bluffs* (Iowa) *Nonpareil* when this article first appeared, in 1963.

first editors to call for Iowa to legalize liquor by-the-drink, a job the legislature finally accomplished in 1963.

"Prohibition just didn't work," he will tell you. "Bootlegging and illegal tavern sales were worse than regulated saloons."

His friends at ASNE are responsible for his first drink of liquor—at age sixty-three.

"We walked into the cocktail lounge at the Willard at the close of an afternoon session. Someone ordered martinis. I'd never even seen one before. I must have drunk it too fast. When I got up my feet didn't operate properly."

Mr. Piper has been an ardent Republican since the days of McKinley.

"I became a Republican when I was sixteen. That was in 1896 when William Jennings Bryan ran against McKinley. I just didn't like Bryan's platform of free silver. My family were all Democrats but I wasn't and I'm still not sorry I changed family horses before I was old enough to vote."

Yet he has been known to editorially support a Democrat at the local level. And he voted for Woodrow Wilson for president in 1912.

Many of his friends in government are Democratic. He renews these acquaintances each year in Washington, usually for a week after ASNE meetings.

"This year I told Senator Humphrey the way things were going I had better enlarge my Democratic acquaintances because I have a feeling there are going to be fewer and fewer Republicans."

Some years ago (long before Goldwater), Mr. Piper wrote:

"The more I read of history the more I think Harry Truman will be more highly regarded in the future than when he was president. He had to make many great decisions. They weren't all right ones, but he made them."

Stalwart Republican that he is, he believes the nation's strength lies in a strong two-party political system. To this, he says, you must couple a people with strong religious convictions.

A solid Baptist (they part on the liquor issue), he's the best source in the office for a needed biblical quote. If he doesn't remember it verbatim, he knows in what book to find it. And the same goes for American history.

Each Sunday his lead editorial deals with religion as a philosophy of life. Time and again he has rallied faltering Southwest Iowa Democrats to support their cause. To this free-enterpriser, competition in politics is as essential as competition in business.

He is proud of his friendships on Capitol Hill, the great and near-great, which span such political chasms as former President Hoover, Senator Taft, Richard Nixon, Vice-President Johnson, and Sen. Harry Byrd.

"The last time I saw Senator Byrd I told him one of my greatest regrets is that I never had the opportunity to vote for him for president.

"Before Nixon was nominated for president I told him I had two words of advice for him in his campaign. The words were, 'Be yourself.' If he had been himself I believe he would have been elected.

"I also told Sen. Bill Knowland before he retired that I believed the near future of the Republican party might depend on California, and I hoped the party leaders in that state wouldn't get into a hassle among themselves. He didn't answer, but began to talk about other matters. His candidacy for governor later upset the party applecart."

Great presidents?

"Washington and Lincoln, and maybe Andrew Jackson, Theodore Roosevelt, Wilson, and Franklin D. Roosevelt."

You understand the importance of the political scene in Mr. Piper's life when you learn that twice it has been instrumental in separating him from a job. And twice it has returned him to work.

At twenty he left Iowa Wesleyan College at Mt. Pleasant, near his birthplace, to become a reporter for the *Iowa State Register* at Des Moines.

A year later, the opposition *Des Moines Leader* printed an editorial on the death of McKinley. It drew warm praise over the state.

Acting on a tip, Mr. Piper did a bit of research.

"It was practically word for word parts of Beecher's famous oration on the death of Lincoln. The *Leader* editor had substituted McKinley's name for Lincoln, and Ohio for Illinois.

"I called this to the attention of my editor. He had me do a story, and we printed it along with the *Leader's* editorial and Beecher on Lincoln side by side. It created quite a stir.

"Later, when the papers were combined, the editor of the *Leader* was made city editor and assigned the task of reorganizing the staff. He knew I had handled the story about his editorial, and when the names of the new staff were posted I wasn't surprised to find I was not on the list."

Des Moines was the home of *Peoples Popular Monthly*, a family magazine circulated throughout the nation. Mr. Piper joined the staff, soon became editor, and later business manager.

"We had no trouble getting subscriptions, it was fifty cents a year. But we lost money on each subscriber. Our problem was advertising—the lack of it. We went along for over twenty years, making some money one year and losing it the next. Depression spelled death in 1931."

It was a time to do some thinking. He had saved some money, so the family headed for its favorite vacation spot, Estes Park, Colorado. In a short time he joined the *Boulder* (Colorado) *News-Herald*, a Republican paper. Later he was to play a part in its merger with the *Boulder Camera*, Democratic.

"It was a situation not unlike Des Moines. Both papers were getting along, but neither making much money. The *Camera* name prevailed, and I was retained as a Republican columnist."

The bank holiday closed two of Boulder's institutions. From Washington came an edict they could not reopen without merging and increasing the capital stock by one hundred thousand dollars.

"Getting the money was slow. I had an idea I could get the job done if I could be temporarily relieved of my newspaper duties. My publisher agreed to let me try.

"I had just one sales talk. I told depositors their money was tied up and they wouldn't get it unless we could get a new charter. I urged them to take 10 percent of their deposits and buy bank stock.

"We raised the money, at the rate of ten dollars a share, and ended up with fifty-eight hundred stockholders in the new bank."

Boulder congratulated him on a civic job well done.

"Then, to my amazement, I found I was through at the *Camera*. The *Camera* was becoming even stronger Democratic, and I was told that as a Republican I was becoming too well known."

The Republicanism that had cost him two jobs now brought a new one. He went to work for the GOP in Colorado, and later for the National Committee, touring Nebraska, Kansas, and Colorado.

After this job ended he learned the *Nonpareil* was seeking an editor, a man with Republican "proclivities." He joined the paper in 1937.

Prolific, his agile mind produces about a thousand editorials a year. While politics is his true love, Mr. Piper's interests are broad; economics, history, the fine arts. He loves music and the theater. Living in the nation's fifth largest railroad center, he is an oftquoted authority on the problems that beset this industry.

Whatever the subject, his basic philosophy is best summed in his Freedom Foundation award editorial of 1960, the last sentence of which reads:

"The United States will be a great and prosperous nation only so long as the state is the servant of its citizens, not the master of its subjects."

On May 2, 1857, in Vol. 1, No. 1, the *Nonpareil's* first editorial stated:

"In politics the *Nonpareil* partakes of the Republican cast—that party being nearest representative of our political proclivities. Yet we do not wish to be understood as committing ourselves totally to the policies of that organization, but reserve the right to adopt whatever coincides with our views, and to condemn what we cannot reconcile with our beliefs, in an independent way, dealing plainly but kindly with all. . . ."

This is our man.

John N. Popham, Managing Editor
Chattanooga Times

By Eugene Patterson

J ohn N. Popham looks like a larcenous choirboy, a weathered cherub hunting—but not very hard—for a return to innocence.

The Marine Corps haircut is a gesture to his colonelcy, though the wall-to-wall grin is a denial of sternness. The records show he made nine Pacific landings and got decorated at Tarawa. But Pop is really a very peaceful newspaperman—until somebody shoves somebody.

He has been managing editor of the *Chattanooga Times* for going on a decade now. Before that he put in twenty-five years as a *New York Times* reporter, twelve of them on the Southern beat before anybody else discovered Negroes are news.

He never did look like a *New York Times* reporter. He wears striped suits, tells improbable stories, and never made an intentional understatement. He savors hyperbole the way some men use whiskey (he takes coffee only), and if he went to Hanoi he would probably punch somebody in the nose.

Popham is, on the whole, as much a Southern institution as Old Grand Dad or Turner Catledge. Virginia-born and yard-raised in a career-marine family, he speaks that bent Tidewater accent with the brokeback "about." And how he does speak.

When Johnny Popham turns on it's a happening.

He is one of the great talkers in the Wurlitzer tradition. Ask him a question and step back. His eyes flash as if you'd turned up the lights. He emits a guttural preparatory sound of some deep pleasure, the smile breaks, the hands come up, and the music begins. No simple melody for him. As he warms to the theme he begins to weave in the variation, put in the counterpoint, and soar now and then in a golden cadenza of such virtuosity

---

Patterson was editor of the *Atlanta Constitution* when this article first appeared, in 1967.

that you realize you have activated the master. One of the truly entertaining raconteurs of this mute generation, Popham is a rebuke to the terse and a scourge to the literal. He wants to get it all in—the fact-enwrapped whole in its natal mood, with Muzak.

And to know the whole Popham you have to take him the same way. Wise, warm, and gifted, he's held in deep affection. But beyond and behind that, among those who know him, is a regard and respect for the remarkable integrity of the work he has done. Selma, Stokely, King, and Colonel Penn came way after he and the *Times* were on to the South story. He was down here before they were, laying down the background whole. He is one of those who did serious work early.

Popham got his Southern insight in New York, of all places. True, he went there with a Southern heritage. His family had used the tools of its Virginia social setting—good conversation, love of reading, respect for intellect. Moreover, the Pophams had a streak of liberalism in them. During Reconstruction his great-grandfather had published his own newspaper in Richmond, the *Southern Intelligencer*. The paper tried to heal war wounds and build some kind of new society for the defeated Southerner and the new freedman. Great-grandPop had even been campaign manager for the Confederate general, Billy Mahone, who became Virginia's first postwar senator, running on the Readjuster ticket.

"I guess there was always the thread in the family that the monolithic South was not completely true," he says. Yet few understand the Southerner better or respect him more. New York formed Popham for that.

He discovered the multicultural society on the pavement beats for the *Times*. He absorbed the Irish agonies in the saloons, the Jewish loneliness walking the East Side streets eating knishes. He learned a great sympathy for the ordeal of a cultural grouping that is tearing down its myth and discovering new American truths.

With that resource from his New York days added to his inborn Southernness, Popham came South like a William Tecumseh Beauregard to watch the destruction of his own home myth.

"You learn [in these groups subjected to change] that the right or wrong posture or stand is something you must take when human beings are opposing tyranny and violence," he says, "but not when they are simply shedding myths that were warming though inadequate. I learned a lot about the phantoms that walk through a man's mind all his life; when he comes to terms with them he builds his structures out of them."

He struck out to know the Negro—a pretty much unthinkable mission in the middle 1940s. He drove fifty thousand miles a year around the South, stopping in the towns, standing on the corners, visiting the Negro churches, campuses, and political meetings.

When the usual celebrated white was imported for a day to make a commencement speech at Tuskegee or Morehouse, Popham covered the speech like the others. But he went back then to the campus and stood by the punch bowl and listened to the unheard people. He wound up in professors' homes for talk into the night, and he began to know and tell the truths white America hadn't known.

Armed with the trust of Southern Negroes, Popham turned to the Southern whites and began trying to put the story together. He gives credit for his own insights to the interpretive help he got from those native newspapermen he calls "the lovely ones"—the Ralph McGills and Hodding Carters and Pete McKnights and Harry Ashmores, and the Harold Flemings and George Mitchells and the young professors who had studied under Odum. He traded his shoe-leather information with them in return for an interpretive "brilliance I could only borrow from them," and he wrote his journalistic synthesis for the nation.

He went hunting his own white child-friends of the 1920s—

the lovely young girls who went to Lake Junaluska in the summer for the Methodist assemblies, the girls and boys who wore on their Sunday jackets the markers that showed their accomplishment as Bible readers, the boys and girls who dreamed and who talked far into the summer night about the world they would explore, the care-free and happy ones—where did they go, how did they feel; did the seeds of their churchly background and courteous Southern manners always fall on barren ground?

I went searching for them in the sense that I visited with white Southerners everywhere, stood in packed halls making what we call our Southern conversation—the little references that permit you to trace the early life rather swiftly—his recollection of Hi-Y days, of football games, of dancing the Charleston, of wringing the head off the chicken in the backyard to prepare for Sunday dinner, of freezing the ice cream on the back porch in summer—and of course the intimate expression, at this point, of how he really feels about race.

He quickly found those who made the segregationist South less than monolithic—

the agronomist at the state university experiment station, the nutritionist in the high school system, the dedicated church worker, the unassuming technician in a host of new industries and installations. And often it would be a topflight businessman, one of that breed with vision who could take some local challenge to ameliorate things or harmonize the race relations, and would carry it as far as he could go before he lost his "safe" ground.

It was in those years that Pop learned the white South was not a monolith and the Negro was not a mute, and he laid down the background, for what was to come, as it surely did.

Through all those years, and now at Chattanooga, Pop kept coming back and back to his chief conviction that education is the liberating factor for a group in change. "This more than anything else allows a man to shed that myth and take on new views without too much hurt and with no need for any organized violence."

And he has backed up his work as a managing editor—"one tries to shape a newspaper to the needs of the community"—with outside service on countless committees that support Southern education programs. When he's not hustling off to the corners of the South to help boards plan the programs, he's beating off invitations to talk about them from program chairmen who know of his golden oratory.

He loves to bulge the eyes of young managing editors with tales of his days covering Dewey's gangbusters, Tammany Hall, the Lindbergh kidnapping, and Murder, Inc. But he is, above all, one of those really good men who came to the South to see it through—to apply his understanding and his gift to helping his kinfolks at least see things clearly through the ordeal of shedding a myth.

His boy, John N. IV, and his girl, Hilary B., are teenagers making splendid records in Chattanooga. With their getting older, he hopes to get out of the office and visit around the South more. He'll be welcome wherever he goes.

Joseph Pulitzer, Publisher
St. Louis Post-Dispatch

By Ben Reese

J oseph Pulitzer was a magnificent chip off the old block.

If I were asked to write his epitaph those ten words would suffice.

In 1949 I sensed the time had come to prepare a full-dress obituary of my chief, then sixty-four. To him I said:

"Ordinarily the subjects of obituaries never get a chance to know what the *Post-Dispatch* will say of them, but in this instance I am going to permit you to edit your own obituary."

Gifted with the art of understatement, and possessor of a reserved sense of humor, Mr. Pulitzer replied:

"Ben, I feel some delicacy about editing my own obituary."

During this conversation Mr. Pulitzer said:

"If my value to the paper has been anything, I like to think it has been as an active everyday working newspaperman. You of all men on the *Post-Dispatch* know my heart has been in the editorials and the news, and that the commercial departments have been of secondary interest. If somehow you could establish my identity clearly as an active newspaperman, contributing with suggestions, criticism, editing, and occasional rewriting, to the news, features, and editorial contents of the paper from day to day, I should be glad to see that done."

All he wanted was a fair break on the facts.

I wrote my own estimate of his contribution to the newspaper. It filled a half-column and was published in the *Post-Dispatch* in a two-column box as part of the obituary and with this introduction: "How does a great editor appear to the men who work with him?"

Reese was co-chairman of the Advisory Board, American Press Institute, when this article first appeared, in 1955.

When Joseph Driscoll had finished writing the obituary, I edited it and took it to Mr. Pulitzer.

"How long is it?" was Mr. Pulitzer's first question.

"About twelve columns," I replied.

"My God, Ben, I'm not worth all that space."

Eternally, or so it seemed, Mr. Pulitzer was needling his editors to keep them on their high-priced toes. This needling, though occasionally exasperating, was healthy for the newspaper. It took the form of countless slips of yellow memorandum paper. The yellow color signalled an alert from J. P.

If he was in a critical mood, I read, "Please forgive me, but . . . "

Usually his memos were worded in the form of a very polite question. But it was a question that could not be shrugged off unless the recipient checked carefully to be sure he knew all the answers. And once the question had been put, the responsibility was on the receiver.

A classic example of the working of the Pulitzer mind and conscience developed after the Centralia Illinois coal mine explosion of 1947 in which 111 miners lost their lives through the negligence of the State Mine Inspection Board, hamstrung between politicians and mine owners who had contributed to Governor Green's campaign fund. J. P. dictated the customary yellow memo to me, in which he said: "Has not the time come for a concise, terse review of the Centralia tragedy, covering these angles . . . the responsibility of the governor . . . what is likely to be done, and how, to improve and enhance safety through federal and state government . . . what may be done for the miners' families . . . are the guilty likely to be punished?"

Never in the thirteen years I was his managing editor, and this included the period of World War II, did Mr. Pulitzer ever send me an order. Not one of his voluminous suggestions was a "must." "If you don't like my ideas, toss them into the waste basket," he said.

Many of his memos went just there, in the waste basket. Sometimes, after a lapse of days, Mr. Pulitzer would say: "I guess you didn't like such-and-such an idea?" Always I was prepared to tell him why. That ended it.

If, by chance, four or five of his suggestions in a row were accepted and published, he became uneasy and would hasten another yellow memo saying, "Don't forget, there are no J. P. musts. You are responsible for everything in the *Post-Dispatch* except the editorial pages and the advertising."

One morning, about three months after Pearl Harbor, Mr. Pulitzer phoned from his home.

"Will you permit me to give an out-of-town assignment?" he asked. (This was something new.)

"Certainly, you're my boss," I replied.

"I want Ben Reese to take his wife to Palm Beach at office expense and as early as possible. He is to stay at least two weeks."

Two days later I was cleaning up my desk so as to take a train that night. That forenoon a constant stream of yellow memos, twelve in all, were dropped on my desk by one Pulitzer secretary after another Pulitzer secretary. Suggestions for the Washington bureau, suggestions for the state capital bureau, suggestions for the city editor, suggestions for the Sunday Pictures sections, suggestions for the sports department. I was boiling mad, for there was I, trying to clear my desk and start for Florida.

About two o'clock Mr. Pulitzer seated himself at my desk, happily remarking, "Ben, you're on your way tonight?"

"I doubt it."

"What's the matter, you don't sound very happy?"

"God damn it, if I get another yellow memo today I'll scream!"

After a moment's reflection Mr. Pulitzer said, "Perhaps I'd better change the color to orchid."

I related this anecdote to more than one thousand members of the *Post-Dispatch* family who attended Mr. Pulitzer's sixtieth birthday dinner.

About six months later an oil portrait of Mr. Pulitzer was hung in the reception room of the news department, where J. P. and J. P., Jr., had their private offices. Painted by Wayman Adams, it was the staff's birthday gift to the editor and publisher. In posing at his summer home at Bar Harbor, Mr. Pulitzer held a slip of yellow memo paper, which appeared duly in the picture.

On the day the picture was hung, Mr. Pulitzer called me to his office.

"Did you see my portrait?"

"Yes."

"Did you see the yellow memo I held in my hand?"

"No, I missed that."

"Well, next time you pass through the reception room please note the yellow memo. I held it several days in your honor."

Nothing was too small for his attention. He was eager to get everything worthwhile into the paper. Always the good reporter he would phone in little tips to the managing editor or the city editor. The daily magazine editor hailed him as the most prolific fountainhead of ideas.

Even when at Bar Harbor J. P. was thinking constantly about the newspaper. As a secretary read to him, he would sit with eyes closed, but invariably he would discover gold nuggets in the news.

Example: On hearing two boys had stolen a plane in Oklahoma and actually flown it, he telephoned editors to get on top of the story and develop it for the daily magazine. This was on a Saturday. The *Post-Dispatch's* own plane, with reporter and photographer aboard, took off immediately for the scene, and the fully illustrated story appeared the following Monday.

The Pulitzer thinking was national and international as well as local and regional.

The *Post-Dispatch* platform includes this statement: "Never be satisfied with merely printing news." Once, in a moment of irritation, I told J. P. that his platform was: "Never be satisfied period."

On the day I dropped twenty-four-point captions from the top of cuts I had lunch with Mr. Pulitzer. At the table he placed the first edition close to his eyes and, with his magnifying glass, tried to scan the headlines.

"What's this picture about?" he asked, referring to the page one illustration. I told him.

"Where's the caption?"

"In smaller type under the picture."

"Please put the twenty-four-point captions back as before, and over the pictures, so that I can read them."

Throughout his long term as editor of the *Post-Dispatch* Mr. Pulitzer had only three managing editors—Oliver K. Bovard from 1908 to 1938, Ben Reese from August 1938 to July 1951, and Raymond L. Crowley, who succeeded Reese. All three were promoted from city editor. Bovard had been city editor eight years, Reese twenty-one years and Crowley thirteen years.

John C. Quinn,
Chief News Executive
Gannett Newspapers

By Michael J. Ogden

F irst things first. What's that funny squiggle? Well, it's allegedly a phonetic signature and is the way ASNE's fifty-second president winds up almost everything—letters, memos, instructions, whatever—and he says there's an "O" with a tail in the middle that somehow makes it come out John C. Quinn.

Maybe. But when you're dealing with the senior vice-president and chief news executive of the Gannett papers (eighty-five dailies as of this morning) with a total circulation of 3,600,000 and a national newspaper, *USA Today*, projected for this fall; with an operation of twenty-four thousand employees, four thousand of them in the news, you really don't have time to fiddle with things like what's the "C" for.

What you do is write in breathless short takes to get in even a part of what you want to say. Like this:

Okay. The "C" is for Collins (a grandfather). Wife the former Lois Richardson, number four of six sisters, all registered nurses, all born in Canada (ask any one of them to pronounce "about"). Before he met her he was running around with a woman named Phyllis, but Loie, compassionate, heart-of-gold, butter-wouldn't-melt Loie, got rid of "that sneaky little blonde," and they were married twenty-nine years ago in Carolina, Rhode Island, a town too small even to support a Gannett paper.

It's their home away from their Rochester, New York, home. Their house was built in 1850 and seems to be full of ancient artifacts and rippling floors. On a mantel the clock reads 10:14 as it strikes the hour. Question. John, defensively: "We've got twelve antique clocks here. They're all set differently. If all of them sounded the hour together we'd have chaos."

Ogden had retired as editor of the *Providence Journal and Bulletin* when this article first appeared, in 1982.

How do you know the right time? He pulls out the famed Uncle Denny phony gold turnip (only his wedding ring is genuine).Was there ever an Uncle Denny? "He's a composite." How do you know the right time? "I carry a wrist watch in my pocket."

Next subject. Four children: a daughter, Lo-Anne, and three sons, improbably named Kiffer, R. B., and Chips. Kiffer chases girls. R. B. would have been my godson if I could have remembered the Act of Faith, not just the Act of Contrition. Chips is working on the *Providence Journal-Bulletin* after a stint with the Gannett paper in Guam.

I know what all the names actually are but there isn't the space. I also know that a biographer shouldn't be using "I" so much, but John worked for me so long I'm responsible for many of his troubles in early life.

Chips got the job on his own, as did his father, but for a different reason. And John started a little lower, night copyboy on the *Journal*, Easter Sunday night, 1943. In the process he appalled his grandmother by joining an outfit that not only worked on Easter, but on any Sunday, and at night. Grandma went to her rest not knowing that it could have been worse. She could have been confronted with the truth behind John's decision.

His previous job had been delivering groceries. Making his first call on a new customer, he apparently chanced upon her as she was stepping out of her Saturday afternoon bath. "Ooh," she squealed, seizing the nearest covering, a very brief hand towel, "The grocery boy. I thought you were the newsboy."

At that moment John decided on his career—newsboy. When he made it past the first night, during which the city editor's bellow of "Copy!" scared John into tipping the glue pot over the picture editor's desk, he was on his way.

He had twenty-three years on the *Journal-Bulletin*. Not once did we introduce him—later Al Neuharth did, frequently—as "the man with the nearsighted hair." Why, I asked John, do you forever push your glasses to the top of your head? "Because," he said, "you were always muttering 'Where the hell did I put my glasses?'"

He taught himself more than that.The progression went like this: From copyboy to the Columbia School of Journalism for his master's (B. A. at Providence College). Supported himself in New York by walking landlady's dog in the morning, working as a page boy at NBC from midnight to eight o'clock, classes presumably after the dog. That doesn't seem to allow for sleep so must have gone without until he returned to *Journal*.

Loie, who thinks it's important, interpolates:

"Meanwhile, he sent a dollar a week to his great uncle; once a week he had bacon for breakfast and the other days he had porridge."

You see where the space goes?

Okay, he's back at the *Journal*. And I decide he might as well become thoroughly rounded now that he's a master. He's tossed around from general assignment to city hall to state house to Sunday department to real estate editor to religion editor to night financial to copydesk to a couple of years in the Washington bureau to assistant day city editor in no particular sequence. Finally, inasmuch as I'm managing editor, he becomes assistant managing editor.

As my great strength is delegating, I delegate everything to John and scurry around making speeches. Also, we take turns going to symposiums in New York City teaching us, among other things, how to make up Sunday papers without dinky sheets and balloon formers. This impresses us, but not the pressroom, so we turn the job of making up the Sunday paper over to the secretary we share.

When the publisher suggests we both stay in town, we sequester a pair of desks just next to the men's room. Because I'm the boss, I give him the outside desk so that staffers en route can bother him, not me.

In that spot I can hear him educating his children over the phone. Educating them in what? How to answer the phone. And, on the subject, today John must be one of the few newspaper editors in America who has two 800 Enterprise phones, one to his office and one to his home. You want to speak to him from anywhere in the world, get his number.

Also, in that area I had some of my better ideas for news stories. We both smoked too much in those days. Somewhere I came across the information that a now-forgotten solution of silver nitrate applied to the tongue could break the nicotine habit. I told John to try it and to write a story on the results. We didn't get a story but John got a small hole in his tongue and continued to smoke until he suffered a small heart attack (this significant; see major result farther on) while trying to ski or toboggan or something else he couldn't master (this also of note later on).

Admittedly, some of my better story ideas frequently involved John's life and limb. Some worked, some didn't. There was the time I told him to check out my hunch that the downtown Providence traffic lights didn't allow enough time between green and red for the average pedestrian to cross. He went out, equipped with a stopwatch. I was right, of course. John almost got run over three times but all that his story got me was a nasty note from the Highway Department.

Another memorable assignment. Publisher Sevellon Brown could not locate one of his chief aides. Said find him. I say yessir, turn to John and instruct find him. He turns, but no one on way to men's room, so sighs and takes up pursuit. He finds missing aide in local bar with local hooker. Calls desk for help in rescuing aide, then assumes chore of escorting hooker to unluxurious hotel across street from *Journal* building. Entire newsroom hanging out third-floor windows cheering John on as he tries to steer, support, and unload gal of ill repute in hostelry of no repute.

When John gets what he asks for, like it or not he damn well swallows it.

First, you'd have to be told about his favorite eating place back in the Providence days. Then you'd have to understand the easily rumpled dignity of the proprietor, a cross between Jeeves and a Roman Fatty Arbuckle.

One dinnertime, John complained bitterly to him about the lack of couth in the city's restaurants, without one of them boasting of a sidewalk cafe. Our restaurateur drew himself up. He ordered a table put on the sidewalk, forcing all pedestrians into the gutter, placed a candle and a rose near the silver and the napery, and had three waiters serve John al fresco. The one slight drawback was that the month was January and a near blizzard was making up. But with the proprietor beaming nearby and surrounded by irate, displaced passersby, John proceeded to brush the snowflakes off his brochettes and dine with aplomb.

Well, obviously, one doesn't achieve John's niche in life without going to more professional behavior and learning other tricks of the trade. In time he achieves one of the two or three great journalistic honors. He is elected president of APME in 1973. From his first post with Gannett, as executive editor of the two Rochester papers, he moves up rapidly in the corporation. His progress is seldom without comment from his new boss, Al Neuharth, chairman and president of the company, even in the early stages.

John has been in Rochester but a brief time. While settling in, he attempts the task, atop a long ladder, of cleaning the drains on his roof at home. The ladder topples and the next time Al sees John in the office, his new prize catch is heavily bandaged and on crutches. "So," says Al cryptically, "One more thing you can't do."

Only Loie remains loyal. Her staunch defense: "But you know—as he was falling he remembered to swing his body to the left so he could keep his right hand uninjured for driving and typing."

Maybe that did it. As he heals, his responsibilities increase until he is handling a mighty big news operation in an organization that this year has revenues of about $1.4 billion and something over $170 million in net income. The four score and more dailies range from the Virgin Islands to Guam and the circulations from 4,000 to 226,000. There are ten women publishers (one black) and two black male publishers.

He also heads the Gannett News Service and, in the words of one editor in the organization, "brought it from nothing to something. It is sizable and does some good work. The Pauline Fathers story ran much too long, but it won a Pulitzer. Quinn later said publicly that Gannett would win other Pulitzers, and he added that he hoped it would not take as many words to do it."

With all the people and all the responsibilities, how does John operate? Not like old W. R. Hearst spreading his papers out on the library floor in San Simeon and crawling on hands and knees from one to another, dictating observations over his shoulder. John doesn't have a floor big enough at home or at his office, where he works at his centerpiece—a copydesk. Why? "Because I always wanted to sit in the slot."

What he does is get out in the field at least 60 percent of the time, frequently using one of Gannett's four corporate jets. He gets all the Gannett papers in his office every day. Over the space of about every two weeks he gets to see them all—"Somehow. While I'm on the plane or in bed or on the phone. Then again, all editors and publishers go to ASNE or APME or ANPA and we get the chance, wherever they're held, to have subsidiary meetings at least once a year."

In addition, there are regional meetings, and there's a ten-day session in Rochester in the fall when John goes through all the budgets of all the news departments. So he goes to the editors and publishers or they come to him or he's on the phone with them—"maybe one hundred calls a day in or out."

And such is his devotion to breaking news that he keeps four television sets tuned to the news channels at home and another four in his office, at the edge of the copydesk. This is probably better, at least from Loie's point of view, than the early days at Rochester. Then, he used to keep an Associated Press machine and a Gannett wire service machine, both complete with round-the-clock mechanical chatter, in their bedroom.

About here ought to be enough on Quinn and Gannett. It's almost beyond belief that one man is going to keep an eye on eighty-five daily papers and a news service, anyway. But I know Quinn. And if Neuharth told him to look in on some other facets of the operation, too, I guess he'd find room.

Among the overflow are twenty-three nondailies, a magazine, a research outfit, seven television stations, eight radio stations, a satellite information network, a slew of outdoor advertising sign companies, and heaven-help-us, a corporation involved in silk-screen printing.

But let's say his principal focus is only on the dailies and the news service. In addition to nurturing them, he puts out a weekly publication of about a dozen pages, called *Wire Watch*, which tells all eighty-five what everyone else is up to.

Finally (or as final as you can get with him), he puts out a yearly publication called *The Best of Gannett*. Which is what it says it is, and John adds that he takes "a certain private satisfaction in spending about as much on this publication to proclaim news-editorial accomplishments as the company spends to proclaim its fiscal accomplishments in the annual report."

It's on heavy gravure stock, maybe book page thick, much of it in color, has its own editors and designers, and his remark on cost may be the only understatement in this piece. As an outsider, I'd equate the cost roughly with putting out *Time, Life* and *Fortune* for one full cycle.

But with it all he doesn't make out his job to be second-guessing the news people. "The better I do my work, the less I get noticed," he says. "Put it another way, too. I give them a job and get out of their way. They don't want me leaning over their shoulders and I'm perfectly willing to let them be the heroes. I keep out of sight. When I drop in somewhere, I'll listen to the problems, figure out what's needed, if anything."

It pays off. One of his editors says, "We don't see him much. I regard that as good. He goes where the fires are burning. Newspapers generally considered to be okay are left alone . . . . He's still a hero among the newsrooms. No applause at corporate meetings is as loud as that for Quinn, who takes on the image of the people's representative, the newsroom's friend."

To the outsiders, or even some of the insiders, who think the Gannett papers lack quality, that while the organization may take some bad papers and make them better they have never produced a great editor or an outstanding newspaper, there can be all kinds of answers.

A pragmatic one—great papers don't get sold. Quinn argues that the critics are mainly those who are used to metropolitan journalism. "The readers in Fremont, Nebraska, want to know what's going on in Fremont. What we're principally doing is putting out tough, aggressive newspapers in the smaller communities. If it were a choice of putting a new bureau in Springfield, Illinois, or Rockford or Danville, or having our own man in Paris, we'll take the local bureau every time."

He's been with Gannett sixteen years and in the sixteen years the papers have gone from twenty-five to eighty-five. And that brings us back to the ski slopes and the heart attack.

After his recovery John goes to Miami for R and R. Coincidentally, Al Neuharth, now head man at Gannett, was then with the *Miami Herald.* Fortuitously, they chance on each other. Al, who had visions of his own, remembers "planning and plotting John's escape from Providence" for some years.

But, like a pro football team seeking the okay of a university to seize their coach, Al defers making a pass until he is given the go-ahead years later. When it comes, Al, out of Miami and out of Detroit and into Rochester, invites John and Loie to visit, tells his secretary to send a *bottle* of champagne while they deliberate. She, a Britisher, misunderstands, sends them a *case.* Al's version.

"Overkill," says John. He murmurs to me, "I don't know. My roots are awfully deep in Rhode Island."

"Time to go," I tell him. "Forget your roots."

He mulls it over. I throw in the final dart:

"And remember—when you answer him. Hold out for three hundred dollars a week."

He must have got it.

Benjamin H. Reese, Managing Editor
St. Louis Post-Dispatch

By Ben McKelway

O ne of the pleasures of advancing age is the privilege of offering advice to the young. For most of us, unfortunately, the pleasure too often is marred by disillusioning rediscovery that youth is bored by what we have to offer.

Benjamin Harrison Reese (Harry to his family; Ben to everybody else) is a happy exception to this rule. Those to whom Ben offers his advice not only ask for more—they take it away with them and actually use it. One of Ben's great contributions to the American Press Institute, on whose Advisory Board he serves as co-chairman and as a regular participant and discussion leader in its seminars, is his repeated demonstration that "The words of the wise are as goads."

Ben is wise in the ways of newspapering, with some forty-five years of it behind him. For twenty-five of those years he was city editor and for thirteen years managing editor of the *St. Louis Post-Dispatch*. His is, indeed, the voice of experience. He retired from the *Post-Dispatch* on June 1, 1951. But his distinguished career on that newspaper continues to envelop him in a certain aura of prestige quickly recognized by a younger generation of newspapermen whose attendance at API seminars enables them to sit at his feet.

His size undoubtedly helps. Whoever coined the phrase—"a man of stature"—could have had Ben Reese in mind. Six feet two inches tall, carrying his 250 pounds with grace, he stands out when he stands up, the commanding figure of any landscape he adorns. He looks now very much as he looked a good many years ago when, as the *Post-Dispatch's* new managing editor, he first began attending ASNE sessions in Washington. His entry into the meeting place always made at least one observer think of the mountain

McKelway was editor of the *Washington Star* when this article first appeared, in 1960.

coming to Mahomet.

His is not the voice of an angel, but it does have a strong resemblance to the voice of a city editor. Subdued as it is by the acoustics of API's seminar room, there was still something about it that inspired reminiscence by one who attended a recent seminar for city editors. Now a city editor himself, this man once worked for Ben Reese as the *Post-Dispatch's* correspondent in Alton, Illinois. They did use the telephone, but looking back on his experience, this ex-correspondent is not convinced that this device was really necessary. Had Ben merely stuck his head out of the city room window and yelled, his correspondent in Alton, some nineteen miles away, would have heard him.

There is not room here, nor is it necessary to review Ben's career with the *Post-Dispatch* which received so many laudatory reviews when he retired. The *Bulletin* asked for a sketch of Ben Reese at API. But a part of this story is that Ben, after forty-five years of deadlines, healthy, full of vim at sixty-two, and already eligible for a special pension, decided not to wait for the calendar to fix the date of his leave-taking and retired ahead of normal time.

One of the conclusions of Britain's Royal Commission on the Press was that "there is still widespread among pressmen a sense of vocation, somewhat as sailors feel a call for the sea." Another similarity between newspapermen and sailors is a common disposition to build castles in the air to which they plan to retire. Tastes in such architecture may differ. What Ben wanted was to sit and look at the ocean. He was familiar with Spring Lake, New Jersey. His son, in business in New York, lived nearby and wanted his father to join him. So Ben and the late Mrs. Reese bought a home in Spring Lake near the sea and there they came to live when he left the *Post-Dispatch*.

The API's Advisory Board had been looking for some retired newspaper editor of distinction who might be retained to spread the API gospel. There were promising prospects, but the search was in vain. Then Ben turned up. The late Sevellon Brown, principal founder of API and chairman of its board, and Turner Catledge, member of its board, decided to talk to him. Each in his own right was a number one persuader. Together they constituted an irresistible force. It turned how, however, that Ben was the immovable object.

"Listen," said Ben. "You two slickers are not going to lasso me into any kind of a job. I am living where and as I want to live. I have earned retirement and I am going to have it. Thank you but the answer is no."

As Stell, Ben's wife, once confided to a friend, she knew all along that Ben's idea of how he would spend his retirement would never work. He soon discovered that the life of a businessman, even in association with his beloved son Ben, Jr., was not for him. He was hungry for newspaper talk but he had removed himself beyond reach of such fare. As Stell described it—

> It was a beautifully clear, sunshiny day and we were looking out over
> the ocean which had brought us to Spring Lake. Suddenly Harry
> turned to me and said, "Stell, if I have to spend the rest of my life
> looking at the goddamn Atlantic Ocean, I'll go crazy."

Turner and Sevellon talked to him again. This time they won. On
October 8, 1951, four months and seven days after a retirement that was to
be free of the pressures of any job, Ben finally cast his lot with the American
Press Institute.

In retirement, Ben has found his niche and the API has found a wise
counselor. He wears three hats. With Paul Miller, chairman of the Advisory
Board and Turner Catledge, a longtime member, he completes a three-man
executive committee that transacts most of its business over a three-way
telephone and consults with Monty Curtis and his competent staff on
matters of policy or new undertakings. He is as quick to make a decision as he
is, on the basis of new facts, to modify or reverse it. What he says is blunt and
direct. He does not feel his way to a point of view. He says what he thinks
without waiting to hear himself say what it is that he's thinking.

His second job is to lead the discussion for one session at each of the
seminars for publishers, general managers, business managers, circulation
managers, and such. He makes a presentation under the heading, "What
Makes a Newspaper Tick." What makes it tick, to the surprise of some
members of these audiences, is the quality of its unpaid content, and not
gadgets or lucky bucks.

But Ben is in his glory when he's talking with his brethren—editors, news
executives, managing editors, city editors, women's editors, editorial writers,
and his favorite people, the reporters. He takes part in all their seminars. At
one session in each seminar he presides as discussion leader. His lecture on
"The Newspaper's Responsibility for Public Service to Its Community" is
drawn from his own rich experience at the helm of a crusading newspaper
which during his regime won four Pulitzer Prizes.

When others are leading a seminar discussion, Ben sits halfway down the
left side of the oval table, leaning slightly forward, alert to everything
anybody says, quick to ask a question designed to amplify or debate some
point, and ready with an illustrative anecdote. When he is pleased, he beams,
and laughter shakes his big frame. In disagreement, he puts into motion the
offense mechanism of a city editor. He is not rude but by nature he is
emphatic. He shares with an attentive audience his own ideas of the right way
and the wrong way to discipline a reporter. He expounds the virtues of a
good human interest story at the bottom of page one. He scorns inaccuracy
as a cardinal sin and would roast the sinners in fire and brimstone. The

newspaperman's greatest asset? "Common sense, just plain common sense." When asked how to obtain and preserve that asset, he looks up in surprise. "If you don't have it, you can't get it," he replies, thus washing his hands of further responsibility in that field.

Ben spends many hours in preparation of his formal lectures and reads them to avoid extemporaneous error. They are full of sound, down-to-earth advice in the unequivocal spirit of the Old Testament and the Ten Commandments. The lectures are delivered with an earnest conviction that leaves no one in doubt as to Ben's firm belief in every word he utters.

He does believe it. That is one quality of his character that endears him to those who know him. There are other qualities which made him a first-rate newspaperman and executive. He was tough. He was thorough. He was tenacious. When he retired from the *Post-Dispatch*, *Time* magazine, in one of the kindest pieces it ever ran about anybody, referred to him as a "bedrock newsman." The affectionate flavor of that accolade was, no doubt, fully merited. It is, however, an interesting coincidence that a number of men on *Time*, including its then managing editor, were trained as reporters under Ben. One of his great satisfactions has been the advancement of good newspapermen whom he started on the road as reporters.

One finds in Ben many of the characteristics associated with a good newspaperman. But one of them, so often attributed to his fellow craftsmen, is not a part of Ben's makeup. His outlook is never blurred by cynicism. When he talks about good newspapers and good newspapermen, he talks with no inhibiting "ifs," "buts," or "howevers."

The impression he leaves on those who hear his lessons of experience is reflected in the hundreds of letters that come back to API after the seminars are over. To quote from a few: "It was like having the old admiral walk the deck again." "It was gratifying to have my newspaper philosophy reaffirmed by a real giant in the profession." "Enclosed are some tear sheets that will show our efforts to be 'the guardian of the town.' " "I spoke at Palo Alto to a group of editors . . . I openly cribbed from Ben Reese's talk." ". . . as a result of your stimulation I've had more stories developed by the staff in the past two weeks than I can recall." "One of the really good things . . . was the inspiration of hearing a campaigner whose results represent American journalism at its best." "You had a tremendous impact on the advertising managers . . . you gave them an understanding about newspapering that they never had before."

Such letters and the warmth of spoken tributes that usually mark the conclusion of a seminar are among the things that make Ben weep and thus reveal that he's really not tough at all. As a matter of fact he's a sentimental old softie. He takes deep pride in what he is doing.

It has been said of Plato that when he gave up politics and turned to teaching he never thought of himself as retiring from public service. As Edith Hamilton has noted, "To find young men capable of leading and to develop to the full their capacity by the right kind of education was now his object."

Ben shares that object, in line with Sevellon Brown's concept of what API should undertake and the skill of its staff in giving it effect. Those most familiar with Ben's work at API take considerable satisfaction in the thought that some 1,885 newspapermen and women, including 675 executives from the business side, plus 126 foreign newspapermen from Latin America, Asia, and the Middle East, have been exposed to his common sense.

His admonition to those nearing retirement: "Get yourself something to do that will keep your mind active and get you out of the house. Hang around the house all day with your family and the smallest domestic annoyance can become a major catastrophe. I am lucky to be with API. It keeps me thinking about newspapers, learning about newspapers, and associating with newspapermen."

Oxie Reichler, Editor
Yonkers (New York)
Herald Statesman

By William I. Bookman

O xie Reichler's son Merton who, significantly or not, is not a newspaperman but a college teacher, shivers a little every time he tells the story about his walk through the snowy hills of Yonkers one Christmas Eve to return a payola gold watch.

Someone who didn't know Oxie very well had left the offering at the editor's apartment and Merton, who knew his father pretty well but not the circumstances of the innocent-looking package, accepted it. Oxie came home from his daily stint of trying to make Yonkers make itself a better city, and saw the watch.

If it had been a grenade timed to explode in seconds, it couldn't have been tossed out of the apartment faster. But Oxie saw it more as poison gas—as any of his associates will readily understand—and Merton became a decontamination squad of one.

The would-be payola dispenser lived across and up—almost vertically—town. It was snowing, the trolleys weren't running, but off Merton went.

Reaching the home of the malefactor, he found that gentleman out, but his mother at home. She was a kindly soul, but she didn't understand English too well. She thought Merton was bringing a gift for her son. Merton spent the remainder of the evening trying to extricate himself from marzipan, lavender, and maternal gush.

People looking for the source of Oxie's vivid moral sense can look up the vitals and learn that he was born the son of a rabbi in Utica, New York, on Christmas Day, 1898. One of Oxie's brothers became a rabbi, and Oxie's own syndicated, "Editor's Moments of Meditation" (he's written about seven thousand of the daily prayers for newspaper readers in the twenty years of

---

Bookman was editor of the *White Plains* (New York) *Reporter Dispatch* when this article first appeared, in 1962.

the feature), show a sincere, vibrant, yet practical religious conviction.

Oxie's sometimes melodramatic incorruptibility has overtones of stubbornness, too, as it finds its primary outlet on the editorial page of the *Herald Statesman*. His devoted readers will sometimes open to the editorials and groan, "Oh, for heaven's sake! Is he still on *that* subject?" Well, *that* subject is much more often than not one which has been blazoned forth initially by the editor, dragged through the three-dimensional maze of Yonkers politics, and made the subject of diatribes against the ol' debbil editor, various kinds of whispering and shouting campaigns, and maybe even a libel suit or two.

Yes, Oxie is still on *that* subject, and he usually prevails, too. If he doesn't—and his most bitter defeat was the voters' rejection of proportional representation and a retreat from this form of citywide elections to the old ward system in 1948—it's usually because the folks in Yonkers can't ante up the same old idealism their editor can. If there's any bitterness in Oxie's soul today, it's probably because few people seem willing to stand shoulder-to-shoulder with him for a fight any more. And his own shoulders are no longer as broad as they once were.

Oxie's adventures in municipal-land all started, he likes to recall, with a woman named S. Alice Smith. She was in charge of Americanization for the Utica, New York, public schools when Oxie was a fledgling reporter with the *Utica Daily Press*.

"When I made my daily stop at her office, she'd grab me and chew my ear off," he told a couple of *Herald Statesman* staffers once. "I remember her pet theme was, 'You can't have citizenship without sidewalks!' She meant that the housewives in East Utica, a big Italian district, couldn't keep their houses clean because their families kept tracking in dirt from the nonsidewalked streets.

"She wasn't a journalist, but she knew how to keep after a subject. She kept giving me stories about those sidewalks, and I kept putting them in the paper. Soon, as S. Alice Smith no doubt knew but as I had to learn, the sidewalks appeared.

"This was something new—you could plant news items and grow sidewalks!"

Oxie has been "planting" news stories ever since—mostly just the ordinary but cumulatively important grist of municipal affairs—and his garden has grown some pretty hardy perennials such as honest government, strict enforcement of laws, and good citizenship. A few varieties, like *proportionalis representum*, have withered and died, but Oxie just digs them up and makes a compost of experience to better nurture his next seedlings.

It comes as a surprise to people who have seen ruddy-faced politicians turn white under a Reichlerian editorial blast, but Oxie was once a public official himself. It was shortly after Oxie wrote a story for the *Utica Observer-Dispatch,* based on inside information, that Fred J. Rath, a former chauffeur and Cadillac salesman, and now a state senator, would be the GOP nominee for mayor. Oxie's editor called him in, barked that he "didn't run fairy tales"—and the next morning saw the competition come out with the story.

As mayor, Rath appointed Oxie deputy public safety commissioner. "Everyone thought I was crazy to take the job," Oxie has recalled. But he had been hired, he knew, to help publicize the administration and to rout scandal from the police department. Working with the paper which was obtaining a portfolio of affidavits, Oxie saw this groundwork turn into sixty-three indictments from a grand jury. "And," adds a finger-wagging Oxie, "sixty-three convictions!"

Oxie came New York Cityward in 1930 with a pocketful of letters of introduction. At the apogee of an erratic orbit among the big city news plants, he checked in at the *Yonkers Statesman* and met Lewis S. Dayton, the editor. Someone had told Oxie that the Yonkers paper might be a greener pasture for not having any sacred cows in it—a refreshing change, to hear Oxie tell it, from some upstate meadows at that time. After persuading Dayton to take him on as associate editor, he found this to be refreshingly true.

That green pasture was to become a battleground.

Oxie's first big campaign was supporting the introduction of the council-manager form of government in 1938, with the proportional representation method of electing councilmen. But he knew that this was just the opening tussle in a long war which, with minor variations in alignment and emphasis, is still going on.

The two major political parties were winking at each other over those headlines that proclaimed the enlightened vote of the people for city manager-P.R. government. The politicos still controlled their organizations and, by God, they'd control any city manager too.

To keep the political boys at bay, Oxie knew he had to arouse support for the new set-up between Election Day in 1938 and the date the manager system went into effect in January 1940. He decided that what was needed was a simple, nonbombastic, nonpartisan interpretation that anyone could understand. To a young reporter on his staff, Ed Schlesinger, he assigned the task of writing four or five questions and answers a day, designed to ring out the meat of the manager plan. The Qs and As were printed in fourteen-point type and put in a prominent page one box.

It was a hit. Sales of the paper actually zoomed from this. The school system made the series required reading in current events classes. In the political clubs the articles were circled in black and the bosses saw red.

The *Herald Statesman*, probably the first paper in the country to do so, later ran a full list of municipal employees when it found that there was no such list available for public perusal at city hall. (And incidentally uncovered the fact that there were blatant sinecures on the city payroll, such as a complete Department of Water Extension whose 273 employees were doing exactly nothing and getting paid for it.)

These disclosures and other developments dismaying to both parties led in 1942 to a victory by the forces the newspaper supported which was even more smashing than that of 1938, when the bosses had stood tolerantly and patronizingly by. Now both party machines put separate petitions on the November ballot, both of them calling for a repeal of citywide council elections and the P.R. system. (The manager they evidently decided they would let stay, since they could always boot him out!)

George H. Hallett, Jr., secretary of the Citizens Union of New York City, recalled the newspaper's part in the campaign. "I have never seen a more vigorous and convincing presentation of fundamental issues in an electoral campaign. It was a daily inspiration to the defenders of good government."

Even for turbulent Yonkers the conflict was historic. Old-time political leaders with customary iron control on their bailiwicks found to their dismay that—on the issues defined dramatically in the newspaper—some of their stalwarts were deserting and lining up on the other side. But even so, never for a moment did they doubt that one or the other of the parallel repealer propositions would sneak by the voters at the polls.

It was a two-to-one landslide against the bosses. Citywide elections and P.R. were safe—at least for the next six years. In 1948 the voters of Yonkers hatcheted proportional representation, largely because they had become convinced that it was too representational. They responded in horror—despite the newspaper's rebuttal—to the election of two Communists in New York City during that town's fling with P.R.

With P.R. also went citywide elections in Yonkers.

It was in 1951 that the *Herald Statesman* won the Polk award for its editorial campaign against a goofy but insidious referendum on the ballot to amend the city charter to remove all control over salaries from the city and have pay raises voted on by the people, who were presumably more tender hearted but who, of course, didn't know the financial ins and outs.

Only the paper and maybe the city manager (who didn't have any power) seemed to be against the referendum. Both political parties were for it, and all the candidates. Oxie knew that there would be chaos if the referendum went through, and he said so in six-column-wide editorials on page one.

Even so, Oxie expected to get licked.

But when the votes came in 99 election districts out of 101 in the city had voted the newspaper's way. One of the other two districts went the other way by nine votes. The last district approved the petition by two hundred votes. Oxie still thinks he may have missed the story of his life by not sending a reporter into that maverick district to find out why it thumbed its solitary nose at the paper and the rest of the city.

The police and firemen were understandably furious when their little plan was thwarted. "It's a good thing Oxie doesn't drive a car," remarked one associate when the police went on a traffic ticket binge to convey their feelings.

There have been many other battles, some of which have earned national recognition for the *Herald Statesman* and its editor. Perhaps the greatest honor came in 1956, when Oxie won the La Guardia Award for Outstanding Achievement in Municipal Affairs. It was the first and only time the award was given to a newspaperman.

Seated in his spartan office at the *Herald Statesman* squeezed between city editor Dave Jensen's newsroom and the clattering TTS workshop, Oxie often pauses nowadays to take a deep breath and wonder a little about what the hectic scene of battle holds next. Relaxation? He and his wife delight especially in their two grandchildren.

Oxie still looks hale, still the plump little man with the steel rimmed glasses who looks less like a forceful editor than the kindly neighborhood druggist or stationery store proprietor.

He still looks like the benign fellow who wouldn't dare hurt anyone's feelings by not . . . well, by not accepting a gold watch, for instance! But don't let appearances fool you. This man is one of the staunchest—and we hope for the sake of American journalism far from the last—of the Incorruptibles.

Vermont Royster, Editor
The Wall Street Journal

By William H. Fitzpatrick

By all odds, the *Wall Street Journal* is the newspaper phenomenon of the last quarter century. Certainly not very many newspapermen, thirty years ago, would have been willing to wager that what then was considered hardly more than a good trade journal would today occupy the prestigious place it does. Surely none of the handful of students in the journalism department of the University of North Carolina in the 1930s would have so bet, any more than they would have predicted that Vermont Connecticut Royster would rise to edit the *Journal* and become the first *Journal* man to head the ASNE.

Not that they would have bet particularly against Bunny, as they called him. It was just that the thirties were star-crossed years for young men. Or so it seemed at the time; to them, the odds that they'd see their first by-line before the first breadline were about even for all.

But if the *Journal*, which as late as 1941 had only 32,600 circulation and in 1965 ranks third in the nation in that regard (870,000 Monday through Friday) and perhaps even higher in both influence and affluence, is a phenomenon, so is Royster if solely by his standing in what is quite likely the most phenomenally successful group of young men ever to argue about writing and editing on one campus.

In those days, Chapel Hill's journalism school must have had, to richer ones with more renown, something of the look of Mark Hopkins's log without Mark Hopkins on the end of it. But it did have O. J. Coffin, described by one of his now successful boys as "a sort of one-man Bible-reading, whisky-drinking journalism department." Coffin is still legendary in editorial rooms in the Upper South and journalism deans today might well inquire, as Lincoln threatened to do in answer to complaints about Grant, what sort of whisky that was. For while his department seldom

---

Fitzpatrick was editor of the *Norfolk* (Virginia) *Ledger-Star* when this article first appeared, in 1965.

numbered over a dozen students per class, in 1933–35 Coffin sent out into the tender world of city editors these then young men:

- Don Shoemaker ('34), editor of the *Miami Herald*.
- Robert Mason ('33), editor of the *Virginian-Pilot* of Norfolk.
- Robert Ruark ('35), a Scripps-Howard columnist and author of *Horn of the Hunter* and *Something of Value*.
- E. C. Daniel, Jr. ('33), managing editor of the *New York Times*.
- And Royster ('35).

In any man's book, that's quite a collection of talent.

When Royster reached Chapel Hill in 1931, neither he nor the place were strangers to one another; there had been Roysters there, off and on, for more than a century as students and professors. While Roy was there, one of his friends recalls, he "was as busy as the bumblebee he resembled. If an activity was thoroughly nonathletic, he went out for it and made the grade. As was inevitable for a Carolina boy who itched to write, Royster fell under the influence of Coffin." He was on the *Daily Tar Heel* for four years. His freshman year he wrote racy stuff for the *Buccaneer*. Later, he adjusted his style for the sedate *Carolina Magazine*. His editor recalls him as a "hell of a good reporter." He was on the debating squad and a member of the Carolina Playmakers. He played in the band one year—the clarinet and the French horn, the latter because there was no one else around to play it. "What could I lose?" asks Roy.

The world of the early thirties Royster and the other bright young men entered had an unchancy glitter about it. Those of them who could latched on to jobs on North Carolina newspapers as soon as possible. Vermont Connecticut Royster did not; and after a bit he headed for where the action was. He arrived in New York with his Phi Beta Kappa key, a Diamond Jim Brady appetite for the world as his oyster, and a name nobody could ever forget.

Vermont Connecticut is the last male in a North Carolina family line known as the "States" Roysters. He says that to the best of anyone's knowledge, the practice of naming children after states of the Union began in the 1800s when two Royster brothers, David and James, went to Carolina from Mecklenburg County, Virginia. David wanted to give his children distinctive names so his offspring could be more easily differentiated from their cousins. So he named them after states, and some of them are lulus: Vermont Connecticut, Iowa Michigan, Arkansas Delaware, Wisconsin Illinois, Virginia Carolina, and Georgia Alabama. (The slight preponderance of Union names may or may not have embarrassed the Roysters during the Late Unpleasantness of a century ago, but it shouldn't have; Iowa Michigan died at Gettysburg and another branch of the family redressed the balance nicely by naming one of its sons Nathaniel Confederate States

Royster, taking in all eleven Southern states at once.)

Royster was named for his grandfather; his own father, Wilbur High Royster, was a lawyer in Raleigh where Roy was born April 30, 1914. In addition to giving the young feller the kind of a name a man has either got to live up to or forever live down, the father, himself a former professor of law, Latin, and Greek at Chapel Hill, gave the son a first-rate classical education.

Before Chapel Hill, Royster attended the Webb School in Bell Buckle, Tennessee, and altogether studied Latin for about ten years and Greek for six. Since one cannot study the languages of Rome and Athens without learning a great deal about the history of those twin cornerstones of Western civilization, it is no wonder that Royster believes it is wise to be slow to accept, without asking why, the cure-alls proposed by government for all the ills that plague mankind. He believes most of the nostrums have been tried unsuccessfully before.

Asking "Why?" is, in fact, Royster's chief characteristic. He has a nonconformist mind; some of his acquaintances may think that his habit of playing devil's advocate—"I have heard him launch an attack or defense of something that came as a complete surprise," says one—is just the gambit of the poseur. But while Roy is no more in the habit than most of the rest of us of asking the operator to please turn off the spotlight because it's getting in his eyes, the actual fact is that Roy is a born doubter and nothing makes him more gleeful than to take apart a proposition that, to more conformist minds, might seem perfectly logical. Once he answered a rather wide-eyed essayist who concluded that all editorial writers ought at all times to be "responsible" by pointing out that there was a need for irresponsibility, too, because after all who could say which was which man's meat and which another man's poison?

Among Royster's doubts is that anything he can do you can do better; or, perhaps more precisely, he has no doubt whatsoever that anything anyone in his trade can do he can do as well, or better, given a little time and the chance. He had hardly moved to the *Wall Street Journal* ("I was a sort of glorified copyboy, keeping a records room straight with a broom") from his first job with the New York City News Bureau when he heard of an opening in the *Journal's* Washington bureau. He asked for a chance at the job and got it, and he had hardly hung up his hat when he wanted to cover the Supreme Court, the Congress, and the White House. Barney Kilgore, now Dow Jones president but then Washington bureau chief, told Roy he was a little too big for his britches. "I guess I was," Roy says.

Anyone with less confidence in the future might have waited a while longer to take on family responsibilities; but not Roy. He and Miss Frances Claypoole of New Bern, North Carolina, whom he had met at a Fourth of July dance in Morehead City just after finishing prep school, were married

July 5, 1937.

As it turned out, there were britches on the *Journal* big enough to fit Roy. He covered the Supreme Court, the Congress, the White House, and the Treasury, too. During the war he served in the navy (ensign to lieutenant-commander). Roy ended up, characteristically, as captain of his own vessels, one of which, uncharacteristically, he ran into a bridge one dawn in Miami harbor—an occasion brought about, one of his sourer friends insists, because the damn bridge wouldn't get out of his way.

After the war, he became Washington bureau chief himself and in 1948 he returned to the New York office as associate editor. His boss now was William H. Grimes, who the year before had brought the *Journal* its first real recognition in the trade when he was awarded the Pulitzer Prize for distinguished editorial writing.

Mr. Grimes had continued the scholarly, philosophical, moral tone of the editorial page established in the 1930s by Thomas F. Woodlock, but he had both broadened and sharpened the attitudes.

In 1953, Royster was awarded the Pulitzer Prize for distinguished editorial writing himself. Whoever wrote his citation certainly caught the full flavor of Roy's work: ". . . an ability to discern the underlying moral issue" in a style marked by "warmth, simplicity and understanding." Those who have worked closely with Royster might agree on two other characteristics of his work—principles and logic.

Some of the principles Grimes had laid down: "We oppose all infringements on individual rights whether they stem from attempts at private monopoly, labor-union monopoly, or from an overgrowing government." Royster says it this way: "Nothing is so corrupting to a man as to believe it his duty to save mankind from men. He comes to evil because he must first usurp the rights of men and finally the prerogatives of God."

But if one is to stand by principles, especially when they have been under constant siege by the movers and shakers of a generation of government activists, Roy believes it is not enough just to repeat them as an act of faith or a litany; they must be presented in a context with which the reader can identify and the point to be made must be reached in logical steps. The writing thus must be simple and clear. "I don't understand this," Royster will quietly say to someone of his work while requiring, when necessary, that it be said of his own. The cardinal sin anyone on the page can commit is to fail to point out obscurities or logic that goes awry, for the first rule is that while it is necessary for the writer to know what he wants to say, it is even more necessary for the reader to know what the writer wants to say. This continual search for clarity has made the page a model of editorial craftsmanship even for those who disagree with it. Another Royster rule: Since clutter is the antithesis of clarity, limit each editorial to one subject. If you want to discuss two subjects, then write two editorials.

Royster succeeded Grimes as editor of the *Journal* in August 1958. That year he won Sigma Delta Chi's award for editorial writing. He's a Fellow of Sigma Delta Chi, and the years have brought him other recognition. (Having achieved them, he wears his honors lightly; a college classmate recalls that when Royster made Phi Beta Kappa, "he never told his mother and she had to read it somewhere.") Royster is also an honorary Doctor of Laws, UNC, and an honorary Doctor of Letters, Temple. In 1956 and 1957 he served as chairman of the National Conference of Editorial Writers, having reached the top by hard work, just as in ASNE—board member, secretary, vice-president. He manages quietly to leave his mark on whatever he touches, and he has already done so on ASNE.

It was Royster who spotted, a board member says, an "inconsistency and injustice in the nominating and voting system. Thereafter, he was the one who thought it all out, prescribed the new wording in numerous parts of the constitution, and thus made it quite painless for the directors and membership to remedy a serious defect in the organization." He adds, "If it didn't risk insulting Vermont, I would say that in knowledge and mechanics of the operation of ASNE's government, he is our LBJ."

For seventeen years the Roysters lived in Hastings-on-Hudson, a pleasant town in Westchester County. But now that their daughters, Bonnie, teaching speed reading in Boston, and Eleanor, married to Robert Hutton III, administrative aide at the University of Hartford, are away, Roy and Frances live in a New York apartment with a beautiful view of the East River. They have a Hatteras-built cabin cruiser and all of the local bridges know about it. Roy plays a little golf; Frances is pretty sharp at bridge, and knows what to do with fried chicken, blackeyed peas, and spoonbread.

Their first grandchild, a girl, was born in January, and she was not out from behind the glass of the hospital's newborn nursery before Royster was writing about her in his column, "Thinking Things Over." He called the piece "A Moment in Time"; it was about intimations of immortality and the hopes with which men try to build a better world for their children's children. And it shimmered and shone with loveliness.

But no man can look upon a grandchild and think, like Wordsworth, of immortality in terms of family roots without looking back also upon his forebears. Royster's ultimate ambition, after he has fully tasted the triumphs that come with success where the action was, is to add one more generation to the century-old line of Roysters who have taught at the University of North Carolina. Mr. Grimes would say it would serve them both right well, whether Roy was teaching English or philosophy or economics. Or maybe just the French horn.

Werner Rupp, Editor
Aberdeen (Washington) World

By J. M. McClelland, Jr.

T he ideal editor, Henry Watterson once said, is a man of salient characteristics who owns a majority of the stock in the newspaper. On the coast of Washington, almost within sight of the sea, lives a man who this year rounds out a full fifty years operating as editor according to the Watterson definition.

He is Werner Rupp. His paper is the *Aberdeen World*. He has run it as well as owned it since shortly after he quit his job as a reporter and editorial writer on the *Tacoma News* in 1908 and joined with that paper's cartoonist in purchasing the Aberdeen paper for twenty thousand dollars.

The cartoonist didn't take to publishing and soon sold out to his partner whose salient characteristics included a knack for hiring able people to run the business side while he concentrated his time and efforts on putting out a good newspaper and producing one of the most consistently good one-man editorial pages ever seen in the West. Congressman Russell Mack was one of his business managers for years.

"I don't know anything about the business side," he has said any number of times and still says so. When he built the present *World* building about thirty years ago, he put his office in a corner on the second floor, next to the newsroom. The business office is down a flight of stairs and around a corner on the first floor.

For many years it was a daily routine for him to spend part of each day in the newsroom working with copy and proofs. But his main task—one that has never ceased to hold his interest and enthusiasm—is the writing of editorials. His page carries two columns of editorials set eighteen pica measure. It takes three, four, or more editorials to fill. He doesn't attempt to write them all now, but he did up until a few years ago.

The Rupp editorial page is widely read and quoted. A woman who

---

McClelland was editor and publisher of the *Longview* (Washington) *Daily News* when this article first appeared, in 1958.

moved to another town in Washington was heard to remark that she hardly knew what to think about anything any more now that she didn't have Werner Rupp's editorials to read.

Next to writing Rupp likes best to talk. He'll talk about anything and the listener usually learns something when he does. He talks fast—so fast he sometimes stumbles over his words. His dark eyes shine as he speaks and his face, beneath a perfectly smooth bald pate, usually relaxes into a smile as he gets off a quip or tells a story to illustrate a point. His sense of humor is strong. He delights in good humor and in getting those around him to share his mood.

Around the *World* office he is known simply as "the Boss." Staff members describe him as a kindly and considerate man who hates to fire anyone. Many *World* employees never intend to work anywhere else.

Among fellow newspapermen Rupp has a reputation for being a scholarly type, despite the impression he gives that everything in life is somehow at least mildly amusing. He graduated from Whitman College when he was nineteen years old and has two degrees. He believes an editor needs to do a great deal of reading and he does.

Participation in politics—from the sidelines—was for long a consuming interest with the Aberdeen editor. He served a term as Republican state chairman and became something of a "king maker" in political circles. He was a delegate to the national convention when Hoover was nominated.

One of the founders of Allied Daily Newspapers of Washington, the state's daily organization, he has served as its president more often than any other, partly because of the way he can make the dullest business meeting seem like fun.

The Alaska-Yukon-Pacific Exposition of 1909 brought a young lady, Lyda Cox, from Boise to serve in the Idaho building. There she met the young editor from Aberdeen and they were married in April of that year. They still live in the house they built in Aberdeen soon afterwards. In addition they have a summer home on the shore of Hood Canal, an arm of Puget Sound, where their green lawn, extending down to the oyster beds of the beach, is cut by a brook bordered on either side by one of the Northwest's most colorful floral species—the begonia. A pond is full of trout, but they hate to catch them. Here the Rupps have made it a tradition to entertain the state's newspaper fraternity that gathers for a meeting each fall at a nearby lodge.

Just as Rupp has always found there is more to publishing a paper than making money, he discovered early that there is more to living than publishing a paper. Until recent years he played golf regularly. For several years prior to the war he donned a jaunty yachting cap on weekends and piloted his forty-five-foot boat on long cruises through the Sound. He belongs to numerous clubs, including the famous Bohemian Club of San Francisco.

Till he was told emphatically to quit, Rupp smoked a large daily quota of long, thin cigars. He has always had a convivial approach to the cup that cheers but treats it respectfully. For those who do get aching elbows, however, he has a certain tolerance.

A careful comparer of newspapers, Rupp has always been a student of newspaper composition and makeup. He was preaching shorter sentences to the Associated Press before it ever heard of Dr. Flesch.

No newspaperman in the state is more widely known or more respected. Henry Watterson would have loved him.

Dwight E. Sargent, Editorial Page Editor
New York Herald Tribune

By Vermont Royster

T he taxi that pulled away from the Denver station was loaded with editors gathering for the 1953 combined convention of Sigma Delta Chi and the National Conference of Editorial Writers. As it headed toward the city's center, the snow-capped peaks of the Rockies to the West formed a majestic backdrop, sharply etched by the autumnal morning sun.

From the back seat a soft but slightly twanging voice spoke with deadpan seriousness. "Driver, what are those hills over there?" The cab swerved as the startled driver looked over his shoulder. "Why, they're the Rocky Mountains!" "Pretty nice hills," came the kindly reply. At the hotel the driver was still too shaken at this lese majesty to count his fare.

Dwight Emerson Sargent, eyes a-twinkle, emerged from the back seat with the satisfaction of a man who had started a day right, deflating the Rocky Mountains before breakfast. Puncturing pomposity, in people or in mountains, came naturally to the editorial page editor of the *Portland* (Maine) *Press-Herald*. And it's a habit he hasn't lost since he became editorial page editor of the *New York Herald Tribune*.

New York is considerably more puffed up than either Portland or Denver, and four months is too short a time for even so skilled an iconoclast as Dwight Sargent to make himself felt throughout the metropolis. But in that short space of time the man from Maine has swept out a few of the pomposities that filled the *Trib's* editorial sanctum in days gone by, and at least one of the city's political icons has felt the prick of outspoken truth.

Example: When Nelson Rockefeller caught the pundits off-guard with his decision, one Saturday afternoon, not to accept the presidency, the *Trib's* editorial writer on duty called Dwight at home. A few minutes discussion

Royster was editor of the *Wall Street Journal* when this article first appeared, in 1960.

sufficed to decide on the *Trib's* editorial reaction; the writer wrote his own editorial, and it appeared on page one Sunday.

Simple? Routine? Perhaps so; but Tribster survivors of the old days say that such a decision then would have required hours of conferences and many phone calls to political elder-statesmen for "guidance"—all amid a self-conscious air that the *Trib* was producing a State Paper. The new herald of the *Trib* is not likely to ever take himself so damn seriously.

Example: When Manhattan borough president Hulan Jack was caught up in some financial peccadillos, several New York newspapers that never had any editorial trouble making up their minds about the home freezers of Truman's cronies or the home furnishings of Sherman Adams, fell into a funk of indecision. For Mr. Jack is a Negro. The new *Trib* never hesitated. Mr. Jack was a public official, and on those grounds his dubious activities were promptly condemned. The other papers, in time, also got around to this commonsense view.

But if the *Trib's* new editorial top sergeant is something of an iconoclast, he is also a diplomat. Indeed, his diplomacy is at least partly responsible for his move from Maine to New York.

Bob White, the man from Mexico, Missouri, whom Jock Whitney picked to revitalize the *Trib* tells the story himself. Some years ago Bob served a term on the board of directors of the Editorial Writers Conference. Then one day his time ran out, and Dwight Sargent took on the chore of telling him that he was being retired to the rear ranks. "Dwight impressed me right then," Bob says, "as a man with his feet on the ground, who wouldn't duck an unpleasant chore but would do it with consideration for the other fellow. He 'fired' me in the nicest way."

The manners which impressed Bob White also impressed Jock Whitney, who's betting millions on the *Herald Tribune*. But it was not of course the only reason why they turned to Dwight Sargent as the man to give the *Trib* a new voice. Dwight had a lot of other credentials.

Born (April 3, 1917) in Pembroke, Massachusetts, Dwight got himself liberally educated at Colby College (A.B., M.A.) and later at Harvard, where he was a Nieman Fellow. From the Colby College paper he moved on to the *Biddeford* (Maine) *Daily Journal*. Thereafter he reported for the Associated Press, learned makeup on the New Bedford paper, dabbled as a radio commentator on station WGAN, and then in 1949 took over as editorial page editor of the *Portland Press-Herald*.

Out of this background Dwight acquired a political viewpoint that seems conservative to a liberal Democrat but perhaps a bit liberal to a conservative Republican. Thus while his party orientation is Republican (as is Mr. Whitney's) he's never hesitated to toss his editorial barbs at Republican icons, something the old *Trib* rarely did. In the Sherman Adams affair (as in that of the Democratic Hulan Jack) Dwight had no trouble making up his mind; on the *Portland Press-Herald* he was one of the first to call editorially for the departure of his fellow New Englander from the White House staff.

He also acquired the view that an editorial page ought to say something, and that what it should say should be forthright and honest. He became a founding father of the National Conference of Editorial Writers, a group dedicated to driving dullness and pomposity off editorial pages, and later became its chairman.

Along the way he acquired too some other assets that never hurt anybody, even an editor—a charming wife and three children. Elaine Cass Sargent, so his college friends report, has softened his wit and kept him from acquiring any pomposities of his own.

The rest he was born with. Despite a somewhat disproportionate nose, he's the best looking editor in New York. Despite his iconoclasm, there's a gentleness about him that may prove an unexpected asset in the jungle of Manhattan. But despite his New England reserve and youthful appearance, there's also a suspicion of toughness in the jut of his jaw.

All these characteristics, natural and acquired, will come in handy. New-owner Whitney is determined to rescue the *Herald Tribune* from its sad estate, but he's no newspaperman. The triumvirate that ASNE has provided him for the rescue team (Bob White, Sargent, and managing editor Fendall Yerxa) are equally determined, but in New York they are up against some very tough economic facts and some journalistic problems for which nobody has any ready answers.

As the herald of the *Trib*, the new editorial page editor has some especial problems of his own. Of late years the paper has had no real political philosophy; its voice has commanded no real respect. The editorial writing staff, like that in the newsroom, has been demoralized by confused and changing policies. It's not going to be an easy resuscitation job.

But the *Trib* has already started to breathe again, even if it still has some pretty steep hills to puff up before it's in a position to trumpet as in the days of Horace Greeley, James Gordon Bennett, and Ogden Reid. And the skeptics had better not underestimate a man who will take on the Rocky Mountains before breakfast.

Louis B. Seltzer, Editor
The Cleveland Press

By Richard Peters

Most of the exaggerations about Louis B. Seltzer are the truth. He may not make five speeches in a single evening, but he often makes four.

He may not own seventy-eight suits, but the figure isn't off a dozen, either way.

He may not write all the paper every day, but some days he fills a couple of columns in about ten minutes. And gets a stack of admiring letters for his efforts.

A skilled writer for *Life* magazine spent five weeks trying to find out what made Louie tick. He wrote a long and glowing piece called "Mr. Cleveland," but he never really explained the phenomenon.

Same with the *Saturday Evening Post*. Their piece, "The Noisy Newsboy of Cleveland," based on shorter research, was longer, but still missed the secret.

On the *Press* his own devoted slaves and fellow toilers are no wiser.

They've worked with him for a long time, their ties with him in many cases are amazingly sentimental even in a sentimental business, but they can't completely understand where he gets the steam.

This baffling dynamo is short, blond, and bald.

He neither smokes nor drinks. He seldom sleeps more than a few hours a night, never in the day time.

He always orders a vegetable plate and tea at a restaurant, and only nibbles a little fancy food on the banquet circuit.

He seldom raises his voice to his employees, reserves angry shouts for the wrong kind of politicians and phonies in general.

He makes preposterous promises, and quite often keeps them.

He keeps his watch forty minutes ahead, so he'll get where he's going.

Peters was chief editorial writer for the *Cleveland Press* when this article first appeared, in 1956.

He lavishes enthusiastic praise on people he likes—and he likes almost everybody.

He is a baffling and usually pleasant blend of sentimentality and shrewdness.

Louie's Horatio Alger story began modestly on Cleveland's West Side nearly fifty-nine years ago.

He was a boy wonder then, and he still is.

He quit school at eleven because cash was short at home. He has been working on papers ever since.

And since 1928 he has been editor of the *Press*, an extremely vigorous and equally local newspaper which is read by seven out of ten families in metropolitan Cleveland.

He operates the paper in the tradition of its founder, E. W. Scripps, who launched the Scripps-Howard chain with it in 1878.

Louie is lively and positive. So is the *Press*.

In and out of the paper, Louie worries about the community he loves.

His day starts before five-thirty. He reads papers, magazines, and books and then begins to funnel ideas to his staff by telephone about six-thirty. Sometime around seven, he's at his desk.

He gets his mail out of the way, letters written and maybe a piece or so done, before the daily staff meeting at eight-thirty. That's when department heads report—and argue.

About ten after nine, Louie ends the meeting with a bellowed, "Okay, let's go."

That's about all the routine his day has. The rest is strictly by ear and improvisation.

Except for his speeches and his meetings.

They are many and scattered.

He presides at this do-good meeting, speaks to that luncheon club, chairs this panel, lectures to those youngsters, even takes the rostrum in churches.

Sometimes he gets home for a few minutes in the late afternoon, but usually he stays right through.

He almost never takes a vacation, and almost never takes any real exercise.

Somehow he stays lean and healthy. Nobody can remember his taking a day off for illness.

In the midst of all this, he has accumulated national awards from the National Conference of Christians and Jews, three doctor's degrees, all kinds of prizes for his paper.

He also has won the affection and loyalty of lots of people, both on the paper and outside.

Forrest Wilson Seymour, Editor
Worcester Telegram and Evening Gazette

By Leslie Moore

B eguiled by the advice of the late Greeley, some aspiring young men went West. But Wog came East. He came East in response to a call by the late George Francis Booth—whose half century of newspapering in New England was, incidentally, not without a Greeleyish touch.

Wog came from Des Moines to Worcester in 1953, and surely no man went West more thoroughly or with more grace and dispatch, than Wog came East.

The Wog is, of course, Forrest Wilson Seymour. Newspapermen west of Buffalo don't need the explanation. From Ohio to the Pacific, Forrest Seymour is Wog. The nickname, its origin lost, was conferred on him during a South Dakota boyhood by his father, and has stuck tenaciously to Forrest ever since like a—well, like a wog.

But to the East he is Forrest, and is hereafter so designated.

In Des Moines he was editor of the *Register and Tribune* editorial pages, and deep also in a score of important civic activities, some statewide.

In Worcester, now sporting a ten-year pin quietly handed him in August by publisher Dick Steele, he is editor of the *Telegram and Evening Gazette*, and deep also in a score of important civic activities, some statewide.

Three assorted honorary degrees, a Pulitzer Prize for editorial writing, and a long list of influential chores and chairmanships testified to his rank as editor and citizen in Iowa.

He moved to Worcester to become associate editor in 1953, rising to the editorship when George Booth died two years later. Nobody now observing

Moore was executive editor of the *Worcester* (Massachusetts) *Telegram and Evening Gazette* when this article first appeared, in 1963.

Forrest at work and noting his grasp of regional affairs past and present, his easy absorption of a way of life that has neither Iowa's spaces nor Iowa's corn, would suspect that he was not born and reared in the Northeast corner.

With a nondescript little sailing dory, he has become a familiar figure at certain points on Buzzards Bay. Cape Cod knows him, and he it. Beacon Hill politicians are sharply aware of him. A lover of mountains, he will one day broaden his acquaintance with Green and White and Berkshires. Meanwhile, he has not forgotten the West as a fine place to visit. Nor can he. Hallock, son, is on the editorial page staff of the Cowles papers in Minneapolis. Peter, son, runs the Associated Press bureau in Centralia, Illinois. Constance Thompson, daughter, is an Iowa University student (and charming young mother) at Iowa City.

So there is plenty in the West to look back to. Pearl, wife, indefatigable correspondent and distinguished hostess, faithfully maintains many associations out thataway, even as she is busy in community and social matters in Worcester. Life requires so much living in the East that there isn't much opportunity for anything else. Sue, daughter, who works in New York for the Time-Life outfit, is aware of that.

A biographical word will save hauling out *Who's Who*. Born in South Dakota, Forrest was the son of Arthur Hallock Seymour, a professor of history and government. During a first year in college, he worked part-time as a reporter for the *Aberdeen Journal*. Meanwhile older brother Gideon, who later reached journalism's topside with the Associated Press overseas and as executive editor in Minneapolis, was a reporter in Des Moines. He got Forrest to Des Moines as a summer copyboy. Then, after a sophomore year in Aberdeen, and another part-time go on the *Journal*, the younger Seymour went to Des Moines for twenty-eight and a half years of newspapering.

The word prodigy would make him squirm, but it's near fact. After a stretch of reporting, he moved to the desk. And at nineteen, an age when most kids are still learning to fill a pastepot, Forrest was in the slot. By 1927 he had become state editor of the *Register and Tribune*. By 1930 he was an editorial writer.

Meanwhile, he had acquired his A.B. from Drake University. Meanwhile, too, he had married. In 1946 he succeeded the late W. W. Waymack as editor of the Des Moines editorial pages, adding steadily to his own and their distinction.

A small but meaningful footnote should be recorded. In 1947, when the late Floyd Taylor was setting up the first seminar for editorial writers at the infant American Press Institute, the two men he called upon to open that memorable meeting were the brothers Seymour. Gid, then editorial page editor of the *Minneapolis Star*, was in the chair the first day. Forrest took over on the morrow. (The four weeks of that seminar, incidentally, mustered as noteworthy a procession of the great and near-great as any API seminar has enjoyed before or since.)

Somebody there, I recall, raised a point which still agitates newsmen hanging over a bar on a dull day: Can a newspaper editor maintain his independence unless he shuns community involvement?

So far as I know, Forrest Seymour has never fretted about that. But he lives an obvious answer. His sense of community responsibility is so acute that he will not turn down a request to do a useful job within the scope of his abilities, whether as trustee of Andover-Newton, president of the Red Cross, member of the Massachusetts Council on Crime and Delinquency, or any one of a half dozen obscure assignments that are all drudgery and no glory. He vows, almost daily, that he will take no more chairmanships or board memberships. And he doesn't—except when he is persuaded that there is a needful work to be done which his energy, talent, and schedule will somehow permit him to take a crack at.

All this, however, is never at the sacrifice of his task as an editor. His philosophy, unspoken but in plain sight, is that in off-hours a newspaper editor has responsibility to his community, as does any other citizen. The editor whose professional integrity and independence are solid need not crawl away into isolation. Nor should he so crawl. If he can be pulled around by the wires of influence and privilege, he is going to be pulled around anyway. Better for him to understand his community and watch it at work while being a part of it.

Forrest knows perfectly well, as do all of us anywhere, that baleful pressures seeking to undercut an editor's professional integrity don't wait for him to join Kiwanis or become chairman of a charity fund-raising.

Pursue that discussion if you choose, but Wog of Des Moines and Forrest of Worcester will let you split your own hairs. He is too busy to prolong the debate. He is too busy because, notwithstanding his extracurricular load, he works like hell all day every day being the best newspaper editor he knows how to be. And that, in the opinion of those who work for and with him, is a very good best indeed.

He loves ideas. He's a stickler for good writing. He fights for the proper comma. Inaccuracy in the news makes him sick. He insists on quality in reporting and editing. He looks jealously on the daily newspaper as an absolute essential to an informed compassionate society of free men. The newspaper is his religion.

He will not, however, insist that the press has the right to ride roughshod over everything else. He believes simply that the press can do its job well without invading or exploiting the privacy of decent and innocent people. He believes that the newspaper, no less than any other instrument of a free society, must be subject to law.

There is a lot more to say about him. Terrific bridge player. Once played a battered trombone. Loves music, and listens long to symphony—but, curiously, is cool to Beethoven and Mozart. Thinks he is a much better ping-pong player than he really is. Pretty fair carpenter and house painter. Kids himself that he can drive anywhere in record time without speeding. He has traveled a good deal abroad.

The sense of humor is lively, and sometimes on the wry side, featured by a wizonic lackardry with spoonerisms.

He can turn out a pretty good speaking job. His talks on newspapering are thoughtful and effective.

That's because he takes his talks seriously and works them over carefully.

One off-beat mark of the man, which made clergymen and a lot of laymen in Central New England rub incredulous eyes, is his profound knowledge of St. Paul and other angles of the New Testament. Forrest insists that this interest in Paul is neither spiritual nor theological, but historical and human. Whatever it is, it brings requests for speeches, and gets him a reputation for being a hotter churchman than he concedes he is. The Seymours are, by the bye, probably as strong at Central Congregational in Worcester as they were at Plymouth in Des Moines.

If, however, your Soroptimist Club program this year is already topheavy with speakers on the press and St. Paul, how about a nice talk on wooden clocks?

A year or so ago, although he knew little about wooden clocks except to tinker with one at home—and although he was deep in a navigation course at the time so he could sail his sixteen-foot dory in Buzzards Bay the next summer—Forrest was asked to fill a program spot for a small club he belongs to.

All public library books on wooden clocks were swiftly and heavily thumbed, and he whipped up a talk about them that captivated the club.

He is not, though, about to become curator of wooden clocks at Old Sturbridge Village, fortunately for Worcester, New England, and journalism.

Don Shoemaker, Editorial Page Editor
The Miami Herald

By C. A. McKnight

Profiles ought to be written with some detachment, and I confess that I am something less than objective about my moon-faced friend, Don Shoemaker.

From 1947 to 1955, I read, admired, respected, and often reprinted the editorials that he turned out, without help, six days a week for the *Asheville Citizen.*

When it came time to select a successor as executive director of the Southern Education Reporting Service in Nashville, Tennessee, he was my number one candidate for that difficult assignment among the many competent Southern editors.

And a few months ago, when Jack Knight and Lee Hills were looking around for a top editorial page man for the *Miami Herald*, I could say nothing but the best about Shoemaker.

So today Don finds himself in balmy Miami, where he divides his time between his job as editorial page editor of the *Herald* and his hobby—sailing Biscayne Bay (and frequently running aground) in his Rebel Class *Elizabeth*, officially named for his bright, tow-headed seven-year-old daughter, but unofficially referred to as the "Mrs. Nathan Bedford Forrest."

Don's return to newspaper work brings him back into full and active ASNE membership. This is by way of welcome.

The Shoemaker story is quite as interesting as the man himself.

A native Canadian, he was graduated from the University of North Carolina, where he had written editorials for the student *Daily Tar Heel.*

Following a short trick as reporter and deskman for the *Greensboro Record*, he went to Asheville in 1937 as telegraph editor of the *Asheville Times.*

McKnight was editor of the *Charlotte Observer* when this article first appeared, in 1958.

He became associate editor of the morning *Asheville Citizen* in 1941. Six years later he became editor. Singlehandedly, he produced six editorial pages a week, doing much of his writing after hours at home where his smart and attractive wife, Lyal, had read and clipped newspapers and magazines for good editorial ideas.

Somehow he found time to found and serve as first president of the Thomas Wolfe Memorial Association, to raise the money to buy as a memorial Wolfe's old homeplace; to chair the Buncombe County Planning Council and head the Community Chest; and to dabble in many other community and civic activities including the Chamber of Commerce and the U. N. Association in western North Carolina.

He also kept at his steady, if unspectacular, game of tennis.

The SERS job in Nashville was his biggest challenge to that point. A unique journalistic venture, conceived by Southern editors and educators, it had set as its goal the factual and objective reporting of the school desegregation story following the 1954 Supreme Court decision.

A single bobble in handling explosive stories in *Southern School News,* the monthly SERS publication, or the inadvertent expression of opinion by SERS personnel, would have quickly brought criticism and discredit.

A measure of Don's judgment and wisdom is the continued acceptance of SERS by White Citizens Councils and the NAACP as the best source of authoritative, balanced information on the complex race story.

A measure of the authoritativeness and completeness of the SERS files is their almost-daily use by scholars, journalists, and writers from all over the United States and many foreign countries.

From this experience, Don planned and edited *With All Deliberate Speed,* published by Harper's in 1957.

In Miami, Shoemaker is teamed with veteran associate editor John Pennekamp in the conduct of the editorial page and the formulation of the day-to-day editorial policy.

Since he reported for work on August 1, leaving SERS in the capable hands of the Associated Press's Ed Ball, Shoemaker has developed a flexible opposite-editorial page with a neat balance between hard news and commentary and lighter froth.

The editorial page has been redesigned to give it more eye-appeal, the writing and editing tightened, the range of subject matter extended, and the page brought closer to the news.

Through the years, Shoemaker has cultivated a bland, urbane, imperturbable front, complete with sports jacket and pipe, which belies the inner drive and tension in every good editor.

Given to understatement, his sly and waggish sense of humor adds zest to his conversation, his letters, and his editorials.

His large library reflects his varied and voracious reading. And finally, he prefers Scotch, with just a touch of water. Especially if it's your Scotch.

Dolph Simons, Publisher
Lawrence (Kansas) Journal-World

By W. L. White

Perhaps we should play the biography of Dolph Simons backwards, starting with the fact that he is about to end nine years service on the board of the Associated Press. Roy Roberts, whose term on this board overlapped that of Dolph Simons, points out that this service covered a "very crucial and important time—a change in management, plus a change in the presidency. Kent Cooper went out and Frank Starzel went in. Robert McLean resigned and Ben McKelway went on."

For the AP it was, continues Roy Roberts, "a period of expanding the news service abroad, and the building-up of interpretive writing: Dolph made a good contribution to it. Although he was on there to represent the small papers, he paid particular attention to the file, and to the development of news—he added a lot to the discussions. While smaller members are often concerned only with themselves, Dolph was interested in the whole service."

Ben McKelway, AP's current president, says Dolph Simons "impressed somebody on the board with his fine sense of balance," perhaps because he is "one of the kindest people," but still has "a very stubborn streak in him, too. He takes a point of view, sticks to it and presents it well; he was a most articulate member of the board."

On what problems in particular? Well, President McKelway found Dolph Simons to have "a very fine understanding of the small newspaper, which comprises the heavy majority of AP members" and was always quick to look out for their interests. But above all he found that Dolph Simons had "a damned good sense of news" which made him "a very good judge of just the sort of job the AP did," which even in New York, "impressed the staff there."

If Dolph Simons, in spite of his editorial halo and his purple toga as

---

White was editor and publisher of the *Emporia* (Kansas) *Gazette* when this article first appeared, in 1960.

publisher, still has the respect of the working press, it is only because he has always been one of them.

Back, now, to Chicago in 1924: There he is at a courtroom press table, covering a fast-moving story which got, in that day, far more columns than Sputnik—the trial of Leopold and Loeb. Although Dolph Simons insists that he was only "the second man for AP at the trial," still "I was nineteen and I got a tremendous boot out of it!"

Dolph Simons knows a news story; knew there was one in the high price of drugs several years before this occurred to Sen. Estes Kefauver, and so one afternoon on his *Journal-World* typewriter, tapped out an editorial on "The High Price of Pills." And then? "We were threatened with boycotts. The Pharmaceutical Association and some of those people went after us a little rough. Druggists were called together and told what bad boys we were."

Ben McKelway, who has visited both the *Journal-World* and Dolph Simons in Lawrence, says that he is "very definite in his convictions that a newspaper must take a stand, and not straddle the fence."

Dolph Simons is also challenged by the fact that he publishes his *Journal-World* in Lawrence, Kansas, at the foot of Mount Oread, on which is perched the University of Kansas and so has, as Ben McKelway points out, "a very intelligent readership." How does his paper measure up?

Frank Murphy, the university's chancellor, finds the *Journal-World* "an amazingly modern small-town newspaper, in that it does give its readership a window to the world." As one example "he deliberately sent young Dolph [his son] off to work on the *London Times,* and still later for another year on a Capetown newspaper."

Dolph Simons's second love is this university from which he graduated. "One might assume," continues Chancellor Murphy, "that he would have a special interest in our Department of Journalism, but as a matter of fact his interest is very comprehensive, very broad."

It includes a constant defense of the university against the onslaughts of Kansas Gov. George Docking, himself a Lawrence boy and one of its graduates. "George and I," Dolph Simons remembers, "were in school together, I think since the fifth grade. I never had a feud with him. But I think Docking is wrong as he can be about the university, and about the faculty and about Murphy. We've had numerous editorials sticking up for Murphy; it has been awfully easy to do, because Murphy is such a great guy. Only last week he was offered the presidency of another state university— with a $12,500 boost in salary. Why did he turn it down? Because he didn't want to run from a fight! Why wouldn't you be loyal to a fellow like that?"

Now for Dolph Simons and his town of Lawrence, Kansas. A Massachusetts Street merchant will tell you that while he is "one of the most considerate of men, the Simons family are aristocratic: not the easiest people to get acquainted with." Lawrence is, perhaps, a little in awe of them. By contrast Ben McKelway, visiting the Simons newspaper, was "struck with the completely friendly and first-name basis that he is on with everybody on his newspaper."

Dolph Simons's friend Clyde Reed, editor of the *Parsons Sun* and, in 1958, the sacrificial lamb offered by Kansas Republicans to the voters in the gubernatorial race, points out that Dolph Simons has been "primarily responsible for Lawrence's spectacular industrial growth in recent years, bringing there manufacturing branches of nationally known firms"—another reason why Massachusetts Street holds him in some awe.

So now for the Simons home. Ben McKelway, who was recently a guest in it, finds that "one of the best things about Dolph is his wife, Marie." It was she who recently redecorated the stately old ancestral house, shaded by elms planted by the Yankee pioneers who founded Lawrence. Both of them planned every square foot of the *Journal-World's* new plant, a gem of streamlined modernity, and she is helping put aside the money for the big new press, which is just around the corner.

And it is Marie who sits beside him on the piano bench when they thunder and tinkle out duets of light music; they so love it that there is even a second grand piano (with a double bench) in their summer home on Gull Lake in Minnesota, which now is beginning to teem with their two sons, daughters-in-law, and three grandchildren.

But the old Lawrence home is a Kansas social center, particularly when old friends come tramping onto its floorboard-to-floorboard carpets for the inevitable party after every big football game. The chivalry and beauty of Kansas are to be found there, furtively dropping olive pits into Marie's vases—fellow editors (from far away, like Palmer Hoyt), old classmates, the commandant at Fort Leavenworth, on occasion Roy Roberts or some of the boys down from the *Star* in nearby Kansas City, and a tasteful selection from the university faculty.

For an account of what may well have been Dolph Simons's greatest service to his university and his town, we are indebted to Ben McKelway. In a glass case in the foyer of the university's Museum of Natural History stands—grand, gloomy, peculiar, and only slightly wall-eyed—General Custer's horse; a monument to the taxidermist's art, and an idol for all the school children of Kansas when they come to visit this seat of learning.

It happened in this wise: After the battle of Little Big Horn, where Gen. George Armstrong Custer and his 266 men were massacred by the Sioux, the only survivor was a solitary saddle horse, presumably that from which Custer was shot down. This was then taken to Fort Leavenworth and, in due time, full of years, bluestem grass, oats, and honors, the horse expired.

The military post was about to take up a collection to have it stuffed, but found the price too high. Custer's horse was headed for a glue factory had not Kansas University saved the day with the following offer: Its ever-alert medical school would stuff the horse, provided that the university in return got the right to exhibit the remains at the Chicago World's Fair.

But, once this festival had closed, the new generation at Fort Leavenworth seemed to have no interest in General Custer's stuffed horse, so presently it was returned to the rotunda of the university's Museum of Natural History in Lawrence, where it could lie in state as do the remains of Napoleon in Les Invalides. "Stand in state" is maybe a shade more accurate.

So now, more decades, and then comes to Leavenworth an unusually truculent general who, full of beans and after searching the archives, serves on the natural history professors in Lawrence what Ben McKelway describes as a "writ of habeas corpus equinus" accusing them of being feloniously in possession of government property: to wit, a stuffed horse; notifying them that, on D-Day at H-Hour, a Repossession Task Force would arrive in Lawrence, seeking lawful custody of the deceased.

While the faculty trembled, Dolph Simons saved the day. Zeroing in on Leavenworth, he let fly at the general an editorial broadside of stately but thunderous Johnsonian prose. Let them come! But, if they dared, the Bluecoats would find that there would be even less left of their Leavenworth task force than the Sioux had left on the bloody field at Little Big Horn!

Dolph Simons today drips with every honor in the power of Kansas, its university, or its press, to bestow. He has headed the Kansas Press Association. He has presided over the University Alumni Association. He has received, in lieu of an honorary degree (none are ever given), the University's Award for Distinguished Service to Mankind.

Yet, as compared with the great love his town and his school bear him, for having led the van and beat off the foe in the battle for General Custer's stuffed horse—all this is nothing!

Charles A. Sprague, Editor and Publisher
(Salem) Oregon Statesman

By Robert C. Notson

C harles A. Sprague was summoned last September from his post as
editor and publisher of the *Oregon Statesman*, Salem, Oregon, to Colby
College in Waterville, Maine. There he was designated as "1955 Lovejoy
Fellow" and awarded an honorary doctor of laws degree.

How did it happen that the editor of a modest-sized daily in an Oregon
city was invited across a continent to receive such recognition? J. Seelye
Bixler, president of Colby, said it was for "significant contribution to
American journalism through editorial courage and forthright liberalism."

Not many men have used the editorial pen to unlock the doors to success
in politics and public office. Mr. Sprague found the way opened for him with
unexpected ease. It was in 1938, deep in the heart of the New Deal years, and
the Republican party was still mired in the mud of defeatism and numbed by
Depression shock. The party needed a spokesman and nominee for
governor in Oregon, one untainted by Old Guardism—one who spoke with
the voice of a "liberal conservative." Editor Sprague was the man.

He was nominated and elected by wide margins. He led an
administration of progress and rectitude. He rallied citizens to the tasks of
war. But his term was not altogether a happy one. Governor Sprague had
been accustomed in his writings to setting forth truth as he saw it. The
exigencies of politics, the pressures of groups, and politicians annoyed him.

He declined to temporize. He appointed the best men to office
regardless of political considerations. At the end of four years the party men
were in another camp. His bid for renomination fell short.

Without rancor, he resumed his editorial duties. Both on the platform

---

Notson was managing editor of the (Portland) *Oregonian* when this article first appeared, in
1956.

and in his writings he continued to speak out sincerely and honestly on issues.

The life of a newspaperman is filled with paradoxes but none more striking than that which has marked Sprague's postpolitical career. "Mister" Sprague began to exercise greater influence in public affairs than "Governor" Sprague.

He instituted a semieditorial column on page one of the *Statesman* known as "It Seems to Me." He wrote in a direct, informal style. Sometimes it was narrative but generally it was clear, easy but concise exposition. He had the faculty of sorting out the facts, pointing up the conclusions, and exacting from readers the exclamation, "Now that is what I think!"

His column became widely quoted. Since Salem is the state capital, his writings were perused carefully by state officials. Legislators of both parties alluded to his writings or proudly claimed his support. As usual, he was not tied to the Republican party line.

Mr. Sprague has been described as an "elder statesman" but such a title belies the youthfulness of his viewpoints and the vigor of his bearing, physically and mentally. The national press has quoted him frequently of late. Under appointment of the president, he served as alternate delegate for the United States in the United Nations.

In his busy schedule he has found time to serve as president of the Oregon Council of Churches, the Oregon Chest, the Oregon-California Advisory board. He has been active in the Presbyterian church, the YMCA, and all sorts of civic enterprises. He has been building chairman during construction of six new structures on the campus of Willamette University, of which he is a longtime trustee.

Mr. Sprague is on the board of the Carnegie Foundation and takes a guiding interest in the *Presbyterian Life*, national publication of his church. In the past year he has served on government boards to examine labor relations in atomic plants and to study facts in recent railroad disputes.

But his chief interest lies in his writings. His style is direct but always well tempered, well considered. He is basically kind and seldom launches personal attacks. He feels that a writer who marshals the facts is thrice armed. Although personally conservative, he regards himself as a "little left of center" in his economic and political writings. Many persons have believed Sprague to be stiff, unbending, or aloof. Actually, he is none of these things. He has a warm interest in others but his busy mind lacks time for many of the social amenities.

No man in Salem is more approachable and it is said that he insists on answering every telephone call and seeing every caller, no matter how crowded his schedule. He believes this is part of his job, and he will not permit the normal secretarial screening. He feels that he is anchored too much to his desk, as are most newspapermen, and these contacts are valuable, the visitors his "antenna."

"They bring me information, opinions, schemes, and often downright prejudices," Mr. Sprague observed. "But out of this I sift something which approximates truth."

Mr. Sprague enjoys the impact of ideas from others, invites well-considered opposition, and appreciates quality where he finds it. He neither smokes nor drinks but makes no attempt to impose his personal habits on others. He attends cocktail parties, cradles a glass of 7-Up defensively against those who proffer lustier libation. He engages in animated conversation until the first signs that alcoholic stimulation has modified sober logic. Then he excuses himself.

Sprague has few hobbies outside his work. He likes sports but seldom attends. In the Cascade Mountains, thirty-six miles east of Salem, he and Mrs. Sprague have a chalet-type cabin on the Little North Fork of the Santiam River. He fishes infrequently, but he enjoys the worry-free solitudes of the forests and an occasional dip in the icy stream which flows by the cabin. Guests frequently shiver in the cool morning air fully clothed, while Sprague thrashes about in waters newly born of mountain snows. He chops wood, assists with meals, and takes long hikes. Although not athletic, he likes mountain climbing and he has planted his crampons on the summits of Rainer, Hood, and Jefferson. Lately many of his weekends have been spent in catching up on his reading which he greatly enjoys.

Sprague's desk is usually littered with more work than he can attend. He writes about fifteen hundred words daily for the *Statesman*, in addition to his duties as publisher and his public activities. He is a frequent speaker on various occasions.

His style is terse, compact. He assiduously distills unnecessary words out of his copy. Although meticulous with facts and phrases, he gives his copydesk full authority to change his material in the interest of accuracy, clarity, or grammar.

"And don't think they don't catch me," he confessed. "There are bound to be bugs occasionally."

The Spragues live in a New England–type brick house. Their family life is pleasant but somewhat spartan. Mrs. Sprague does most of her household tasks. They are very proud of their son, Wallace, managing editor of *Parade* magazine, and visit frequently at his home in Short Hills, New Jersey.

Mr. Sprague is interested instinctively in young men, particularly those with promise in the newspaper or political fields. At sixty-eight he has foresworn further political ambition for himself and contents himself in stimulating others. Recently he was approached to enter the lists for United States senator. He declined. He is satisfied with his job as an editor.

Dale Stafford,
Editor and Publisher
Greenville (Michigan) Daily News

By E. C. Hayhow

T here's an ancient story about one man's joust with fate. In a horrendous chain of events, Old Dobbin ran away with the son and heir, grievously wounding both; the cat tipped over an oil lamp starting a fire which destroyed the house; a smooth-talking salesman seduced the beautiful daughter and as an appropriately fiendish finale, Mama ran away with a guitar player.

Greenville, Michigan (population seven thousand) has a newspaperman who would find nothing incredible in such a tale. He has had his own troubles.

Dale Stafford, former big-city editor, is now publisher, editor, managing editor, chief editorial writer, business manager, etc., of the *Greenville Daily News*. Last year he gave a talk before the APME meeting in New Orleans on the joys and blessings of operating a small-city daily. Returning home to the *Daily News* (with its work force of twenty), he faced up to the following blessings:

● Linage was down—way down—the ultimate for any publisher, but to a Stafford the end of the world. (Events spared him the heartbreak of worrying about his fiscal position.)

● An outgrown flatbed refused to accommodate itself to a new newsprint supply and web breaks jumped from two or three daily to eight or nine with the inevitable delays and the consequent howls from outraged subscribers who received no papers.

● The female reporter who covered most of the spot-news beats became suddenly smitten, married, and took off on a month-long honeymoon.

Hayhow was editor and publisher of the *Hillsdale* (Michigan) *Daily News* when this article first appeared, in 1958.

- The office manager took ill and went to the hospital.
- One of two clerks quit without notice to have a baby.
- One of two display advertising salesmen left on a honeymoon.
- Subscribers on a motor route reported no papers and a check with the woman driver's home brought the incomplete information that "she had gone to Grand Rapids." She turned up three days later lugging the bundle of now-somewhat-late intelligence and vital information and announcing she was quitting.

As all small-city publishers know, there is an automatic procedure for handling emergencies on small newspapers: the boss goes to work. And he better be prepared, through background or experience. Dale Stafford was prepared on both counts.

Stafford took over the untenanted news beat and lent a hand in the display ad department. He handled the most pressing bookkeeping matters and made up the payroll. He hired a new rural delivery driver. Meanwhile, he was continuing his regular chores, including the writing of his column, "Personally Speaking."

The best he could do with the web break problem was to commiserate with his pressman, for Stafford is no mechanical genius. A couple of years ago, we dropped by his summer home on Lake Charlevoix to find him making a great to-do about mowing the lawn. It was like a man running his head off but making no progress. Stafford was covering the ground all right, but the grass was merely bowing its head as he passed. It developed that he had discovered a new talent for his rotary mower, leveling the water front, and it hadn't occurred to him that the blade might need sharpening. He didn't even know the machine carried a blade.

A native of St. Louis, Michigan, Stafford attended Michigan State, serving as athletic publicity director while a student. He began his professional career as sports editor of the now extinct *Lansing Capitol News*. In 1929 he moved to the *Pontiac Press* as police reporter, later becoming sports editor. In 1937 he joined the Associated Press as a rewrite man in the Detroit bureau, leaving in 1941 to become sports editor of the *Detroit Free Press*. In 1945 he became assistant managing editor and later managing editor of the *Free Press*. His purchase of the Greenville property came in 1951.

Stafford is among the publishers who feel that newspapermen should contribute to civic affairs in an active capacity. Thus he is vice-president of both the Greenville Memorial Hospital and the Greenville Chamber of Commerce. A job with wider implications is his chairmanship of the Advisory Committee of the Michigan Vocational Training School, a school for veterans and disabled persons.

Professionally he is a director and secretary of the Inland Daily Press

Association and chairman of its Freedom of Information Committee. He is also a director of the Michigan Press Association. Before moving from Detroit to Greenville, he headed the Michigan Associated Press Editorial Association and was active in committee work of the APME.

In September, October, and November of 1956 he was in Indonesia, conducting seminars for Indonesian publishers under sponsorship of the Indonesian government.

Stafford is a big man. He'll go six feet, three inches and about 240 pounds when he's dieting, which is most of the time now. Like most big men, he exudes good nature. In thirty years we've never seen him outwardly ruffled. His friends know that he courts ulcers and/or high blood pressure by permitting himself to boil inwardly, particularly when the monthly profit sheet is not to his liking. But it never shows. Careless of dress, his stature and manner makes him a man to remember, and this has helped him immeasurably in business and professionally. He makes friends easily and has a genius for keeping those he makes.

His hobbies include golf, fishing, puttering around his spacious yard, and gin rummy. He is by far the most adept at the latter. Some of his customers insist he makes more money at the card table than from his newspaper. This he denies, with the logical explanation that it wouldn't be good business. We recall an incident at the Grand Hotel on Mackinac Island a few years back. A traveling wire service representative, bored and somewhat lonesome, expressed a wish for a friendly game of gin, boasting casually that he was the "champion of Indiana." We introduced him to Stafford. An hour or so later, the championship of Indiana and forty-seven dollars of the traveling representative's dough reposed with the gentleman from Greenville.

We asked Stafford two questions:

One: What compensations impel a man who "has it made" in the big time to willingly . . . even eagerly . . . accept the hard work and uncertainties of the journalistic hinterlands?

It isn't, we learned, entirely a matter of compensation. A goodly share of the motivation is challenge . . . a desire to test one's knowledge and ability against a new, somewhat different force. But there are compensations, mostly other than monetary. This is not to say that very many publishers of small dailies are on welfare. It is to say that there is as much or more money available in top metropolitan positions.

But where is there satisfaction to equal a successful campaign for a new charter, or a new school or highway, when it is a personal, one-man effort, as it must be on a small daily? Or the satisfaction of a testimonial from an advertiser about the pulling power of one's own newspaper? Or the satisfaction of increasing one's circulation from 3,900 to 5,200 in six years in

the face of stiff big-city competition?
   Two: Would you do it again?
   Answer: (With emphasis and feeling) Yes.

William P. Steven, Executive Editor
Minneapolis Star and Tribune

By Daryle Feldmeir

A man who paid Bill Steven's salary for fourteen years, and who ought to know, claims the executive editor of the *Minneapolis Star and Tribune* is the profession's number one "No!" man.

"Bill Steven," says editor Jenkin Lloyd Jones of the *Tulsa Tribune*, "is a constant questioner and a chronic disagreer. If you suggest stepping outside a burning building, he will first want to argue the subject.

"This characteristic of mind springs not from a perverse desire to oppose," Jones adds, "but because Bill never believes anything until it has been examined. No process of journalism is sacred to him just because it has always been done that way."

While Jenk Jones wrote those words, 650 miles north of Tulsa the presses were rolling out another "first" in American journalism: the "new" *Minneapolis Star*, a newspaper planned for a year by fourteen staff members, primed with a host of Bill Steven ideas, which has received wide attention.

When the late Gideon Seymour and John Cowles, president of the *Minneapolis Star and Tribune*, returned from the ASNE convention in 1944, they brought back a thirty-five-year-old managing editor for the *Tribune*, and told him to start recruiting a separate staff (some of the *Tribune* beats then were "covered" by the afternoon staff on a rewrite basis).

Bill recruited young staffers from the colleges' postwar crops.

"I wanted bright, young people," he says. "I think an awful lot of the newspaper business is energy, and just sheer energy will get you a hell of a lot of stories."

It became standard practice to hire a young man and throw him in the

---

Feldmeir was managing editor of the *Minneapolis Tribune* when this article first appeared, in 1956.

drink. If he swam, or looked as if he might learn rather quickly, he was saved for seasoning.

Bower Hawthorne, then city editor, recalls that at one point he had twenty-nine staffers; and in the same period, seventy-one others had either resigned or been cut loose.

As the staff was winnowed down, Steven turned them loose. He looked around for areas the other news media were slighting. First it was the local schools, then Community Chest agencies, the University of Minnesota, state mental hospitals, the atom. The *Tribune* plunged for all it was worth and, following suit, the community nudged itself into action.

Steven needled his staff to come up with ideas. Except for a handful of specialists, whose work was heavily promoted, no one was allowed to get too set on his beat.

Staffers called their life a game of musical chairs. Steven conceded that constant shifts from beat to beat meant missing a few stories, but he was willing to in order to get the extra stories that came from a fresh pair of eyes on an old beat.

Nothing was sacred. The society page died, and was reborn as a woman's page for the average housewife. The food editor began trudging "Around the Block" for homemaking hints and recipes (and readers, too) from housewives who never had had their names in the paper before.

The telephone technique took a licking. "A wonderful invention and the worst thing that ever happened to newspapering," says Steven. *Tribune* reporters began traveling like salesmen.

Even the *Star and Tribune's* contribution to the mammoth Aquatennial parade—Minneapolis's annual ten-day summer festival—fell victim to the idea men. Gid Seymour, Steven, and other executives were dissatisfied with the standard papier-mache float the newspapers entered.

Steven suggested, "We ought to rent three live elephants for the parade, call the little one the *Minneapolis Tribune*, the middle one the *Minneapolis Star*, and the big one the *Minneapolis Sunday Tribune*." But unemployed elephants, during the summer months, simply were not to be had.

Someone else suggested clowns to represent the papers, and another added, "Why not ask the Jaycees to march in the parade as clowns?"

What developed is the *Minneapolis Star and Tribune* Aqua Jesters, one of the most phenomenally successful amateur clown organizations extant. A hundred young businessmen—mostly business and a slice of ham—entertain at hundreds of Upper Midwest functions, and promote the *Star and Tribune*.

Steven, naturally, is a member of the clown brigade. But the parade means miles of marching and Bill loathes exercise. Since each Aqua Jester develops his own act, he became the Queen of the Jesters, a big-bosomed, frowsy witch of a femme fatale. He has never walked a step in any parade.

None of his relentless, driving, assertive nature is news to fellow editors. They have known about it since he first showed up at an APME convention in 1937. "Having that delightfully relaxed manner of knowing how to run everybody else's business," an APMEer recalls, "Bill made some programming suggestions."

In 1938 he was elected to the APME Board, and in 1948 president. He was the first chairman of the APME Continuing Study Committee, the extracurricular newspaper activity, of which he is most proud. "When AP gains an inch," he explains, "hundreds of papers gain an inch."

And he found time to marry and rear a family. His wife, Lucy, and their four children (Margaret, eighteen; Sarah, fourteen; Lucinda, twelve; and James David Ritchie, ten) fit nicely into a ten-room colonial home and a frenetic newspaper career.

On a recent Saturday, a large delegation from the Minnesota AP Circuit dropped in for glasses and good talk after an AP banquet. On Sunday, Lucy, who is active in the American Field Service, had a hundred guests in the house. On Monday, she managed a Girl Scout cook-out, then arrived downtown just in time for a banquet of the World Affairs Program, a project enlisting students and teachers in 120 high schools.

Bill met Lucy on his first day on the *Tulsa Tribune* in 1930, at the YMCA, where she was a secretary. He promptly dated and married her.

Honeymoons were hard to negotiate in those Depression days, but Bill managed. Gypsy Smith, the old-time evangelist, was in Tulsa and the *Tribune* offered a third of a day off for every night a staffer covered one of the revival meetings. Bill earned a two-week honeymoon on Gypsy Smith (after a delay to permit him to cover the Oklahoma primary election).

There is some talk among staffers that Bill has shortened his pace a bit since he became executive editor. They point to the fact that when the new *Star* touched off a basket of protests from some readers who couldn't find their favorite television listings in the new format, Bill wrote more than a hundred letters soothing ruffled antennae.

This was a cry-and-a-half (at least) from a couple of years back when his pungent pen was turned on some excessively irate readers, like the man who spelled out his dissatisfaction with a *Tribune* columnist in a two-page letter and got this reply:

"Dear Sir: Oh come now. Sincerely, William P. Steven."

When Bill left Tulsa for Minneapolis, Jenk Jones recalls, "I wondered how long he would last. For only the employer who would rather be right than comfortable could put up with Bill." But Gid Seymour could take it and apparently, so could John Cowles.

Edward T. Stone, Managing Editor
The Seattle Post-Intelligencer

By Julius Gius

O ut in the northwesternmost corner of America, the *P-I* (pronounced Pee-Eye) is a breakfast staple. It comes with the morning coffee, to be chawed on, consumed, or challenged in 190,000 homes every weekday and a third that many more on Sundays.

The *P-I*, the only morning daily in all the vast expanse of western Washington, is officially the *Seattle Post-Intelligencer*. The managing editor of this far-ranging, lusty, and influential member of the Hearst organization for fourteen years has been Edward Thoburn Stone.

Tall, angular Ed Stone, fifty-seven this month, has been with the *Post-Intelligencer* since he broke in as a cub in 1926, and he's made every working moment count.

"He's a hard man to work for because he moves at only one speed, full ahead," says one of Stone's veteran deskmen. "I'm sure he begrudges every hour he spends in sleep because it's unproductive time."

With Stone in the saddle, the *Post-Intelligencer* never has been static. His staff knows that the newspaper is subject to constant change and improvement. The poorest excuse any staffer can offer for doing a job in a deadly routine fashion is, "Well, that's the way we were doing it last month."

Stone keeps himself close to the newsroom's operation (there is no door on the managing editor's office) for, as he puts it: "I have always felt that news is the sole reason for a newspaper's existence."

He keeps a steady stream of ideas pouring into the city desk (often more than they can keep up with, his city editor will tell you) and has an unfading memory of stories suggested and left undone. He knows his circulation area like the back of his hand, because he's handled every job on the city

---

Gius was editor of the *Bremerton* (Washington) *Sun* when this article first appeared, in 1958.

side—and thrived on them all.

His intense, detailed preoccupation with the news prompts Stone to wonder if perhaps he's a different breed than the customary managing editor. "Occasionally I have been surprised by other editors who express wonderment at my methods," he recalls. "Having been pitched into the job with some suddenness, I had to evolve my own methods and newsroom policy as I went along. It's nothing you learn in school."

As he did when he first took over the managing editor's chair, Stone still faithfully scans all dupes from the wire services and the city desk and frequently calls attention to a story overlooked or underplayed.

"I think the news editor is sometimes irked at this detailed supervision over his job. He's even hinted that I ought to be sitting back in my office Thinking Big. I tell him that my report card is the newspaper on the doorstep, and the subscriber doesn't give a damn for any Big Thoughts of mine that aren't in the paper. My primary function is to see that our readers are reasonably well informed on the news of the day, and to me everything else in a newspaper's operation is secondary.

"But others may disagree—and rightly so—with that conception of the job."

On Stone's versatile staff there is a deep loyalty born of respect and nurtured by his very real interest in their welfare and well-being. One of them put it this way: "I've worked for him nearly twenty-two years. I curse him roundly at least once a week and threaten to quit once a month. But I never quit because I like the guy personally, I admire him as a newspaperman, I like the way he backs up his staff—and I want to be around to see what idea he comes up with next."

Stone firmly rebuts his staff's accolades. "I'm one of the laziest guys I know . . . probably one of the laziest men alive."

Ordinarily quiet and easygoing, Stone will explode a full head of steam to support his men in legitimate pursuit of the news. Many a self-appointed censor or misguided bureaucrat has "heard from" Ed Stone in crackling terms as he waged, and generally won, his part of the FoI fight. He does all of his business at the *Post-Intelligencer* building and has short shrift for the politician, flack, or self-server presumptive enough to think Ed Stone will listen more sympathetically over cocktails or steak.

Outside the office there is a touch of shyness in Ed's nature. The town's favorite watering holes hold small allure and he abstains from civic affiliations and club life. "I just don't happen to believe a newspaperman at the policy-making level should get tangled up in community affairs," he contends. So he belongs only to ASNE and APME, having carried his share of responsibility in both.

Ed Stone's roots are deep in the Pacific Northwest. His grandfather Asa

Stone came west by covered wagon from New England in 1845 and homesteaded at Oregon City, not far from Portland. Ed was born and reared across the Columbia river in Vancouver, Washington, and took an early interest in newspaper work because his father handled assorted circulation and advertising chores on the *Vancouver Columbian*.

He made his way through the University of Washington, then returned to his hometown to take over the news side of a weekly. That lasted a year. If his partner hadn't been a problem drinker, Stone might never have left—and the *Honolulu Star-Bulletin* wouldn't have flubbed, as it did, the chance to get a good hand. Stone was hired by the *Post-Intelligencer* as a temporary general assignments reporter while waiting the promised "next opening" at the *Star-Bulletin*. He still hasn't heard from Honolulu, but the *Post-Intelligencer* took him out of the temporary category after a five-month trial period when Todd Moss, then city editor, told him: "Instead of a raise, consider yourself on the permanent staff." Forty-dollar-a-week Stone thanked him and went on from there—to assistant city editor, then city editor in 1937, managing editor in 1943.

His wife is the former Bertha Dewey; she was in library school when he was studying journalism at the university. From their first meeting they have enjoyed common interests in history, literature, good drama, subdued home life—and newspapers.

They have one son, Francis, twenty-nine—"Frank" to the *San Diego Tribune* news staff, which he joined five years ago after a two-year indoctrination superintended by Fay Blanchard at Rochester, New York. Frank has had the good sense to make Ed twice a grandfather.

Stone's hobby is books ("I know that sounds awfully stuffy"), but he has little room for modern fiction. In earlier days he restricted his lunch outlay to fifteen cents in order to accumulate the price of a book. His library now has well over one thousand volumes, predominantly history, some of which he has read more than once and a few, he admits sadly, that he hasn't yet read at all.

It was Stone's interest in literature and in the antiquity of the Mediterranean countries that fostered an eight-month adventure abroad in 1957. He had reread Washington Irving's *Life and Voyages of Christopher Columbus* and Samuel Eliot Morison's biography of Columbus, *Admiral of the Ocean Sea*. This fired an interest so overpowering that Stone arranged leave from the *Post-Intelligencer*, took a night school course in Spanish and, with his wife, set out for Lisbon with the primary mission of retracing Columbus's career—in fact, his very steps—prior to his voyage of discovery.... But that is quite another story from this one.

Walker Stone, Editor in Chief
Scripps-Howard Newspapers

By Earl H. Richert

W alker Stone, who has been editor in chief of Scripps-Howard Newspapers since 1952, is one of that rare species in the journalism of any era who has spent all his professional life with one employer and in one city—the statistics being thirty-nine years with Scripps-Howard in Washington.

And after four decades of seeing the big and little rise and fall, wars start and stop, Walker isn't exactly a fellow to jump out of his chair when some big news comes along. But then he never was.

The adjectives for him are "deliberate, unruffled, serene." And stories which illustrate these characteristics are legion throughout Scripps-Howard.

There is, for example, the one about the time he was at a hotel in Fort Worth and told the clerk he was dissatisfied with his room and was checking out at once. The clerk, eager to appease, asked solicitously what was wrong. "The room's on fire," Walker allegedly replied.

Dick Thornburg, editor of the *Cincinnati Post and Times-Star*, who once served as Walker's managing editor, describes his old boss as a typical sensible Southwesterner who "walks slowly and on the shady side of the street."

Charles Lucey, editor of the *Trenton Times* who served many years as Scripps-Howard's political editor under Walker's direction, can never forget how completely unflappable Walker was when they were both being carted off to jail in Caracas three years ago after having interviewed Venezuela's Communist boss. (They were soon released and received an apology from President Betancourt.)

But these characteristics are deceptive. As Dick Thornburg also says,

---

Richert was editor of Scripps-Howard Newspapers when this article first appeared, in 1967.

"Anyone who concludes that his drawling speech and leisurely pace reflect like qualities of mind is being fooled."

There is much more inner excitement in Walker and he feels more deeply than his cool and somewhat detached attitude would indicate.

Walker was born in Okemah, Oklahoma, in 1904. While in college at Oklahoma A & M (now Oklahoma State), he was editor of the college daily and brought to school and pledged to his fraternity, Kappa Sigma, one Paul Miller, now president of Gannett Newspapers and of the Associated Press. During his senior year, 1925–26, Walker was secretary of the student senate and general manager of college publications.

Walker's college years were, as they are for so many, most influential on the later course of his life. He formed scores of friendships that have lasted over the decades—and one that ripened into marriage. Pretty Donna Smith, a campus coed, later became Mrs. Walker Stone, mother of his two daughters and, recently, partner with Walker in the high estate of grandparenthood.

Most of us who know Walker intimately never have seen a man who, far removed from the scene of his college campus, has held so firmly to the friends he made in college. Hardly a week goes by that some old college friend—from ambassador on down—doesn't drop into Walker's Washington office to visit.

After college, he came to Washington with the primary purpose of studying law and enrolled at George Washington University. But, to eat regularly, he found it necessary to get a job. He landed on the *Washington Daily News* as a copyreader. The fact that he was a complete greenhorn on a copydesk was no special handicap. "I just looked over the other guy's shoulder and watched what he did, and caught on," Walker says.

Walker was soon switched to the city side as a reporter and there developed many of the acquaintanceships which have proved fruitful news sources over the years. It was during this period that he became acquainted with LBJ, then a congressman's assistant. Among his colleagues on the *News* was Ernie Pyle.

From reporter he became city editor of the *News* and later transferred to the Scripps-Howard Newspaper Alliance where he served as Washington correspondent for the *Evansville* (Indiana) *Press* and three other papers which since have been discontinued. The demise of these papers was in no wise chargeable to the quality of Walker's representation in Washington.

By 1935, Walker was writing editorials for all Scripps-Howard newspapers, and in 1936 he was given charge of Scripps-Howard's Washington bureau (SHNA) with the title of associate editor. He was named editor of SHNA in 1943 and editor in chief of all Scripps-Howard newspapers nine years later.

His writing talents are a thing of envy to many of us in Scripps-Howard. In editorials he has authored some of the most graceful prose ever to move out of Washington to our newspapers. Not language that was artificially prettied-up or lacquered, but words and sentences that were strong and clean-limbed—bearing a definite relationship to an upbringing in the open country in Oklahoma. In this category, for example, was his nationally quoted "Ike is running like a dry creek" line in a 1952 editorial urging General Eisenhower to get cracking on his campaign.

Taxes have been a specialty with him and he wrote the first Scripps-Howard editorial of January 1966, saying the time was now to raise taxes—a position little heeded then but now generally agreed by economists to have been the right thing to do. He still is old-fashioned in thinking that someday, somehow, we've got to start making payments on the national debt. The "new economics" have not converted him.

Over the years as head of SHNA and as editor in chief, Walker has traveled extensively abroad, absorbing background for foreign policy editorials and doing considerable reporting himself. "There is," he says, "no substitute for having been there."

A detailing of his foreign travels would fill the space remaining. But for example, he inspected the atrocity camps of Buchenwald and Dachau, interviewed Nehru on the day China invaded Tibet (concluding Nehru had no guts), has known and interviewed every chief of state of the Philippines since before it became a republic, has been to mainland China, twice to the Congo, etc.

On his second trip to Russia, in 1962, that time with an ASNE group, he got into an argument with then Premier Khrushchev. Mr. K. said there would be no trouble about atomic bombs, except for the United States refusal to ban them.

Walker asked why, in 1946, the USSR had vetoed the United States-Baruch proposal to turn over to the United Nations all atomic secrets, which were then a United States monopoly, plus control of all fissionable material.

Mr. K. promptly stated Walker had misstated the Baruch plan and offered to have the Kremlin foreign office set him straight.

Walker replied, "I do not need to use your foreign ministry; I was there."

For once, Mr. K. had no ready answer.

The foregoing story with its mention of Baruch prompts me to say that although Walker has never to my knowledge named the public servant he admired most in his Washington years, I would guess it would be Bernard Baruch. They were good friends and Baruch's counsels were most valued.

Walker takes much greater pride in the men he has brought into the organization and developed over the years than he does in his own writing.

In one week at the end of World War II, he brought into the bureau Jim G. Lucas and Robert Ruark, both of whom became stars. Names of editors cited above also are illustrative of his talents in this field. And there are many more Stone-products who can be named.

Walker always has loved the outdoors, and hunting and fishing. Before Bob Ruark's death, Walker went on a couple of African safaris with Bob. He also is a devoted poker player, but he says he hasn't been drawing well in recent years.

Four years ago he bought a 520-acre tract of land in Virginia, about two hours drive from Washington and with a breathtaking view of the Blue Ridge. It is stocked with horses, cattle, quail, and bass and Walker has been devoting much time to making it livable for the day he retires.

He calls the place Hawthorn Farm. Staff members, noting the speed with which he takes off for the country on weekends, call it Shangri-La.

Thomas Hazzard Thompson, Editor
Amarillo (Texas) Globe-Times

By Charles E. Green

O ne of these days Thomas Hazzard Thompson, editor of the *Amarillo Globe-Times*, may decide to write a book about a West Texan newspaperman who gets embroiled in a cloak-and-dagger act with a county judge. Its setting will be in a Panhandle town near the beautiful Palo Duro Canyon where nature has painted walls with colors no human would dare try to imitate.

His hero will be an erudite man in his low fifties, who edits an afternoon newspaper and writes a column just for the kick. He will either like to hunt and fish, or else he thinks he should—let's simply say he does a great deal of both.

So the day the story opens, the hero will be dressed to go hunting. Then, as any true-to-life editor would do, he drops by the office to check his mail. While he is sorting the letters, the telephone rings and this boyish voice that is talking scared tells him he must see him at once. It's a life and death matter. "If they knew I was calling they'd shoot me down like a dog."

It will turn out to be a story of bribery in high places, and a sordid alliance between the underworld and men selected to protect us from such. It will involve a prostitute so pretty she could pass as the girl who used to live next door. It is she who will rise above the decor of her life and show the courage needed to break open a very nasty case.

The scared boy will also prove his weight in gold. He'll have to go in hiding as the villains of this piece are after him with loaded side arms. His young wife will live six months in mortal terror, her only hope the West Texas editor, who by now has called in—not the Texas Rangers—but a

---

Green was executive editor of the *Austin American-Statesman* when this article first appeared, in 1960.

legislative investigating committee headed by an ex–football star who's big and rough and brave enough to wade right in where angels fear to tread.

In spite of anonymous threats and strange cars passing the house all hours of the night, the fight against corruption will continue until enough evidence is found to bring the judge to trial. On a change of venue the case is moved to a distant town. The defense has a fistful of money, so they hire a couple of brains to spring the judge.

They do. They not only win the case because there's no corroborating witness, but have someone testify that the editor is a sort of educated fool. This gets in all the papers, so when the hero returns home he gets a lot of kidding; loses some face in the community. He's pretty cut up about it. It does hurt, and way down deep.

He begins to wonder if it's worth the effort. Somewhere on his desk is a personal motto which reads like this: "If you know something is rotten in the community, you have two choices: (1) air it (2) cover up." This belief, and a strange type of faith that sustains most honest men, keeps him from quitting.

Then when it seems that nothing on God's green earth can save the situation, he gets this second phone call.

It turns out to be the corroborating witness he's needed, a pretty prostitute. A woman who had the courage to tell her gambler husband that he didn't have the guts to pull the trigger when he stuck a gun in her ribs.

Our hero is back in business. With this new evidence the legislative committee moves in and takes charge. The county judge resigns in the face of massive protests by the people. The bar association brings charges to disbar him as a lawyer. The grand jury assembles to consider the new evidence. The slate of officers recommended by the once-discredited editor is swept out of office.

The manuscript would make the rounds and be given an appreciative reading. The best New York publishers would write pleasant rejection slips praising the style but pointing out the weaknesses in plot structure; too contrived, with coincidence overemphasized. Would the author care to make certain revisions . . ?

Thomas Hazzard Thompson of Amarillo, Texas, declines. The first reason being he'll never write the book. The second reason being the plot is real. The third and best reason, he's the hero of what you've just read.

Tom Thompson is the last man you'd pick to lead a crusade. He dresses neatly. Brown is his favorite. He's six feet tall and often looks as if he's just come in out of the wind and is still slightly ruffled. He now has some of those half-glasses over which he peers, usually benevolently. He can be impatient, and from time to time scares the distaff side of the staff into tiptoeing. But with it goes a certain courtliness which is not, reports Louise Evans, editorial page editor of the *Globe-News*, a hallmark of the shop.

"He wants his staff to be a great deal more erudite and scholarly than it is. By now I think he has settled for what he has. But," adds Miss Evans, "he is constantly on the lookout for that certain spark and when he finds it, he fans."

When Tom got his degree from college, he marched back to Amarillo intent on going to work for the newspaper. He had scored well in English, written a number of short stories that received special mention, and one novel. But those were the ugly thirties when footing was scarce and each new applicant was viewed with suspicion by those who still held down jobs.

He didn't get to first base, although he offered to work for nothing.

His parents were salt of the earth people from Kentucky who came to the Texas Panhandle in the early 1900s, just as Amarillo was changing from a cow camp to a cowtown. Tom's father was one of the smart young businessmen who acquired a reasonable amount of money and property before he was struck down in the flu epidemic of World War I.

So like all High Plainsmen, the Thompsons were land-poor during the Depression. But Tom didn't exactly go hungry. He got a job teaching English in Amarillo Central High School and his mother, who had turned out to be an excellent businesswoman, provided him with a rather small but elegant studio-type apartment in the backyard.

You must drag this part of his life from Tom, but he became the center of a group of young intellectuals who made his place their headquarters. Again quoting Louise Evans:

"Studio-type apartments were fairly heady stuff in cowtown country. But I remember going there with some friends and getting into a discussion with Tom. My memory of the meeting is clouded by the fact that he was discussing Thomas Mann as the greatest literary giant of the century and I thought he was talking about Somerset Maugham. We argued at great length and since I seemed to be making no headway in convincing him Maugham was a crack storyteller but scarcely a giant, I went away."

She was weeks getting invited back.

Later, Tom finished his master's at the University of California, became an instructor in English at Louisiana State University. He was recalled by his mother to take over the management of their property. Learning this business, collecting rents, wasn't enough and he developed a novel which was practically accepted with some changes. Unfortunately the manuscript was lost and Tom never quite recovered from his shock.

It was about this time that Paul Allingham came into the picture.

Paul Allingham is president-publisher of the Atchinson, Kansas, *Globe*. At that time he was with the *Amarillo Globe-News*. "Since he wasn't too busy," says Paul, "I talked Tom into joining the staff as a part-time reporter. He clicked, although there was the usual run of smart-aleck reporters who couldn't get used to a 'professor' on the staff. Tom had the ability to meet and talk with topside people."

The war separated Tom from a promising career. Again quoting Paul Allingham: "I'll never forget Tom and several of us listening to Sibelius's 'Finlandia,' which has a martial air and makes a man want to join something. Tom announced he was going to Dallas to see about joining the navy. We killed a fifth of bourbon with our hero then put him on the train."

Paul's next communique from Tom was a postcard mailed from El Paso. All it said was: "Jesus." Tom was headed for boot camp without even getting to come home.

Here I am reminded of something Helen Thompson once said about her husband. Helen is a dark-haired, dark-eyed beauty who was a photographer-reporter with the Amarillo paper during the war.

"Truly, I don't think Tom ever went out of his way to make a crusade. He sees an apparent injustice or inequality, and does something about it. He can't ignore it or back off."

So in boot camp when he read in a Los Angeles newspaper that the navy was advertising for more storekeepers to volunteer for training and then had called a large group of storekeepers to be assigned to other duties, he became the first known man in navy history to pass and sign a "petition."

He had officers running in all directions. They dropped him like a hot rock. Even the fine old chaplain who was nearing retirement age asked Tom to lay off. It was mutiny, according to the rules. The fifty who signed the petition were taken up by the navy and scattered to the four winds. Tom drew Washington where he was well hidden in the insurance and death payment division. Later he grabbed a chance for officers' training and made the grade.

After the war Tom returned to Amarillo and took over the job as business editor of the newspaper. Shortly after the consolidation of the *Globe-News* with the *Amarillo Times*, and the subsequent death of T. E. Johnson, Tom was made editor of the *Globe-Times*. For years Gene Howe had taken over "page two, column one" with a famous column known as "The Tackless Texas," devoted to the doings and philosophies of old Tack.

Gene Howe had been dead a couple of years when Tom was assigned the spot. It took a brave man to move in but Tom did.

Tom's "Turnstile" column made a hit. He knew Amarillo from a small town, and most of the people. He has a reporter's contacts still. Even in the office he has a reporter's attitude. As soon as he has finished with the detail work, he takes to the street and to the clubs to find out what is going on.

This, as briefly as I can tell it, is the Amarillo story, and something of editor Thomas Hazzard Thompson who brought it about. It might not have been told except the now discredited Judge Roy Stevens himself pointed an accusing finger at Tom and said, "But for that man I would not be in this trouble."

Yet Tom is no real Javert dogging his enemy with plodding tenacity, but a real live guy, a human being. One you'd like to take a drink with or play in a round of golf. A sort of windblown image of impeccability.

Perhaps this, written by Louise Evans, best illustrates our man. She reports:

"Our new and shiny building faces directly into the east with windows half a block wide. The morning sun was too much. Bamboo-type curtains were hung. 'Looks like a Samoan cathouse, doesn't it?' said Tom. But I hadn't seen Samoa, so I cannot vouch for the metaphor."

Philip M. Wagner, Editor
The Baltimore Sun

By Price Day

Philip M. Wagner, whose profession is that of editor and whose avocation is the growing of wine grapes, holds strong opinions both on newspaper work and on viticulture.

From nineteen years of experience in running editorial pages for the Baltimore Sunpapers—first for the *Evening Sun* and since 1943 for the *Sun*—he has decided that if a single proposition is to govern an editorial page, the proposition is that the page must be believed. Beyond that:

"I look for consistency in a newspaper, not personal journalism. The *Sun* has had men who were conspicuous as personalities—notably H. C. Mencken, who by the way was not an editor and did not want to be an editor, because he was just temperamentally not an editor—but the editorial pages have been collaborative. People outside may have thought of the *Sun* as 'Mencken's paper,' but editorially, except once for three brief and curious months, it was not so.

"Papers of our sort emphasize the quality of the writing. We want a civilized job. Our policies are libertarian, which means that sometimes we are called liberal and sometimes, as the world changes, conservative. The point is that we ourselves strive for continuity.

"One isn't likely to find the sensational and extreme editorial position that gets you into the stream of the news generally. We are not seeking to take positions on immediate situations that will merely call attention to ourselves. The *Sun* and papers more or less like it try to illuminate what's happened, and, of course, try to help steer events insofar as we can."

Such papers, Wagner believes, are able to exert their greatest influence locally, their next greatest within their states, then nationally, and then internationally.

"We are extremely unambiguous on state and local issues," he says. "On national issues we try to mingle opinion with illumination. Internationally,

---

Day was associate editor of the *Baltimore Sun* when this article first appeared, in 1957.

we do not try to tell Khrushchev what to do, on the modest assumption that he is not a regular reader, and is not conditioned to take our comments in a serious way anyhow."

He realizes that the reading public asks a newspaper to take a stand in national elections (though the *Sun* in 1936 declined to advise its readers as between Roosevelt and Landon), but says:

"Nevertheless, this is the least congenial part of running an editorial page. The position of advocate always carries with it a temptation to forget the other side. Being an advocate is an unnatural business. It's always a real relief to have an election over and resume our prime function, that of disinterested criticism.

"If the record may show that our readers sometimes fail to follow our advice in national elections, our record on local issues, notably on the important questions of public borrowing, is excellent. With rare exceptions, the local public votes on loans as we advise it to. This is what I mean in saying that an editorial page must be believed."

As for viticulture: It began in the days of Prohibition when Wagner decided that a table wine was a pleasant thing to have on a table, and began to explore the subject of wine making. The explorations have led to an enterprise called Boordy Vineyard. The labels on the bottles bear the further legend, "J. & P. Wagner, Props." It is a joint endeavor. The "J." is Jocelyn, Wagner's wife.

On a small place in the country a few miles north of Baltimore the Wagners have established what amounts to—what in fact is—an experiment station in hybrid vines developed in France by a crossing of the classic but disease-prone varieties with the hardy vines of the eastern United States.

"Some people play golf and others go fishing," Wagner says. "We play at grape growing and wine making, with the emphasis on the growing. It's ideal for an editor, since a grapevine has no moral problems. You can start the day with it, then drop it, and nothing morally awful or internationally disastrous will have happened before you pick it up again. And of course at dinner time you have a dividend to help still further to ease the pains of the days.

"Ours is a real horticultural enterprise, with the purpose of introducing into this country a whole new range of plant material of big potential value to American agriculture—grape varieties hitherto unknown in this country which in half a century might transform viticulture east of California.

"The vineyard has been made self-sustaining primarily to demonstrate that wine growing is a practical possibility in this country."

Out of Wagner's grape growing and wine making have come two books, *Wine Grapes*, published in 1937, and *American Wines and Wine Making*, first published in 1933 and continuously in print ever since, in many editions. It is the standard work on the subject.

The Wagners vacation in Europe every other year or so, spending the larger portion of their time in the wine regions of France. They last went, however, at the time of the Suez crisis and the Hungarian rebellion, when editorial work for the *Sun* altered the character of the holiday.

As for violins, not heretofore mentioned: Violins come into it only incidentally, as a by-product of an intense interest in music. Wagner once studied the subject of violin-making, and then made two.

This and other interests are reflected in some of the names over which he has written in the *Sun* and the *Evening Sun*: Musicus, Hortus Minor, Agricola, Jr., Classicus. He is considered something of an authority on pokeweed in cookery, on the chronic shortage of piano tuners, and on Mexicatessens in California.

As for background and dates: Wagner, born in New Haven, Connecticut, in 1904, grew up in Ann Arbor where his father, now retired, was professor of romance languages at the University of Michigan. He himself received his A.B. at Michigan in 1925, having as an undergraduate held the post of managing editor of the *Michigan Daily*.

He came into the nongraduate newspaper business in a way rather reverse. He was in public relations first, and is able to turn the tables on publicity men by telling them that he was one once himself. After five postcollege years in the publicity department of the General Electric Company, an experience which he believes gave him a look into the world of business that has been valuable in his work as an editor, he came to the *Evening Sun* as an editorial writer.

In 1936 he went to England to represent the *Sun* in its London bureau, and was there during the constitutional crisis known otherwise as the Simpson affair, and the period when the events that were to lead to World War II were beginning to gather momentum. He returned to the *Evening Sun* in 1937.

That newspaper, in the early months of 1938, went through an interesting interlude. Mencken for the first and last time did become an acting editorial-page editor, with the understanding that he would remain so for three months only, on his own request. Members of the staff recall that their main job was to sneak copy into type in order that the page should not appear on the streets with blank columns: Mencken thought little they wrote fit to print. When Mencken relinquished the unaccustomed chair, Wagner was named editor.

Those were pleasant days on the editorial page of the *Evening Sun*, a page full of surprises and wit and literacy in high degree; but a sterner world was in the making, and for Wagner personally sterner tasks called. In 1943 he moved into the editorial chair of the *Sun*, and has been there since, having strong opinions.

C. G. Wellington, Editor
The Kansas City Star

By Carl E. Lindstrom

His name is Clarence George Wellington. Everyone who knows him calls him Pete while he, in turn, calls everyone on the *Kansas City Star*, as well as a host of other people, by their first names.

His wife, a charming and vivacious lady, is Gladys. His children are four, three boys and a girl. Two are in the newspaper business, one an editor of the *Hutchinson News-Herald*, the other a reporter-photographer on the *Star*.

Pete is dedicated to his family and to the *Star*. He loves to fish but seldom gets away for it except during his regular vacation, usually spent in Wisconsin. Except for "must" appearances at downtown dinners and receptions for visiting dignitaries, Pete and Gladys seldom go out evenings but occasionally entertain at their new ranch style home in Johnson County, Kansas, a twenty-minute drive from his office.

Gladys drives Pete to work in the morning. He is usually at his desk by nine and not infrequently will remain until six or even later. When he arrives he sheds his coat, rolls up his sleeves and calls in various editors to find out what they have in prospect. He likes quick, succinct replies. He usually brings in a batch of clippings, examples of style violation, or of good writing, or a clip on a story which he believes calls for a follow-up.

He is a stickler for accuracy and lucid writing. Often with a few quick strokes of his pencil, he can sharpen up a verbose story. When proofs come down, he scrutinizes them carefully, makes changes, asks questions.

When Pete was sick early in 1953, his bed was covered with newspapers, clips, magazines, and memos. At that time Gladys said she was going to burn his briefcase to prevent his bringing home work at night. He doesn't carry the briefcase now but still goes home with a stack of newspapers and memoranda.

Pete went to the *Topeka Capital* and worked through 1915 after leaving the *Abilene Reflector*. He joined the *Star* in 1916 and had a desk job before the

Lindstrom was executive editor of the *Hartford Times* when this article first appeared, in 1955.

year was out. He had worked up to the assistant city editorship by the time a young hopeful by the name of Ernest Hemingway appeared. After about four years he succeeded George B. (Boss) Longan who had the reputation of being an extraordinarily fine city editor.

Like Longan, he was impatient with slipshod reporting and sleazy writing, but where Longan supposedly worked by ukase, Wellington took the time to go over copy with his staff. Old-timers say he was the better teacher.

Ernest Hemingway credits Wellington with being "a stern disciplinarian, very just and very harsh and I can never say how grateful I am to have worked under him."

That was Wellington the city editor but I know a man who says he "never found Pete as implacable and severe as his reputation." He is Paul Fisher, director of public relations for United Aircraft, who worked on the *Star*, 1931 to 1942, and reports: "Actually, the process of mellowing already had begun for Wellington. Old-timers said that in his city editor days he was thin, tireless, and impatient, but after his marriage to Gladys he began eating more regularly and certainly more richly, and with the establishing of a home and the coming of the children, the *Star* was no longer his single passion."

There are two Wellingtons: the present executive and the former city editor, but as a stylist of news writing and reportorial techniques he never ceased being the latter. A large school of now-famous writers got lessons from him: Russel Crouse, Courtney Riley Cooper, Clifford Knight, detective story writer. Charles A. Fenton in his *Apprenticeship of Ernest Hemingway* writes:

> Hemingway told an interviewer that during his seven months on The *Star* he was trying to tell simple things simply. He remembered that he had been "enormously excited under Pete Wellington's guidance to learn that the English language yields to simplicity through brevity." Hemingway was especially indebted he declared, to Wellington's concept of flexible narrative rather than the rigidly inverted, conventional news story, with its artificial dogma of lead, secondary lead, and key qualification points.

"As night editor," says Fisher, "Pete was actually the top man on the *Times*. The paper, beginning in about 1933, was a good image of Pete's craftsmanship. He had slowly shaped a staff in which there was no doubt he carried tremendous pride. It was young, aggressive, versatile, tough-minded, and tireless. He had taken about eight youngsters with a flair for writing and putting them together with an equal number of veterans, he had a group that could meet the Pendergast situation and the breakdown in the whole political structure of the state on a footing with any metropolitan staff."

Sometimes Pete joined the writing staff at a large round table in Ed's Lunch next door to the *Star* at the coffee break at ten-thirty. He took a spirited part in the discussion, which was mostly shop, and he was treated as an equal.

"No one ever saw Mrs. Wellington out of humor. Often when the staff had done an extremely able job, Pete would take from two to twenty of the reporters to his home for beer and eggs. The group would tiptoe in, close the kitchen doors, and drink a dozen bottles of beer while Pete was getting out the eggs, ham or bacon, and bread for toast. As the voices grew in volume, Gladys would come down in a robe to take over the cooking, because her house man complained that Mr. Wellington's cooking entailed too much dishwashing."

That's the view of a former staffer. One who works for him now says, "He is a great guy, this Wellington. I would go to hell for him as I imagine other staffers would too. I certainly have been lucky to work for him."

James Russell Wiggins, Executive Editor
The Washington Post

By James S. Pope

Dr. Jogtrot tells me James Russell Wiggins will be president of ASNE, and Octopus will win the Kentucky Derby if Wiggins doesn't ride him. Ordered not to, Wiggins instantly will mount any land or sea creature; but that's a problem for Octopus's owner.

The prediction does demand respect. Jogtrot's been hot since he picked Fidel Castro and the American Davis Cup Team. And there's neat symbolism, you have to admit, in parlaying our hero with horses. If he'd been a little older at the time, Wiggins would have outrun Paul Revere by thirty lengths. His known passion for prodding contented citizens into awareness of secret dangers has caused the *Washington Post* and *Times-Herald* to keep standing a ninety-nine-point banner: WIGGINS WARNS.

Wiggins formed his dominant habits early. At zero he got born in Luverne, Minnesota; at nineteen he acquired that town's weekly *Rock County Star*, became wedded the same year to Mabel Preston and to principle. Owing to Mabel's housewifely genius, her shrewd distinction between tolerance and sheer indulgence, this happy triangle has endured. But first there were, for all of them, the formative years.

It was during this period that Wiggins struck his wife forcefully in the nose. He was preparing a speech on preparedness in his sleep, and Mabel, likewise asleep, had no chance to prepare for an eloquent sweep of the Wiggins right arm. She has slept fitfully since.

Undaunted, Wiggins soon aimed a blow for principle. Setting up the *Star's* motto that "Nothing Was Ever Lost by Enduring Faith in Rock County" (a credo that greatly cheered residents during the bank closings later on) he adopted a policy: drunk drivers would get their names in the *Star*.

Pope was executive editor of the *Courier-Journal and Louisville Times* when this article first appeared, in 1959.

His number one and probably only machine operator promptly got convicted, and made a worse mistake. He said to Wiggins, "If you print my name you won't have an operator next week." From that time forward the words "You can't print that" have aroused one of the finest baritone bellows in America.

Wiggins's true ambition was to be a poet rather than an editor, but about 1930 he committed himself fully to journalism and the *St. Paul Dispatch-Pioneer Press*, and soon won the name of "The Black Irishman," a man capable alternately of the darkest thoughts and the most jocund and symphonious laughter. Three years later he laid a fateful trail; he went to Washington.

Wiggins already had more knockouts than Dempsey but he kept swinging. As St. Paul's correspondent he fought for McNary-Haugenism and became so keen a farm expert he was able, with Felix Belair, to become an architect of the Soil Conservation Service to replace the AAA, killed by the Supreme Court. He returned to St. Paul as managing editor in 1938, and naturally became an articulate member of the Committee to Defend America by Aiding the Allies—a name many feel Wiggins must have written.

War found him ready to defend much further. He was a captain and quickly a major in Air Combat Intelligence with brilliant service around the Mediterranean (the exact nature of his exploits are said to be still classified).

He was editor of the St. Paul papers briefly after the war, then achieved that finest of titles—assistant to the publisher—at the *New York Times*. Phil Graham trailed him for a year, finally in 1947 bagged him as managing editor of the *Washington Post* while they sat on a New York subway bench at 3:00 A.M., a favorite hour of Wiggins for any activity. He became executive editor in 1955, after the *Times-Herald* purchase. The distinction of the combined papers owes much to his genius in all the arts of editorship.

Graham ascribes Wiggins's success to luck, first in marrying Mabel and second in avoiding college. He was saved from that peculiarly impervious ignorance bred only in universities. Not having any English instructors, he retained a fresh and measureless appetite for good literature; and so with only one teacher and that the finest anywhere (J. Russell Wiggins), and in one classroom (the world), he polished his mind into a jewel of precision and power.

Wiggins was probably the only managing editor who wrote his own shorthand notes. He kept a pad on his desk in St. Paul, worked late filling pages for his secretary to transcribe next day. His skill at this art made him indispensable after Roosevelt press conferences, before transcripts became available. The whole press corps, and frequently the White House, called on him for exact quotes.

Turner Catledge identifies Wiggins with Demosthenes, contends he "stays perpetually pregnant with quotations from Jefferson, George Washington, Hamilton, Lincoln, Jesus, and others. And he can give more citations of law and precedents than there are laws and precedents. Also, he insists on being very thorough with these citations and will keep his speech going to quite unusual lengths in order to share them with his listeners."

Catledge and Wiggins traveled some six thousand miles in a car covering the 1936 campaign, to their financial improvement, since they accepted Landon bets in just about every state except Maine and Vermont. Wiggins was one of a group of personal advisers around Wendell Willkie four years later, a natural-born one-worlder.

His energy, a confrere says, is "incredible." He reads a page at a time, remembers it. His specialized knowledge awes people. His great intellectual love is Jefferson. He owns a sizable Jefferson library, can quote most of the words written by or about him, including that statesman's garden manual. He is said to know more about 35-mm photography than Mr. Millimeter; spends ten minutes with the light meter, then makes ten shots to get the best.

A conservative dresser, he may turn up at a friend's house Sunday afternoon in old slacks and a beard. He still has the night-work habit. A colleague who found him in his office at 1:30 A.M. stuck his head in the door and said, "If I had a husband with your kind of hours I'd divorce him." "It's been discussed," Wiggins replied cheerfully before turning back to his papers.

He does not smoke, drinks appreciatively, likes to walk to work. He watches his diet, but more with kindly curiosity than with suspicion. An adversary says he "plays a furious game of tennis." (Played?)

Wiggins is a man of magnitude; no small tastes, he. His favorite orchestral work, therefore, is the *1812 Overture*. Friends suspect some conductor probably let the Wiggins boy fire the cannon for him. It's plausible; some of his finest chest tones resemble a sturdy old muzzle-loader at zero plus one, especially when the subject is secrecy in one of our gun-firing departments.

He fiddles with considerable gusto and occasional tunes, preferring "Danny Boy" and other Irish gook. His most recent attachment, said to fascinate his musical biographers, is to the "Chipmunk Song."

He loves to sing, especially after closing time; and especially, according to Pat Wiggins Schroth, his own words. He has been noted to smile with such joy while rendering one of his own lyrics at a gridiron show as to lose a complete stanza. He writes also for his five grandchildren, commemorating their important anniversaries in verse they are said to enjoy. He was humming the wedding march so loudly at Pat's recent wedding he had to be shushed as the bride came down the aisle. Pat resented this elation.

He is not above writing like a newspaper fellow, though a society story he

The Wiggins children touch all the bases. Pat sticks to Washington and United Press International. Gerry (Mrs. Rohland Thomssen, Jr.) sticks to St. Paul. Jack, a gifted artist, lies in wait for the family in Maine. Bill's with the United Features Syndicate in Chicago.

Some children are disciplined by trips to the woodshed and such uncouth techniques. The Wiggins tribe had to endure psychological warfare. Father seared one sentence into their brains to create the most upright children on record: "Never do anything you wouldn't like to see in headlines in the morning paper." Try it on yourself when you feel delinquency coming on.

The Wiggins children touch all the bases. Pat sticks to Washington and United Press International. Gerry (Mrs. Rohland Thomssen, Jr.) sticks to St. Paul. Jack, a gifted artist, lies in wait for the family in Maine. Bill's with the United Features Syndicate in Chicago.

Some children are disciplined by trips to the woodshed and such uncouth techniques. The Wiggins tribe had to endure psychological warfare. Father seared one sentence into their brains to create the most upright children on record: "Never do anything you wouldn't like to see in headlines in the morning paper." Try it on yourself when you feel delinquency coming on.

Nick B. Williams, Editor
Los Angeles Times

By James Bassett

Massaging his Eisenhower pate, eyes half-shut, he sits hunched in his chair at the nether end of the big conference table, listening to the airy rhetoric of the editorialists. Suddenly he stops massaging. His eyes open. And he remarks in his Texas-Alabama-Tennessee-Virginia-Maryland drawl, "Maybe we'd better look at it *this* way—"

Wearing his battered good luck fedora, unencumbered by typewriter, disdaining notes, he rambles across a strange continent, then comes up with a series of penetrating commentaries. And all in his own inscrutable longhand.

This man, this determinedly unassuming fellow, is Nick B. (Boddie) Williams, fifty-eight, editor of the *Los Angeles Times*.

For him it was a hard day's journey from the copydesk rim in the Depression thirties to a plush office only slightly smaller than LBJ's Oval Room. Yet he negotiated the course without losing his (a) sense of humor (b) honest introspective ability or (c) literary touch.

This last isn't offered in jest. Williams once wrote sparkling magazine fiction. But he had the solid good sense to remain a moonlighter rather than deserting the craft. Now, today, he's too busy for such sideline stuff.

It's a brave editor, they say, who dares expose himself in print where his staffers can study the end result. Or an immodest one. Williams hasn't an iota of vanity in his makeup, unless you count professional pride a fault.

Thus much of his public writing, and his public speaking, deals with journalism's myriad problems and responsibilities in this era of electronic entertainment, with oddball demands for curbs on untrammelled reporting, with armchair critics of the Fourth Estate and with jungle competition for the reader-viewer's precious time.

In a serious mood a few years ago, Editor Williams sat down with

---

Bassett was editorial page director of the *Los Angeles Times* when this article first appeared, in 1965.

publisher Otis Chandler (who once worked for him as a reporter) to "redesign the editorial strategy of the *Times* . . . to meet the reader-observer habits of the 1960s."

Such a moment of soul-searching typifies this quietly restless man, who is never satisfied even with the commas in a page of copy. (He tortures them into huge comet-tracks, signifying that he's actually *read* the story.)

In "reshaping, simplifying, and expanding" the *Times*, Williams embarked upon a dangerous and precedental course: he paid real money to enlist top talent. Publications that had once used the daily press as a farm club suddenly found their staffs fair game for acquisitive Editor Williams.

Nor was he unduly fazed, beyond losing hair, sleep, and appetite, by the discovery that establishing a foreign bureau in Paris, for example, could mean an out-of-pocket expenditure of seventy-five thousand dollars, just for the first year's operation. Today the *Times* has almost a dozen such enterprises in full swing, from Saigon to Mexico City, with more to come.

In a moment of complete candor, Williams disclosed the kind of person he sought for this refurbished *Times*. Said he: "The exceptional man, the man whose work everyone in town must read, every day, is now an essential."

To downtrodden journalists, this was heady stuff. And it made for keen competition within the *Times's* stepped-up shop itself.

Meanwhile few—make that *no*—details escaped Williams's deceptively placid gaze.

He remained the Great Dissenter at the editorial board's daily pow-wow. He guarded the "balance" of the *Times's* thundering herd of political columnists. He read (and answered) hundreds of subscribers' critiques of the new product. He personally conceived such arresting novelties as the Barry Goldwater column, and, as a change of pace, one by Dr. Robert Hutchins. He midwifed the intercontinental birth of the Los Angeles Times–Washington Post news service.

And he traveled.

Disdaining the full-dress flummery of the usual journalistic "task force" expedition, Williams began to study the globe firsthand with Publisher Chandler and myself. In the first year of traveling, we visited Japan, Hong Kong, Thailand, Malaysia, Cambodia, South Vietnam, Britain, Germany, France, Belgium. Next on the docket: Latin America.

Williams probably wouldn't admit it, but he was deeply flattered at receiving a Knighthood of the Order of Leopold, the highest Belgian honor, for "informing the public of this vast [Southern California] region of developments in other parts of the world . . . with great ability and sincerity." His intimates consider the last to be a highly apt and operative word where he's concerned.

Williams's innate modesty extends to a genial depreciation of his own physical courage. Yet in the course of these journeys, somehow, he managed to get arrested and detained by East German border patrol guards, and to penetrate deep into Vietcong country aboard a pint-sized United States aid plane. (Those who accompanied him to Berlin and Saigon have learned their lesson; he can handle Cuba by himself.)

For all his burning academic interest in such affairs, Williams insists on remaining personally aloof, and on keeping the *Times* disengaged from manipulative politics. Kingmaking, he declares, has no place in a responsible newspaper. Or vice versa.

Detached, indefatigible, inscrutable, secretly amused, Williams watches from his third-row aisle seat, the *best seat*, as befits the editor of a great metropolitan daily.

He carves out time to think, too, about what he sees by delegating authority to subordinates he has handpicked and trained to his satisfaction. He respects their judgment. With rare moral courage, moreover, he accepts responsibility for their occasional blunders. Even the monumental ones.

In vitally statistical conclusion, it should be noted that his all-Southern drawl comes naturally: born in Virginia of Virginia and Kentucky parents, educated in Texas and Tennessee, married to a South Carolinian.

He's a martini-on-the-rocks man and a steak barbecuer.

He likes to fish, shoot the breeze, read two or three books concurrently, and scribble memoranda for improving the journalistic breed in a cryptic code to which only his secretary holds the key.

Off duty, Editor Williams keeps in practice by stablecleaning for a pair of rather evil-looking horses on his vest-pocket rancho in La Canada, whence he commutes to his downtown office in an air-conditioned, telephone-equipped Buick.

Laurence L. Winship, Editor
The Boston Globe

By Carl E. Lindstrom

You can separate the many strata of friendships that make up his life by the names they call him. In the early days he was one of a group of Boston social workers who still call him "Jack." His closest colleagues on the way up called him "Win." In the city room he often is referred to as "The Man" and those who fear to be more familiar may speak of "LLW."

Syndicate salesmen call him "Larry" and so do his grandchildren.

When Laurence Leathe Winship, editor of the *Boston Globe*, was promoted from managing editor he was given a new office, new desk, new chair. But he took with him the same pictures, not of autographed VIPs, but of groups which interested him for their peculiarly human aspect. There's Mrs. Roosevelt striding along at full height beside the shortest reporter on the *Globe*, an unusual play at Fenway Park, a group of Red Sox wives in their box at Sarasota, an excellent picture of James Morgan, the *Globe* editor who died last year at the age of ninety-three.

A photographer moaned, "I've never made Winship's wall."

There's no rug on the floor, no curtains, nothing to encourage a visitor to linger, though Winship's door is always open to anyone who knows how to keep it short. He works in his shirt sleeves.

There's an old, white colonial house on King Philip Road, South Sudbury, Massachusetts, where the Winships live. You'll hear music there, strains of Beethoven, Mozart, or Haydn, for Ruth Winship is an accomplished violinist and has friends who complete a string quartet.

Larry has no musical instincts but obligingly goes to an opera once a year with his wife and facetiously claims to know a good deal about music. He enjoys repeating some of the critics' argot with a knowing look. If he goes to a symphony concert, it is likely to be the Friday matinee at Symphony Hall.

Lindstrom was executive editor of the *Hartford Times* when this article first appeared, in 1956.

Of the three children, at least one went to Henry Ford's Little Red Schoolhouse. John is an engineer, Tom is in Washington for the *Globe,* Joanne is married to a doctor. When Larry baby-sits for their children he is likely to vacuum the living room.

There has always been a tennis court, for Larry plays nearly every evening and sometimes gives tennis parties for neighbors. Not far from the tennis court is a garden in which Winship grows flowers as well as corn and cabbages. In the wintertime he will stuff grapefruit halves with suet and seed and string them on low branches for the birds.

You get to Boston from Sudbury on what is left of the old Central Massachusetts, which still uses steam engines. It is the line Calvin Coolidge rode from Northampton. Larry gets up at 5:30 and walks about a mile to catch the 6:50. En route he picks up a bundle of papers and spends the forty-minute train ride tearing out stories, writing notes to himself and arrives with his pockets bulging with clippings.

Winship moves fast in the office, spends lots of money to get details and takes a hand in the writing. He often rewrites the lead and even the head. He is unorthodox on makeup. He is thoughtful in praise, writing one-sentence notes in a big scrawl on copy paper.

It is a common thing to run into newspapermen who say, "Larry Winship bought the first story I ever sold." A Hartford copyreader during the 1924 Democratic convention doodled a set of whiskers on a picture of McAdoo who was a front runner. There was a striking similarity to Lincoln. His neighbor on the desk shouted, "I can sell that to Winship of the *Globe.*"

"Go ahead—for half."

They shared twenty-five dollars.

His consideration for staffers is exemplary. He is likely to assign a man who is nursing some grief to a story at a distant point. After one veteran employee's wife died he sent him on a trip to Alaska; one man who came back from an illness and did not seem completely recovered was sent on a long trip to South America.

Winship has unbelievable patience with alcoholics. He dried up the *Globe* staff without firing anyone and some of the worst of the problem boys he inherited came to occupy positions of great responsibility. A drinking companion once felt that he had indulged too deeply and apologized to Winship the next day. Larry replied, "My brother told me once never to mention the follies of last night until the sun has gone down."

His usual eating place is Thompson's Spa across the street from the *Globe* office, but occasionally he will drop in at the Tavern Club, a famous old retreat hidden in an alleyway off Boylston Street.

When James Morgan was living there was a threesome dinner at Locke-Ober's once a month—Morgan and Winship and Felix Frankfurter.

Morgan probably was the closest of Winship's friends. The distinguished political editor was still writing leads in longhand on election night in 1952, at the age of ninety.

Let's see what his friends have to say.

Louis Lyons, curator of the Nieman Foundation, is a longtime associate. He writes:

> Larry's talent in journalism is an essential simplicity of interest and style—what Frank Sibley used to call "perennial curiosity." Win is interested in everything and can see a story anywhere. He has an extraordinary talent for friendship.
>
> Winship has made the *Globe* a very human institution. Its strength in the news is fairness, honesty, and a play of human interest.

Up at Deer Island, Maine, Gluyas Williams has this to say:

> Our acquaintance at Harvard was limited to sitting near each other at classes because both our names began with W.
>
> In later years the characteristic that impressed me most was his deadpan approach to humor. He was visiting us here at the time of one of our small-boat races, which, like most indifferent sailors, we take *very* seriously. He was going to crew for me and all morning I got more and more tense and nervous, and explained over and over to him his duties and that he must look alive and keep alert, etc. At last I hoisted the sail bag to my shoulder and trembling with excitement told him it was time to start for the dock. It was then I noticed a book tucked under his arm and asked suspiciously what that was for. "Oh," he said, without expression, "I'm just taking along a detective story to read during the race."
>
> He brought the same deadpan qualities to his acting in amateur dramatics. In a production at a small club to which we both belonged, he had an utterly thankless walk-on part and completely stole the show. He was a lieutenant of the guard, and his part consisted of walking on with his captain, played by John Marquand. He did it without change of expression in face or voice, merely doing exactly what Marquand did, a fraction of a second later; if John bowed, he bowed; if John put his hand to his sword, so did Laurence; if John spoke, so did he, in a monotone. Bit by bit, the audience was looking only at him, and the chuckles became hilarious; he wowed them.
>
> He is an excellent cook and if you drop in at his cottage here, when everybody else is going sailing, you are apt to find him over the

stove making cranberry jelly or raspberry jam. And he turns out a very fine Lobster Newburg.

When the Supreme Court recessed this year, Justice Frankfurter reflected:

> Larry is at once tough-minded and tenderhearted, the latter being, I think, his most striking characteristic. His is a personal world: he cares predominantly about people, and the virtues in them that he admires, and is not much concerned with general ideas or causes in the abstract. He is a man of strong feelings, a man of deep emotions, which he tries to keep well in hand, and generally succeeds in doing so. But his dominant quality—that of admiration of high qualities and the tenderest devotion—was manifested in his relations to James Morgan. Very few sons, it is my observation, are as attached to their fathers as Larry was to James Morgan and far less and fewer so imaginative and so wise in their devotion. As Morgan became advanced in his years, after he passed his eightieth, Larry left no opportunity unavailed of to cushion the strains and stresses of life for Morgan, and in all sorts of ways his imagination contravened the sturdy independence of Morgan, his pertinacious avoidance of being helped and coddled. Larry is a fine exhibit of the fear of a New Englander in showing his feeling, but he is, of course, chock-full of it. What gives special savor to his nature is that, coupled with this strong emotional bent, is a very sophisticated judgment. One might infer that words do not come easily to him, which isn't true, for when he writes, he has the power of conveying much in little. While he doesn't talk much, he has a speaking face—he can look a lot.

Professor Oscar Handlin of the department of history at Harvard writes:

> Winship can see through the sham, the hypocrisy, and the pretense of the false front wherever it may be found. On the other hand, he can understand human emotions and has the kind of sympathy with human failings. To all of this he adds a kind of wry tolerance; as if, knowing that few men live up to ideal standards—which is regrettable—he is capable of treating them with understanding, although without relaxing his own standards.

Doris Fleeson says Winship is a "charitable realist."

> If I had to characterize him as an editor I would call him a humanist. Without being sensational, he always is interested in what makes people tick and with due regard for their personal dignity

tries to help you make them come alive.

John I. Taylor tells of Larry's "finest scoop."

It was the time of the Willkie convention in Philadelphia when it became obvious that Willkie was going over on the fourth ballot as presidential nominee. Winship and three other *Globe* writers were sitting in the press gallery watching the drama when Winship jumped up and said he would be back shortly, and ran out of the auditorium at the moment when every reporter present was spellbound by the drama. Larry made a beeline for the hotel of Wendell Willkie and sat with him while he got the news he was nominated for president. Also in the room was one Willkie volunteer, two schoolteachers from Indiana who had driven to Philadelphia but couldn't get into the auditorium. There were no others, not even a secretary in the room. This story by Winship was possibly the best human interest story I have ever read.

Larry normally leaves the office about two o'clock and upon arriving in Sudbury takes a half-hour nap. He loathes dinners and public affairs of any kind. He invariably responds to invitations with "So sorry—but somebody will be there to represent the *Globe*."

He is usually in bed by nine but is likely to read half the night with a bottle of milk and a box of crackers at the bedside. His reading range is tremendous, with a predilection for Dickens and detective stories.

Once a staff reporter for the *Globe* found himself in earnest conversation with a Sudbury resident who told him of Winship's great interest in town affairs, his assiduous attendance at town meetings, his charities, and much else. Finally he asked the reporter:

"What does Mr. Winship do at the *Globe*?"

Thomas Winship, Editor
The Boston Globe

By James D. Ewing

T om Winship likes to talk about "impact journalism." He is fond of defining the *Boston Globe's* role in terms of its impact on the life and politics of New England. He wants the newspaper to make a difference in people's lives, to be a positive force in the community and region—and it certainly is.

Since Winship became editor in 1965, the *Globe* has made a spectacular climb from the middle ranks of what was then an overcrowded and undistinguished Boston newspaper field. Today it is the largest, most influential paper in New England and on *Time* magazine's list of the ten best in the country, with five Pulitzers and a number of other journalistic coups to its credit.

"Impact" is a good word to describe Winship himself. Wherever he goes and whatever he does, he makes his presence felt.

On a typical day he bursts into the *Globe's* city room at about nine in the morning, trotting, body tilted slightly forward, clearly excited about starting the day's work. In his loud, gravelly voice he hollers his favorite greeting, "Whadya say, pal?" or "Howya doing, pal?" He enjoys using the idiom of the Irish politician.

By then, he and his wife, Liebe, have been up since six. They have either taken an early morning ride on their two Morgan horses, Clancy and Seamus, or jogged two or three miles near their suburban home in Lincoln, Massachusetts. They seem to need no more than six hours sleep a night.

According to Tom, Liebe is a better journalist than he is and has been the most important influence in his life. She writes a syndicated column for young people, "Ask Beth," which runs in forty newspapers, and is the author of two books, with a third in preparation. She is certainly Tom's balance wheel, preventing him from occasionally spinning off into space.

Ewing was publisher of the *Keene* (New Hampshire) *Sentinel* when this article first appeared, in 1980.

After breakfast of half a grapefruit and a cup of coffee, he drives his pickup truck to the Lincoln railroad station to catch the 7:52 to Boston, a thirty-five-minute trip. He tries to perfect his timing so he hits the platform just as the train comes to a halt. He dislikes being early for anything, and rarely is.

The train trip gives him a chance to skim through three or four different newspapers, ripping them up and stuffing notes in his pockets in the process. He also chats with fellow riders, mostly affluent bankers, brokers, and lawyers. "It doesn't do any harm to spend some time with your critics," he says.

Once in his office, he empties his pockets of the torn-out bits of paper, along with a dozen brief memos he has scribbled on the Robinson Reminder pad he always carries with him. They make an untidy heap on the desk, but they are an important part of the day's agenda for Winship and the news staff.

Winship always works in shirt sleeves, and he loves flashy haberdashery: brightly colored shirts, ties, and suspenders. The only flaw in an otherwise modish way of dressing is his habit of wearing brown shoes with blue suits, considered a no-no in fashion circles. It is, however, an honored Yankee tradition (saves buying black shoes), which Winship probably picked up from the late Sen. Leverett Saltonstall of Massachusetts, for whom he worked two years in the early 1950s in Washington.

Within moments after he arrives, the newspaper tearouts and reminder memos sealed in large white envelopes start streaming out of Winship's office to various members of the staff. Some are suggestions for stories; others are praise (only seldom do they contain criticism). The memos are nearly indecipherable, having been scrawled on a swaying train in hen-scratch handwriting. The memos are called "tiger notes," because of Winship's fondness for calling staff members "tiger."

From then on, the average day is a blur of meetings with *Globe* personnel and visitors, a business lunch and dozens of phone calls—as many as fifty or sixty a day. Winship loves the telephone and often conducts an important conversation with the phone cradled between shoulder and ear, using his hands to edit a story on a completely different subject.

Ever since being named *Globe* editor, Winship has maintained an open-door policy. He sees anyone who wants to talk to him, with or without an appointment. That's how he got his first taste of confrontation politics in 1970.

The "Bread and Roses" chapter of the women's movement at Radcliffe College formulated a set of demands that they decided to serve on the *Globe* in the most direct way possible. An angry group of about fifty of them marched into Winship's office and loudly insisted they wouldn't leave until

the *Globe* agreed to give them a regular weekly column (which they would write and edit), remove all "sexist" (especially movie) ads from the paper and abolish all "sexism" from the news columns and photos. They would picket the plant until their demands were met, they said.

With restraint that still earns admiring comments from the staff, Winship heard them out, then politely offered to buy the women lunch in the *Globe* cafeteria. They accepted and eventually left the building peacefully, though without any commitments, apparently convinced that Winship had at least listened—as indeed he had. (Steps were subsequently taken, at his urging, to eliminate certain offensive words and pictures in advertising, though the idea of the column was rejected.)

It is this ability to listen—even under trying circumstances—that is often cited by his colleagues at the *Globe* as one of the main reasons Winship is such a successful editor. "His antenna is always fine-tuned. He's always listening for new ideas, new story possibilities, signs of new trends," one editor says. "He has an almost uncanny ability to spot the ideas and forces that will change society well before they are generally recognized."

Winship relies heavily on young people for this insight. His four children have had a lot to do with shaping Winship's attitudes about desegregation, the Vietnam war, environmentalism, the women's movement, and a number of other major issues of the past twenty years on which the *Globe* has adopted strong liberal stances.

On one occasion, however, Winship's determination to keep in tune with young people almost got him killed. A couple of youngsters turned up one summer Sunday on motorcycles. Winship asked to be shown how to ride one.

Following brief instructions, he took off. A short distance down the road, feeling he had mastered the technique, he tried to slow down and turn back for a triumphal return to base. Unfortunately, he opened the throttle instead of closing it, and at the same time steered away from the road, straight toward a corral, picking up speed as he went. The machine smashed through the fence and skidded to rest on its side, throwing the bruised but otherwise unhurt Winship into the dust.

Since then, he has given up motorcycles and turned to horse-drawn buggies for recreational travel. Every summer, the Winships' horses are trucked to their four-hundred-acre farm in East Randolph, Vermont (population about six hundred). Here there is a collection of fifteen carriages and sleighs, including some buggies used for an annual three- or four-day buggy safari through the Vermont countryside.

Winship loves his place in Vermont for its beauty and—above all—for its privacy. There, he can wear his favorite attire, a jump suit, as much as he wants. He maintains a wardrobe of about a dozen of these garments in various colors and materials and has been known to show up at parties wearing one of them with a flaming ascot tie, moccasins, and no socks.

The farm in Randolph supplies the fuel for the wood-fired furnace that heats his big house in Lincoln. Winship is immensely pleased with this answer to the energy shortage. Every time he tosses in a stick of wood, he claims the furnace yells, "OPEC!" and he thumbs his nose.

The Winships have traveled many places abroad for business and pleasure—and, as is true of all his activities, every trip generates at least one colorful story. For example, during the 1975 ASNE China trip, Gene Patterson shared a train compartment with Winship and Dave Laventhol of *Newsday*. One morning shortly after six o'clock, the train pulled into a station in Manchuria. The three men had overslept and got all tangled up trying to rush into their clothes so they could meet the waiting delegation of dignitaries.

It took Winship a little longer than the others because he had to fish around on all fours for a lost shoe. Here's what happened next, according to Patterson.

"Though he was the last man off the train, Winship was as cocky as Mickey Rooney as he lurched down the reception line, shoelaces aflap, giving each of the honchos the big Boston hello. Only later did one of us point out to Tom that he'd greeted the Chinese with his fly open.

"'Oh, no no no, did I do that?' Tom groaned to one of our Chinese interpreters, zipping hastily.

"The interpreter roared with more laughter than Tom thought necessary.

"'What's so funny?' Tom asked.

"'Didn't you see the deputy chairman of the revolutionary committee when you shook his hand?' the interpreter said. 'His fly was open too.'"

In 1964, the Winships went to the Soviet Union with some New England colleagues. Nikita Khrushchev was running the USSR and his son-in-law, Alexei Adzhubei, was running Izvestia, the big government newspaper. Adzhubei was a bit of a dandy, but a rising power in Russia.

The New Englanders had a session at Izvestia with Adzhubei, who opened the meeting with a lengthy monologue about peaceful coexistence, wars of national liberation and other such lively subjects. He also took care to explain that, surprising as it might seem, he had considerable editorial independence at Izvestia.

It was more than Winship could take. With customary directness he said, "That's enough of all this policy business. I want to know whether you have an in-law problem."

Adzhubei flushed, ejected his French cuffs, glared at Winship and thundered pompously: "I hold this job on merit. At Izvestia Mr. Khrushchev is *my* father-in-law, not the other way around." (Just ten days later,

Khrushchev was suddenly ousted from power and his son-in-law was instantaneously fired from Izvestia.)

Winship's ability to make outrageous remarks and somehow get away with them is legendary among his friends.

His insouciance shows up in all sorts of ways and occasions. No one who was there is likely to forget his introduction of Bert Lance at the 1978 ASNE convention as "just a poor country boy who can't tell a southern overdraft from a cold draft from New England."

Nor will Bob Healy, the *Globe*'s political editor, ever forget the time Winship insisted on diving off the high board into a pool at a Miami hotel. The two were covering the 1972 Democratic convention. Late one afternoon, after they'd had a couple of cool drinks, Healy decided to demonstrate his skill off the high board. He had done it before.

Winship, who is extremely nearsighted, wanted to try it too, with glasses off of course. Healy warned him it was pretty scary the first time.

"Hell, I don't mind this," Winship replied. "I can't even see the water."

Miles H. Wolff,
Executive Editor
Greensboro (North Carolina) Daily News

By Michael J. Ogden

A ny newspaperman knows endless ways of preparing a personality piece. One that should prove the most fruitful is to sit with the subject over a drink. It always seems like such a nice, relaxed method.

Any newspaperman should also know that the chances are good it won't work out. Yet, I, for one, never learn.

Take Miles Wolff. At the very least, we've been running into each other for a dozen years. I must have picked up some things. Then *Who's Who* pins him close to sixty-five, names his wife and children, his journalistic background, and offers the specific information that he's Miles Hoffman Wolff, for whatever that's worth. How much more is there to clear up?

My eyes tell me that a movie typecaster could easily put Miles down for a successful, if honest, alderman. My ears tell me that he has a soft accent. Yet I can't isolate it.

He says it's pure North Carolina and I take his word for that. So, figuring the career data can be pulled out of the library, we huddle around the drink. Anything but Scotch for him. Anything for me.

The major difficulty is that his life is longer than one drink . . . or two . . .

What happens in the end is that I wind up with a sheaf of yellow, lined-paper notes. I find in the cold light of day that they start off coherently if a bit spasmodically:

"Amiable . . . portly . . . butch haircut . . . rimless glasses . . . tends to dark suits . . . partial to vests . . . title executive editor *Greensboro Daily News* (A.M. and Sunday—95,000 and 105,000) . . . secretary Mrs. Ruth Laughlin

---

Ogden was editor of the *Providence Journal and Bulletin* when this article first appeared, in 1964.

---

been with him eleven years of the fifteen he's been in Greensboro . . . "she thinks I'm wonderful" (check this with her) . . . he gets to office about nine-thirty, starts with correspondence and exchanges, quits about five-thirty or six . . ."

All that is on the top of the first sheet in a reasonably legible hand. So far, okay. Then the penmanship becomes a bit more sweeping. Someone must have called room service again.

A circle around a phrase that says simply, "Mostly Lutheran." What that mean? Who is?

There's more: "May to October—looked job." First part could be a song title but probably isn't. What rest of it mean? I must have thought it significant when I put it down.

Same with the phrase, "Ben Reese said he'd fix rocker." What's that doing in the notes?

"Remembers girls only vaguely . . . " Well, who doesn't?

What happens is what you'd expect. The whole damn thing has to be torn up and begun again in orderly fashion. It's not as much fun but maybe the perspective gets clearer.

The whole youthful background is in North Carolina, first in Dallas, North Carolina, where Dad was president of Gaston College at the same time that he was a church organist. Mom could paint in oils and pastels and taught at the college. There were three sisters, all of whom eventually married professors, and three brothers, two of whom became surgeons and one, now with the Duke Power Company, who installed an electric elevator in his home by himself. When Miles was eleven the family moved to Concord, North Carolina. He carried the evening paper for a while, and the seed was born. But germination was slow.

There was Roanoke College in Salem, Virginia, where he learned enough to be a high school teacher for a couple of years. More, in fact. By the time he was twenty-one, he was a principal, first in Winecoff, then in China Grove, both in North Carolina, and where at both places "the kids loved me." (How do you go about checking this?)

It was about this time that he asked the *Concord Tribune* whether the paper would take him on for the summer, even for nothing. What could they lose?

"I covered a fire so well that after a couple of weeks they gave me twenty-five dollars a week retroactively. Then I went to the *Charlotte News.*"

"Why did they take you on, Miles?"

"Must have been hard-pressed, don't you think?"

Maybe not that hard-pressed. He lasted five weeks before he was back in Concord.

"Charlotte said I needed experience. Another year in Concord and I went back to Charlotte, to the *Observer* this time. This time I made it. I got my first by-line the first week, on the front page . . . "

"What kind of a story, Miles? Remember it?"

"It was a seventy-two-year-old woman being raped. I guess I couldn't have missed."

Miles was off and running then. Columbia and Charlotte Associated Press, then bureau chief at Baltimore Associated Press beginning in 1932. Two years of that and he went to the *Baltimore Sunpapers* as assistant to publisher Paul Patterson. Worked his way downward through the next four or five years until he was assistant managing editor of the *Evening Sun.*

Then up again. Between 1941 and 1949 he was managing editor of the *Evening Sun.*

"What happened in 1949, Miles?"

"Neil Swanson fired me."

"Why?"

"I remember asking him 'Why?', too, and as near as I can recall it, Neil said, 'Because I always planned to.'"

Which is a reasonable enough, though possibly cryptic, answer. And Miles can't throw a good deal more light on it other than that he thinks Neil resented it when Miles didn't invite him to his wedding.

Of course, Miles had married Nan back in 1940, which would seem to tag Swanson as a man who could harbor a slight for quite a time. But then, I don't know much about Neil Swanson other than he once wrote a book called *Unconquered,* which in the paperback version had a picture on the cover of Paulette Goddard stripped to the waist and tied to a tree.

Where were we? Oh, yes. A few months later saw Miles back in the state of his birth, in Greensboro. He has been there since, putting out the morning and Sunday papers in his shirt sleeves, then putting on his vest and coat and becoming immersed in almost any civic enterprise you can name. Not only immersed but swimming to the top.

At one time or another, he has been president of the United Fund, the Chamber of Commerce, the Rotary Club, the Whist Club, the North Carolina Associated Press Club, the Greensboro Symphony Society, the city Arts Council, and this year he becomes president of the Piedmont Triad Committee, a tri-city organization formed to promote the joint ventures and interests of Greensboro, Winston-Salem, and High Point. There's more: vestryman, Holy Trinity Episcopal Church, president of its Men's Club; on the board of trustees of Maryfield Catholic Nursing Home.

He gets the breaks, too. The year he was president of Rotary he got to go to Switzerland for the international meeting. His immediate predecessor got only to Philadelphia and his successor to St. Louis.

"How do you get mixed up in all these things, Miles?"

"I haven't the slightest idea. People ask me and I accept."

His enthusiasm, or inability to say no, has carried over into the national newspaper organizations. A longtime toiler in the vineyards of APME, he was also for five years chairman of ASNE's *Bulletin* at the same time that he was on his way to the presidency.

There still must be free time. Else, how account for these other matters?

He grows plants all over the white-pillared house at Hendrix and Elm. Upstairs and the cellar and the yard is a veritable jungle of pots, creepers, vines, ferns, orchids, philodendrons, geraniums, hyacinths, camelias, bulbs, begonias, jonquils; it's a tough place to visit without a machete.

And every Saturday morning Miles waters the whole lot of them—bustling about like a genial, bemused scientist—upstairs, downstairs, inside, outside. "I play with them," he explains.

It goes way back with Miles. During World War II he cultivated not one but two Victory gardens. They must have been successful because we did win, didn't we?

If, to anyone else, it's a queer idea of play, there are other pastimes. He's taking up golf again after a long lapse, at least as far back as the meeting of ASNE's directors in Key Biscayne, Florida, a few years ago, when he received a trophy "for not playing golf."

Also, he plays the piano. At least, I think he plays the piano. I have heard him. On the other hand, so has Victor Borge who, unknown to Miles, was observing and listening to him from an adjacent hotel room on the last night of an APME meeting at French Lick. Miles had been giving his all on the keyboard for a considerable time before taking a break so that I might introduce him enthusiastically to Borge as a fellow musician. Borge smiled warmly on Miles and inquired politely, "Ah, yes, and what instrument do you play?"

Well, there's newspapering and civic enterprising and golf and herbiculture and bridge and music and there's the three children—Miles, Jr., twenty, a junior at Johns Hopkins; Lila, twenty-one, in her final year at nursing school; and Ann, married, with two daughters. Nan, who's from Bel Air, Maryland, met Miles, typically, at a bridge table. He wasn't her date and that first night she didn't see what the other girl saw in him. Nor, for that matter, does she think to this day that his bridge is as good as he thinks it is. He says he is "moderately good." If pressed, he will add, "I'm at least as good as Al Friendly," which may be an impressive ticket in the world of bridge.

Beyond that she, more often than most wives, finds her husband either across the bridge table or flailing among his plants or around the house. Miles comes home every day for lunch. One result of that was her insistence a few years ago that he take to wearing vests "to cover your stomach." Another is his ten-minute traditional midday nap. Right after luncheon he stretches out upstairs, lying on his back like a stone carving of an unmitered medieval bishop. No fear of his missing an edition or a meeting of the Rotary or a session at the bridge table. The nap lasts exactly ten minutes. At that point his own snores wake him and the full, busy world of Miles Wolff immediately begins to revolve again.

In Miles's shop, which he oversees from an unsoundproofed room with a little glass window known to the staff as the gas chamber, he is *Mr.* Wolff. Everyone else in the plant is on a first-name basis with everyone else, including the publisher. But there aren't more than one or two who take the liberty with our Miles.

Miles happens to have up his sleeve one more talent. He makes omelets—large, fluffy omelets. "I make them plain," he says, then pauses thoughtfully and adds, "I also make them with parsley, if I have the parsley."

Appendix

ASNE Presidents, 1922-1984

1922-26	Casper S. Yost
1926-28	E. C. Hopwood
1928-30	Walter M. Harrison
1930-33	Fred Fuller Shedd
1933-34	Paul Bellamy
1934-36	Grove Patterson
1936-37	Marvin H. Creager
1937-38	A. H. Kirchhoffer
1938-39	William Allen White
1939-40	Donald J. Sterling
1940-41	Tom Wallace
1941-42	Dwight Marvin
1942-43	W. S. Gilmore
1943-44	Roy A. Roberts
1944-46	John S. Knight
1946-47	Wilbur Forrest
1947-48	N. R. Howard
1948-49	Erwin D. Canham
1949-50	Benjamin M. McKelway
1950-51	Dwight Young
1951-52	Alexander F. Jones
1952-53	Wright Bryan
1953-54	Basil L. Walters
1954-55	James S. Pope
1955-56	Kenneth MacDonald
1956-57	Jenkin Lloyd Jones
1957-58	Virginius Dabney
1958-59	George W. Healy, Jr.
1959-60	J. R. Wiggins
1960-61	Turner Catledge
1961-62	Felix R. McKnight
1962-63	Lee Hills
1963-64	Herbert Brucker
1964-65	Miles H. Wolff
1965-66	Vermont Royster
1966-67	Robert C. Notson
1967-68	Michael J. Ogden
1968-69	Vincent S. Jones
1969-70	Norman E. Isaacs
1970-71	Newbold Noyes
1971-72	C. A. McKnight
1972-73	J. Edward Murray
1973-74	Arthur C. Deck
1974-75	Howard H Hays, Jr.
1975-76	Warren H. Phillips
1976-77	George Chaplin
1977-78	Eugene C. Patterson
1978-79	John Hughes
1979-80	William H. Hornby
1980-81	Thomas Winship
1981-82	Michael J. O'Neill
1982-83	John C. Quinn
1983-84	Creed Black